HOW THE COLD WAR ENDED

Issues in the History of American Foreign Relations

Series Editor
Robert J. McMahon, Ohio State University

Editorial Board
Richard Immerman, Temple University
Melvyn Leffler, University of Virginia
Fredrik Logevall, Cornell University
Nancy Mitchell, North Carolina State University
David Painter, Georgetown University
William Stueck, University of Georgia
William O. Walker III, University of Toronto

Previously Published Titles in This Series

John F. Kennedy: World Leader (2010)
—Stephen G. Rabe, University of Texas at Dallas

The Triumph of Internationalism:
Franklin D. Roosevelt and a World in Crisis, 1933–1941 (2007)
—David Schmitz, Whitman College

Intimate Ties, Bitter Struggles:
The United States and Latin America Since 1945 (2006)
—Alan McPherson, Howard University

The Color of Empire:
Race and American Foreign Relations (2006)
—Michael L. Krenn, Appalachian State University

Crisis and Crossfire:
The United States and the Middle East Since 1945 (2005)
—Peter L. Hahn, Ohio State University

HOW THE COLD WAR ENDED

Debating and Doing History

John Prados

Potomac Books, Inc.
Washington, D.C.

Library of Congress Cataloging-in-Publication Data
Prados, John.
  How the Cold War ended : debating and doing history / John Prados. — 1st ed.
    p. cm. — (Issues in the history of American foreign relations)
  Includes bibliographical references and index.
  ISBN 978-1-59797-174-4 (hardcover : alk. paper) — ISBN 978-1-59797-175-1 (pbk. : alk. paper)
  1. Cold War. 2. Cold War—Historiography. 3. World politics—1945–1989.
4. World politics—1945–1989—Historiography. 5. United States—Foreign relations—Soviet Union. 6. Soviet Union—Foreign relations—United States.
I. Title.

  D849.P66 2010
  909.82'8—dc22

                                                                    2010029048

Printed in the United States of America on acid-free paper that meets the American National Standards Institute Z39-48 Standard.

Potomac Books, Inc.
22841 Quicksilver Drive
Dulles, Virginia 20166

First Edition

10 9 8 7 6 5 4 3 2 1

To aspiring historians everywhere,
especially the young participants
at National History Day

CONTENTS

SERIES EDITOR'S NOTE

FROM THE BIRTH OF THE AMERICAN REPUBLIC in the late eighteenth century to the emergence of the United States as a fledgling world power at the end of the nineteenth century, the place of the United States within the broader international system of nation-states posed fundamental challenges to American and foreign statesmen alike. What role would—and could—a non-European power play in a Eurocentric world order? The combination of America's stunning economic transformation and two devastating world wars helped shatter the old European order, catapulting the United States into a position of global preeminence by the middle decades of the twentieth century. Since the mid-1940s, it has become common to refer to the United States as a superpower. Since the collapse of the Soviet Union, America's only serious rival, and the concomitant end of the Cold War, it has become common to label the United States as the world's lone superpower, or "hyperpower," as a French diplomat labeled it in the late 1990s.

By any standard of measurement, the United States has long been, as it remains today, the dominant force in world affairs—economically, politically, militarily, and culturally.

The United States has placed, and continues to place, its own indelible stamp on the international system while shaping the aspirations, mores, tastes, living standards, and sometimes resentments and hatreds of hundreds of millions of ordinary people across the globe. Few subjects, consequently, loom larger in the history of the modern world than the often uneasy encounter between the United States and the nations and peoples beyond its shores.

This series, *Issues in the History of American Foreign Relations*, aims to provide students and general readers alike with a wide range of books, written by some of the outstanding scholarly experts of this generation, that elucidate key issues, themes, topics, and individuals in the nearly 250-year history of U.S. foreign relations. The series covers an array of diverse subjects spanning from the era of the founding fathers to the present. Each book offers a concise, accessible narrative, based upon the latest scholarship, followed by a careful selection of relevant primary documents. Primary sources enable readers to immerse themselves in the raw material of history, thereby facilitating the formation of informed, independent judgments about the subject at hand. To capitalize upon the unprecedented amount of non-American archival sources and materials currently available, most books feature foreign as well as American material in the documentary section. A broad, international perspective on the external behavior of the United States, one of the major trends of recent scholarship, is a prominent feature of the books in this series.

It is my fondest hope that this series will contribute to a greater engagement with and understanding of the complexities of this fascinating—and critical—subject.

Robert J. McMahon
Ohio State University

INTRODUCTION

THE COLD WAR IS ONE of the most important international conflicts since World War II. It certainly dominated world politics over the last half of the twentieth century. How the Cold War ended remains contested historical terrain. Yet no basic understanding of today's world—or of the past century of historical development—can be complete without attention to this evolution. At a breathtaking pace, the tides of history cast up two superpowers, destroyed one of them, and planted many seeds for the decline of the second. The Cold War's history telescoped into an even more furious last decade in which an empire collapsed, a superpower nation imploded, and another emerged standing, torn between contradictory impulses, on the precipice between triumphalism or consolidation. In the next century, observers of American history, diplomacy, and international politics will inevitably take the decade of the 1980s as a point of departure and the Cold War confrontation between the United States and the Union of Soviet Socialist Republics as a central element in their analyses. The impact of these events is uncontestable.

As Cold War conflict evolved over almost five decades, there were many, many discrete episodes of confrontation, ranging from sharp clashes such as the Cuban missile crisis of 1962 to slowly drawn-out developments such as the entrenchment of human rights values in world political thinking and subsequently in international diplomacy. There were dimly remembered but recurrent crises over Berlin; desert and jungle wars in Africa, the Middle East, and Asia; and a series of diplomatic achievements to reduce tensions, including agreements controlling nuclear weapons, building confidence in superpower restraint, or permitting the United Nations to exercise international peacekeeping functions.

With so much to choose from, I selected the Cold War decade of the 1980s—the end of the Cold War—for four reasons. First, it *will* be a starting point for many future historians. Second, the Cold War ended in a quite unique way: with one side stepping back from the conflict, then transforming itself as a national entity, not as the result of any destructive armed conflict but through a succession of policy choices that brought transformational change. The magnitude of this development was enormous and compels our attention. Third, the era that ended in 1991 marked the birth of the current age and thus a key waypoint for the trends and institutions that operate in today's environment. Last, the application of a variety of techniques of historical study permits a more nuanced understanding of these events to emerge.

In view of the conflict's centrality to past and present, it is inevitable that there would be a historical debate over the way the Cold War ended. Clearer understanding will be important in the years ahead. American historians are divided between those who argue that the United States brought an end to the Cold War by purposeful action and observers who see U.S. actions as a secondary factor. One school of thought is populated by a group we can call "Reagan triumphalists," analysts who believe that President Ronald Reagan consciously sought a victory in the Cold War through a combination of a military buildup and CIA covert operations.[1] Another view holds that President Reagan won the conflict in a different way—secretly harboring visionary views on eliminating nuclear weapons, Reagan's actions toward that goal reduced tensions between the superpowers in a way that permitted the Cold War to subside.[2] Some historians prefer to see the main mover in ending the Cold War as Soviet leader Mikhail Gorbachev, and yet others identify a variety of key figures as critical to developments. We can label this the "Great Leader" school of thought.[3] Additional schools center their interpretations on clusters of situational or structural factors ranging from developments in the third world to the effects of economic, political, cultural, or social trends.[4] Which of these explanations might be nearer to being accurate makes a difference in how we evaluate U.S. actions in the post–Cold War world. The ensuing chapters examine aspects of the history of the final decade of the conflict with a view to evaluating these alternative explanations. The structure of our inquiry is outlined in greater detail below.

A collateral question concerns the impact of the Cold War and whether the United States "won" that conflict. The fact that the Cold War *did* end peacefully has led to certain dangerous assumptions, including that *peaceful conflict* can be pursued without cost. The events of the Cold War's end permit an exploration of some costs entailed in an outcome of this dimension, even though the conflict itself never escalated to the level of an armed clash directly between the superpowers. And I also believe there is a misleading understanding of the way in which the Cold War, in fact, ended. Those observers who argue that the United States won the Cold War by purposeful action tend to present the sequence of events as a smoother, more direct process than it was, and as a more stable conflict situation, less subject to dangerous escalation than it was. This impression needs correction in order to prevent the Cold War analogy from being misapplied in future conflict situations. It would be useful to lay down a baseline to denote our current state of knowledge on how the Cold War ended.

A summary review is also needed because previous studies were largely based on memoirs, interviews, and periodical material. But actual documentary records of governments are becoming available, not just in the United States but in Europe, the former Soviet Union, and other places, which permit us to incorporate knowledge of the inner workings of nations on many sides of the conflict. This new evidence sheds significant light on previous constructions of the Cold War narrative. It is important to integrate the new evidence into conventional views of these events.

A few words on scope: The Cold War is an enormous canvas, with different sets of events in progress all over the globe, each with detailed antecedents and multiple chains of causality. To make this study workable it has been necessary to restrict coverage significantly. The focus here will be on the central arena of Cold War confrontation, that is United States–Soviet bilateral relations, arms control, and European issues, in particular those pertaining to the USSR's cordon sanitaire of allies in East-Central Europe. Regional crises in the third world and development issues have been excluded except where directly relevant to the main story, such as the 1980s war in Afghanistan. There is a school of thought, briefly referred to already, which contends that events in the developing world, the third world, were crucial to Cold War outcomes. I agree that these features of the history warrant attention, but as I argue in chapter 6, the East-West struggle commonly labeled the "Cold War" and the North-South evolution that centered around decolonization and development proceeded simultaneously but had different characteristics. The third world served as a stage on which superpowers acted, and its greatest direct influence on the Cold War conflict occurred in the years before the period of this investigation. I have therefore not attempted such a global study. Thus, this should not be considered a definitive account. Rather, it is intended to convey an understanding of the basic superpower confrontation that created conditions for other global events. This approach also afforded me the space to address the different types of historical analysis that are employed in the text and the issues involved in researching and writing history.

———————

Dispute plays a crucial role in advancing history. Events themselves, and the immediate reporting of them, create a first, rough draft. Events are impressive displays of people and forces at work, from the micro level to the vast expanse of global developments. A certain impression—and presentation—of events usually evolves fairly quickly. The conventional wisdom becomes received history. Details are quickly forgotten. But events are outcomes, and may be intermediate ones at that. Historians typically work at two levels, either placing events within their broader context and explaining their meaning for a larger canvas, or mining below the surface to extract and identify the causes and processes that yielded given outcomes. The present study is of the second type. Mining history moves the discussion beyond the conventional wisdom to reach for a deeper understanding of cause, process, or evolution. As more historians focus on a subject, their varied interpretations trigger disputes over the issues. Observers holding similar views coalesce into schools of thought that continue the debate, ideally leading to a consensus understanding. More often than not, that consensus is then challenged by fresh contingents of historians ranging over the material and rediscovering neglected details, adding new data, or, by the passage of time, casting a different light on preceding events. This is a dynamic process, and the disputes involved are vehicles for the advance of understanding. Thus it is important *not* to shirk from historical dispute, for premature elaboration of a certain consensus—or, worse, a refusal to consider alternative views—is an obstacle to comprehension.

My goals here are threefold. The first is to engage the dispute over how the Cold War ended. That historical terrain is broad enough and thorny enough to furnish ample scope for my second purpose, which is to illustrate—by practical application to a specific case—how our understanding of a subject can be enriched by attention to a broad array of factors. Many issues in the Cold War debate are subsidiary but important in their own right, such as the roles played by factors as varied as foreign adventures, arms racing, economic trends—and their manipulation—mass movements, ethnic identity and expectations, cultural developments, ideas and ideology, spies, or covert operations and secret police. There are also regional and geographic aspects to the debate. In short, the wide array of possibilities could occupy all of us for a very long time. In effect these various elements constitute multiple streams of causality and can be perceived as somewhat like the rings of a tree. In the case of the Cold War, an examination of different sorts of data yields insights that can be fed back into an overall explanation.

To reach this goal, the book is structured in chapters, the first of which presents a bare-bones account of the final decade of the Cold War and identifies several contending explanations for the events discussed. Each of the succeeding chapters takes up one or a few threads of multiple causality and layers that new understanding onto the basic story. The conclusion attempts to put the tree back together, as it were, analyzing the end of the Cold War in terms of what we learn from the different sets of factors. Following the conclusion, there is a section featuring excerpts from key documents and records that bear on our inquiry. Overall, this book is an argument for approaching any subject by means of applying a varied set of lenses, in this case different "types" of history.

My third purpose is didactic. I make an effort to discuss "doing" history. The lens used in each substantive chapter is different, ranging from an inquiry into the role of the Great Leader in history, to the impact of institutional factors, to the effects of Great Ideas and cultural pressures or those of global dynamic forces, to the influence of subterranean elements—in this case military capabilities and intelligence operatives. This set of lenses is not exhaustive. Factors such as the influence of events in the third world, as noted, and the effects of scientific and technological progress have been excluded, but I do cover what I consider the main contributors to this particular historical outcome. Each of the substantive chapters ends by advancing intermediate observations that bear on how the Cold War ended, but then goes on to examine methodological questions of crafting history. The subjects covered include the kinds of data suitable for constructing the different layers of our "tree trunk," sources of that information, particular issues related to the specific type of historical inquiry featured in the chapter, framing a research project, hypotheses, themes in writing, constructing a narrative, and drawing conclusions. Readers who are not interested in these discussions can skip over that material and pick up the narrative at the next chapter. The conclusion of the book pertains solely to our inquiry into how the Cold War ended.

CHAPTER 1

WHAT HAPPENED
Accounting for History

BY 1980 THE COLD WAR HAD BEEN RAGING, at greater or lesser intensity, for decades. Participants, policy analysts, and historians could debate whether the conflict began in 1945, at the instant World War II drew to a close; in 1946 with the powers' disputes over Iran and Turkey and the rise of the Iron Curtain; a year later with Greece and the Marshall Plan; or in 1948 with the Czech coup and the first Berlin crisis. But suffice it to say that as Jimmy Carter's presidency drew toward its end in the United States, patterns of Cold War behavior had become well established. During most of the 1970s a reduced state of tension prevailed—a "thaw" in Cold War parlance called "détente." Impelled by U.S.-Soviet agreements to stop adding to nuclear arsenals, the Helsinki Accords on human rights, confidence-building measures, and other developments that suggested the adversary superpowers could perhaps get along after all, détente became a time of hope. But in the United States conservative reaction imperiled superpower cooperation while other crises, notably the Iranian hostage crisis that began in 1979, fueled charges that American foreign policy was not aggressive enough. Soviet support for revolutionary movements in the third world, which some Americans saw as adventurism, fed a perception that Moscow was on the march while the United States stood still. Many saw America as being like a deer trapped in the headlights, caught on the sill of a "window of vulnerability."

Fast-forward a decade. By 1990 Moscow's Berlin Wall had fallen, an event that symbolized the end of Soviet domination over Eastern Europe, and there were clear signs of trouble in the Soviet Union itself, though as yet little sign of the fissures that triggered the disintegration of that nation not much more than a year

1

later. The nations of Eastern Europe were beginning to emerge from Moscow's tutelage and tried their wings with fresh noncommunist political leadership in new free-market economic systems. The United States, laboring under a mountainous national debt, continued its competition with the Soviets but also found its eyes drawn in other directions, especially to the Middle East, then in the throes of the run-up to the first Iraq War.

Sampling just these two pictures might induce vertigo. The changes were so profound it seemed the world had turned upside down. What accounts for this transformation? Not long after the fall of the Soviet Union, American analysts of what has come to be called the "triumphalist" school advanced the explanation that a clever strategy to weaken Russia, implemented by a steadfast President Ronald Reagan, had undermined the Soviet Union and caused its collapse. Looking at 1980 and 1990, fixed images at points in time, might suggest a steady progression. In fact, that could be history's verdict on the Cold War, though the explanation of its demise will probably be different. Today, even at almost two decade's remove, we remain too close to these events to draw confident conclusions about the historical dynamics at work. It *is* apparent, however, that the period of the 1980s, far from a smooth progression to a transformed and more peaceful world, witnessed turbulence equal to the darkest years of the conflict, a near brush with nuclear holocaust, and a triumph of forces that no one would have predicted. It is not too soon to begin reaching for explanations of how the Cold War ended. This record may serve an important function as a field of inquiry that permits us to show the explanatory value of various types of historical analysis within boundaries set by one of the key upheavals of our time. The present work will review how the Cold War ended along a number of different axes, illuminating the utility of multiple lines of inquiry. We may not obtain a definitive explanation for the transformation, but we will move toward resolving essential historical conundrums, while developing tools for analysis and attaining a better understanding of the end of the Cold War.

The first step along this path is to tell a story, the simple outline of the years between late 1979 and 1991, when the Cold War first flared and finally melted away. In later chapters we will refocus that picture, using lenses ranging from analysis of power politics to the impact of individuals upon history to the operation of the dynamic forces of culture, economics, and nationalisms. But the first step is the story.

Antecedents

President Jimmy Carter, up for reelection in 1980, faced enormous political difficulties attributable to foreign policy. The ongoing and unsolved Iranian hostage crisis, which followed from the Iranian revolution and began with student radicals occupying the U.S. embassy in Tehran in November 1979, making hostages of all the Americans stationed there, posed major headaches for Carter, though they are beyond the scope of this narrative. Some of President Carter's greatest diplomatic achievements had come in the Middle East, on Israeli-Palestinian peace efforts, but hostilities remained intractable and progress fragile. The oil production and pricing effects of the Arab oil embargo during the October 1973 Arab-Israeli War, amid growing U.S. dependence on foreign oil, began generating huge inflationary pressures that sharpened existing American economic problems on Carter's watch, ones that by 1980 were key contributors to recession in the United States. The dawn of the global economy, with corporations increasingly taking wing as "multinationals," had the effect of reducing the economic base from which American presidents had to operate.

The Cold War competition posed another set of problems. The decade of the 1970s saw American defeat in Vietnam, balanced by increasing U.S. involvement in Latin America and Africa, perhaps highlighted by actions in Chile and Angola, and anti-Apartheid efforts in South Africa. The Soviet Union had its own third world ventures in Angola, Mozambique, Zimbabwe (then Rhodesia), Ethiopia, and Somalia. The United States countered. The Indian Ocean became a cockpit of conflict. When Moscow responded to a tribal insurgency—backed by the United States—that was sapping the strength of its client state Afghanistan, by means of a large-scale intervention in December 1979, some in the United States feared that Russia would also invade neighboring countries with the intention of seizing control of the Persian Gulf. That eventuality would directly threaten Western European energy supplies because the gulf nations were among the world's greatest oil producers, but it would also have affected the United States. President Carter termed the East African littoral–South Asian area an "arc of crisis" and declared a doctrine of preventing this area falling to any other power—meaning the Soviet Union. Carter adopted a military strategy emphasizing strategic mobility and began to build a "rapid deployment force" to counter such a development. He also moved to contain the Soviets in Afghanistan by increasing the scale of the covert CIA operation supporting the rebels there. In Latin America, Carter adopted a more active stance in countering supposed Cuban encroachments, including taking a harder line against the soon-to-succeed Nicaraguan revolutionaries, Marxists whom Washington feared were aligned with Cuba and the Soviet Union.

These events took place within the context of a political backlash against détente in the United States. The Nixon and Ford administrations had oversold the progress made on improving relations with the Soviet Union and underappreciated the resistance within the United States to moderating the hostility of the conflict. After the first bloom of détente between 1972 and 1974, darker views increasingly predominated. Amid rapid technological progress on strategic nuclear forces, President Gerald R. Ford's inability to advance from an initial Soviet-American agreement (SALT I in 1972) to an articulated treaty left the playing field open to those who feared the rise of Soviet military power. This element will be addressed separately elsewhere, but here it is important to note that this diplomatic development became the first failure of détente, soon to be succeeded by others. Efforts by American conservatives to manipulate the diplomacy in order to use American commercial concessions, exports, and military competition to force changes in Moscow's domestic policy reduced Soviet incentives for détente and contributed to a cycle of rising hostility. When Jimmy Carter came to office these elements were already present in the global situation. Soviet moves in the third world then sharpened the sense of hostility and further eroded American support for détente, making the cycle a vicious one, at least in the United States.

The pre-Carter period also introduced an element that President Carter himself subsequently emphasized and that has since been enshrined as a key international issue. This element was human rights, to which the powers had long made verbal commitments honored in the breach, in particular of the United Nations' 1948 declaration on the subject. From late 1972 the Soviets had pressed for a major conference on security and cooperation in Europe, where the USSR, the United States, and the rest of the European states would come together and recognize the post–World War II boundaries on the continent. Moscow saw this as making sacrosanct Stalin's border manipulations, which greatly affected Poland and Germany (and to a lesser extent Hungary and Romania), and ratifying the disappearance of the Baltic states. The United States sought to draw the Soviets into a series of confidence-building measures under which the sides could observe each others' military maneuvers, affording greater transparency, reducing the danger of a Warsaw Pact surprise attack on the North Atlantic Treaty Organization (NATO) allies, and, not incidentally, furnishing an intelligence windfall by permitting direct observation of the Soviet military at work. A German settlement, or at least some arrangement to reduce tensions in Berlin and along the Iron Curtain divide, was pursued separately in ambassadorial talks. To induce the participation of the European states, the sides agreed to discuss human rights. The different sets of issues were grouped in "baskets," with Basket 3 as human rights and the Basket 3 features of the Helsinki Final Act reaffirming and extending the UN declaration of years before. At the time, Washington viewed the Basket 3 issues as potentially providing fodder for propaganda attacks on a USSR that paid only lip service to the Helsinki accord. But President Carter, as soon as he entered office, not only made human rights concerns a central element in U.S. foreign policy, he also ranged across the globe, seeking to uphold human rights far beyond Europe.

International sanction for human rights undid much of what the Soviets had wanted from the other baskets of the Helsinki Act, for the increasingly vocal and global movement gave cover to those Eastern Europeans, "dissidents" in Soviet eyes, who wanted to stand for individual and national rights. These dissident movements threatened Soviet dominance and developed throughout Eastern Europe. In then-Czechoslovakia, a group of activists and intellectuals, who became known as "Charter 77," in that year presented their government with a charter demanding Czech adherence to the Basket 3 standards. Carter administration support for human rights prevented the Czech government from acting as harshly against Charter 77 adherents as it—and no doubt the Soviets—wanted, and indeed kept the Soviets from going to the wall against homegrown dissidents as well. Presently there emerged in Poland something unheard of in a communist country, a free labor union, one called Solidarity. Human rights provided a foundation, and the dissident movements a fulcrum, for much that happened in the 1980s. Indeed the decade began with a Solidarity strike and threats of Soviet military intervention that were turned aside in part by the Carter administration's warnings of counteraction.

Another thread helping establish the situation as it existed at the beginning of the new decade was the dynamic evolution of the strategic nuclear balance, as moderated by attempts at arms control. The 1970s had seen what Soviet theorists liked to call a "military-technical revolution." Four essential changes had occurred. Most obviously, both sides in the arms race had attained a state of plenty, with so many nuclear weapons and delivery vehicles that war would be cataclysmic. Second and not so visibly, improvements in nuclear weapons design and miniaturization and advances in computer hardware and programming, plus better scientific understanding of such physical phenomena as the earth's magnetic field, had led to a huge advance in the design of weapons, the numbers of independently targetable weapons per delivery system, and the accuracy of the delivery systems. In both these fields the United States held a major advantage over the Soviet Union. The Soviets led in numbers of land- and sea-based strategic missiles; the Americans in numbers of warheads as well as bombers and cruise, as opposed to ballistic, missiles. Third, America's NATO allies had themselves achieved a certain plateau of nuclear sufficiency. And fourth, growing enmity between the Soviet Union and the People's Republic of China had made the potential for a nuclear exchange between those two powers a matter of significant, though not substantial, concern for Moscow's military planners.

For all the technological advances, the state of the strategic balance was fundamentally ambiguous. On one level, it could be said the Soviets were ahead because they had more missiles. On another, the leader was the United States, which had larger numbers of warheads and greater accuracy. In nuclear exchange calculations, the most frightening scenario was the one in which one side might destroy the adversary's land-based missiles, disarming the weapons considered most accurate and effective, and then threaten the mass destruction of the population in order to preclude any retaliation. By some calculations, the Soviets were approaching this level of capability in the late 1970s, creating for America what pundits termed a "window of vulnerability." Conservatives seized on this issue, with some constituting themselves into a public advocacy group called the Committee on the Present Danger (CPD) to hype the threat. Republicans used the window-of-vulnerability argument to considerable effect against Jimmy Carter in the 1980 election.

Arms control was one way to close the window. In part, negotiations had to attempt to compensate for Henry Kissinger's sloppy work on SALT I. This is not trivial because the issue would bedevil nuclear arms reduction talks right through the end of the Cold War. It was Kissinger who, in designing provisions to curb modernization, had agreed to a loophole big enough to drive a heavy missile through. At the time, U.S. intelligence had known Moscow was developing a family of new intercontinental ballistic missiles (ICBMs), one of which was larger, a so-called heavy ICBM. This missile offered the greatest long-term potential to contribute to a window of vulnerability because its larger payload could accommodate more warheads able to strike different targets. Land-based missiles were housed in underground silos that had to be expanded to fit the heavy ICBM. Kissinger sought to constrain the heavy missile threat by setting a ceiling on silo growth, but he negotiated a simple limit on percentage increase without specifying this applied to all dimensions (depth and width) taken together. With SALT I in place, Moscow maintained it was free to both deepen and widen ICBM silos to the permitted limit, more than sufficient for its heavy missile. When he met Soviet leader Leonid Brezhnev at the Vladivostok summit in 1974, President Ford had sought in SALT II to minimize the damage by adding a separate subceiling on numbers of heavy ICBMs, and Brezhnev had accommodated him, but it fell to Jimmy Carter to consummate the SALT II agreement. Carter promised that SALT II would be a formal treaty ratified by the U.S. Congress, which required a two-thirds affirmative vote in the Senate. The political headaches attached to generating that vote led Carter down paths inimical to détente.

The Carter administration's initial push to complete the SALT II treaty foundered on the rocks of audacity. The Soviets were startled when the U.S. secretary of state, sent to Moscow by Carter to negotiate a "comprehensive" agreement in March 1977, seemed to bring up new issues and sought to reopen elements the USSR considered settled. This meeting coincided with the first bloom of Carter's human rights policy, which also annoyed the Russians. As a result, the Soviets rejected the entire package, and over two years were spent regaining the lost ground. A final SALT II treaty was signed in Vienna at a 1979 summit conference, but ratification became stalled in the U.S. Senate. In the midst of the resulting political push for congressional action, there was a spurious "crisis" over Soviet troops in Cuba and the Russians invaded Afghanistan. Carter subsequently removed the treaty from Senate consideration. This widened the field for Republican proponents of the window of vulnerability and helped Ronald Reagan, Carter's opponent in the 1980 election.

Another sharpening military issue concerned the nuclear balance in Europe. The Soviets had long had an arsenal of medium-range missiles—of the same types that had figured in the Cuban missile crisis—aimed at NATO. Now, more than two decades later, Moscow had modernized, using another of its family of new missiles. Unlike its predecessors, this weapon carried several warheads and was considered threatening. Both Britain and France had their own nuclear deterrents—in the French case an articulated "triad" (land- and sea-based missiles plus aircraft) like that of the United States—and there were also American weapons in Germany plus nuclear-armed tactical aircraft, both land- and carrier-based, collectively termed "forward-based systems"—which the *Soviets* had tried to constrain through SALT. To counter the Russian theater weapons modernization, the Carter administration moved ahead on two new intermediate-range nuclear force (INF) systems, a ground-launched cruise missile and a ballistic weapon called the Pershing II. The Western European countries themselves were reluctant to accept these U.S. weapons as NATO forces, but the Carter administration finally got NATO to agree to deployment toward the end of 1979. These advancing programs on both sides of the Iron Curtain would figure importantly in the events of the final decade of the Cold War.

Apart from these kinds of issues central to the superpowers was ferment across the globe. In Latin America, Central America especially, restive peoples were increasingly opposing traditional oligarchs. In Nicaragua, these opposition forces were about to triumph, overthrowing a dictator long aligned with Washington. In Africa, the residue of colonialism had yet to be worked out of the system, and internal struggles were still in progress in Zimbabwe and the former Portuguese colonies of Angola and Mozambique. Other struggles were under way in Ethiopia, Yemen, and, of course, Afghanistan. Global hotspots offered stages for superpower competition.

In addition, there is the issue of internal developments in the Soviet Union. Its planned economy remained subject to many artificialities, too rigid to respond effectively to the rapid pace of global change, poor on meeting the needs of Russia's consumers, and disproportionately slanted toward the production of military goods. An earlier Soviet leader, Nikita Khrushchev, had promised that the USSR would catch up to the United States by 1980. Yet when that year dawned the Soviet Union remained far behind—its economy perhaps half the size of America's—peopled with better-educated, better-heeled citizens whose rising expectations were fueled by both ideology and want. Despite propaganda and efforts at information control, Russians could see something of the advances in the West, and their lives of store lines and shoddy goods compared poorly. Agricultural production suffered in the planned economy, grain in particular being insufficient to feed Russia's people. And the predilection of Soviet planners for heavy industries such as steel production increased the rigidities of the nation's economic system. There was also a problem inherent in the many ethnic groups, "nationalities" in the Soviet system of internal "homelands," whose demands for recognition and a certain autonomy could undermine national unity. Security services and the political controls of the Communist Party of the Soviet Union (CPSU) maintained stability, but these structural factors existed and would ultimately have to be accommodated.

In addition to the direct costs of Soviet military programs, there were expenditures for aid to allies in Eastern Europe. These were rising as a consequence of restiveness—exemplified by the August 1980 Solidarity strike at Gdansk in Poland—and local economic weaknesses. Subsidized aid to pro-Soviet third world countries, including Iraq, Syria, Cuba, Vietnam, Somalia, and Ethiopia, and to several African national liberation movements also drew on the Soviet budget. And the cost of the Soviet war in Afghanistan, which had risen gradually in the late 1970s, ballooned with Russia's open intervention in December 1979.

During the 1970s the Soviet Union massively expanded its imports of Western and Japanese goods, from American wheat to European consumer goods and Japanese electronics. For a time the imports were bought using hard currency earned from oil exports, grace to the oil boom of that time. The Soviets also earned money from gold and weapons exports. But weapons exports were limited to a relatively narrow range of customers, primarily Soviet allies; gold was a limited quantity; and maintenance of oil production was dependent on Western tools and investment capital to develop newly discovered Siberian oil deposits. The Russians had also found large deposits of natural gas and hoped a gas pipeline under construction to deliver the material to Western Europe would supplement its foreign earnings.

As the United States came to its presidential election in 1980, a number of significant factors thus influenced global developments. Superpower competition continued in the third world, the Iranian hostage crisis seemed to show American weakness, nuclear arms control had become a casualty of technological progress and superpower hostility, and conservative political forces in the United States were on the march under the banner of the window of vulnerability. Jimmy Carter proved unable to hold the center in American politics, and the election went to Ronald Reagan, who came to the White House committed to challenging Soviet power. The issues would play out over the next decade.

The Bare-bones Narrative

The story proper begins as President Reagan takes office, having chosen select advisers, all dedicated to the cause. Reagan had to deal almost immediately with his first crisis, over Poland. During the waning weeks of the Carter administration, the CIA had received evidence that, amid Solidarity troubles in Poland, the Soviets were deploying military forces to intervene there as they had in Afghanistan. Solidarity called a new strike a few days after Reagan took office. President Carter had warned Moscow against precipitous action, then handed the ball to Reagan, who repeated and strengthened the warnings. The Russians stood down, at least for a time, trusting a new military-led Polish regime under Gen. Wojciech Jaruzelski. The new leader made some concessions, permitting not only Polish workers but also farmers to create unions, aggravating Moscow to the point that the Soviets were openly calling for a crackdown on Solidarity and again rattling their weapons by the fall.

General Jaruzelski moved ahead, banning Solidarity and assuming the leadership of the Polish Communist Party in addition to heading the government, and finally the Soviet Union called on him to prepare for a joint military intervention. Jaruzelski preempted the Soviet move by declaring martial law on December 13, 1981. Thereafter Polish security forces conducted an on-again, off-again effort to suppress Solidarity and like-minded Polish dissidents.

Informed of Polish and Soviet plans by a spy, a senior officer on the Polish general staff, the CIA kept the administration appraised of these events, and President Reagan issued more and sterner warnings that helped dissuade Moscow from an intervention. Reagan also ordered the agency to try and help the Polish dissidents. Under the activist director William J. Casey, the CIA hardly needed further encouragement. Casey not only contrived an operation to help the Poles, he expanded U.S. covert operations in Afghanistan, resumed a previously abandoned secret war in Angola, and initiated fresh operations in Cambodia, the Horn of Africa, Mozambique, and Nicaragua. Agency propaganda reached into Eastern Europe and the Soviet Union itself. By the mid-1980s covert action consumed the majority of the CIA budget. During the latter half of the decade, tentative efforts were made to do even more in Eastern Europe, including launching covert efforts in Czechoslovakia and Hungary.

The Reagan administration matched CIA secret operations with a widening stream of public cultural and educational contacts, what has come to be termed "public diplomacy." At the State Department, an official office was created for this purpose, moving outside the traditional framework of the U.S. Information Agency, the first time American statecraft had possessed a tool of this sort, for a multi-tiered effort to employ people-to-people contacts and information services as a form of offensive psychological warfare. In 1983 the president issued a national security directive specifically governing a public diplomacy campaign. Its fruits would be most evident in Latin America, where public diplomacy was harnessed in service of the CIA operation in Nicaragua. In many other parts of the world, this tool was not appreciably distinguished from conventional propaganda efforts. Anemic foreign aid budgets during the 1980s, meanwhile, severely limited the impact of that facet of U.S. international activity. In the global arena, therefore, the Cold War competition of the 1980s on the American side was characterized by strong CIA covert action, a major push on propaganda, and limited U.S. foreign aid.

In Soviet-American bilateral relations, the arms race dominated the first half of the decade. Though Mr. Reagan talked of restraint and reciprocity, within weeks of taking office he approved huge increases in U.S. military spending and increased these budgets further in later years. Under Reagan, the U.S. Navy implemented a new "maritime strategy," the Army added divisions, and the Air Force deployed additional aircraft. In the summer of 1981 the president approved the production of a new type of nuclear weapon (the "neutron bomb"), and he continued with the NATO programs for new intermediate-range missile forces. Both of these became targets of major public protest in the United States and Europe. In the spring of 1982 a defense planning guidance document set the administration's basic strategic doctrine: to prepare to wage, rather than simply deter, nuclear war and to prevail under the circumstances of such a conflict. The window of vulnerability suddenly disappeared, though more will be said about this elsewhere. The triumphalist version of how the Cold War ended, however, is based on the argument that the Reagan administration had an explicit strategy to defeat the USSR through the compound effects of raising the conflict's costs for Moscow with the buildup of U.S. defenses and covert programs, using public diplomacy to weaken internal Soviet cohesion, and initiating economic denial policies to foreclose foreign sources of credit for Russia and limit its ability to earn hard currency through exports.

In the meantime the Cold War went on. The major arena for potential amelioration continued to be superpower accommodation, and the area of deepest engagement remained negotiations on arms control. Talks on the intermediate-range missile forces began in late 1981. But the bargaining positions the Reagan administration adopted for these and other negotiations sought unilateral advantage for the United States. Meanwhile, both Reagan and Brezhnev separately vowed to observe the SALT II limits, although that treaty had not been ratified. President Reagan rejected the rubric of strategic arms *limitation*, enshrining a new goal of strategic arms *reduction*. Negotiations thus left SALT behind and instead became known as Strategic Arms Reduction Talks (START) when they opened at Geneva in February 1983. Six weeks later President Reagan announced that the United States would begin a crash project to develop ballistic missile defenses, the so-called Strategic Defense Initiative (SDI). Soviet officials attempted to take the SDI into account in negotiations only to find their American counterparts intransigent. Facing one-sided U.S. arms proposals and uncompromising negotiators, the Soviets walked out of both the INF and START talks once the United States actually began deploying its first INF missiles in October 1983. But a strong antinuclear movement in the United States and Western Europe contributed to Reagan's decisions, demonstrating that political obstacles also lay in the path of further arms racing.

At the moment of this nadir in negotiations, a series of events occurred that shook Moscow profoundly. One of these the Soviets brought upon themselves, when air defenses shot down a civilian airliner, Korean Airlines flight 007 (KAL-

007), which blundered into Soviet airspace on September 1, 1983, triggering a massive U.S. propaganda effort, including attacks at the United Nations, to paint the Soviets as bloodthirsty aggressors. Coming on top of a March 1983 speech in which President Reagan termed the Soviet Union an "evil empire," his inauguration of the SDI program shortly afterward, the continuing U.S. military buildup, and Washington's intransigence in arms talks, Moscow found the propaganda offensive ominous.

The impact of all these factors was magnified by the Soviet Union's own aging leadership and its succession problems. Leonid Brezhnev had passed away in 1982 and been replaced by former intelligence chief Yuri Andropov. But Andropov had only a few months of good health before he suffered a relapse of kidney and other ailments. By the fall of 1983 the Soviet Union was basically being governed from a hospital room, and Andropov lacked both full access to the sources of information that he might have used to better interpret events and the bureaucracy through which he might have exercised closer control. Other members of the Soviet collective leadership, the Politburo, expressed great fear of the Americans in their speeches and public pronouncements. Suddenly the United States and NATO began an exercise, code-named Able Archer, designed to rehearse the system for ordering the use of nuclear weapons in a war. Soviet military doctrine held that initiating war in the guise of an exercise was a good way to attain surprise. The Russians put their intelligence services on alert to detect any sign of a move to war and took other measures to signal to the United States their determination. A nuclear-armed attack aircraft unit in East Germany went into combat mode, and Soviet nuclear forces staged missile and defense tests that activated all elements of the system that could actually launch a nuclear war.

Washington became aware of these Soviet actions only in retrospect. A Soviet intelligence officer who doubled as a British spy informed London—and through it Washington—of Moscow's demands to know if the West intended war. Scattered indications of Russian military moves, joined with this information, were assembled into a picture of Soviet anxiety and briefed to President Reagan. He ordered a complete review of the intelligence and, more important, arranged with Moscow to address the Russian people directly. In January 1984 Soviet media broadcast the speech, in which Reagan assured Russians that he had no intention of making war, indeed that the two nations had a shared interest in avoiding it. The CIA intelligence review confirmed that the Soviets had indeed been frightened and on the brink.

After the War Scare of 1983, President Reagan modified U.S. policies in important ways. The hardest of hard-liners, figures the opposition liked to call "Reaganauts," found themselves increasingly isolated in the White House. Although he continued to pursue aggressive covert confrontation in the third world, even escalating the secret wars in Afghanistan, Nicaragua, and Angola, Reagan became noticeably more cautious on nuclear weapons issues. The president responded to a conservative push to tar the Soviets with systematically violating arms control agreements by saying the United States would not feel itself bound by agreements and would plan forces based on military requirements, thus calling into question future negotiations. But President Reagan then ordered certain submarine missile launchers dismantled to keep U.S. forces within the SALT II limits. Reagan also proposed a comprehensive ban on chemical weapons, rejected deployment of the neutron bomb, and agreed with Moscow to modernize the emergency communication system between the two superpowers, known as the "hotline." Change in the Soviet Union also contributed to the developing dynamic. Andropov died soon after the war scare and was replaced by the aged Konstantin Chernenko, who himself passed away early in 1985. The Soviets returned to arms talks shortly before Chernenko's death. His successor would be the reformer Mikhail Gorbachev.

The ascendance of Gorbachev became a key moment in the decade. Less interested in adulation or a new cult of personality than in problem-solving, the new Politburo chief had previously been responsible for trying to rectify the shortfalls in Soviet agriculture. These, he learned, could hardly be addressed without more extensive changes in the planned economy overall. Soviet economic difficulties had persisted and by the mid-1980s were sharpening, with oil production reaching a plateau, agriculture stalled, and military production continuing to consume a large proportion of available resources. Taking a broad view, Gorbachev believed that transforming the "Soviet Man" was necessary to cope with the nation's difficulties. He tried to do this by tamping down on alcoholism—a significant Soviet problem—with little success. Glasnost, an opening of the society to what Gorbachev viewed as Soviet-style democracy, was something he hinted at as early as December 1984 and instituted once he took the reins of the Politburo. He unveiled its companion, perestroika, a restructuring of the society and economy, in an address before the Communist Party's Central Committee in April 1985, barely a month after becoming the party's general secretary. These twin concepts became pillars of Gorbachev's effort to accelerate economic growth and revamp Soviet culture.

But the Soviet system embodied a defined hierarchy of relationships. The dominance of the party bureaucracy, whose Marxist ideology might have been progressive in rhetoric but was conservative in action; the matching conservatism of the security services, exemplified by the KGB; the comparative weakness of parallel government structures; the rigidities of the five-year plans with which Moscow governed its economy; and the relative paucity of resources given the burden of military production—all militated against the social and economic breakthroughs Gorbachev sought to achieve. At the same time—and unappreciated in Moscow as well as in Washington—dysfunction within the Soviet Union was attaining levels that actually threatened the nation's viability. Gorbachev began as a reformer of Soviet state structures but was eventually forced into virtual warfare with those very mechanisms.

These things took place within the framework of the Cold War competition. The Soviet Union remained mired in a counterinsurgency war in Afghanistan, its costs in blood and treasure increasingly unpopular at home. Within months of assuming full power, Gorbachev led his Politburo to a decision to "resolve" Afghanistan, which meant either win or get out, and the leadership gave the generals two years to attain victory; failing that, the Soviet Union would withdraw. Before the end of 1986 the Politburo consensus shifted to one of abandoning the quest for a military solution, with a withdrawal mediated by United Nations negotiators. In February 1989 the last Russian troops left, though Moscow continued to supply aid to its client government in Kabul.

Elsewhere Soviet aid sustained Saddam Hussein's Iraq in a war with Iran, though in this case, remarkably, Saddam was also quietly helped by Washington, putting the USSR and U.S. on the same side of at least one third world conflict. Moscow also aided Sandinista Nicaragua in its struggle against CIA-supported *contra* rebels and continued to fuel and finance Fidel Castro's Cuba in the face of a U.S. economic blockade. Eastern Europe also drew on Soviet resources, with dissidence a growing factor in Poland and a nascent one in other lands.

On the military side, Gorbachev initially followed a course similar to that in Afghanistan, investing more in defense research and production while simultaneously pursuing arms talks. Here he changed tack even more rapidly, with the 1985 Geneva summit meeting marking the onset of a fresh intensification of negotiations. This led to even more ambitious arms reduction proposals the following year, culminating in a 1986 summit at Reykjavik, where President Reagan and General Secretary Gorbachev only just failed to agree on measures that might actually have ended the nuclear arms race. Subsequent to that the Soviets abandoned their opposition to the INF Treaty with the United States, and it was signed in 1987. A strategic arms reduction treaty, START I, was finalized in 1991. In December 1988, at the United Nations General Assembly, Gorbachev revealed that Soviet military doctrine had been modified to emphasize defense, not offense, and announced major unilateral troop withdrawals, starting with East Germany. Parallel negotiations on conventional forces in Europe led to agreement on reductions, cuts even beyond the unilateral ones. But negotiations, which had perhaps been the key pressure valve for moderating Cold War hostilities at the beginning of the decade, increasingly took a backseat to political developments.

Transformation began with Eastern Europe. The Jaruzelski government in Poland, which had alternated repression and accommodation in its efforts to cope with the rise of a noncommunist opposition, installed a reformist cabinet in the summer of 1988 and began roundtable talks with the opposition early the following year. That April the sides agreed on measures including the legalization of Solidarity and democratic elections in which the opposition would offer its own candidates. A month later the government conceded a right to free religious worship and recognized the Catholic Church. In Czechoslovakia, mass demonstrations against the communist government marked the twentieth anniversary of the 1968 Soviet intervention against the Prague Spring, and a fresh outbreak of popular unrest followed early in 1989. In Hungary, a study commission reported in January 1989 that the Uprising of 1956 had been a true expression of national will rather than an isolated revolt. Mass demonstrations occurred there too. In a festive summertime rite, the body of Hungary's leader in 1956 was reburied with the equivalent of a state funeral. These signs signaled that in Hungary too the Soviet sun was moving into eclipse. The scope and pace of change was accelerating.

Soviet domination of Eastern Europe had been unquestioned since the dawn of the Cold War. It had been maintained by force when necessary, notably in Hungary in 1956 and Czechoslovakia in 1968, after which the "Brezhnev doctrine" had claimed a right to intervene to preserve Moscow's control. The almost-intervention in Poland in 1980–81 had been the latest manifestation of this predisposition. But by the late 1980s Soviet leaders were conflicted about enforcing Russian hegemony. Warsaw Pact meetings and KGB approaches to the security services of the satellite nations had had some tamping-down effect at mid-decade, yet now the signs in several nations showed that dissidence had become generalized. Intervention throughout Eastern Europe would be a massive proposition. And the satellite nations were a constant drain on the economic resources Moscow wanted to focus on the transformation of Soviet industry. Rather than intervene, in early 1989 Moscow agreed to withdraw its military garrisons from Czechoslovakia. That March the Soviets formally renounced the Brezhnev doctrine. Gorbachev acknowledged change, at least rhetorically, while visiting West Germany, saying publicly of the Berlin Wall that nothing in life is eternal and telling a Warsaw Pact conference in July that pact members, which included all the Eastern European countries, were free to choose their own paths to socialism. In Poland just a few weeks later, President Jaruzelski resigned his post as head of the communist party. Late in August Gorbachev, far from denouncing the move, advised the Polish communist leadership to join in a coalition with Solidarity. The stage was set.

Coming up in the fall of 1989 was the fortieth anniversary of the creation of the German Democratic Republic (GDR), East Germany, a Warsaw Pact member and Soviet ally. Festivities were planned for East Berlin with Gorbachev in attendance. Shortly before the event, the East Germans suddenly informed Moscow that their land, long considered a socialist economic showcase, stood at the brink of bankruptcy and within two years would definitely succumb. This bombshell shattered Moscow's last illusions. In October Gorbachev told the East German party bosses that they had better join the parade of reform. The advice came as the GDR witnessed a growing stream of immigration to West Germany, the very thing the Berlin Wall had been created to prevent. East Germans were traveling to Czechoslovakia or Hungary and asking for political asylum in the West, and ultimately just passing on through to West Germany as those countries responded to the flow by simply opening their borders to immigrants. Mass demonstrations in favor of the GDR simply opening its own borders began around mid-October. Warsaw Pact powers put the GDR on notice that it would get no help by issuing a declaration renouncing intervention in each others' internal affairs. On November 1 the GDR opened its border with Czechoslovakia, further increasing the immigrant flow. A week later the cabinet resigned. As demonstrations continued, the East German Communist Party, attempting to reach decisions on a new government and a crackdown on the protests, made a huge error, mistakenly announcing that the border with West Germany would be opened. Within hours, during the night of November 9–10, 1989, crowds in both East and West Berlin began to dismantle the Berlin Wall. This symbolic act marked the end of Soviet Eastern Europe. Though change would consume many more months, the Soviet empire effectively ended that night. In Czechoslovakia, a "Velvet Revolution" overturned the old communist government; in Hungary, the communist regime simply melted away, agreeing to free elections that would end its reign; in Romania, a communist dictator was literally swept from power in a week's time; and in Bulgaria, the communist regime attempted an orderly transition to democracy.

Moscow's own effort at reform without political transformation, already beset by obstacles, was greatly influenced by the fall of the satellite states. Gorbachev had first attempted to overcome resistance by securing an overall mandate, pushing radical economic reform through the Twenty-seventh Party Congress in early 1986, introducing a plan a year later, and securing Central Committee approval that summer. He looked forward to using resources freed up by the end of intermediate-range missile production and tried to rally public support with a book-length explanation of his approach titled, unsurprisingly, *Perestroika*, and, as had Khrushchev before him, by denouncing the evils introduced into the communist system by Stalin. But inertia remained. In March 1988 a controversy followed publication of a letter by a chemistry professor who termed Gorbachev's criticism of Stalin "obsessive" and who expressed nostalgia for the presumed days of Soviet power. The letter carried weight because it expressed views privately held by many Soviet hard-liners, party ideologists, and military officers. Gorbachev came to regard it as a good thing, a "teaching moment" that enabled him to again address the necessity for reform, but the Soviet leader also appreciated that he needed to outflank the old party stalwarts by weakening the Communist Party of the Soviet Union. In June 1988 he presented political reforms that established a presidency and a Congress of People's Deputies to be elected by secret ballot. The election took place in March 1989.

Political reforms that constrained the CPSU, in a one-party state, in a context in which the party had substituted for a deliberately emasculated government bureaucracy, had the effect of weakening central control over the system. In effect Gorbachev had begun dismantling the very control he needed to implement radical reform. These developments also afforded greater sway to the nationalities grouped in their republics within the Union of Soviet Socialist Republics. This factor began to surface in November 1988, when the Baltic state Estonia declared its autonomy and right to override all-union laws made in Moscow. Estonia, followed by Lithuania, moved away from so-called Russification by making their own languages official ones. From that moment the power of the nationalities grew, further eroding Gorbachev's power. Gorbachev also conceded the force of cultural factors, abandoning the anti-alcohol campaign in 1988 and restoring freedom of religion in April 1989.

But perestroika and glasnost suffered from the economic rigidities that continued to make the Soviet Union incapable of meeting its consumer demand, and despite economic reform efforts, and Soviet disarmament initiatives, little new capacity for growth was created. In fact, the need to provide new bases for Russian troops repatriated from Eastern Europe and Afghanistan and jobs for soldiers being demobilized required *increasing* expenditure rather than liberating resources. West Germany furnished the USSR important aid in cash contributions specifically to accommodate the withdrawing troops, but the overall effect was that economic reforms remained stalled and public confidence in Gorbachev diminished. Freeing up resources by reducing or eliminating aid to Eastern Europe and Cuba was also of limited benefit. To a degree the Soviet leader tried to generate domestic momentum with his treaty-making and foreign policy achievements, but that too did not suffice. At a certain point Gorbachev became more popular in the West than he was in the Soviet Union.

Except, for a moment, in Washington. In January 1989 George Herbert Walker Bush, the first President Bush, took office in the United States. Some thought of Bush as marching in place, though in terms of foreign policy at least, he was the best-equipped person to occupy the Oval Office in many decades. Bush had been vice president throughout the Reagan administration and knew the backgrounds of every issue then on the table; he had served as CIA director, U.S. ambassador to the United Nations, and plenipotentiary to the People's Republic of China. Bush could have hit the ground running. Instead, he used the policy reviews that every president orders upon entering office to stall any approach to the Soviet Union. He seems not to have known quite what to do with Gorbachev, who had gone out of his way to meet with Bush as president-elect, when the Soviet leader was in New York for the historic UN speech where he revealed Moscow would unilaterally cut its troops in Eastern Europe by the hundreds of thousands. George Bush became president about six weeks after the meeting, then took more than that many months to craft a Soviet policy. True, in May 1989 Bush stated an intention to move beyond the traditional U.S. strategy of containment, but in fact, Bush remained immobile in July, when he made a brief visit to Poland. It was the Poles who finally convinced Bush that movement in Soviet-American relations would afford them—and other Eastern European lands—wider scope for change in their own relations with Moscow. Shortly thereafter, President Bush invited now-president Gorbachev to the summit conference held at Malta in December 1989. As it turned out, they met in the immediate aftermath of the fall of the Berlin Wall.

The Malta summit achieved little of a concrete nature, but like Reagan's 1985 Geneva meeting with Gorbachev, it had a catalytic effect. Subsequently relations between the superpowers warmed considerably, to the extent that Washington and Moscow sometimes seemed, if not boon companions, at least willing collaborators. Bush made no move to impede the Soviet Union's forging of a new framework for its own relations with Eastern Europe; he even made moves to discourage Russian dissidents from upsetting the Soviet apple cart. Negotiations on START continued—still bedeviled by the same modernization issues Henry Kissinger had permitted into the mix as far back as the early 1970s—and finally produced a pair of treaties that truly took the edge off the nuclear arms race. Even more significant, Bush and Gorbachev combined to achieve a four-power treaty on the status of Berlin that marked the juridical end of World War II. In a parallel measure, in cooperation with German leaders, especially Helmut Kohl, Moscow agreed to a scheme for the reunification of Germany under the *Western* auspices of NATO, a move unthinkable to Soviet leaders before Gorbachev. In fact, Gorbachev's actions here bordered on the heroic—and Kohl's on the statesmanlike—and completed the peaceful transformation of Europe.

But at home Mikhail Gorbachev could not match his achievements on the global scene. The nationalities were more and more restive, still led by the Baltic states but now joined by Ukrainian mine workers, Belorussians, Azerbaijani dissidents, Georgians, Moldovans, and others. Even Communist Party cadres began calling for greater pluralism. In March 1990 the CPSU Central Committee agreed to end the party's dominant role in government while a simultaneous reorganization endowed the president's office with greater power. President Gorbachev needed that to energize his stalled economic reforms, but he presently discovered that Soviet government structures atrophied by party rule simply lacked the necessary administrative capacity and organizational capability. Meanwhile, party hardliners and military officers became increasingly restive amid the sea of change. Led by the Baltic states Lithuania and Latvia, various Soviet republics moved toward declaring themselves independent of Moscow. Gorbachev responded by negotiating an all-union treaty to define relationships between the increasingly autonomous republics and the center. Gorbachev barely retained control of the Twenty-eighth CPSU Congress in July 1990. He began making a series of concessions to the hardliners. But party organs were in decline and faced with surging demands from the national groups. Into 1991 the cleavages grew deeper. The Soviet people voted to accept Gorbachev's all-union treaty in March 1991, but implementation immediately stalled, starting with the Baltics. Gorbachev opponent Boris Yeltsin, who had called for his resignation, won election as president of the Russian Federation, the largest of the republics. On August 19 a cabal of generals, KGB officers, and party officials mounted a coup d'etat to overthrow the Soviet government. Boris Yeltsin won his spurs defying that coup and defeating it. Gorbachev thereafter lived on borrowed time; he had been eclipsed by Yeltsin, who abolished the Communist Party that November. Ukraine declared its independence by referendum on December 1. Mikhail Gorbachev resigned as president on December 25, 1991, marking the Soviet Union's final disintegration. The Cold War ended with a whimper, not the bang so many had feared for so long.

Issues for Historical Inquiry

Even from this summary presentation, it is clear that the end of the Cold War represents a huge canvas, spanning continents and many issues, each of which could (and does) fill entire books. It is also clear that any adequate explanation for how the conflict terminated will be far more complex than the claims of the Reagan triumphalists. Indeed, their explanation demonstrates one of our basic propositions: *historical explanation is critically dependent on the manner and procedure of inquiry.*

The answers you get flow from the questions you ask. When did the Cold War end? Several answers are plausible. The fall of the Berlin Wall in November 1989 immediately comes to mind. It marked the demise of the Soviet empire, or at least the security zone along the Russian periphery. The August 1991 coup attempt in Moscow is another endpoint, the moment when a reversion to the traditional style of Soviet leadership was revealed to be impossible. But the Russian Federation did not really supplant the Soviet Union until Gorbachev's final resignation toward the end of that year. And an alternative date is December 1988, when Gorbachev went before the UN to announce unilateral Soviet withdrawals from East-Central Europe and military doctrinal changes. How did the Cold War end? Exploring the variety of potential explanations is our purpose here. Ask "Who won the Cold War?" and Ronald Reagan is one possible answer. There are others. The essential meaning, however, is that the events of the 1980s offer evidence for the continuing importance of individual agency in historical events. Without Reagan—or Mikhail Gorbachev, Lech Wałęsa, Václav Havel, Pope John Paul II, or a host of other characters—these events would have turned out differently. Those who argue that only dynamic forces determine historical outcomes work from a narrow perspective that ignores key explanatory elements.

Before proceeding further a word is necessary about one element of the research question posed. Asking who "won" the Cold War in some ways prejudices objective inquiry. Aside from putting the debate on predetermined ground, the question is value-laden. In addition it assumes there *had to be* victor and vanquished, winner and loser. Sometimes that is true. World War II, the preceding cataclysm, did have clear winners. But that is not always the case. History is not a zero-sum game. Outcomes are more often a matter of judgment than clear demonstration, and this was the case with the Cold War. The question will be engaged in the conclusion, once a broader evidentiary base has been laid to address it. Bear with me in the meantime.

Another thing apparent from this bare-bones recitation is that historical conditions in any particular period are established by what has gone before. The backstory of the Cold War in both the United States and Soviet Union determined a range of possible actions for leaders of those nations, set the terms of internal debates, provided a given resource base, furnished a given set of technological and political possibilities, and also created competing agendas of other issues with which leaders had to cope. Beyond the quick rundown above, there will be no effort in coming chapters to analyze the backstory as an independent variable; rather, the narrative will refer to earlier developments only when necessary to explain the peculiar factors influencing particular choices or events.

The remainder of the text will present a sourced, nuanced reformulation of the story told above, one that brings to bear documents, technical studies, memoirs, and other evidence to break out individual aspects and show the special contributions of different agents of change. In effect, each chapter will ask how the Cold War ended in another way, using a different lens and illuminating how historical inquiry, by changing focus, lends weight to different elements of evidence and arrives at different conclusions. The final chapter will weigh our results, attempting to judge the merits of the various arguments introduced, describing how the Cold War ended as a function of the relative importance of the factors adduced here.

Because many proponents of arguments on the end of the Cold War insist upon the centrality of Ronald Reagan or Mikhail Gorbachev, the first lens applied will be that of the role of individuals. A subsequent chapter will analyze the contributions of political movements in the United States, Western and Eastern Europe, and the Soviet Union. Another cut at the story will focus on the importance of organizations and bureaucracies. Several chapters deal with a succession of dynamic forces, including economic trends, technological developments, and social and cultural factors. The individual chapters will discuss aspects of the character of historical research that are illuminated by the text, in effect treating the methodological element common to all work in the field. Following the conclusion will be an appendix excerpting a number of the key documentary sources important to understanding how the Cold War ended.

CHAPTER 2

PLAYERS, PROGRAMS, AND PLOTS

BRITISH PRIME MINISTER MARGARET THATCHER is rumored to have once said that President George H. W. Bush took up the gauntlet to oppose Saddam Hussein's 1990 invasion of Kuwait after she had performed a backbone transplant on him.[1] While this tale may be apocryphal, it suggests that very great events still happen because individuals will them so, and the point applies as well to the final years of the Cold War. A number of people played key roles in this era, either as prime movers in events or as catalysts of change, not least Lady Thatcher herself, whose influence on Ronald Reagan should not be underestimated. The players in the Cold War story range from national leaders in several countries to subordinate officials, particularly in the U.S. government, to private individuals. They came from many backgrounds and had a variety of motives. Their actions, prodding, or facilitation of moves in a number of places add several important layers to the bare-bones account already related.

This chapter focuses on a certain number of these characters. There are many more people whose roles or functions were important to developments of the 1980s than can be included here, but this recitation includes the central figures as well as a number of secondary characters whose impact is illustrative of the kinds of effect similarly situated officials had in nations other than the United States. The important point is that despite the weight of historical forces, the role of the individual remains important in judging causality.

Margaret Thatcher

Maggie Thatcher is a good person to begin with. Called the "Iron Lady" for her steely determination, set views, and ability to hew to a course of action, Thatcher became prime minister in 1979 and was the first woman to hold that post in Great Britain. She had led the Conservative Party in opposition since 1975, been a member of Parliament for two decades, and served as a junior minister in previous Conservative governments. As Thatcher put it, "From the first I regarded it as my duty to do everything I could to reinforce and further President Reagan's bold strategy to win the Cold War."[2] She had no doubts and met with Reagan officially barely a month after his inauguration. Thatcher resisted bringing up issues that she knew Britain and the United States would disagree on. Nothing stood to be gained by raising matters that the United States would not concede and that might damage the "special relationship," the informal Anglo-American alliance that has bound the two nations together since World War II. But not all conflicts could be avoided. When Washington reacted to the suppression of Solidarity in Poland by imposing sanctions on the Soviets, British corporations with contracts to help build the Russian gas pipeline stood to suffer. Thatcher pushed a law through Parliament *requiring* British companies to ignore U.S. sanctions and made her rejection of the U.S. approach plain. The same strategy Reagan supporters claim furthered economic war against Moscow was not acceptable to Washington's closest ally, and Thatcher made that clear without creating a cleavage with President Reagan. In the spring of 1982, moreover, Thatcher took the helm of the British war against Argentina over the Falkland Islands, a fight against an American ally important to Reagan's secret war against Nicaragua.

On other things the superpower and its special ally agreed. Among these was the Polish question. Thatcher countenanced cooperation between her Secret Intelligence Service and Reagan's CIA on efforts to secretly support the Solidarity movement. She kept up and enhanced that cooperation even during the period of London's widest differences with Washington, possibly to show that the governments retained common goals despite their differences, and certainly with the effect of creating that impression.

The American president appreciated Thatcher's refusal to squabble publicly with the United States as well as her backing on most Cold War matters. He had met Thatcher, to whom he was introduced by mutual friend Justin Dart, on a trip to Great Britain before his election campaign. "I liked her immediately," Reagan recounted. "She was warm, feminine, gracious, and intelligent—and it was evident from our first words that we were soul mates."[3] Now Washington engineered a compromise over the Soviet pipeline business and papered over differences on Argentina as well as possible. Thatcher drew even closer to Reagan. Her invitation to the president in 1982 to address British notables at the Guildhall, a kind of equivalent to speaking to a joint session of Congress, cemented the relationship. Thatcher was palpably angry with the United States over Reagan's invasion of Grenada late in 1983, but the swiftness of that action minimized damage to their relationship. Reagan's confidence in Prime Minister Thatcher put her in position to play a crucial role as intermediary when new leadership took control in Moscow in the mid-1980s.

Lech Wałęsa

When new leadership came to the helm in Moscow, the Soviet dominance of Eastern Europe had already been shaken by events in the satellite countries, most notably Poland at the beginning of the decade. There too individuals were of crucial importance. Were we to select one, the Polish labor leader Lech Wałęsa would have to be that person. Wałęsa stood at the center of a series of events that nearly sparked a Cold War crisis and certainly did shake the Polish communist government and, through it, the Soviet Union. The background of these events begins in 1970, when economic troubles in Poland triggered food riots, eventually forcing the nation's communist government to promise a series of reforms and replace leaders who had been in power for more than a decade. But the new communist party first secretary, Edward Gierek, had not fully implemented the reforms and, in 1976, sought to avert new protests with a further wave of repression. Thus the decade of the 1970s witnessed a buildup of frustration in Poland, pent up by government security measures.

The unrest in 1970 had begun with actions by workers at the Lenin Shipyard in Gdańsk on the Baltic Sea. Lech Wałęsa, son of a carpenter, had graduated from trade school, repaired cars, and became an electrician at the Lenin yard several years earlier. Like other Polish youths, he had been through the army. The 1970 troubles upset his world. Lech served on the underground committee leading the strikers. When the government cracked down that December, killing eighty workers, Wałęsa was arrested for "antisocial activities" and spent a year in prison. But he returned to the yard and rose to shop steward, starting a petition drive for a memorial to honor the slain workers. Living on earnings from temporary jobs, he became even more the activist, editing newsletters and making fiery speeches. In 1978, in direct response to a fresh 60 percent price increase, the thirty-five-year-old Wałęsa joined with other activists to form an underground entity they called the "Free Workers of Pomerania." Over the next year security services apprehended Wałęsa several times, but when he was tried for creating an anti-state organization, the court acquitted him. Wałęsa's fiery 1976 speech at an impromptu commemoration of the 1970 uprising at the Lenin Shipyard got him fired from his latest job.

The Gierek government's security measures were more effective than its economic policies, and by 1980 its foreign trade balances had shrunk and its debt mushroomed. Foreign debt increased by more than an order of magnitude between 1973 and 1980, and Poland's $27 billion debt at that time was greater than that of the much larger Soviet Union. To some degree Warsaw had done this deliberately, allowing rising consumption as a substitute for social reforms, but by 1980 the bills were coming due. On July 2 the government declared massive increases in the prices of many products, the largest since 1976. Wages, also set by the government, did not offset the cost of living. Labor protests began with railroad workers in the city of Lublin and soon spread to include more than 150 enterprises. On August 14 the strikes reached Gdańsk with a walkout at the Lenin Shipyard. Wałęsa climbed over the fence around the yard to join the workers and soon became a strike leader. Two days later the Gdańsk workers inaugurated the Interfactory Strike Committee, including shipyard workers in the ports of Gdynia and Sopot. The movement spread to many more industries—over three hundred factories and businesses within a week—and soon membership was more than 10 million workers. They organized around demands set within days of the Lenin Shipyard strike. Rapidly crystallizing groups of workers joined in a National Committee of Independent Autonomous Trade Unions, or the Solidarity (*Solidarność*) movement. The initial Solidarity statement was issued on August 23, 1980.[4]

Lech Wałęsa tirelessly spoke to audiences to induce them to join the movement and worked to prevent Polish labor from diluting its impact by adopting too many goals. Though a strong proponent of free labor, Wałęsa at this stage retained a socialist perspective and believed labor reform could be accomplished within the existing state structure. The Gierek government could not stand up to the widening circle of labor unrest. Obliged to compromise, it negotiated an agreement with the workers, signed by Deputy Prime Minister P. M. Jagielski on behalf of the government. Lech Wałęsa signed for Solidarity. The government recognized the right of workers to form associations, but it did not specifically recognize Solidarity. A week later Gierek resigned. The Polish United Workers (communist) Party was taken over by Stanisław Kania. Specific recognition of Solidarity and its acceptance as a partner for collective bargaining became the next focus of the Polish labor movement. This struggle continued for months.

Moscow instantly recognized the potential of Polish events to affect its Eastern European satrapies. On August 25, before Warsaw had gone very far in its dealings with Solidarity, the Soviet Politburo established a special commission on Poland chaired by Mikhail Suslov, the Soviet communist party's chief ideologist. Commission members included many of the most powerful figures on the Politburo, among them Foreign Minister Andrei Gromyko, KGB chief Yuri Andropov, Defense Minister Dmitri Ustinov, and party official Konstantin Chernenko. The group debated the Polish troubles and toyed with plans for military intervention. It drafted a single-page memorandum, together with a resolution for adoption by the full Politburo, ordering preparations to include mobilizing Soviet reservists and drafting vehicles away from Russian civilian users.[5] The group originally considered almost immediate action, but this was preempted by the Polish government–Solidarity agreement at the end of August.

Thereafter Soviet military forces were demobilized, and the plans were altered, but not cancelled. Rather the military option appears to have been used as a tool to pressure the Polish government to keep the lid on Solidarity. Within months Minister Ustinov, for one, is known to have advocated more strenuous action. The full Politburo met on the Polish question on October 29 and decided that "counterrevolution" was taking place. Renewed military preparations followed. In early December the Soviets were ready to activate their Warsaw Pact forces for a joint intervention in Poland, and a pact conference was held in Moscow on December 5 to sanction that course. The record of that conference shows that Polish communist leader Kania, while conceding that other Socialist parties might be unhappy with developments in Poland, reminded the pact members of the situation's complexities and argued that Warsaw itself had taken a variety of precautions to prevent matters from getting out of hand. The communist leaders of Bulgaria, Hungary, and Romania all counseled against outside action. Even East Germany, often pictured as Moscow's closest ally, proved reluctant. Only Czechoslovakia provided even lukewarm support for the preferences of Moscow hard-liners. In view of the discussion, Soviet leader Leonid Brezhnev, while insisting on the serious nature of the situation in Poland, refrained from demanding immediate military intervention.[6]

Military action would have enforced the Brezhnev doctrine, set by the Soviet intervention in Czechoslovakia in 1968, which maintained that Moscow had a right to employ force to prevent its Eastern European allies from deviating from the socialist line. Czech leader Gustav Husak in fact used the troubles of 1968 as his basis for supporting action at the Warsaw Pact meeting. But the Soviets—even before the advent of Gorbachev—did not take that course. When U.S. photographic reconnaissance satellites succeeded in surveying Soviet military dispositions opposite Poland, the CIA discovered that far fewer troops had been made ready for combat than it had expected. The CIA duly reported both events in Poland and the Soviet military posture to President Jimmy Carter.[7]

Washington took seriously the signs of Soviet action in Poland and reacted to Soviet military maneuvers and preparations by warning against any intervention. It was precisely at this moment that the Carter administration gave way to the presidency of Ronald Reagan, who continued the policy of warning off Moscow. The evident American awareness of the interventionist tendencies in the Soviet Union served to accentuate Moscow's reluctance to act openly. In this sense, U.S. policy helped preserve an atmosphere in which Solidarity could continue its struggle. Lech Wałęsa's private knowledge of Soviet and U.S. moves cannot have been much, but his understanding of conditions in his country proved acute enough to enable him to take full advantage of the maneuvering space accorded him.

The Soviet or Polish armies were not the only parties that could threaten. Solidarity did the same by staging an hourlong general strike, simply to remind the Warsaw government its demands were not being met. The workers resisted appeals for compromise from Polish Catholic figures. The labor groups staged a national convention of Solidarity at which Wałęsa was elected its first chairman. Henceforth he became chief negotiator. But talks with the Polish government dragged, and in their midst came new Warsaw measures signaling its intransigence. The most important was on February 11, 1981, when the Polish defense minister, Gen. Wojciech Jaruzelski, became the new prime minister. Through much of 1981 Wałęsa refused to back down, to such an extent that Moscow again considered countering continued unrest with military intervention. Alerted by Ryszard Kuklinski, a Polish general staff officer and CIA spy, the Reagan administration issued further warnings. But Prime Minister Jaruzelski saw that Moscow had neared the end of its tether, and to forestall Soviet action, on December 13, 1981, he declared a state of emergency, outlawing Solidarity and imposing military rule. Security services arrested Wałęsa, who was subsequently held at a prison in southeastern Poland close to the Soviet border. The unfolding Solidarity crisis, of which Lech Wałęsa had been a prime catalyst, in turn framed the field for foreign policy action at the moment Ronald Reagan became president of the United States.

Ronald Reagan

Ronald Reagan is a central character in this story and, in some ways, the antithesis of the archetypal individual who makes history. Such a person—more like Thatcher—most often has acute political perception, a capacity for calculation, sharp bureaucratic skills, plus a certain personal charm. Political and policy agendas are finely calculated, then carefully compromised to obtain forward movement. Reagan was long on the charm but guileless. He lacked many of these other attributes. His thought process was intuitive, and he relied on emotive power more than logic. President Reagan was a master of projection who could appear sympathetic to many even as he went his own way. He did this with the Polish crisis, rhetorically backing Solidarity even while he adopted sanctions against the Warsaw government that had their main impact on the Polish people. But complementing Reagan's charm was a way he had of *hoping*, of embracing a dream or goal with such enthusiasm that he brought others to his side, or at least induced them to refrain from obstructing his course. And in the case of Poland, Mr. Reagan softened economic sanctions with a covert program of help to Solidarity.

Ronald Reagan came to the presidency from the state of California, where he'd been governor for two terms in the late 1960s and early 1970s. He emerged on the national scene in 1968, when Richard Nixon overmatched him for the Republican presidential nomination, and solidified his standing among conservative Republicans in 1976, when Reagan lost the nomination to Gerald Ford by a surprisingly narrow margin. Reagan won on his third try, once conservatives had become dominant within his party. It did not hurt that a Democrat had occupied the White House during the inflation of the late 1970s and the Iranian hostage crisis. Reagan had come to office in California as something of a conservative firebrand, jumping into the storm over free speech at the University of California, opposing Vietnam War protesters, and cutting back welfare programs. His years in politics, especially those in dogged pursuit of the presidential nomination, taught Reagan the art of compromise, and at the White House he would do that when necessary. Tip O'Neill, a Democrat and Speaker of the House during Reagan's first term as president, enjoyed warm and enduring personal relations with the president in spite of the partisanship beginning to intrude into American politics at that time.

Little in Reagan's background suggested he might make a great president, though he revealed political interests early in his almost three-decade-long career as a Hollywood actor. While still a Democrat, Reagan supported Dwight D. Eisenhower in both his elections, and he campaigned actively for Richard Nixon in the

1960 match against John F. Kennedy. One thing Mr. Reagan did do, as a radio broadcaster in the late 1930s, indicated the boldness with which he could proclaim the correctness of visions he adopted. On the radio, the future president, then covering baseball games "live," would take bare summaries off the news ticker and make up the details he broadcast to his audience. Conjuring images, Reagan would eventually be called the "Great Communicator." As a political device, this facility with visions would be useful, but in interstate diplomacy, particularly amid Cold War conflict, Mr. Reagan's low reality threshold became problematic. As an official of the Screen Actors' Guild over a period of years in Hollywood, Reagan also acquired some experience with contract negotiations that might have helped his diplomacy, except his notion of bargaining was to lay down a marker and then talk until the other side gave up, by either agreeing or walking away.

The vision that Mr. Reagan adopted for American-Soviet relations was engaged and proactive but not substantive. He wanted action—action to defeat the communists and reverse what he saw as a tide of Soviet ascendancy, without being too concerned with specifics. There were a few concrete items on the Reagan agenda, including his fear that nuclear arms agreements favored the Soviets and his sense that defense against nuclear weapons was the way out of the Armageddon conundrum. Nuclear weapons in general troubled him.[8] Beyond that, bringing the president action meant opening the door for a cadre of "policy entrepreneurs" and their various schemes. Reagan himself expressed this style of policymaking in his explanations to the Tower board that later investigated the Iran-contra affair. Drawing upon an article he had published in the magazine *Forbes* in 1986, Reagan explained, "My management style has always been to choose good people, to establish clear policies and directions, and to provide those I have appointed with the authority to make the subordinate and secondary decisions to carry out my policies."[9] Soviet diplomat Anatoly Dobrynin recounts, "The Reagan I observed may have been no master of detail but he had a clear sense of what he wanted and was deeply involved."[10] President Reagan supplied the vision, his entrepreneurs the details—at least until events shocked Mr. Reagan out of complacency.

Having a stable of operators beneath him, free to make "subordinate and secondary decisions," frequently meant the administration was riven with intense bickering. At the beginning, Secretary of State Alexander Haig fought with almost everyone. Conservative but pragmatic, Haig clashed with an official family of true believers and crippled his cause with an early effort to seize hold of the policy machinery and then a grab for the White House itself, when President Reagan was wounded by a gunman in March 1981. At the Pentagon, Defense Secretary Caspar Weinberger presided over factions warring among themselves and with the diplomats at the State Department. Later Weinberger fought George Shultz, Haig's replacement at State. Reagan deliberately restricted the role of his national security adviser only to discover, first, that the security advisers—he had half a dozen of them (a record), seven if you count Alton Keel, who served only as acting security adviser—could not rein in the entrepreneurs; later, the advisers and their National Security Council (NSC) staff became entrepreneurs on their own account. More often than he liked, President Reagan became the man forced to decide among the competing agendas. And decisions could be tough. The president recounts that, after listening to the debate at meetings, he would sit at his desk to consider problems, although sometimes he did this before going to sleep or while standing in the shower. "If a horse was nearby, that always helped my decision-making," Reagan wrote.[11] He loved to ride and adored Rancho del Cielo, his California spread nestled in the hills above Santa Barbara, where the Secret Service installed television monitors disguised as rocks and wore out dozens of vehicles negotiating the steep climb from the coastal plain. Maggie Thatcher was nearly stranded at mid-climb on one visit when her car dropped its transmission on the rocky road up the mountain.

In the spring of 1983 President Reagan gave a speech charging the Soviet Union with being an "evil empire," a play on avid discussions on Soviet intentions and "imperialism" within U.S. defense and foreign policy circles.[12] Only weeks later he announced the Strategic Defense Initiative program, intended to create a defense against ballistic missiles. This was urged on the president by outsiders, in effect policy entrepreneurs among the general public, and represented one of Reagan's few personal programmatic proposals. During these months the United States completed preparations for deployment of its "Euromissiles." At the same time, Washington remained intransigent in arms control negotiations and—at least as measured by budgets—was proceeding with a broad-based military buildup.

An autumn of discontent began on September 1, when Soviet air defenses, operating under rigid procedures with antiquated equipment, misidentified a civilian airliner as a spy plane and shot it out of the sky. Downed over the Soviet Far East, Korean Air Lines flight 007 had been carrying 269 people, among them ten Canadians and sixty-one Americans. Grasping for political advantage, Reagan's subordinates played the incident for everything it was worth, revealing U.S. intelligence intercepts of Soviet air defense controllers' messages, doctoring them to make the Russians look even worse, and relying upon them at the United Nations

Security Council to justify a condemnation of Russia. Public charges about Moscow swirled in the United States. Soon to follow would be the Euromissile deployment, the War Scare of 1983, and the president's growing consciousness that relations with the Soviet Union could not be permitted to deteriorate indefinitely if he expected to achieve progress in international relations. Reagan changed course.

There are a number of such episodes. These include not only Reagan's shift after the war scare but also his opening to Mikhail Gorbachev at the Geneva summit in 1985 and his championing of the Intermediate-Range Nuclear Forces Treaty in 1987. There were other instances in which the president sat inert, however, even during those same time frames. Thus it is not plausible to conclude that Reagan underwent some transformation that compelled him to change styles. Nor would it be accurate to say that President Reagan engaged on those issues that mattered the most to him and let others go by because his involvement remained quixotic throughout. Explaining presidential behavior is always problematic, but in the case of Ronald Reagan it is especially so.

Reagan's management style and the atmosphere surrounding his White House often made him seem a curious leading figure, the front man for institutions, interests, and the policy entrepreneurs. Observers frequently characterized Reagan as passive and his management style as insensitive to real world factors. The way the Cold War ended suggests that characterization is not accurate. More precise analysis of instances where Mr. Reagan took the lead in changing course in the face of interests and entrepreneurs suggests that the president overrode his own managers at those moments when he realized that existing courses of action threatened his goals or beliefs, or offered only possibilities that fell short of them.

Coming to the White House at age sixty-nine, Ronald Reagan was the oldest person ever to become president of the United States. This was more than a historical curiosity. It meant a chief executive who might nod off during discussions at key national security meetings, read the policy papers but remember little from them, and often agree with the last official who spoke to him. In the realm of nuclear weapons, for example, Mr. Reagan remained unaware of basic differences between U.S. and Soviet strategic forces and thus unable to discern that arms restraints the United States proposed might be construed in Moscow as a bid to secure relative advantage. These attributes were exploited by the policy entrepreneurs. Age also meant the president had a reduced attention span, which constrained his ability to enforce a course of action where it differed from those preferred by his associates. Mr. Reagan had an aversion to conflict among his official family, which restricted his ability to enforce discipline because he was reluctant to knock heads together or fire recalcitrant officials. Thus disputes among subordinates—or even between his own goals and those of the entrepreneurs—remained unresolved and could continue to rage beneath the White House level. The conflict between Secretary of State George Shultz and Secretary of Defense Caspar Weinberger, famously, persisted to the end of Reagan's presidency. Once his attention flitted elsewhere, even Reagan's own preferred policies could fall into the gaps created by the shifting phalanxes of power asserted by the entrepreneurs.

A key feature of Reagan's—contradicting his own reluctance to countenance conflict—was his ability to hold passionate beliefs but connect them to conflicting lines of policy simultaneously pursued. A good example is the SDI. President Reagan believed very strongly in affording people the possibility of a true defense against nuclear weapons, which was what his SDI was to be. He championed that program as though he could simply *will* it into being, even though no existing technology could bring the SDI to fruition and the promises made by Reagan and military officials rested on a very narrow base of actual achievements. Reagan's commitment to his belief in the SDI proved so strong that at the Reykjavik summit he rejected a proposal that could have rid the world of the very nuclear weapons he intended the initiative to neutralize. Yet the president permitted various officials to craft arms control proposals that used the SDI as a bargaining chip—thus anticipating trading it away—or that relied upon the demands of the SDI to sustain high defense budgets—anticipating forging ahead with the program. With similar conviction, the president believed that the Russians were violating arms agreements—"They do just plain cheat," as Reagan put it to his diary in January 1984.[13] The president sent numerous reports to Congress alleging Soviet violations, put allegations of cheating into speeches as late as 1987–88, and yet felt no contradiction in seeking new arms treaties with Moscow. It was Reagan himself who popularized the phrase "trust but verify."

As befit a Hollywood leading man, Ronald Reagan expressed his approach through speeches. Drafting them represented much more than intuiting the right imagery and crafting language to represent policy. Rather the policy was frequently settled in the course of preparing for the speech, at times even so a speech could be made. This was no novelty for presidents, but the practice was especially prevalent on Reagan's watch. President Reagan invariably worked to personalize his speeches, inserting examples or text of his own, and in doing so he created moments when he was especially open to new ideas. The SDI program, for example, had its genesis as a Reagan emendation to one of his speeches.

Ronald Reagan's published memoir and diaries are oddly opaque, detailing quotidian comings and goings but rarely expressing his private thoughts. Court historian Edmund Morris, with better access to this president than any professional since Arthur M. Schlesinger Jr. in the Kennedy White House, said of Reagan's diaries, "Not one sentence, not even the odd stray phrase, was colored with original observation."[14] The man was like his record. For his biography of Reagan, Morris resorted to inventing a fictional character whom he inserted as spokesperson for Reagan's thoughts and motives.

Other observers read into Reagan, attributing rationale, seeing in him whatever they would. For journalist Lou Cannon, Reagan was a puzzle, someone he was still trying to understand despite having written two biographies of the president.[15] Historian Richard Reeves, to judge from the title of his Reagan biography, *President Reagan: The Triumph of Imagination*, thought the president a wizard of imagination.[16] Peter Schweizer, early popularizer of the triumphalist vision of the end of the Cold War, saw Reagan as a master of political maneuver, notwithstanding that many of those maneuvers were contrived by the operatives around the man, not the president himself.[17] For political scientist Paul Kengor, Reagan was the Crusader, heroically assuming a position and standing upon it until others rallied around him.[18] For Republican speechwriter Joseph Shattan, Reagan differed from every other American political figure because "he had boundless faith in the strength of the free enterprise system and boundless contempt for Soviet collectivism."[19]

Mr. Reagan so frequently articulated his belief in free enterprise, and often enough his faith in a transcendental God, that some came to view him almost as a mystic. Nearer to the truth might be the idea that Ronald Reagan functioned as a vessel, a repository in whom many players in this drama vested their own agendas, claiming legitimacy from the imprimatur of the president's general pronouncements. But after 1983 these characteristics of President Reagan's served to facilitate a different sort of entrepreneurial activity. In fact, they made Reagan more open to a relationship with the Soviet Union. In this he marched in step with another major figure of the age, a man of the cloth.

Pope John Paul II

Pope John Paul II seemed to have perceived the danger. The Roman Catholic pontiff told an audience in early September 1983 that the world might be transitioning to "a new prewar phase."[20] The expressed fear was highly significant coming from this Polish pope, the former Cardinal Karol Wojtyła, whom some perceived as a cold warrior in his own right and who indeed had been the subject of recruitment efforts by President Reagan's policy entrepreneurs. John Paul II had supported Solidarity's efforts in Poland over appeals to back down from his Polish colleague, Stefan Cardinal Wyszyński. The pope received Lech Wałęsa at St. Peters in 1981. At the height of the Warsaw government's crackdown against the popular movement, John Paul II made a pastoral visit to Poland in which the huge public turnout and fervid Catholic response put a shot across the Warsaw government's bow, serving notice that the Catholic Church in Poland and Solidarity were really the same—the Polish people. It could hardly be otherwise in a land where to be Catholic was to belong to the overwhelming majority, to such a degree that communism in Poland had never attempted to suppress religious exercise, as had been the case in the Soviet Union.

This predisposition was not evident in Wojtyła's early years as a parish priest, as professor at a Catholic university in Lublin, or even as bishop and then archbishop in Krakow in the 1960s.[21] A cardinal after 1967, Wojtyła steered away from politics. The motherless child of an army officer (his mother had passed away when he was eight years old), both of whose siblings had also perished (his sister before he was even born and his brother, a young doctor, from infectious disease contracted from one of his own patients), Wojtyła had retreated into prayer. And his studies had been of literature. His World War II experience had been in a chemical plant, secretly studying for the priesthood while shying from the Germans, whose persecution of the Church, though wavering more than its war against the Jews, had been equally fierce when it was "on."

The sacred, and the defense of human dignity, were at this man's heart. All this suggests his predisposition to avoid controversy, which was, in fact, demonstrated in Wojtyła's early Church career. But Wojtyła strongly opposed the Vatican reforms instituted by the council Pope John XXIII held in the early 1960s. *That*, rather than communism, in this analyst's view, is what energized Wojtyła's later activism. It was on social-ethical grounds in 1976, during Warsaw's renewed crackdown against the popular tide rising from the beginning of that decade, that Cardinal Wojtyła took the field in what can be construed as a political role. Once he ascended to the papacy in October 1978, John Paul II had the tools of the Roman Catholic Church available to him. The defense of human dignity in communist Poland was not only a desirable goal, a victory for the popular will represented opportunity to restore the freedom to exercise the Catholic faith in Poland. Religious aims, pursued by religious means, could contribute to political ends.

Soviet authorities, not to mention Polish ones, were concerned from the beginning of John Paul's pontificate that he might prove a disruptive influence. Party official Oleg Bogomolov, in an assessment for Soviet leaders barely two weeks after John Paul II's christening, predicted that the Church would adopt "a new aggressiveness" in its policy toward the Soviet bloc.[22] Indeed Wojtyła made his first visit to Poland as pope in June 1979. The Warsaw government had no alternative but to accept his visit, rejecting Soviet advice not to do so. Some observers credit this visit as John Paul II's most important contribution to the Polish revolution for his admonition to the people to "be not afraid."[23] When the strikes began at the Lenin Shipyards in Gdańsk a year later, the workers swiftly erected religious symbols, among them a portrait of John Paul II. The pope kept a watching brief on subsequent developments. The KGB and Bulgarian intelligence were widely accused of playing a role in Turkish terrorist Mehmet Ali Agca's May 1981 assassination attempt against the pope, in which John Paul II was gravely wounded. Though this was not the case,[24] the assertion was strongly made at the time and could easily have led Wojtyła to adopt an even fiercer anti-Soviet role. And the pontiff did keep up the pressure, with weekly radio broadcasts to Poland. He also supported an Italian charity, Parcels to Poland, which sent care packages to addresses supplied by Solidarity, and reportedly made cash donatives from the Papal Treasury to Solidarity accounts. In June 1982 he hosted President Reagan at the Vatican—another event that passes with the barest of mentions in the Reagan diaries. After John Paul's June 1983 pastoral visit, the Warsaw government felt obliged, finally, to lift martial law, though it kept up certain security measures against Solidarity.

Conversely, Pope John Paul II remained silent on the Euromissile deployments that rent the Western societies all around him and said practically nothing about the U.S. Strategic Defense Initiative, which had had a gravely destabilizing impact on arms control negotiations if not yet the strategic balance itself. He also intervened to soften the appeal against nuclear war issued by a conference of American bishops. And the pope's failure to criticize the Reagan administration's October 1983 invasion of Grenada, his philosophical offensive against "Liberation Theology" in Latin America, combined with a 1983 pastoral visit to Nicaragua, had the effect of supporting Reagan's covert war in Central America.

This context makes John Paul's late-1983 fears of the world entering a prewar phase of history quite striking. No hard evidence is available to help interpret the origins of this stark warning. Only conjecture is possible. The American bishops' statement may have accomplished more than has been thought, leading John Paul to reflect on the increase of hysteria across the globe, especially in the wake of the KAL-007 shootdown. One concrete datum relates directly to the Church—John Paul's first and dearest concern—and resides in the murder, allegedly by Polish secret police, of the popular priest Father Jerzy Popieluszko. This may well have led the pope to reconsider his political activism. It is notable that through the remainder of the decade John Paul's actions were more muted. The pope's warning may also have helped President Reagan see the consequences of the War Scare of 1983 more clearly. Reagan's change of course the following year thus owed something to the close relationship the president felt he had forged with the pontiff. When Prime Minister Margaret Thatcher told Reagan that a new Soviet leader, Mikhail Gorbachev, seemed to be a person with whom one could really do business, the combination of the new general secretary and the pope, both American friends, indeed swayed the president and changed the course of history. This construction is different from the triumphalist narrative of the relations among the three leaders but has in common an understanding that individual action has real historical meaning.

Mikhail Gorbachev

Without Mikhail Gorbachev this history would have evolved very differently. If the inquiry came down to a demand to nominate *the* most important individual involved in the final decade of the Cold War, Gorbachev would have the strongest claim to the title. Of course, he had unique advantages in that the political process was so different in Russia and the powers of the chairman of the Politburo and general secretary of the CPSU were so broad, but Gorbachev's consciousness of the need for reform in Russia, his intelligence and willingness to entertain radical proposals, his ability to engage in political maneuver to achieve goals, and his lack of a stake in the old ways were all key elements in the Cold War's outcome. Many Soviet citizens exhibited determination, as did Gorbachev, but only he put that determination in the service of imagination.

Gorbachev was no radical, at least not at the beginning. He was a committed Marxist-Leninist steeped in CPSU traditions and the protégé of Yuri Andropov to boot. But the Soviet leader was also a pragmatist and a problem solver, and his goal—achieving a new dynamism in Soviet society—eventually led Gorbachev down paths not trodden since Lenin's abortive "New Economic Program" of the

1920s, then to roads never taken at all. It may fairly be said that Mikhail Gorbachev began as a communist reformer and ended up a social democrat.

The new Soviet leader was a man of the land—and of the party. Born to a peasant family in the North Caucasus in 1931, Gorbachev had worked on a collective farm. His undergraduate degree had been in agriculture. His party work had, among other things, focused on organizing farmers, and he had risen to agricultural secretary of the CPSU apparatus in Stavropol, Gorbachev's native region and the focus of his entire career before his Moscow days. At the apex of the power structure, as a Politburo member, his portfolio had been agriculture.

Beyond that, Gorbachev had been a quintessential party apparatchik. As a youth in secondary school, he had penned an award-winning essay on the glories of Stalin. His work as a stalwart of the Komsomol communist youth organization had stood out—enough to earn him the prestigious Order of the Red Banner at the tender age of eighteen. Gorbachev studied law at Moscow State University and graduated in 1955, but then he abandoned the field to turn to party work. He clearly intended to make his life in the CPSU and was sent by the party to Stavropol, no doubt because he came from that *kray*, as the Soviets termed this regional area.[25] There he functioned as a CPSU chapter secretary and Komsomol organizer. In 1960 he rose to the *kray* staff as first secretary of the Komsomol, and a year later he became deputy chief (second secretary) of the regional party committee, which he led by 1970. Gorbachev became a member of the CPSU Central Committee in 1971. He arrived in Moscow in 1978 as a party secretary—for agriculture.

Andrei Gromyko tells the story of how, one day that November, Soviet leader Leonid Brezhnev telephoned him to ask his opinion of Gorbachev, whom he was considering elevating to the Politburo. Both had heard good things about the man. Gromyko responded, "He sounds like a communist—straightforward, honest, and very well-trained." Gorbachev became a candidate member (nonvoting) of the Politburo in 1979 and a full member a year later. "I watched him work, and not from the sidelines," Gromyko observes. "We worked closely together in the Politburo and many times had intensive discussions. . . . [He was] skillful not only at identifying problems but at exposing the facts which make it plain that a decision has to be taken and determining the solution he sees as most appropriate."[26] In deliberations, Gorbachev was a persuasive advocate and a consensus builder. Historian Vladislav Zubok believes that this man "attacked a problem like a tank attacking enemy defenses."[27]

The new Soviet man's weaknesses were less apparent than his strengths, or to be more precise, became apparent to outside observers only much later. Gorbachev lacked patience and a certain steadfastness. He was perfectly willing to question previous wisdom and order modifications and willing to change direction again if a different course offered better chances for progress, but the other side of that coin was the danger of prematurely abandoning a line of action that, given more time, could have worked.

Gorbachev's background in agriculture helped him develop his approach to problem solving. In farming the relationship between inputs and outputs is direct, and results are apparent within the space of a few months. In the Soviet context, in which agricultural production had lagged at least since the 1960s, solving problems was very necessary. Gorbachev experienced this firsthand—the USSR Food Program he inaugurated soon after arriving in Moscow proved yet another failed solution. Col. Gen. Dmitri Volkogonov, subsequently a prominent commentator, maintains that this Gorbachev initiative "collapsed spectacularly."[28] Perhaps because Soviet agriculture was so chronically challenged, the setback does not seem to have hurt Gorbachev with his Politburo colleagues.

The man from Stavropol was notable too for being twenty years younger than most other Politburo members. And his Stavropol background served Gorbachev another way—senior Soviet leaders Yuri Andropov and Mikhail Suslov since the 1960s had often vacationed at spas in that area, where party official Gorbachev had been responsible for their care and amenities. Both subsequently took an interest in his career, and in fact he became known as a protégé of Andropov. With the support of the then-KGB chief, the protégé became head of the CPSU Central Committee secretariat. By the early 1980s Brezhnev was old and senile. He passed away in 1982. Andropov replaced him, but his strained kidneys finally gave out. He died in early 1984. Close Brezhnev associate Konstantin Chernenko took the helm then, but Gorbachev was given new responsibilities as chairman of the Politburo committee on Poland, and he often presided over the full body. Like his predecessor, Chernenko was sick and succumbed to heart failure in March 1985. The need for stability at the head of the Politburo naturally brought forward Gorbachev's name. Andrei Gromyko nominated him for the top job. Gorbachev was confirmed in less than twenty-four hours, and the succession was announced on March 11, 1985. His arrival on the scene came at a difficult moment for the Soviet Union.

Russia's problem with agriculture was merely symptomatic of a much wider set of economic woes that gravely weakened the Soviet state. This was not a mystery to Politburo leaders. A top Soviet analyst, Georgi Arbatov, writes of Andropov, "I am convinced that he was aware that the state of the country . . . had been abnormal, and that something serious had to be done, beginning with the economy."[29]

Arbatov believes that Andropov had no real interest or understanding of economic matters and that his "solutions" were limited to such things as halting the construction of monuments and memorials (which Chernenko reversed). But Andropov had commissioned a wide range of studies of restorative measures, and Gorbachev would later affirm that many actions he took were based upon the investigations undertaken at his mentor's behest. Chernenko had spoken of the need to accelerate the Soviet economy in early 1984, though he had not returned to that issue. Gorbachev began by talking of acceleration but swiftly moved beyond that to consider transformation. His earliest measure, a bid to end alcoholism by restricting liquor sales, not only proved unpopular and counterproductive but also hurt the state treasury, cutting receipts from excise taxes. That course was abandoned. Increasing the production of consumer products proved difficult given the USSR's rigid economic structure. Simple measures would not work. Moreover, Russians' expectations for their quality of life were tremendously higher than they had been in Stalin's time, or indeed in that of Brezhnev. The conspicuous consumption of the *nomenklatura* (the communist elite) was visible to all. Gorbachev moved to more radical reforms. His heralded perestroika program was explicitly aimed at breaking down barriers to change. Fast-forward several generations of reform formulas, and ultimately Gorbachev found himself aiming at a market economy. But he repeatedly dismissed his top advisers, and by dumping their schemes, he often sacrificed what limited progress had been achieved thus far. Gorbachev's weaknesses were most evident in his handling of the Soviet economy.

The Polish troubles, familiar from Gorbachev's Politburo work, were merely one facet of Moscow's strained relationship with Eastern Europe, which remained an economic drain on the Soviet Union while its contribution to Soviet security had become increasingly questionable. Here too change had already begun. In Poland the Jaruzelski government ended martial law, released Lech Wałęsa, and made at least some concessions to the popular will. Other Eastern European states were also moving toward limited accommodation with their dissidents. Moscow looked on uneasily but made no effort to enforce the Brezhnev doctrine.

The stalemate of the Soviet war in Afghanistan continued as Gorbachev came to power in Moscow. Here he was determined to change the equation. Georgi Arbatov of the influential Institute for U.S. and Canadian Studies gave the new leader a blueprint, recommending not only a withdrawal from Afghanistan but unilateral reductions in Warsaw Pact forces and troops posted on the Chinese border, but that proved too much for Gorbachev.[30] Instead, within a couple of months of taking the reins, Gorbachev set a time limit for the Soviet military in the war. Either

Russia would win in two years, Gorbachev ordained, or it would get out. He gave the military a bigger budget for the war, sanctioned a revised military strategy, and looked on as the Afghan political leadership was replaced, but before the clock ran out on the deadline, Gorbachev changed course. In 1986 he decreed the withdrawal would proceed.

Gorbachev had expressed orthodoxy in security matters at the time of the KAL-007 incident, arguing in the Politburo that the shootdown had been a legitimate defensive action, but the aftermath called into question the honesty of Soviet military reporting channels and the flexibility of its command arrangements. The replacement of the hard-line Soviet chief of staff, Marshal Nikolai Ogarkov, had come in 1984 under Chernenko. Ogarkov had been a proponent of military expansion and higher defense budgets. His successor, Marshal Sergei Akhromeyev, though holding many similar views, proved more amenable to political direction. The Chernobyl nuclear accident also helped clip the wings of the Soviet military. Gorbachev would be more skeptical than his predecessors and also had more room to move.

Mikhail Gorbachev first met Ronald Reagan at a summit conference in Geneva in 1985. He had previously corresponded with Reagan on possible arms-control measures, and in earnest of Soviet intentions came with a Politburo decision to hold up deployments of medium-range SS-20 missiles (the systems corresponding to the U.S. cruise missiles and Pershing IIs), shifting the emplacement of new rockets from European Russia to sectors opposite China. But the real test came at Geneva. There the CIA had mounted a special effort to induce public manifestations of disdain for the Soviets as their leader arrived. Gorbachev and Reagan began on a poor footing, with the president reading from note cards and reciting boilerplate U.S. arms-control positions. Pavel Palazchenko, one of Gorbachev's translators, saw Gorbachev's frustration. The Politburo chief managed occasional sallies where he intimated flexibility on arms and such regional issues as Afghanistan. Gorbachev and Reagan then held a private session during which both put some cards on the table, and by the second plenary the ice had broken. The banter at the dinner Gorbachev hosted later revealed that clearly, Palazchenko recalls. Talk of the countries' respective problems—drugs in the United States, liquor in the Soviet Union—led someone to quip that drinking was still a good idea if it meant a toast for peace. "Oh yes," Gorbachev shot back. "It is only drinking without a toast that is called alcoholism."[31]

Gorbachev went on to quote the Bible—Ecclesiastes, on there being a time for everything—and reflected on the need to think more of the future than about the past. President Reagan returned from Geneva and demanded that his bureaucracy study whether U.S. arms control positions were self-serving, a major Soviet concern. Although Reagan's policy entrepreneurs crafted reports that rejected that charge, Gorbachev had gotten through to Mr. Reagan. He and Gorbachev would do business.

At one stroke Mikhail Gorbachev had moved the negotiating process off ground zero even without any actual agreement. Gorbachev soon began to appreciate that he *needed* progress in foreign affairs—to offset bottlenecks in domestic reform, reopen the spigot on multilateral credits, and create a path to economic gain by reducing military spending. Before the end of the Reagan presidency, there would be more summits and agreements, and Gorbachev would have taken every one of the steps Arbatov once recommended but that he had rejected out of hand. With Gorbachev's determination to move ahead began the move to superpower accommodation, and ultimately the end of the Cold War.

The Role of Individual Agency

"Individual agency" is the current term of art, but the notion that Great Leaders make history has a long and storied tradition. Although it has become fashionable to attribute events to systemic forces, global trends, institutional dynamics, security imperatives, cultural constraints, and other overarching causes, explanations of causality that emphasize individual agency have not lost their potency. The end of the Cold War is a good example. Without Margaret Thatcher, Lech Wałęsa, Ronald Reagan, John Paul II, and Mikhail Gorbachev, the decade of the 1980s would have evolved very differently. Nor are these the only important characters. They have been selected here to permit layering in some key facets of the story. The insertion of Václav Havel, Hans-Dietrich Genscher, François Mitterand, George Shultz, Egon Bahr, Gustav Husak, Erich Honecker, William J. Casey, or any of a host of others would have enabled the narrative to bring in alternate developments, some of them quite important. Individuals still have a crucial role in history and in explanations of causality.

But did Great Leaders end the Cold War? A cadre of Reagan loyalists would answer in the affirmative and claim the honor for the president. Some observers would agree with the general point but award the mantle to Mikhail Gorbachev. Or they could share the glory. James Mann, who writes of President Reagan's quiet rebellion against the restraints that bound him, puts it this way: "Unquestionably, Gorbachev played the leading role in bringing the four-decade-old conflict to a close. Yet Reagan, overcoming considerable opposition of his own at home, played a crucial role by buttressing Gorbachev's political position."[32] Historian Melvyn Leffler expresses a similar view: "No one, then, was more responsible for ending the Cold War than the Soviet leader. Reagan was critically important, but Gorbachev was the indispensible agent of change."[33] This sense of shared credit, with Gorbachev in the lead, has become the consensus.

Yet there are analysts who would spread the renown more widely—hence Thatcher, John Paul II, Wałęsa, or any of the other figures one might care to nominate. Every one of these persons contributed something to the outcome, helping to structure the intervening events that led from high Cold War to none at all. And what of the person who took the first brick out of the Berlin Wall? In his most recent effort to assay the Cold War, John Lewis Gaddis puts this thought nicely:

> What no one understood, at the beginning of 1989, was that the Soviet Union, its empire, its ideology—and therefore the Cold War itself—was a sandpile ready to slide. All it took to make that happen were a few more grains of sand. The people who dropped them were not in charge of superpowers or movements or religions: they were ordinary people with simple priorities who saw, seized, and sometimes stumbled into opportunities. In doing so, they caused a collapse no one could stop. Their 'leaders' had little choice but to follow.[34]

The huge edifice of perceptions, expectations, policies, war plans, collections of armaments, and national objectives that was the Cold War lay beyond the individual agency of Great Leaders. Put another way, the ship of state was a supertanker, not a sailboat, and responded to the tiller quite differently than a small craft. Neither Gorbachev nor Reagan aimed at ending the Cold War, at least not until late in the game, and perhaps not even then. In fact, Reagan, owing to his methods of management, did not really even have his hand on the tiller; and Gorbachev, faced with the increasing inertia of the Soviet bureaucracy, gradually discovered the connection between tiller and rudder on his ship was being severed. Their agency was invaluable in recognizing the evolution of the situations they faced and in responding in ways that avoided further deterioration of the situation, but the forces acting upon them were greater than their span of command. Individual agency is logically necessary but not sufficient as an explanation for how the Cold War ended, the investigation of which therefore entails examining more factors that bear on these events.

Examining the Impact of Characters

It is nevertheless apparent that the Great Leader is a primary character in understanding the world and its progress, and certainly biography is a staple of historical inquiry. For the purposes of diplomatic history, this kind of approach is not mere biography, not even a rendition of the Great Person and Their Times. It is important to situate a figure in his or her milieu, as it is important to establish essential biographical information, but the core analytical problem is to ascribe motive. The point is not simply to say something about the individuals involved in an episode. Understanding milieu, context, and biographical detail, the standard methods of biography, are the techniques to use here as well. The analyst is not researching a character simply to describe them but for the ultimate purpose of explaining something else, a historical development. The observer's challenge is to set her eye for detail on identifying the motives, attributes, and characteristic practices that affected the outcome of specific events or sets of events. The object is to find the key factor that helps explain why the person acted a certain way. The relevant source material is conventional: memoirs, reflections by others, meeting records with their notes of the words of the person, decision documents, contemporaneous accounts, speeches, and media commentary. For this particular period, television and radio coverage, including speeches and press conferences, most particularly anything off-the-cuff, are also important. This is the raw data that needs mining.

In the case of how the Cold War ended, the set of individuals covered here was critical to setting in motion two of the central dynamics of the decade. The first, the "troubles" in Poland, helped catalyze parallel movements in other Eastern European lands, eroding the dominance of communist parties throughout these Soviet allies. Lech Wałęsa, who had his eyes only on the conditions for workers in his native Poland, was motivated by that labor struggle. His drive to establish labor power in the form of collective bargaining collided with the concept of state power in a communist nation. And the gradual success of that drive—about which more will be said in a later chapter—meant a loosening of state power. There were special conditions in Poland, the most important of which was the fealty and religiosity of the Roman Catholic majority. The tenacity of that religious penetration, which prevented the Warsaw government from perfecting its state power, also opened a wedge for the workers. Pope John Paul II's purpose was to widen religious freedom, but in the Polish environment Catholic action had a natural harmony, a synergy, with labor activism.

The narrative assessed John Paul's sudden fears of a growing prewar situation as flowing from his appreciation of a growing desperation in Warsaw, suddenly prepared to countenance the murder of Catholic priests, as well as the shock of the KAL-007 incident. His warning, in turn, had an impact on President Ronald Reagan, helping the president understand that international conditions were more serious than he had imagined. The effect of the War Scare of 1983 was to startle Reagan out of the diplomatic deadlock produced by his policy entrepreneurs, who were driven by their visions of acquiring strategic superiority. This, the second key dynamic of the decade, was the move from a stance—in the capitals of both superpowers—of escalating confrontation to one of incipient and then accelerating accommodation. Reagan acted from dedication to a dream, finally discarding a stream of policy advice that viewed negotiation as a vehicle to attain superiority or, failing that, to score propaganda points. Margaret Thatcher's central role lay in making the link between Mr. Reagan and Mikhail Gorbachev. Responding to the long British desire to preserve a special relationship with the United States, her own disquiet over rising hysteria in Western Europe and the arms race complications she saw growing from the Strategic Defense Initiative, Thatcher played the role of facilitator.

Mikhail Gorbachev's motives were more basic. Pragmatist that he was, Gorbachev understood that some progress in international relations would help him in the struggle to restructure the Soviet Union, and subsequently that foreign policy movement was crucial to domestic reform. Gorbachev proceeded quite straightforwardly to ensure that that movement occurred. Later the narrative will display more evidence of Gorbachev's actions in a variety of contexts, but that first sally at Geneva in 1985 effected a tipping point that set the dynamics of international relations in a new direction. Still, both Reagan and Gorbachev were subject to the activities of the officials and bureaucracies that worked for them. The end of the Cold War cannot be understood without examining the impact of government structures on policy outputs. These are a vital field of inquiry.

CHAPTER 3

ALICE IN WONDERLAND

Institutions, Operators, and Political Prerogatives

MANY CHALLENGES CONFRONT THE HISTORIAN who sets out to explain a chain of events. Beyond the detective work of assembling the material—hopefully unearthing new data—and the need to bring a fresh perspective to the subject lie a number of obstacles. It is often the case that describing the major players and their motives plus rendering their goals fails to explain events adequately. This is true of the end of the Cold War. President Reagan's command of the issues and his attention to management were not enough to determine the evolution of events on his watch. As a rule, no leader has full command, of course, but for illustrative purposes the Reagan administration supplies historians a particularly rich field of inquiry. Alongside the president labored a crowd of like-minded individuals whom Reagan brought with him to power, who had savvy and implemented their own agendas within the rubric of his world vision. This group will be called "policy entrepreneurs," for their efforts were very much entrepreneurial in nature and the image fits precisely with the free-market theories championed by the president. The entrepreneurs were responsible for much of the concrete content of Reagan administration policies in almost every field from supply-side economics to defense and foreign policy. It is notable that the administration's most troubled policies—such as the Strategic Defense Initiative—were those few initiated by the president himself.

What distinguishes the policy entrepreneurs of the Reagan era from any collection of senior government officials is the uncommon range of their license to act—given by the president—and single-minded dedication to their particular agendas. Political loyalty to "Reaganism" plus conservative principles purchased this freedom. Officials always have policy views they try to enact, but in most cases actors shape their proposals to fit the president's program, work to enshrine those prescriptions as policy, and loyally act to implement them. Individuals who stray off the reservation are drummed out of the group or left isolated. In the Reagan management scheme, by contrast, individuals competed to seize issue areas and became the authorities in those fields, and their predilections became *the president's* policy, so long as they remained loyal to Mr. Reagan. The president's reluctance to impose discipline on his official family signaled to the entrepreneurs that such behavior was acceptable. The system flourished because President Reagan relied on his vision of where he wanted to go but had no articulated road map for how to get there. The entrepreneurs supplied the policies to go with the vision.

In the Soviet system, collective action was more important than individual initiative, so there the relative importance of institutions was much greater. But even in Ronald Reagan's Washington the freedom of the policy entrepreneurs was not unfettered. Institutions still figured in the mix: the entrepreneurs were only so many, embedded within much larger bureaucracies that had to be drawn in, pulled along, or convinced to support particular agendas. And there were other power centers besides the White House. The most important lay in Congress, whose role was considerable. Both in the political world and within the bureaucracy there existed previous understandings on policy consensus, standard procedures, and acknowledged arrangements on turf, some of which stood to be subverted by the entrepreneurs' agendas.

Neither President Reagan nor the policy entrepreneurs were unitary actors. They could not simply issue orders and expect them to be carried out in the way they preferred. The same was true of the Soviet general secretary and members of the Politburo. In both America and Russia, leaders faced the need to act through a diversified collection of departments and ministries, bureaus and offices, even individuals. Ministries had their standard procedures, ones that might or might not be suited to the contemplated action. Individuals had their own viewpoints, and these could differ from those of top officials. Actions at both governmental and individual levels could be modified by political considerations. During the Cold War of the 1980s, the activities of bureaucracies and bureaucrats, on both sides, had an important impact on events, sometimes moderating them, occasionally aggravating outcomes.

In many cases, a few of which will be examined here, enshrining a policy meant running roughshod over all opposition, internal and external. In turn this necessitated keeping hold of the tiller as the ship of state entered the rapids of policy dispute and ignoring all obstacles as the transit was made, in essence donning blinders. President Reagan was vital to the policy struggle because his vision could be cited as justification for the measure proposed. Historian Richard Neustadt long ago concocted the image of the "president in sneakers," the man who despite supreme command needed to bring along the lowest level officials, such other organs of government as the legislature, and the people.[1] Neustadt concerned himself primarily with the presidency as a political process, but the essential concept applies also to government bureaucracies. The president sells his policy, using the bully pulpit of office, his ability to grant favors, and his political strength to build consensus. Practice during the Reagan years was mostly different. Here the entrepreneurs struggled to gain the president's agreement so he might intercede in favor of a given policy agenda. Compromise was to be avoided. The purpose of invoking the president was to override objections.

The remainder of this chapter will present a series of events of the decade from both sides of the Cold War. These will add layers of meaning to the barebones account of the first chapter, fleshing out key episodes in this evolution. Equally important, the framing here will demonstrate kinds of insight that can be provided through analysis of the behavior of institutions and actors other than principals (such as the policy entrepreneurs), and of political factors. The levels-of-analysis approach is used here primarily because different types of developments better account for certain events than others. All add to the overall picture, producing an integrated narrative with greater explanatory value. The first, which shows the policy entrepreneurs in action, is the story of how the Reagan administration came to offer an arms control proposal known as the "Zero Option."

Reagan's Entrepreneurs and Arms Control

The Zero Option began as a device to try to ameliorate the arms race in Europe. As noted in chapter 1, the nuclear balance in Europe had been complicated during the Carter administration when the Soviets began deploying a modern medium-range missile armed with multiple warheads. President Carter had countered with a plan to deploy a corresponding force within NATO Europe composed of fast-acting Pershing II missiles plus slower ground-launched cruise missiles. West German chancellor Helmut Schmidt played a key role in convincing other NATO partners to accept the program by giving a speech that presented the missile deployment as a last resort, to be undertaken only if negotiations failed. NATO accepted a "dual-track" program that explicitly provided for a negotiation, with missile deployment contingent on that outcome. It thus became incumbent on the United States to engage the Soviet Union in talks on this subject. When Jimmy Carter lost the 1980 election to Ronald Reagan, it fell to the Reagan administration to fulfill that commitment.[2]

The negotiation entailed by the "Euromissiles," as they became known, proved to be the defining moment for one of the officials who established themselves as policy entrepreneurs, Richard Perle, the assistant secretary of defense for international security policy. The State Department was assembling a bargaining position that aimed at stabilizing the European nuclear balance at an equal level, the lowest one negotiable. From Perle's perspective that was not acceptable since the Euromissiles were single-warhead weapons while the equivalent Soviet system, known to NATO as the SS-20 (and to Russians as the RS-20), carried three. Some deemed this acceptable because the British and French had nuclear forces, so far outside the arms control arena, for which the Russians presumably wished to compensate. Perle took the idea of "equality" and proposed zero missiles, a concept that became known as the Zero Option. In practice, the Zero Option meant the United States would forgo deploying the Euromissiles if the Soviets reduced their intermediate-range force to zero. Since the Soviets were deploying SS-20s to replace older missiles that had been in the field since the 1950s, an agreement on this basis amounted to the Russians dismantling their entire theater missile force while the British and French retained a substantial nuclear capability aimed at Moscow. As Thomas Graham Jr., a senior official with State's Arms Control and Disarmament Agency (ACDA), put it, "This was a proposal claimed to be inspired by Dutch peace groups, but in actuality it was devised by . . . Perle and was intended to be unacceptable."[3] President Reagan recognized this.[4] (Perle's competitor, State Department official Richard Burt, told British peace activist Mary Kaldor that the "zero" device had been lifted directly from banners carried by the Campaign for Nuclear Disarmament (CND) protest group.[5]) Soviet rejection would then legitimate deployment of the Euromissiles, among which the Pershing IIs posed a direct threat to Soviet leadership and military command centers. Perle outmaneuvered State Department officials who proposed alternative approaches. Then–secretary of state Alexander M. Haig opposed the proposal precisely because he knew the formula would be nonnegotiable. Defense Secretary Caspar Weinberger sided with Perle. Mr. Reagan calls this "one of many instances I faced as president when my policy of encouraging cabinet members to speak freely and to fight for their points of view put me in the middle." He mulled over the alternatives during a cross-country flight aboard the "doomsday plane," a specially built Boeing 747 aircraft configured as an airborne command post to serve the president in case of nuclear war. At a National Security Council meeting on November 5, 1981, President Reagan approved the Zero Option. He then used a televised speech divulging details of the proposal as a device to lock it in. As Reagan later wrote, "I'd learned as a union negotiator that it's never smart to show your hole card in advance." Of course, the curious thing was that there *was* no hole card, no bottom line to be "tipped off," as the president put it, because there was no intention of compromising.[6]

The negotiation opened on November 30. After listening to U.S. proposals, in a second round early in 1982 the Soviets responded that they wished to take British and French forces into account. American negotiators rejected that possibility. The Russians came back with a series of proposals, each seeking compensation for the British and French, offering reduced levels of Soviet missiles but never zero. As time went on and a succession of Russian formulas was rejected, American intransigence became increasingly visible. Meanwhile, opposition in the form of the "nuclear freeze" movement (which will be discussed in chapter 4) in both Western Europe and the United States created political difficulties for continued American stonewalling. At length Paul H. Nitze, U.S. delegation chief and another of the policy entrepreneurs, decided to try to craft a compromise proposal with his Soviet counterpart in these Geneva talks that each would then attempt to sell at home.

Nitze's initiative led to the episode afterward known as the "Walk in the Woods," as he and Soviet diplomat Yuli Kvitsinsky, literally on a walk in the woods at Saint Cergue, sitting on a log during a rain shower, cobbled together an alternative on July 16. The Nitze formula involved equal numbers of intermediate-range-missile warheads set to a low level, but most importantly, the United States would not field the Pershing II, thus answering the Soviets' strongest objections. In August Nitze returned to Washington to secure backing for his proposal. By cutting Richard Perle out of the loop and restricting information to those who might inform Perle, Nitze succeeded in lining up substantial backing for his idea. He presented it to Defense Secretary Weinberger, another powerful entrepreneur, while Perle was out of town. Nitze also sought support from Perle's boss, Undersecretary of Defense Fred Iklé. According to Thomas Graham, the Joint Chiefs of Staff appeared to have no objections; Nitze's own direct superior, Arms Control and Disarmament Agency chief Eugene V. Rostow, supported the idea; and President Reagan expressed interest at an initial NSC meeting on August 9. According to George Shultz, just coming in as secretary of state, the proposal "was well known to the president and all his top advisers," and it "was studied throughout the rest of the summer."[7] President Reagan was away at Rancho del Cielo from August 20 to September 7, a fatal lapse for Nitze's entrepreneurial effort.

Richard Perle was in Colorado, on a working vacation at an Aspen Institute workshop on arms control, when all this began. Alerted by an assistant, Perle counseled delay, which fit with Washington's summertime tempo and people's vacations, but also afforded him time to line up opposition to the Nitze formula. After his return, Perle was able to reverse the playing field, bringing Secretary Weinberger into his own camp, convincing the Joint Chiefs that Nitze had falsified their opinion in an early memorandum, and backing down Fred Iklé. Formerly a powerful legislative aide in Congress, Perle could also mobilize Capitol Hill figures to put additional pressure on the administration. When the National Security Planning Group, an NSC offshoot, met to consider the formula on September 13, Perle had his ducks all lined up in a row. Paul Nitze made the strongest presentation he could, but this time there were few on his side. With Weinberger and the Chiefs united in opposition, President Reagan bought the dangerous reasoning that *because* the Russians were most afraid of the Pershing II the United States ought not to give it up. New instructions for the delegation chief were not to raise the proposal on his own and to reject it if the Soviets did so. President Reagan told Nitze that if he were asked why the United States was refusing to negotiate on this proposal, he should reply, because "I am just one tough son of a bitch."[8]

A few days later President Reagan sealed the U.S. position in concrete with a national security decision directive that specified zero missiles as the goal. Just to add clarity, the old moniker of Zero Option suddenly mutated into the "Zero-Zero Option"—in other words no missiles on either side—making clear the goal for the Soviets was zero only and preserving the unacceptable nature of the U.S. bargaining position. George Shultz was reduced to arguing that private informal contacts were useful in negotiations, and Mr. Reagan agreed with that, but Paul Nitze ended up with a letter of reprimand from the president. As for Nitze's direct boss, according to Shultz, "Rostow let his disappointment show and eventually was asked to resign."[9] Richard Perle continued his entrepreneurial ways. Negotiations on intermediate-range nuclear forces remained stalemated.

The Zero Option episode shows the policy entrepreneurs in stark relief. Both major proposals in this case were tabled by subordinate officials and maneuvered through the bureaucracy in such a way as to avoid the normal interagency process. One became official U.S. policy and the second almost did so, except that it was derailed by a further set of deft maneuvers. The episode also shows President Reagan agreeing with mutually contradictory initiatives. In the Reagan era, personal agendas clearly held sway. But sometimes depth of commitment to an agenda could obscure real global dangers. That would become clear in the case of Able Archer 83.

A Moment of Terror

Ronald Reagan's image of morning in America and his unabashed acceptance of his policy entrepreneurs' proposals did not so much end the Cold War on Washington's terms as threaten its intensification and perhaps climax in an act of thermonuclear madness. Unintended consequences abound in history, yet the logic of events often diverges from linear progression. On the cusp of monumental confrontation at the moment of the NATO exercise Able Archer in 1983, the sides turned away. Afterward, the well-entrenched policy entrepreneurs in the Reagan administration found themselves increasingly isolated. This occurred despite President Reagan's success at marshalling political support for his stance and the unity of vision among him and the entrepreneurs. How does one account for this? When in doubt, dig deeper. In the case of the Able Archer 83 turnaway, two elements afford the best insights. One, intelligence on the adversary, will be discussed here for its relevance but reserved mainly for a subsequent chapter. The second determinant of action showcased here is the impact of institutions.

In Able Archer, the effect of bureaucracies on the Soviet side created the potential for crisis, and the complete insensitivity of U.S. officials exacerbated that situation, but the operation of a different U.S. bureaucratic structure—for intelligence warning—ultimately served to calm the waters.[10] Able Archer was a standard NATO exercise, its 1983 scenario modified to feature a full rehearsal of the decisions required to approve the use of nuclear weapons. For at least two years before the exercise began, the Russian spy apparatus had been highly concerned that the U.S. might initiate a surprise attack. Ronald Reagan's March 1983 inauguration of the Strategic Defense Initiative fueled Soviet fears of a U.S. first strike, and his condemnation of the Soviet Union as an "evil empire" was incendiary in Moscow. Soviet commanders had also been spooked that fall when the Russian warning system had erroneously produced indications of a massive nuclear attack.[11] Soviet intelligence had already created a special collection program called Operation RYAN to try to glean advance warning of attack. Soviet allies, including the East German and Czech intelligence services, were also drawn into the collection program. The Soviet military, whose theoretical studies into the role of deception in warfare included the notion that surprise could be gained by initiating military operations under the guise of exercises, was willing to believe in that threat. Given his KGB background, Soviet leader Andropov was naturally suspicious. He had himself initiated the RYAN program (with Brezhnev's approval) while he still headed the KGB. Andropov's control was also blunted by the kidney problems that ultimately brought his demise. With Andropov working out of a clinic, the Politburo was spearheaded by even more suspicious characters such as the military boss, Dimitri Ustinov, and party ideology chieftain Mikhail Suslov. Russian leaders were already making speeches acknowledging the red-hot situation and their problems with the United States.

The level of international tension was high owing to stalled arms talks—deadlocked over the one-sided demands of the American entrepreneurs who dominated Reagan administration policies—and the beginning of actual deployment of America's new intermediate-range missiles. The Euromissiles, especially the Pershings, posed a major threat in the event of war, of which the Soviets were well aware, and in the United States, there had been talk of incorporating attacks on leaders into war plans. American military spending had attained higher levels than during the Vietnam War. Tensions were exacerbated by U.S. fleet maneuvers in the Pacific that spring and then by the unfortunate September 1983 incident in which Soviet air defenses mistakenly shot down Korean Air Lines flight 007, an episode the United States shamelessly exploited for propaganda advantage.[12] Under these circumstances, Able Archer could indeed have appeared threatening, especially given organizers' early plans to have President Reagan personally participate. According to some sources, German leader Helmut Kohl and British prime minister Margaret Thatcher actually did play roles, though in different facets of the exercise and not simultaneously. Had the United States actually intended to launch a bolt-from-the-blue surprise attack, the president could have been protected under cover of the exercise, which would have afforded the opportunity to spirit Reagan out of Washington in the doomsday plane. Only about a week before Able Archer, the United States invaded the Caribbean island of Grenada, a member of the British Commonwealth. The sudden spike in top-secret-coded cables that passed between London and Washington as Prime Minister Thatcher protested the action must have seemed highly suspicious in Moscow.[13]

The rigidities of command in the Soviet system played a central role in the KAL-007 shootdown. The Soviet military also hewed to its fixed idea—which subordinates were unable to challenge—that war would begin in a certain way. The same was true of the Russians' intelligence community and Operation RYAN—considered very time-consuming by KGB and military intelligence field stations. Unable to turn up any explicit indications of a U.S. intention to attack, the field could not get the center to reconsider its basic instructions. Prerogatives of leadership and accepted modalities in foreign affairs were similarly decisive in the Soviet walkout from the intermediate-range-missile negotiations. All these were products of institutional interests and standard procedures.

Despite the defects of their system, the Soviets did make efforts to bring their concerns to U.S. attention. A week after the KAL-007 incident, meeting with American secretary of state George Shultz at a European security conference in Madrid, Soviet foreign minister Gromyko expressed fear that the world "is now slipping toward a very dangerous precipice," and added, "It is plain that the great responsibility for not allowing nuclear catastrophe to occur must be borne by the U.S.S.R. and U.S.A. together. In our opinion the U.S.A. should re-evaluate its policies and the President and his administration should look at international affairs in a new way."[14] Shortly after the meeting, Mr. Shultz denounced the Soviets as intransigent. Journalist Don Oberdorfer, in Madrid to report on the conference, recorded in his diary that day, "Shultz' indignant denunciation of Gromyko within 2 or 3 minutes of the Soviet's departure was human and admirable at one level—the personal and narrowly political—but it was chilling at another . . . its implications for the veneer and fabric of dialogue between the superpowers. It may be difficult to get this back on track."[15]

Moscow's ambassador to Washington, Anatoly Dobrynin, recalls both the general problem and the specific. Dobrynin writes, "I can testify that the possibility of a nuclear war with the United States was considered seriously indeed by Khrushchev, Brezhnev, Andropov, and Constantin Chernenko, who was the last leader of the old school." In fact, Andropov told Dobrynin, "Reagan is unpredictable. You should expect anything from him." Soviet leaders did not really believe a nuclear war was winnable, the ambassador notes, "But they were by no means confident that their potential opponents felt the same way, and the incessant American attempts to attain strategic superiority made them fear otherwise." By his own account, Dobrynin and his KGB station chief were both skeptical, but "it was most difficult for us to fathom" President Reagan's repeated public attacks on the Soviet Union. During a 1983 home visit, Ambassador Dobrynin reviewed the situation with Marshal Sergei Akhromeyev, by then chief of the general staff but at this time already the deputy. Dobrynin asked him flat out, "Do you indeed believe the United States and NATO could attack us some day?" Akhromeyev dismissed the importance of beliefs in intentions. He replied, "Soviet military doctrine can be summed up as follows: 1941 shall never be repeated."[16] But the perception of threat was no mere invention of a cadre of Soviet generals alarmed at America's evident hostility. Vladislav Zubok, at that time a junior researcher at Moscow's Institute for U.S. and Canadian Studies, today believes Able Archer may have been the most dangerous moment of the Cold War.[17] Don Oberdorfer expressed the fear succinctly in his journal on September 20: "Incidents can occur which can be interpreted as a grab for advantage or a deliberate or special attack on the other party, and in that way can provoke a major reaction beyond the situation itself."[18]

President Reagan did not take the Able Archer war game seriously and let other commitments preclude his participation, but the exercise went ahead on November 2. At just that moment, the first of the ground-launched cruise missiles were being deployed in Great Britain. The first Pershing IIs would reach West Germany at the beginning of the new year.

The Russians telegraphed their concerns both in private and openly and continued even after Able Archer 83 ended on November 11. The Soviets tested the first of the new generations of intercontinental and submarine-launched ballistic missiles, including one test that demonstrated a capability to intercept incoming missiles. Such missile tests were routinely monitored by U.S. intelligence. Ominously, and in a move they must have believed would be detected by the CIA, the Russians put a regiment of nuclear-armed bombers on alert in East Germany. On November 26 the Soviets walked out of intermediate-range-missile talks. In another move the United States must have detected, the Soviets ordered nuclear missile submarines out of their protected bastion in Arctic waters to cruise off the U.S. coast. Warsaw Pact members were informed on December 1. The Soviets took measures to increase the readiness of pact forces in East Germany, Poland, and Czechoslovakia, as well as Russian troops in the Baltic Military District. They also drilled the communications links that activated Soviet nuclear forces. And they conducted an exercise of their own, its scenario built around a U.S. attack answered by Russian preemption. American officials, intent on their propaganda campaign, did not notice the Soviet signals.

In the midst of Able Archer 83, the KGB sent out a super-alert message noting a change in NATO message formats and instructing all Soviet intelligence personnel to report any signs of war. In the United Kingdom, Harry Burke, a senior analyst at Government Communications Headquarters, the British code-breaking agency, who had the Soviet–Eastern Europe portfolio, was in charge of warning intelligence. Burke actually had no knowledge of Operation RYAN or the KGB alerts, but he observed unusual features in Soviet exercises and wrote a paper cautioning that something might be up. Then Oleg Gordievsky, the KGB's deputy chief of station, who secretly worked as a British spy, told his controllers of the Russians' fears.[19] The British shared this information with Washington several weeks later through the CIA station in London, startling the U.S. intelligence officials responsible for warning of war. CIA Director William J. Casey traveled to Britain to hear Gordievsky's tale firsthand. The CIA then informed the president. This tip-off built upon data already briefed to Reagan in September. It is said that Casey approached Nancy Reagan to reach her husband. It is also reported that Mr. Reagan met secretly with Gordievsky in the White House.[20]

Gradually President Reagan came to appreciate the danger. Secretary of State George Shultz spoke to the president on November 18 about creating an in-house group of experts on the Soviet Union. After the meeting the president confided to his diary, "I feel the Soviets are so defense minded, so paranoid about being attacked that without being in any way soft on them we ought to tell them no one around here has any intention of doing anything like that."[21] Returning from an overseas trip in mid-December, Shultz found a changed tone in Washington. There had been talk at the White House of Reagan delivering a speech directly to the Russian people. After a December 22 meeting with CIA Director Casey, the speech, originally conceived as another move in the propaganda war, was suddenly reframed as a confidence-building measure, a talk to be delivered directly via global satellite link. National Security Adviser Robert McFarlane confirms the unease at the White House, and NSC aide Jack F. Matlock Jr. helped draft text that did what Reagan had speculated about in his diary. On January 16, 1984, the president delivered that speech. Reagan spoke of two peoples who after all did have common interests, "the foremost among them to avoid war." In his memoir, the president would reflect on this period. "Many people at the top of the Soviet hierarchy were genuinely afraid of America," Reagan wrote. "Perhaps this shouldn't have surprised me, but it did."[22]

There may have been quiet feelers from the White House as a result. In his diary a week ahead of the speech, Reagan noted information from George Shultz that Moscow might be interested in a private channel. A meeting of Soviet bloc ambassadors in Washington at the end of January yielded comments from all, save the Cuban representative, that their American interlocutors had lately become more conciliatory. According to Soviet ambassador Viktor Israelyan, in March 1984, during a standing international negotiations group on disarmament in Geneva, his American counterpart took him aside and attempted to arrange a private meeting between Vice President George H. W. Bush and Soviet Politburo member Mikhail Gorbachev. The Americans were convinced, Israelyan relates, that Gorbachev would emerge as the next Soviet supreme leader and wished to open a channel. When Bush appeared in Geneva for his scheduled speech on chemical weapons, he pressed Israelyan on the same point.[23] Ambassador Dobrynin records that "through the first half of the year, the most intriguing challenge for Washington in general and our embassy in particular was to determine just how serious the president was in reaching out to the Soviet Union."[24]

During the intense public discussions of the prospects for the SDI, the Soviet Defense Ministry published a slick pamphlet titled *Whence the Threat to Peace?* that drew attention to the U.S. military buildup.[25] Russian chief of staff Marshal Nikolai Ogarkov underlined that presentation with a paper of his own intended for Western consumption. Soviet scientists had publicly critiqued the feasibility and purposes of the SDI. These commentaries underlined the Russians' fears. Both Soviet scientists and generals blanched at the possibility that an American SDI could function to make a U.S. nuclear first strike feasible, or, equally anxiety-provoking, that space-based SDI weapons utilizing directed-energy principles might actually assume a primary offensive role in striking at targets on the earth's surface.[26]

American officials had difficulty recognizing that there had been a near-crisis with Able Archer or indeed that anything had happened at all. This was the case for U.S. defense and foreign policy officials, enamored of their particular agendas, and especially for the CIA, wedded to its secret wars against the Soviets. In December 1983 Herbert E. Meyer, a conservative journalist and editor whom Bill Casey had brought in to ride herd on the national estimates and act as a political operative, wrote a memo describing the Soviet Union as entering a terminal phase of its history, in which dangers of confrontation might be greater than ever, but refusing to link this point to the Soviet moves during Able Archer. The wake-up call came, again, from the British, who shared a March 1984 review that concluded Moscow might have feared imminent nuclear war. Two months later, the CIA compiled a special national intelligence estimate to assess whether there had been a war scare. It essentially punted, noting many signs of the high tension but refusing to draw out the larger meaning, instead referring to precautions and military prudence.

That fall, the CIA leaked a further Herbert Meyer memorandum, similar to the one from the previous December, again making the end-of-empire argument without understanding that the United States might already have witnessed a crisis episode.[27] Meanwhile, certain agency analysts, among them Soviet expert Melvin A. Goodman, had spoken to Gordievsky directly. "My own meeting," Goodman recollects, "convinced me that the extraordinary alert, which seemed implausible to many, was genuine and that the confrontational style of the Reagan administration was partly responsible."[28] Six years later, during the first Bush administration, the President's Foreign Intelligence Advisory Board reviewed the evidence on the war scare, and its staffer Nina Stewart wrote a paper that archly concluded the CIA had been far too complacent in dismissing Soviet fears. Robert M. Gates, in 1983 the CIA's deputy director for intelligence, frankly admits, "We in the CIA did not really grasp how alarmed the Soviet leaders might have been."[29]

The War Scare of 1983 suggests important features of bureaucratic action. Its impact can vary in both direction and effect. Institutions can also screen out larger considerations, here reinforcing the blinders American policy entrepreneurs had donned earlier. In this case, the shock of going too near the brink had a key effect on an individual—Ronald Reagan—who stepped back from the precipice. Political scientist Beth A. Fischer terms this passage the "Reagan Reversal" and proposes a theory of leader-driven decision making to account for it.[30] From that moment, the sway of hard-line cold warriors in the Reagan administration began to fade. But President Reagan's attention faded too, and the pattern became one step forward and two steps back. The United States did not stop seeking unilateral advantage or, for that matter, pursuing the Cold War—the CIA in particular continued its Polish, Afghan, and Central American operations with enthusiasm. But the war scare did cue President Reagan to the need to offer positive incentives. Reagan rose to the occasion again at the Geneva summit in 1985, but the pattern did not change to one of two steps forward and one back until after Reykjavik a year later—and Mikhail Gorbachev had the most to do with that. Having considerable institutional strength and fighting hard for their positions, the policy entrepreneurs succeeded for a time in ensuring the incentives remained cosmetic, but once momentum built for arms agreements and moves that actually reduced hostilities, Mr. Reagan quickly put his weight behind the drive to reduce tensions in international relations.

The Turning

Other episodes produced different results. Able Archer 83 unfolded rapidly, behind veils of secrecy, too quickly for political factors to apply. But politics is a favorite component of historical analysis and, in many cases, an important, or even the most important, driver in events. It affects institutions, as bureaucrats strain to position themselves amid shifting political currents, as well as the great individuals in history, who strive to stimulate, lead, or follow the existing currents or to fashion new ones. In significant ways politics define the boundaries of permissible individual or institutional action. This is especially true when discrete events form part of a more extended evolution. The Cold War as a whole is one example, as are myriad lines of development within that overall construct. A useful illustration for present purposes is the story of the issue of Soviet compliance with existing arms control agreements, which had policy implications both for negotiation of further accords and for U.S. military programs. On this issue American hard-liners fought to tar the Soviet Union as inherently untrustworthy and use such a determination to unleash new arms buildups. Debating a series of more or less ambiguous charges, the hard-liners eventually won their point when Moscow gave them a clear violation to exploit. But a combination of political trends and institutional factors precluded the outcome the hard-liners sought to achieve. The net effect was to help preserve a path for successful Soviet-American negotiations and consequent progress in reducing Cold War tensions.

From the beginning, Reagan's entrepreneurs, many of them stalwarts of the Committee on the Present Danger, sought to make issues of compliance with arms agreements an irritant for the Soviets, even if that soured the pot for new treaties. And the entrepreneurs controlled the U.S. machinery for verification, so they had means to make their views heard. The ACDA, by law a key actor in negotiations, was put under Eugene V. Rostow, a former CPD principal. The ACDA Verification and Implementation Bureau, which Carter had abolished, was resuscitated under Fred Eimer, among the most conservative arms control professionals. Staffers, including Michael Pillsbury and David Sullivan, the latter a primary exponent of the thesis that the Soviets had aimed to subvert the SALT treaties from the beginning, held key positions. The General Advisory Committee of ACDA, a public review board, was packed with like-minded individuals, then asked to find the Soviets in violation.

Although in February 1981 the administration had decided it would observe the unratified SALT II treaty, just a few months later presidential counselor Ed Meese asserted publicly that the United States was not bound by it. At that moment, State Department lawyer Thomas Graham had just finished a legal analysis for Rostow that showed that under international conventions on diplomatic agreements the opposite was true. President Reagan, who agreed with those who charged Moscow with cheating, was forced to declare that the United States would comply. Thereafter several of the entrepreneurs bent considerable effort to reverse that policy.

A key avenue for this endeavor became the U.S. Congress. The conservative shift of the 1980 election resulted in a Republican Senate with a number of members quite willing to press on Soviet compliance issues. In fact, when operatives such as Pillsbury and Sullivan left the administration, they went to Capitol Hill. Richard Perle, who had come from the Senate office of conservative Democrat Henry Jackson of Washington, moved easily in those circles as well. The political thrust, in the idiom of the day, was to "let Reagan be Reagan." Charges that the Russians cheated on arms agreements were grist for that mill. The KAL-007 shootdown furnished opportunity. Soon afterward, Republican Senator James A. McClure added an amendment to the defense appropriations bill requiring the administration to submit an official report on Soviet compliance; this quickly became an annual exercise.

At first these reports focused on issues left over from the 1970s. David Sullivan had originated some of the charges himself while he was at the CIA a decade earlier, and he joined the administration after a stint on the staff of conservative North Carolina Senator Jesse Helms, who presently emerged as chairman of the powerful Senate Foreign Relations Committee. Many accusations concerned the generation of ballistic missiles the Soviet Union began deploying in 1973–74 and involved their size, weight, and the number of warheads they carried. Sullivan had pressed these issues as violations when he was a CIA analyst. But the charges were no more than political litmus tests because the relevant agreement, the SALT I treaty, contained no provision regulating these characteristics. (At the last minute the United States had inserted a "unilateral statement" attempting to restrict missile size by constraining the dimensions of launch silos containing the rockets, but that had not been agreed to, and the restriction itself was gravely flawed because it specified a general percentage increase rather than explicitly restricting cubic size.) The real fight was not with the Russians but with Henry A. Kissinger, since the flaws traced to his sloppy negotiating while he served as Richard Nixon's national security adviser and since he conducted these talks secretly.[31] A related allegation, that the Russians had tested certain missiles with more than the number of warheads agreed upon, was ambiguous because constraints of this type were not enacted until the SALT II treaty, which remained unratified, and also because Soviet encryption of radio signals (telemetry) from their missile tests (also prohibited only as part of the SALT II treaty) prevented the United States from being certain of the loads the Russian missiles carried. Other compliance charges were similarly ambiguous, and the Soviets had certain charges of their own regarding U.S. practices.

The first report filed as a result of the McClure amendment came in January 1984. It pushed the ambiguous charges for everything they were worth and prejudged the issue even by title—these reports were about "Soviet noncompliance," not about degree of cooperation with the treaty regime. Subsequent reports in February and December 1985 and March 1987 were pitched the same way, though by the last the United States had a real Soviet violation to protest. Meanwhile, the ACDA's General Advisory Committee produced its own reports along the same lines.

President Reagan clearly accepted these arguments. In his January 1984 speech that turned down the heat in the Cold War, he also claimed to have mounting evidence of violations and said, "In recent years we've had serious concerns about compliance with agreements." National Security Adviser McFarlane added, in a November 1984 speech of his own, "We learned that Soviets violate treaties." Reagan made additional claims of the same sort in speeches in Quebec and to the UN General Assembly in 1985, and in others as late as 1987 and 1988. And elsewhere in the administration these charges were widely parroted. Soviet violations became a staple in speeches by CIA Director William Casey, for example. Early in 1985, with SDI feasibility in question and the administration's Peacekeeper missile program still mired in controversy, Caspar Weinberger used violations charges to shore up flagging support for continued high defense budgets.

But despite official reports and violations rhetoric, Ronald Reagan resisted taking the actions that corresponded to the supposed provocation. The administration announced it would not consider itself bound by the SALT II treaty and then in 1985 began to convert or dismantle older ballistic-missile submarines to stay within SALT II treaty limits as new ones armed with the Trident missile put the United States up against those limits. Late in 1985, as Reagan was about to meet the Soviets at a summit in Geneva, he delayed release of one of these violations reports so that it would not complicate the talks. In a clear manifestation of the policy entrepreneurs' work, Defense Secretary Weinberger released a similar report from the Pentagon on the eve of the meeting and accompanied it with a letter to the president—one the secretary made public—offering the advice that the Geneva summit would provide an opportunity to confront the Russians on their violations.

The policy entrepreneurs showed their hand most blatantly in 1985 and after in their attempt to reinterpret the meaning of the Anti-Ballistic Missile (ABM) Treaty of 1972. In this they were abetted by like-minded politicians in Congress, which held hearings on the subject and tried to popularize it. Not long before the Geneva summit, out of the blue, Richard Perle devastated a routine meeting among U.S. officials by questioning the meaning of the ABM Treaty. A lawyer in his office, a man with no arms control background, from a plain reading of the treaty text, professed to find no language that would prohibit exotic missile defenses of the sort contemplated under SDI.[32] Flummoxed officials ordered a legal review, itself carried out by a State Department counselor who was a former district court judge with no international, much less arms control, experience and who sided with this "broad" interpretation. Before that inquiry had even been finished, and days before an NSC meeting on the subject, National Security Adviser McFarlane startled the public by citing the "broad" interpretation in a television interview. The NSC decided in favor of the broad interpretation. Given the public posture already assumed by a White House adviser, President Reagan announced that the United States accepted that broad interpretation but would continue to adhere to the treaty—a carbon copy of his actions with respect to SALT treaty violation charges.

This strange stance on the ABM Treaty upset America's NATO allies, who saw their own nuclear deterrents threatened by a potential Soviet missile defense that could have resulted from the virtual U.S. abrogation of the agreement. It also terrified Moscow. And it concerned Congress members, who worried about the nation's reputation for upholding its treaty commitments. As Capitol Hill hearings threatened to box in the Reagan administration with legislation mandating a traditional interpretation of the treaty, early in 1987 Defense Secretary Weinberger moved to get President Reagan's approval for an *immediate deployment* of the SDI despite the fact that no hardware actually existed. Both the State Department and Joint Chiefs of Staff opposed the move. Reagan liked the idea but postponed a decision. Protests from many allies followed. Congress then enacted its legislation.

By this time, the policy entrepreneurs had a real Soviet violation to exploit. The ABM Treaty had also enacted restrictions on radars, and Moscow had a large early warning radar under construction at Krasnoyarsk in the Urals. The location of that radar violated treaty strictures that required any such installation to be on the nation's periphery. The Soviet military evidently decided that construction would be easier in the Urals. The Krasnoyarsk project had been approved under Brezhnev and had simply moved forward without challenge until the structure was far enough advanced that U.S. reconnaissance satellites could capture detailed photographs that identified its purpose. Moscow reacted to the Krasnoyarsk issue first by denying the radar's existence, then by protesting that it was inoffensive and complaining of similar U.S. radar improvements, and finally by inviting a delegation of American legislators and technical experts to examine it. In 1988 Gorbachev offered to convert the radar for international space research and ordered some other, less controversial systems taken off-line as a sop to the Americans. Two years later, the Soviets unilaterally declared they would dismantle the Krasnoyarsk radar as a confidence-building measure. In this case, Russian-American relations had been set back by institutional factors on the Soviet side—the independence and rigidity of the Soviet military.

Crafting history is an exercise in accounting for results. Even where the observer determines what figures the most in an outcome, he or she must remain alert to the operation of ancillary elements. With Krasnoyarsk, the ability of the Soviet military to get its way created an irritant to reducing international tensions. Both political and institutional factors are important. In Able Archer, politics applied only at the margins, in the sense that officials acted within their understanding of existing trends. In the longer-run debate over Soviet arms control compliance, American political reluctance to exacerbate Cold War tensions combined with institutional commitment to preserving a negotiating process to defeat the hard-liners' larger aims. In this sense, the hard-liners won their debate but lost the policy dispute because President Reagan had moved beyond a stance of confrontation to one of engagement.

Gorbachev's Epiphany

Mikhail Gorbachev had an epiphany concerning institutions on the Soviet side. That happened at Chernobyl in 1986. Not far from Kiev, in what is now the nation of Ukraine, Chernobyl was a major Soviet nuclear power plant. During the early morning hours of April 26, 1986, an experiment was under way with a turbogenerator during what was supposed to be a down period. Reactor no. 4 at Chernobyl, "Block 4" in Soviet parlance, experienced a power surge.[33] The emergency core cooling system had been disconnected for the experiment and had not been reengaged when a regional network dispatcher asked operators to continue generating power for the grid. The night crew proved unable to stem the resulting chain reaction, leading to a reactor accident that literally blew the top off the containment vessel housing the nuclear pile. Staff had rejected orders to shut down emergency apparatus, then management proved unable to respond in a timely fashion. Evasion of responsibility predominated.

The Soviet government at first made no public announcement. Then Sweden and Finland reported detection of elevated levels of radioactivity in the atmosphere. Moscow made a perfunctory statement about the accident on April 28, following the standard rubric of saying little. Gorbachev rejects accusations that the Soviet government misled its public. But mass hospitalizations, heroic first responders who performed feats that were literally suicidal, and the size of the eventual emergency effort—more than a half million people by some accounts, including Chemical Troops of the Soviet military—could not be denied. Radioactive debris from Chernobyl not only contaminated the immediately surrounding area but was also picked up by the prevailing winds and blown far and wide through Europe, while the land within several dozen kilometers of the plant became uninhabitable. More than 200,000 Soviet citizens had to be evacuated, half that number permanently relocated. Over the long term, eight thousand died, and the health of over 435,000 more was permanently affected. Costs of dealing with the mess were later estimated at nearly 20 billion rubles, money Moscow could scarcely afford.

Simply getting information from the system became a headache. The Ministry of Medium Machine-Building did not inform Soviet leaders in Moscow of the accident until the next day. By some accounts the information was relayed in the morning, but Gen. Dmitri Volkogonov, who attended a conference for senior officers at Lviv that day, was informed of the accident by Marshal Sergei Akhromeyev during a break in the sessions. Volkogonov established later that the report did not even reach the ministry until midday and was given to the general secretary only after that. Defense Minister Marshal Sergei Sokolov left the Lviv conference for the meeting called by Gorbachev. When Gorbachev convened the Politburo, Party Central Committee Secretary Vladimir Dolgikh reported no information beyond generalities. Gorbachev sent a special commission to Chernobyl to supervise efforts and identify problems there, but their bulletins were light on details and minimized the scale of disaster. Only a few months earlier, the general secretary had presided over a communist party Congress that had included a doubling of electricity generated by nuclear reactors among its goals in a new five-year plan. In only a moment, nuclear power stood revealed as the opposite of a panacea.

General Secretary Gorbachev made no statement on Chernobyl until a May 14 speech, in which he complained that the West had overreacted to Chernobyl. He still fell short of acknowledging the severity of the incident, but he sympathized

with victims and described countermeasures. By then Russian engineers were using helicopters to dump loads of concrete into the mass of steaming material inside the melted reactor core. As Gorbachev later noted, "The scale of the disaster
became clearer every day."[34]

Details of the Chernobyl tragedy are stunning, but there were dozens of Soviet nuclear plants of the same basic design, with others already under construction and more intended by the five-year plan. Physicists approached Gorbachev
to tell of flaws in some of these plants. The general secretary finally ordered
experts to make personal inspections, and he was warned of the potential for explosions elsewhere. Some nuclear projects were halted as a result, but the general
secretary determined that Russia could not do without nuclear power.

Gorbachev eventually admitted that "it is necessary to say with all honesty
that in the first days we just did not have a clear understanding." He does not
fault individuals but blames "the closed nature and secrecy of the nuclear power
industry," burdened by bureaucracy and nepotism; "the Cold War and the mutual
secrecy of the two military alliances"; and, again, "departmentalism," with its "fear
of showing initiative . . . dread of authority and the desire to avoid responsibility."[35]
In all, Gorbachev writes, "Chernobyl shed light on many of the sicknesses of our
system," and it "made me and my colleagues rethink a great many things."[36] But the
severity of the event was not so difficult to appreciate. Pavel Palazchenko, a transla-
tor who often assisted the general secretary, was in Bangkok on assignment for the
UN when he learned of Chernobyl. He had been in New York in 1979 when there
was a nuclear accident at Three Mile Island in Pennsylvania and watched Soviet
government handling of the accident with that index for comparison. "Moscow
was close to panic," Palazchenko found upon his return. "Few people believed the
official version of the events." The mood was gloomy and often angry. "I think
it caused a rift between the people and the government that never quite closed."[37]
Palazchenko translated for Gorbachev at some of the general secretary's most important meetings with foreign figures and felt him engaged in a delicate balanc-
ing act. In contrast, Gorbachev's close aides, such as Anatoly Chernyaev, defend
Gorbachev's handling of the events, finding that he never avoided dealing with the
issue and made many forthright statements.

In the Soviet Union, nuclear power was a by-product of the nuclear weapons
program. The military held the major responsibility, and the Ministry of Medium
Machine Building was in part a creature of the military system. "One can blame
Gorbachev for trusting those responsible," notes Chernyaev. "But since nucle-

ar energy was directly linked to the military-industrial complex, it was taken for granted that everything was in perfect order." Chernobyl changed that. Chernyaev writes, "Again we saw that the military-industrial complex was in fact a 'state within a state.' And that the safety of nuclear power was not its top priority. . . . The accident, like much else, was a product of the Soviet system as well as of a patriotism twisted by the Cold War."[38] Gorbachev may not have blamed individuals, but within days of his speech, a further incident occurred in which a German man flew a small plane from Finland into the Soviet Union to land in the middle of Red Square. Gorbachev fired his defense minister and other military officers. He also realigned the Politburo, elevating loyalists to several key positions. Chernobyl may not have been the cause of this shake-up, but it certainly furnished the opportunity. Within a year, the minister responsible for nuclear matters was also replaced.

Like Reagan, Gorbachev changed. He became more willing to override the Soviet bureaucracy, and soon thereafter he moved to add the social revolution of perestroika to his reforms. From this perspective, the function of perestroika very much seems to have been to create a political counterweight to the party apparat, thus enabling Gorbachev to mobilize public opinion to force change in the institution. But the social forces unleashed were a double-edged sword. As Palazchenko puts it, Chernobyl "was perhaps the beginning of a powerful wave of rejection of authority and the loss of legitimacy of the country's leadership in the eyes of the people."[39] Unhappy citizens could complain not just of the apparat but of Gorbachev's own leadership. The day would soon come when, stymied in efforts at domestic reform, Gorbachev would seek foreign policy achievements to open his way forward, but what is important here for how the Cold War ended is the way Chernobyl made General Secretary Gorbachev confront the realities of the Soviet bureaucracy and polity. For the Soviet-American relationship, that would have huge implications indeed.

New Thinking and Reykjavik

Less than a month after the great disaster, General Secretary Gorbachev made an unusual personal visit to the Ministry of Foreign Affairs (MFA) on Smolenskaya Square. There he encouraged the diplomats to craft new positions for negotiations with the United States. "Today," Gorbachev recounts, "I consider this meeting the starting point for the full-scale implementation of our 'new thinking.'"[40] The occasion was billed as a conference on the role of Soviet diplomacy, and the speakers were chosen by the foreign minister himself. In Gorbachev's keynote address, he used the vocabulary of "new thinking" and related it specifically to the nuclear arms race, appealing for deeper reflections and complaining about past practice. "The overwhelming majority of us," recalls Victor Israelyan, who was in the audience, "welcomed Gorbachev's speech. It struck a responsive chord and was in line with our own wish to see diplomacy fulfilling its natural function—that of working for honorable, mutually acceptable agreements."[41]

All the top MFA officials and many of Russia's ambassadors, senior party officials, and Central Committee members were in attendance. The MFA had already begun to re-create itself, and the May 1986 conference reflected the coalescence of that process, not its beginning. The Soviet military had been humbled by the Red Square airplane affair and the Chernobyl disaster. Stalemated relations with the United States had to be overcome. It was a moment of possibilities. The road to Gorbachev's radical proposals at Reykjavik began here.

Befitting the search for a new approach, Andrei Gromyko, just shy of three decades at the helm of the ministry, went on to a sinecure as chairman of the Presidium, in effect the Russian chief of state, in July 1985. Gorbachev brought in Eduard Shevardnadze to replace him. Shevardnadze had no foreign affairs experience. He was a party leader from Georgia, but he and Gorbachev had been friends since the 1950s, they had served together on the Central Committee and Politburo, and the general secretary knew they thought alike. Shevardnadze was a quick study and problem solver, could learn on the job, was friendly where Gromyko had been dour, and would be absolutely loyal to Gorbachev.[42]

Minister Shevardnadze swept away an entire constellation of top MFA officials. His possible replacements were the first to go. Anatoly Dobrynin, recalled from Washington, became chief of the Central Committee's International Department. Georgy Korniyenko, first deputy foreign minister, though an arms expert, was steeped in anti-U.S. ideology, so Shevardnadze replaced him too. The Central Committee supplied staff support to Gorbachev but was isolated from policy, increasingly so as Shevardnadze solidified his own control over foreign policy. Preoccupied with domestic reform and trusting Shevardnadze, Gorbachev was content to let that happen. Shevardnadze surrounded himself with professional diplomats, with very few exceptions leaving behind his old Georgian coterie. The lead deputies were Yuly Vorontsov and Anatoly Kovalev. Vorontsov had spent ten years as Dobrynin's top aide in Washington. Kovalev was a proponent of troop reductions in Europe, the cockpit of the NATO–Warsaw Pact confrontation.

Facing his first meetings with American diplomats, the foreign minister pulled in the chief of the MFA's U.S. section, Alexander Bessmertnykh, and for days on end, they talked endlessly of the arcana of arms negotiations until mastering the subject. The new minister was straightforward with his subordinates. He recalls telling them, "I am completely in your hands, and my situation is as bad as you can imagine. I can only promise that I will work in such a way that I won't be ashamed of myself, and you won't be embarrassed by me." Shevardnadze went on to make Bessmertnykh a deputy foreign minister with responsibility for arms talks. This was a new unit of the MFA, the Department of Arms Limitation and Disarmament, one of a set of offices that focused on issues, not regions. Another important center was a unit to focus on human rights issues. Shevardnadze cut back the regional bureaus, while adding a new office for Eastern Europe and an institute for Europe as a whole. He demanded accurate reporting from the field. Shevardnadze's reorganization became the first MFA shake up since Stalin's time. He could not eliminate, even within the Foreign Ministry itself, all opposition to an arms deal with the United States, but Shevardnadze created substantial room to move and the reorganization favored the general secretary. As the major U.S. Congress analysis of Soviet negotiating behavior put it, "Gorbachev's restructuring of the foreign policy establishment and his criticism of past Soviet policy seemed to have two principal purposes: to strengthen his hold on the formulation and implementation of Soviet foreign policy; and to ensure the execution of his foreign policy agenda set forth at the 27th Party Congress, especially on arms control."[43]

Minister Shevardnadze did not presume to compare himself with Gromyko— he was a rowboat whereas Gromyko had been the battleship of Soviet foreign policy. But Shevardnadze's rowboat had a motor and swiftly picked up speed. As he set the tiller, Shevardnadze turned toward the most important and most difficult task, "our participation in the practical realization of the new foreign policy strategy, closely linked with the efforts of perestroika and democratization of society." He aimed to rein in the arms race, to establish peaceful means as the mechanism to resolve security issues, and to work on international cooperation on technology, economics, and the environment. To put relations on a new basis it seemed necessary to do away with the communist ideological notion that "peaceful coexistence" was "a specific form of class warfare." The program adopted by the Twenty-seventh CPSU Congress in early 1986 seemed to make that possible. Then came Chernobyl. A few weeks later Gorbachev, in concert with Shevardnadze, ordered a unilateral halt to nuclear weapons testing, a sign, if one cared to read it, that the Soviet Union had indeed embarked on a new path.

At the party congress, Gorbachev had put forward a proposal to abolish all nuclear weapons by the year 2000. Regarded as propaganda in the West, his idea became something to be fleshed out by the foreign policy apparat. At Geneva, Gorbachev had personally seen Ronald Reagan's deep commitment to the Strategic Defense Initiative, and an offer that could pull the president off that stance had to be irresistible. The abolition of nuclear weapons was such a proposal. It met Shevardnadze's concerns that both sides gain equal security and that global security be a priority. A trade of nuclear weapons for the SDI met Gorbachev's concern to head off a technological competition that threatened to soak up whatever economic progress the Soviets achieved.

The military resisted. Many times Shevardnadze stumbled into the general secretary's office to complain he could not work with it any more. Gorbachev would remonstrate, or if necessary call in Lev Zaikov, who had replaced Boris Ponomarev at the head of a Politburo unit charged with coordinating arms negotiation issues. If necessary, the general secretary would intervene himself. The Soviets produced several intermediate proposals dealing with missiles alone by the summer of 1986, when Gorbachev received a letter from President Reagan advancing the latest American scheme to negotiate to U.S. advantage. On vacation at his Black Sea retreat, Gorbachev rejected the pro forma MFA draft reply and resolved to suggest a summit conference. The sides soon agreed to meet at Reykjavik, in Iceland, in October.

Soviet intelligence was also not happy. The KGB was wrapped in embarrassment resulting from the recent disruption of its attempt to install electronic monitors in the new American embassy under construction. Headaches worsened when the Americans arrested a KGB officer assigned to the UN. A week later, the KGB retaliated, seizing Nicholas Daniloff, an American journalist resident in Moscow, on a trumped-up espionage charge. The Daniloff affair poisoned Soviet-American relations and threatened the summit. It consumed a great deal of the top diplomats' energy and was resolved just two weeks ahead of the Reykjavik meeting by an exchange that both sides denied was a spy swap. The KGB's motives in this affair have never been clearly established.

General Secretary Gorbachev told the Politburo on October 4, during an intermediate phase in preparation of a negotiating position, that his ultimate goal was the total elimination of nuclear weapons. Four days later, when the Politburo met to approve the Soviet proposals, Gorbachev warned that agreement was *necessary*: "Something needs to be done. . . . The United States has an interest in keeping the negotiations machine running idle, while the arms race overburdens our economy."[44] The offer needed to be bold but realistic: "If the Americans accepted our initiatives, it would indeed mean a fresh start in disarmament and normalization in world politics. If they rejected them it would show the true intentions of the Reagan administration." The stakes were high.[45] The Politburo overrode the oppositionists within the military and MFA. It understood that Russia's Euromissile deployments had been counterproductive. Soviet leaders now accepted a scheme under which Moscow would first trade a 50 percent reduction in all strategic weapons, plus an agreement banning the long-disputed INF missiles (essentially accepting the American Zero Option), for limits on the U.S. Strategic Defense Initiative that took the form of strict adherence to the ABM Treaty.

The summit took place on October 11 and 12. Gorbachev presented the Soviet proposal. He alluded to a goal of abolishing nuclear weapons, starting with reduction by half. President Reagan at first spoke of elimination of land-based missiles only, the formula Weinberger's Pentagon had been pushing, which favored the United States. The Soviet leader held fast to the 50 percent across-the-board reduction. That night a working group of subordinate officials, men such as Paul Nitze and Richard Perle on the U.S. side and Marshal Akhromeyev heading the Soviet team, met to flesh out the general proposals. The Americans put on a disturbing show: using the rhetoric of "50 percent," they spoke of details indicating smaller reductions of only about a third on the U.S. side. They also attempted to snare the Russians into agreeing to the broad interpretation of the ABM Treaty.[46] General Secretary Gorbachev upped the ante on the second day, accepting the principle of equal limits that the U.S. working group had been reaching for but holding to his SDI restrictions during a period of strict adherence to the ABM Treaty. On the second day, Gorbachev negotiated at length on a complete abolition. Pavel Palazchenko was translating. He recalls, "To my surprise, Reagan answered that he would not be against the destruction of all nuclear weapons, including tactical and battlefield ones."[47]

The memorandums recording these conversations from *both* the Soviet and American sides have been declassified and are available, in addition to Soviet notes recording the working group meeting on the previous night. These make clear that Gorbachev indeed offered, and Reagan accepted, a formula for the total elimination of nuclear weapons.[48] Ronald Reagan supplies more confirmation, writing in his diary for October 12, "Our team had given us an agreement to eliminate entirely all nuc[lear] devices over a 10 yr. period."[49] But the implication here that abolishing nuclear weapons had been a U.S. offer is not accurate.[50] Despite his abhorrence for these absolute weapons, President Reagan walked away from the deal because of his enchantment with the Strategic Defense Initiative and refused to meet Soviet desires for SDI constraints. He offered treaty adherence but with less restrictive provisions on technological development than Gorbachev needed. Indeed Gorbachev warned Reagan that he could not return to Moscow without an understanding on SDI. The negotiation collapsed.

Reykjavik proved a great success for the policy entrepreneurs. In an international forum, the president of the United States had agreed on a principle that subordinates had taken back. They had also manipulated what *had* been proposed, substituting a previous U.S. arms formula for the Soviet offer that was actually on the table. Reykjavik led to public embarrassment as U.S. officials, starting with White House press secretary Larry Speakes, asserted that Reagan had never agreed to eliminate all nuclear weapons. Other spokesmen maintained it had all been a misunderstanding, that Reagan had only been talking of land-based missiles. Charges flew back and forth for days until the Soviet Union released a transcript of the negotiating session that explicitly showed Mr. Reagan's approval. After that, commentary on Reykjavik became notable for its absence.[51] The policy entrepreneurs were saved from deeper difficulty only by the president's mystical dedication to SDI, which was perplexing since there was little chance that technological development, no matter how fiercely pursued, could have yielded a workable ballistic missile defense during the time frame the Russians wanted for strict ABM Treaty compliance.

The Importance of Institutions and Operators

Understanding the impact of governmental institutions on historical outcomes is a central problem of analysis, not confined to time or place. Institutions may be powerful or weak; their effectiveness is influenced by political factors, the determination of leaders or entrepreneurs, and their standard procedures, values, education, and staffing. A host of factors may apply to the historical analysis. In the case of how the Cold War ended, it must be said that institutions and bureaucratic maneuvers, like individual agency, did not determine the outcome. But they did play a primary role in conditioning intermediate events, sharpening superpower differences, and restricting leaders' range of choice.

It must be concluded that institutions and policy entrepreneurs did not, for the most part, play a positive role. Yet, in at least one case, that of Able Archer 83, information that emerged perforce from the bureaucracy helped convince President Reagan to turn away from a course that might indeed have ended the Cold War—in a thermonuclear conflagration. But, by and large, hoary doctrines and short-range thinking afflicted the institutions. These rigidities prevented recognition of changes that occurred and encouraged traditional hostilities. Policy entrepreneurs, struggling to emplace their own rules of the game, delayed policy formulation and substituted personal goals for national objectives. In some episodes recounted here, like the Chernobyl disaster, these factors led to great national tragedy. In others, like Reykjavik, the result was to close the window on a potential breakthrough limiting the arms race. In one case, the U.S. debate over ABM Treaty interpretation, institutional interests obstructed the path for entrepreneurs who sought to change the playing field to favor their preferred course of action. Political factors played both ways, for example, in the controversy over Soviet compliance with arms agreements (including the ABM Treaty issue), where politics alternately enflamed the issue and imposed limits on government freedom of action.

Entrepreneurs had limited success in their efforts to change institutions to their advantage. This was true for both sides. In the United States, Caspar Weinberger's efforts to exploit arms control issues and the SDI to favor Pentagon programs eventually led him into a stalemate on policy plus open bureaucratic war with George Shultz's State Department. At a lower level, Richard Perle managed to concentrate many of the reins of action, including leading roles in several interagency mechanisms for policy coordination, in his own hands, but he could not override previously established U.S. government procedures. On the Soviet side, Eduard Shevardnadze carried out a wholesale reorganization of the Ministry of Foreign Affairs but could not eliminate certain key officials' long-standing predisposition to resist agreements with the United States on ideological or other grounds.

Historical Research, Analysis, and Projects

Researching institutions and politics is an important task for the historian. Here data collection is less challenging than the extraction of relevant insights. In general, the same source materials that are necessary to examine the roles of individuals remain central. The data exists in memoirs, periodical accounts, interviews and oral histories, and documents. Perhaps research in documents has special value because a given slice of this material, containing successive statements and restatements of an institutional position across a varying range of issues, eventually reveals a core element of consistency. That may be inferred to be the institutional view. Tracking the changes in institutional views or lack thereof, and comparing these to the record of policy decisions, provides a baseline in determining the relative influence of institutional factors in decision making. Comparison with historical outcomes demonstrates impact on diplomatic history writ large.

The analysis of the policy entrepreneurs' role advanced here for the Cold War case is a subordinate theme in institutional history. Individuals play a role in bureaucracies. Sometimes that role rises to the level of the Great Figure in History. More often it does not. Most often individuals work within their institutions, transforming them or not, making them more effective and relevant or obstructing critical actions. In the case of the Reagan-era Cold War, what seemed remarkable is that individuals deliberately went outside institutional boundaries, forging alliances with like-minded officials elsewhere in a sort of free-market approach to attaining goals. This established two tracks in the process of policy formulation: the official institutional process, on the one hand, and a simultaneous sub-rosa extra-bureaucratic track aimed at fixing the outcomes of policy deliberations, on the other. This is an example of insight drawn from evidence. The challenge for the historian as detective is to extract the insight from the mass of data.

Institutions and policies exist within a political milieu. Policy deliberations as well as institutional reform take place within this framework. The political environment establishes a spectrum of what is possible and defines a range of actions feasible only at some level of political cost. Selecting a course that accepts political costs is an especially daring executive choice. That puts a premium on political analysis in any diplomatic research project. In this respect, a word is in order on the use of periodicals and media sources as research material. Executive deliberations most often occur in private while politics are pursued in public forums. Getting out the message is the essence of political communication, and the first expression of that comes in media reportage, including in the way the media covers events. This coverage is also *the* source of success at putting across the message. In addition, journalists are paid to observe, and their commentaries provide a first cut at history. While memoirs, interviews, and oral histories often contain important political observations, there is no substitute for periodical evidence. It is a primary source.

Finally, a word on how much is enough. A key question for the historian lies in how to combine research with analysis. There is a point of departure for every research project. The historian usually begins with some definition of the terrain encompassed by the project and some impression of the relative importance of causal factors. Collection of evidence suggests fresh lines of inquiry and confirms, extends, or modifies impressions of causality. Good history combines research and analysis in an iterative process. But evidence evolves both backward and forward. That is, for most subjects, the researcher can reach back into the past accumulation of evidence and, faced with the mass of that, can actually make choices about how deeply to do so. Simultaneously, new sources that also demand attention will appear. This remains true even at the writing stage of a project since fresh evidence can throw up novel lines of inquiry, entailing additional collection of source material. When to stop gathering evidence is a major dilemma. There are no easy answers since the historian has an obligation to be open to new interpretations and evidence. Not making a choice is often the difference between a completed project and a never-ending quest for the ultimate historical treatment.

My best advice is to have at the outset some set of objectives that includes determinations of scope of the project, how definitive the result is intended to be, and what must be excluded. These criteria need to be put before the reader when rendering the final product. In the case of how the Cold War ended, as noted in the introduction, the historical analysis is not intended to be definitive so much as illustrative of the understanding that can be conveyed by examining different pieces of the puzzle. And that riddle goes beyond institutions and politics. An examination of the impact of international factors adds important insights to our picture.

CHAPTER 4

"THE MOST DANGEROUS DECADE IN HUMAN HISTORY"
Popular Movements and Global Outcomes

IN TRUTH, BY THE TIME OF THE REYKJAVIK SUMMIT, the moment was late for both superpowers in the Cold War—not so much so that arms agreements could not help, but both the United States and the Soviet Union confronted restive nations within their alliances, and the centrifugal forces pulling those alliances apart were greater than perceived in either superpower capital. The role of systemic forces in such tectonic shifts as the end of the Cold War is quite critical, and the historian labors under an obligation to evaluate them. This is often not so easy. There is a temptation toward overdeterminism, making judgments that a single factor is sufficient and necessary to account for an outcome. There are times when such an analysis may apply, but *especially* at those moments the historian needs to ensure that trends working in parallel are not equally or more central to events. For this, it is incumbent on the historian to establish the spectrum of systemic forces in play and then make some judgment as to relative weight.

In the case of the end of the Cold War, at least four elements rose to the level of systemic factors. One was psychological: a generalized dread of nuclear war, which led to a popular mobilization against war and applied primarily within the Western alliance. The second factor applied directly to the Soviet bloc, as the Central European peoples became increasingly restive, tired of their long subjugation to Moscow, and contrived to utilize universal norms, in particular the deepening global acceptance of human rights strictures, as the basis for increasing their nations' autonomy. Both shall be dealt with here. One aspect that is not a systemic force, but rather a long-term foreign policy strategy—containment—is also most appropriately covered in this discussion. Two additional systemic factors—international economic developments and ethnic nationalisms in the Soviet Union—will be the focus of the next chapter. All these forces contributed in varying measure to the Cold War's demise.

Fears of Nuclear War

The Reykjavik summit actually turned out to be the penultimate way station for a disarmament agreement, a treaty that went beyond arms control to actually eliminate a category of nuclear weapons. General Secretary Gorbachev's acceptance of the principle of dismantling the Euromissiles survived the failure of the summit and became the basis for intense negotiations. President Reagan, who had been prodded by his policy entrepreneurs to preserve the most dangerous weapons, the Pershing II missiles, also acceded to this principle. The willingness of the leaders of both superpowers to break with their previous policies had largely responded to public opinion, indeed a mass mobilization, which government policies had been unable to manage. The origins of this shift lie in the Carter-Brezhnev years and the beginning of the Euromissile problem, which accentuated fears of nuclear war.[1]

In the West, including in the United States but particularly in Western Europe, the Carter era brought heightened security concerns. Many put their hopes in the arms control process that brought forth the SALT II treaty, others in new weapons under development. The Soviet intervention in Afghanistan at the end of 1979, President Carter's decision to respond by withdrawing the SALT II treaty from ratification, and the subsequent onset of the Solidarity crisis in Poland stoked fears of confrontation. In the United States, this reinforced the proclivities of the conservatives who made up the Committee on the Present Danger, but on the Left, it also energized antinuclear activists. In mid-1979 political scientist Randall Forsberg, responding to a major nuclear reactor accident at the Three Mile Island plant, had proposed a "nuclear freeze" and quickly created a public advocacy organization to press for it. This marked the point of departure for what became a public political initiative.

Western Europe's response embraced these elements too but was more complex. Among the Carter administration's weapons programs was one that became known as the "neutron bomb," conceived as a tactical nuclear weapon with enhanced radiation but limited blast effects, which military experts believed would be useful in a NATO defense against any Warsaw Pact attack in Europe. The weapons program, conceived as a way to make tactical nuclear munitions more useful and to blunt a pact attack by eliminating its manpower, had unintended consequences.

Europeans, especially in West Germany, feared that with the neutron bomb the United States intended to defend NATO by destroying the continent. Though the program was cancelled, it had already shaken the alliance.

American officials came to excessively narrow beliefs on the nature of their alliance problem. They viewed European doubts as stemming from fear that the United States would not defend the continent in the event of war. This problem was squarely posed in 1976, when the Russians first began to deploy the SS-20 missile. West German chancellor Helmut Schmidt's 1977 speech to the International Institute for Strategic Studies, which raised questions regarding the "Eurostrategic balance," made the doubts explicit. Americans framed the concept as "decoupling" and saw in it the heart of NATO's troubles. Washington's answer took the form of the "two-track decision," which the United States induced NATO to accept in December 1979.[2] Under this formula, the Americans would deploy their Euromissiles (track 1) unless in a negotiation the Soviets agreed on limits to these forces (track 2). Emplacements of Euromissiles were planned for Great Britain, Holland, Belgium, West Germany, and Italy. The wide dispersion of the weapons would have the military effect of complicating Soviet countermeasures in the event of war plus the political result of tying the United States more directly to each of these alliance partners, seeming to bind NATO. But Washington wholly failed to take into account the extent to which European peoples would be troubled at being made targets for nuclear attack as the result of the presence of these weapons, and it made facile assumptions that NATO governments could squelch opposition to the move.

Moscow had its own role to play in the drama. The SS-20 missile, in development since the late 1960s, had been conceived simply as a replacement for obsolete INF missiles that had long been aimed at Europe. But the SS-20, with multiple warheads and instant launch capability, proved far more threatening than the older forces with their lengthy preparatory sequences and poor accuracy. The Soviets then scared everyone with their Afghan intervention, and the seeming evaporation of the hopes for the SALT II treaty suddenly cast a very somber light on the Cold War situation. By early 1980 détente had effectively disappeared and was replaced by fresh fears of crisis and nuclear confrontation. Like the Americans, the Soviets failed to anticipate the effects their moves, particularly the SS-20 deployments, would have on the Western Europeans.

A rising tide of public concern and the mass mobilization that followed overtook military and diplomatic developments. The nuclear freeze campaign begun in the United States coincided with a reinvigoration of secular and religious opposition to nuclear weapons in both the United States and Western Europe. The Committee for a Sane Nuclear Policy (SANE) in the United States had four thousand members in 1977 and ten times that number by the end of 1980. The Physicians for Social Responsibility dramatized the physical effects of nuclear weapons, Mobilization for Survival formed to engineer a broad-based national public campaign against nuclear dangers, and the Quakers' American Friends Service Committee and many more religious groups took up the banner of the freeze as well. David Cortright, the SANE president at the time, recalls that many of the letters he sent to Congress had as many as a hundred organizations as signatories. In polling the American public, the percentage who viewed the dangers of nuclear war as the most pressing national problem grew from less than a quarter in 1981 to over half two years later. A massive rally for the nuclear freeze that took place in New York's Central Park in June 1982 drew a crowd variously estimated at between 750,000 and 1 million people.

Policy entrepreneur Caspar Weinberger reacted to the huge demonstration by declaring that it would have no effect on administration policy, but by the fall there had been some six hundred appearances by senior officials to talk down the freeze in designated media markets alone. Ensconced in the White House, Ronald Reagan worked hard to build support for his policy. In October 1982 he actually baited the protesters, saying they were inspired by "some who wanted to weaken America." In May 1983, when American bishops released a pastoral letter explicitly asserting moral objections to the arms race as leading to dangers of nuclear war, the Reagan White House created a high-level group under the president's national security adviser specifically aimed at counteracting these objections. Certain public declarations, lines in the president's speeches, even the name of the zero-option arms proposal, were designed to still public opposition. Until President Reagan actually began to produce arms agreements, he remained unsuccessful at halting the growth in antinuclear sentiment.[3]

Trends in the United States, significant as they were, were dwarfed by developments in Western Europe. As in the United States, European church groups assumed a leading role, pressing for disarmament on moral and religious grounds. They were closely followed by political alliances. In the Netherlands, for example, the Interchurch Peace Council argued on biblical grounds that there had been a time of "mercy"—now ended—during which deterrence could be tolerated pending disarmament, but that the moment had come to move on. Public support for neutron weapons as measured in opinion polls had peaked at 28 percent. The council had over four hundred active chapters across the country by the end of 1977, and these were so strong that the group, combined with the opposition of the Social Democratic Party, made the government reject deployment of neutron weapons on Dutch territory and loath to accept the NATO two-track decision. When Reagan took office, "many Dutch feared that the daredevil Reagan would bring nuclear devastation to Western Europe."[4] The politics of the Euromissiles in Holland played out over the next five years. In 1985 as many as 3.75 million Dutch—of a population of 14 million—signed a petition against deployment. In Belgium, where a plurality of citizens had supported missile deployment in 1980 (and many had yet to make up their minds), opinion polls through 1981 recorded opposition levels rocketing past the halfway mark to settle at 88.9 percent late that October and hovered around the 80 percent level right through the NATO deployment.[5]

In Italy, the government's December 1979 decision to accept deployment triggered an immediate swell of opposition and split Catholic groups, some of which objected to Europe being made the target of nuclear forces, others of whom argued the Euromissiles might redress a strategic imbalance in favor of the Soviets. The Church hierarchy stayed out of the debate, which, with the advent of Reagan, shifted in favor of opponents.[6] A half million Italians marched against the Euromissiles in October 1981, a performance matched two years later as U.S. cruise missiles were about to arrive at their base in Comiso. Two-thirds of the citizens of Comiso, long host to a NATO base, petitioned against stationing the missiles outside their town. In Greece, Spain, Switzerland, and Scandinavia, smaller but still significant protest movements incorporated the same moral themes with political ones.

In the United Kingdom, the Campaign for Nuclear Disarmament, like the American SANE, underwent a rejuvenation through the late 1970s. Membership reached 75,000 in 1983 and 100,000 by 1985. Labor unions signed up in force. There came a moment early in the decade when unions participating in the CND represented more than half of all British workers. In fact, a longtime CND activist, Michael Foot, emerged at the head of the Labour Party, which went into parliamentary elections in 1983 on a platform promising to terminate NATO Euromissile deployments planned for the UK. Foot lost to Maggie Thatcher's Conservatives, but agitation continued at a very high level. Among the creative demonstrations mounted by British peace activists was one in which protesters joined hands to form a human chain linking several planned NATO missile bases and the Greenham Common women's encampment, which continued for months to blockade the base at which the first cruise missiles were to appear.

West Germany was the planned deployment zone for the Pershing II missiles as well as a substantial number of cruise missiles, and as such it was a key front in the struggle for public opinion.[7] Here too religious and political groups united to stop the Euromissiles. Chancellor Helmut Schmidt had been the key mover in the original NATO elaboration of the two-track decision, but his notion of restoring a European strategic balance centered more on the idea that that could be done through negotiation. The Euromissiles themselves were simply the threat that would induce Moscow to agree. Schmidt no doubt responded to Germany's strong aversion to deployment in taking his position. At the political level, Social Democratic Party (SPD) legislator Egon Bahr and the Green Party's Joschka Fischer gave voice to the Euromissile opposition, and Christian Democratic Union general secretary Heiner Geissler to proponents of deployment.

The German Social Democratic Party, much as had British Labour, joined the opposition, leading Hans-Dietrich Genscher, in many ways the central figure in this German political debate, to leave the party over its migration toward alleged neutralism. Genscher's move undermined the leadership of Socialist Helmut Schmidt and strengthened the hand of Helmut Kohl, who took over as chancellor in October 1982. A May 1983 election confirmed the parliamentary strength of a new pro-Euromissile coalition, but without convincing the SPD, the antinuclear Green Party, or Lutheran and other opponents of deployment. A half million Germans protested in Bonn that October, during the run-up to a Bundestag vote on the missiles. Proponents won that test by sixty votes, and the first Pershing IIs reached their West German bases on November 26. Two days later, the Soviet delegation walked out of the INF negotiations. Once in power, the German conservatives discovered the Euromissile deployment did not, in fact, end their fears of a "decoupling" of the United States from the NATO alliance, while the antinuclear opposition remained very strong.

High points for movements protesting the Euromissiles occurred in October–November 1981 and again exactly two years later. Almost 1.8 *million* protesters showed up for marches in Holland, Great Britain, West Germany, Italy, Finland, and Belgium. For the 1983 protests—at the point of U.S. Euromissile deployment and on the eve of the hidden Able Archer crisis—the turnout was between 2.1 and 2.5 million, depending on sources consulted, in most of the same countries (less Finland). What was significant about these protests, aside from the huge numbers, was that except in France—where peace protests tended to be monopolized by the French Communist Party—the movement aimed at *both* NATO and Soviet Euromissiles.

The NATO missiles took their places on European bases amid a rippling of protests over the course of the next year. A crucial passage in the Euromissile story took place in the Netherlands. In June 1984 the Dutch government, which, owing to powerful opposition, had been stalling for years on giving final approval to missile deployment, announced it would make its decision—in December 1985. The Dutch made approval conditional on the Soviets' failure to freeze their SS-20 deployment at its current level or reach an INF agreement by that time. If nothing else, the Dutch maneuver re-emphasized the importance of diplomacy. By then, Mikhail Gorbachev had become the central figure on the Politburo and was soon to take over as the top leader in Moscow. In command, Gorbachev proposed a compromise to forestall Dutch approval of the Euromissiles, telling the Dutch government he was halting emplacement of SS-20s at the level that had existed in June 1984. Aware the Soviets might simply move their excess missiles to the Asian USSR, the Dutch rejected that formula and went on to approve NATO deployment in November 1985. Holland was the last NATO country to move forward on Euromissiles.

Notes of Soviet Politburo meetings and memoirs of leaders show clearly that by late 1985 Moscow increasingly felt that the SS-20 program had become an albatross. A product of lockstep development by a rigid Soviet military, deployment of the SS-20 had been given little thought when Brezhnev sanctioned it. Not only had the NATO response been far more destabilizing from the Soviet standpoint, the political impact of the Russian missile deployment in Western Europe had proved far worse than Moscow anticipated, and the walkout from INF talks had compounded the Soviet error. In preparing for the 1986 Reykjavik summit, Gorbachev told the Politburo that developing the SS-20 had been a mistake. Many of the protest groups that had opposed the Euromissiles, from the nuclear freeze campaign to SANE, sent members to Iceland to hold vigil outside the NATO base of Keflavik, the support center for the Reykjavik talks. They were present to witness the near breakthrough and then pathetic end of the summit. One major reason Gorbachev, at the end of Reykjavik, was prepared to leave on the table a possibility that Moscow would accept an INF agreement based on the Zero Option, was precisely because he understood that the masses were exercised as much at Soviet as at NATO missiles.[8]

Echoes of the same realization rippled in Washington. The NATO Euromissiles provided strategic advantage, but the immense political controversy that surrounded their deployment decoupled Western Europe from the United States more surely than if the United States had actually done nothing in the face of the Soviet program. Reagan little understood the military aspects, but he could hear the reluctance of his European colleagues and see the crowds in the streets. Public support for military measures was dissipating in the United States as well. In addition, Reagan was a good politician and appreciated the potential of foreign policy achievements, especially at a time when he was caught in the throes of the Iran-contra affair. Starting in November 1986 and flowing from Reagan's adventurism in the Middle East and inability to control the activities of his policy entrepreneurs in Central America, where he also could not bring himself to abandon pursuit of a secret war against Nicaragua, the Iran-contra scandal increasingly threatened constitutional crisis in the United States. Mr. Reagan's presidency hung in the balance. Thus President Reagan insisted on arms progress in the face of the entrepreneurs, who, as it happened, were not themselves truly committed to a zero-option agreement. They wanted to keep the Pershing IIs.

By 1987 Ronald Reagan needed an INF agreement at least as much as Mikhail Gorbachev. There were two main reasons: one was Reagan's domestic problem; the other the intense public revulsion at the Euromissiles. The opposition was fueled in large part by the mass mobilizations on both sides of the Atlantic. Here the inchoate forces of public opinion had an identifiable impact on the policies and diplomacy of national governments. Actually elaborating what became the INF Treaty consumed most of a year because careful negotiators on both sides wanted to dot every i and cross every t in the diplomatic documents, but after Reykjavik, there remained no doubt such an agreement would eventuate. The INF Treaty was signed at a December 1987 summit in Washington. The powers exchanged instruments of ratification in Moscow in June 1988. On that occasion, President Reagan went so far as to enunciate the words, "The Cold War is over." That was not quite true, yet. In 1989, with the Bush administration in office, only Margaret Thatcher supported completion of the Euromissile deployments that were then to be dismantled. German diplomats went so far as to tell Secretary of State James A. Baker that proceeding with the program would result in the fall of Helmut Kohl's West German government. Other NATO countries were only slightly less distressed. "The alliance may have been able to endure such a crisis in 1983," Baker later wrote, "but it would not be able to survive [another] with the wily Mikhail Gorbachev in power."[9] The popular will had energized the most significant move away from superpower confrontation in many years.

Human Rights Norms

Activists, primarily from the Committee on Nuclear Disarmament, held a Europe-wide conference as early as April 1980 that issued an Appeal for European Nuclear Disarmament, which in turn marked the foundation for the umbrella group END. British participants wanted to stimulate a European movement, indeed a global one. As seen, Western Europe was primed to oppose the Euromissiles, but END wanted to stimulate protests in Warsaw Pact states as well. There *were* East-Central European signatories of the April END manifesto, some of them quite notable, indeed some who would later be cabinet ministers in their countries. But to be a protester in any of the Soviet satrapies was quite different from marching against Euromissiles in the West. Not only did the Russian security services keep a close watch, the Central European states with their communist governments stood ready to quash the least spark of public expression. Given the Brezhnev doctrine and the examples of Russian action against the Prague Spring in 1968 and the Hungarian Uprising a dozen years earlier, plus the Soviets' care to monitor conditions through their ambassadors, bilateral visits, and Warsaw Pact conferences, the governments on Russia's periphery could have no doubt as to Soviet intentions, and their own communist parties had a vested interest in resisting political liberalization. The Solidarity crisis in Poland served as fresh evidence of the strength of the forces ranged against change.

This did not mean that Europeans, East and West, did not share certain views. Soviet forces stationed in East-Central Europe and the delicate balance of forces between the Warsaw Pact states and NATO, plus the emerging American military doctrine of launching deep strikes against the pact, put all Central Europeans at risk. The Soviets' SS-20 deployment, triggering such a vigorous NATO response, could only have put more fear into the hearts of East Germans, Czechs, and Hungarians, not to mention Poles, Romanians, or Bulgarians. But public protests were few and quickly suppressed. Central Europeans expressed their opposition more in political tracts, like the Russian samizdat, that circulated quietly among the intelligentsia. And among them also were complaints about the Western protesters, END and the others, who seemed to fantasize that the Central Europeans could mobilize protesters as easily as the West Germans or British.

The peoples of East-Central Europe had more immediate problems. Political expression was itself prohibited—Euromissile protests would have been just one type. Gaining freedom of expression was essential, and to that end dissenters bent their main effort. Solidarity served as a beacon of hope to Central Europeans precisely because it hinted at winds of change. And the activists had a wedge to use here, courtesy of the Soviets, indeed of Leonid Brezhnev. In 1975, when détente still reigned, Moscow sought a multilateral recognition of the existing boundaries in Europe, which would have had the effect of condoning the annexations and border changes Russia had imposed at the end of World War II and of acquiescing in hegemonic Soviet control over the states of East-Central Europe. The United States wanted security provisions and confidence-building measures such as prior warning of military exercises and an ability to observe them. The European states—the Western ones, at least, but all were represented as thirty-five nations attended the resulting conference—wanted recognition of human rights norms. Helsinki, site of the conference, gave its name to the final agreement negotiated there, which made provision for periodic review by the Conference on Security and Cooperation in Europe, meaning that implementation across the continent would be revisited. The human rights norms of the Helsinki Final Act were grouped together in Basket 3 of the agreement and included a wide range of basic rights, including freedom of expression. This wedge in a basket one day broke the Soviet empire.

Effects of the Basket 3 provisions were seen first in Poland, providing citizens encouragement to seek the labor freedom that led to Solidarity, and in Czechoslovakia, where Czech intellectuals used human rights to demand political change. On New Year's Day 1977 a group of prominent Czechs issued a manifesto demanding that the communist government observe the tenets of the Universal Declaration of Human Rights affirmed by the Helsinki Final Act, which Czechoslovakia had signed according to laws the Czech government had itself recently promulgated. The date and the document defined the group, which became known as Charter 77. The chartists included prominent cultural figures such as playwright Václav Havel, professors such as Jan Patočka, and political figures such as Jiri Hajek, who had been a minister in the reformist government of the Prague Spring. They asserted that they had no political agenda. But recognizing rights, such as freedom of expression, was fundamentally political in a totalitarian society. Charter 77 took off like wildfire, with numerous new figures adding their names to its signatories. The Czech communist government reacted ferociously, tracking down chartists and imprisoning them. The high-security response proved self-defeating. Like Nelson

Mandela in South Africa, Havel and his cohorts exerted more influence as imprisoned martyrs than they would have had they been on the street. Their writings and the charter were eagerly sought, and groups of supporters formed throughout the nation. Havel was released from prison, rearrested, released, sent back, and finally kept there through the spring of 1983. The Czech actions were quietly deplored at home but roundly criticized abroad, including by socialist and communist parties in the West and even in the communist countries Yugoslavia and China.

Czech dissidence, having expressed itself through Charter 77, next took the form of efforts to document government human rights abuses, including "Helsinki Watch" groups in the West, whose reports traveled back into East-Central Europe over Voice of America, BBC, and Radio Free Europe airwaves. Charter 77 representatives also signed the END declaration in 1980. Havel was finally released from prison as Europe moved toward a Helsinki Act review conference scheduled for Madrid in September 1983. The Czech government, in need of foreign loans, was increasingly aware of the necessity of friendly relations with the West, knowledge that acted as a restraint on its measures against dissidents.

Historian Daniel C. Thomas argues that, in Czechoslovakia, the communist government's grip rested on three main factors: the state's security forces and consequent capability to suppress dissent, its ability to supply citizens with a reasonable standard of living, and the support of Moscow.[10] The argument can be extended: identical factors applied in the other Soviet client states. Capabilities for repression diminished as it gradually became apparent that the dissidents were not a scattering of individuals who could be silenced but encompassed a wide swath of cultural and social figures. Support from the Soviet Union also weakened. In the security field, the Soviet KGB supplied technical assistance, specialized help, advice, and intelligence on dissidents and monitored the satrap's efforts. The Soviet leadership was there to encourage action, both bilaterally and through the Warsaw Pact.

But the bonds became visibly looser. That the Soviets did not march their armies into Poland in 1981 cut two ways. Moscow undoubtedly made the correct decision, for intervention would have antagonized the West, stimulated dissent throughout East-Central Europe, and been costly in its own right, but the failure to do so put national communist leaders on notice that they could no longer count on Soviet troops to shore them up. The Russians' own problems increasingly turned them elsewhere. Prodded by Soviet leaders, the KGB focused outward, on finding signs that the United States intended to start a war or on assorted theaters of struggle with the Americans in the third world. While the KGB—at least by CIA lights—had long virtually controlled the satellites' security services, by the mid-1980s their touch had become lighter, confined to technical help and monitoring. The residual mechanism served more to keep Moscow in the picture than as a channel of control. In January 1985, it is said, the Soviets intended to clamp down at a scheduled Warsaw Pact meeting in Moscow by demanding their allies act to destroy the dissident movements. But the failing health of Russian leader Chernenko led Moscow to cancel the conference.[11] When Gorbachev succeeded Chernenko, the accent shifted to benign neglect. Soviet control loosened further once Gorbachev began encouraging the allies to undertake democratic reforms.

Meanwhile, the Basket 3 provisions of the Helsinki Final Act also weakened the capacity for repression because they made clear that suppressing people simply for exercising their human rights was not legal. That was an international norm, which presumably did not matter that much to leaders in Prague, Budapest, or Bucharest; but it was also a matter of domestic laws, not so important per se in a totalitarian state but certainly a potential political problem, depending on the dissidents' strength. Repressive solutions ultimately proved morally and politically unsustainable. This led states such as Poland, Czechoslovakia, and Hungary to an intermediate strategy of pairing limited political concessions with continued security measures, as in the succession of compromises the Jaruzelski government reached with Solidarity. In Romania, the leadership continued to rely on a full panoply of repression, but the result was a surface calm that masked the true popular revulsion at the Nicolae Ceauşescu regime.

Hungary is a mid-range case. János Kádár's regime trumpeted its success in producing a high standard of living and yielding slight but real grants of privacy to citizens in the wake of the Helsinki summit. Kádár counted on Hungary's "new economic mechanism," a policy that sanctioned small private businesses and limited reforms, to satisfy the masses. But the oil crisis of the 1970s greatly increased pressures on Hungary's centrally planned economy, and criticisms by other communist parties forced Kádár to purge the reformers. Moscow's subsidized energy deliveries took the sting out of oil prices until the mid-1980s, while Hungary joined the International Monetary Fund in 1982 and obtained World Bank loans. Yet foreign debt expanded until, late in the decade, Hungary's per capita foreign debt was the highest in the Soviet bloc. Kádár was forced to resign as prime minister, though he retained control of the Hungarian Socialist Workers' Party, and his successor introduced corrective measures that included steep price increases and an income tax to restrain consumption, resulting in intense public dissatisfaction.

Much dissidence in Hungary took the form of a sort of 1956 "truth movement," in which Hungarians pressed the regime to admit that the government overthrown at that time by the Russians, in combination with hard-line Hungarian communists (of whom Kádár was one), had acted in the interests of the Hungarian people and not foreign subversionists. Controversies over 1956 have swirled in Hungary ever since—they continue even today as a historical debate—and would be a major focus of political agitation in the period leading up to the end of the Cold War. Hungarian authorities tolerated the questioning so long as it did not verge on a political challenge but said nothing to resolve questions about 1956.

Meanwhile, Hungarian dissidents formulated a statement of support for Charter 77 in Czechoslovakia and addressed a stronger, similar statement directly to the Kádár government when Václav Havel and four others were sent back to prison in 1979. Hungarian activists soon afterward organized the Foundation to Assist the Poor. It was the first public voluntary entity created outside communist party auspices in many years and an expression of the human right of free association. Hungarians, like Czechs, were among the signatories of the 1980 END manifesto on the Euromissiles. Many more assertions of increased public independence followed, among them the creation of such organizations as the Network of Free Initiatives, the Hungarian Democratic Forum, and the Federation of Young Democrats. The Democratic Union of Scientific Workers challenged the communist trade union system for the first time and made contact with Solidarity in Poland. The security services could no longer suppress these activities without inflaming Hungarians. Other stirrings of public opinion forced new concessions in the religious field. The government permitted the World Jewish Congress to have its annual conference in Budapest in 1987. In 1988 the celebration of Constitution Day, which the communists had co-opted from the traditionally observed anniversary of the death of King Stephen I, who had played a key role in the Christianization of Hungary, coincided with the 950th St. Stephen's Day. The outpouring of religious fervor was such that the religious holiday eclipsed the political observance. Within a year, the 1950 law prohibiting religious orders in Hungary had been repealed. Meanwhile, a unit of the Communist Party's Central Committee was scheduled to take a fresh look at the 1956 overthrow. When the group's chairman, Imre Pozsgay, went on the radio in January 1988 and described the report as a reconsideration of whether 1956 had been a popular uprising or a counterrevolution, Hungarians were thrilled. Quickly publicized, the report became a catalyst for democratization.

By then inflation in Hungary stood at 17 percent, foreign debt totaled more than $16 billion, and the Kádár leadership had been completely discredited. Prime

Minister Károly Grósz succeeded Kádár at the head of the party and brought in economic expert Miklós Németh as his own successor. But, limited by Hungary's highly leveraged situation, the actions open to them failed to stem the tide. In the spring of 1988 a Group of Four—including Grósz and Németh; headed by Rezső Nyers, the original champion of the new economic mechanism; and with Pozsgay as the other member—took over. Again their possibilities were limited. Biting the bullet, the communists rechristened themselves as the Socialist Party, taking the word "Workers" out of their name, and called elections. They calculated they would emerge as the largest single parliamentary bloc and thus remain in power. The political distance crossed had been enormous.

In Poland, discussed in some detail in the second chapter, the Jaruzelski government in the fall of 1986 felt it necessary to grant amnesty to political prisoners, freeing many from Solidarity. Wałęsa demanded the Polish government recognize the right of citizens to form free trade unions. A measure of dialogue followed Jaruzelski's creation of the Consultative Council at the end of the year. By the summer of 1987, internal reports pointed to increased labor unrest, deepening frustration among the intelligentsia, and the declining prestige of senior communist officials, including the party's first secretary. "Consecutive liberalization measures," said one report, "have little resonance within society and render little help in improving the 'reputation' of the government."[12] The regime tried to hold the line, but its domestic policies were anathema to the West, whose credits were vital to Poland, where foreign debt had ballooned to $39 billion, with inflation at a staggering 70 percent. Jaruzelski agreed to a series of roundtable talks with dissidents in the fall of 1988. Preparations for the talks included extended preliminary conversations among the new welter of Polish quasi-political groups and identified issues to raise and common ground for negotiations.

As in Hungary and Poland, partial accommodation bought the Polish communists some time but was vitiated by two other developments. The economic progress of states along the Soviet periphery was hampered by long-ago actions. Because Moscow had encouraged autarky, building self-sustaining rather than mutually cooperative states, the planned economies of the periphery were geared to heavy industry and had matching rather than complementary sectors. They could not easily convert to consumer economies, and the five-year plans for government investment imposed additional rigidities. Gorbachev's advent had the effect of prodding the periphery to move faster, further emphasizing those rigidities. In addition, the East-Central European states were dependent on Soviet energy, long subsidized by Moscow and shored up by Soviet foreign aid. In search of hard currency and afflicted by production shortfalls, Moscow was increasingly tempted to prioritize deliveries, supplying the most to Western European countries that paid cash. During the 1980s Russia successively cut subsidies, cut deliveries, then slashed foreign aid to the peripheral states. Alternative sources of capital in the West, particularly the United States, dried up with the Reaganites' anti-détente backlash and only gradually reappeared. The United States terminated loans or lines of credit to Poland with martial law, and to Hungary and Romania in 1982, while East Germany also lost funding sources. Increasingly, the Central European communist governments were left to their own devices. In the face of a revolution of rising expectations, with few possibilities left other than to reduce existing political and cultural restrictions, the regimes were in a bind. And the fulcrum in these struggles was human rights; its expression, democratization. The accommodation strategy lost viability as dissidence grew amid a diminished stock of concessions remaining for the communists to make.

The climax of the upheaval on the Soviet periphery occurred as the Reagan presidency gave way to that of George H. W. Bush. And the trends were plain, even in the West, even to those without access to secret intelligence. Take, for example, the International Institute for Strategic Studies (IISS) publication *Strategic Survey*, assembled annually by staff plus outside experts. In the edition for 1986, the institute noted Poland's release of political prisoners and termed this a "calculated risk," warning of the adverse effects of Poland's continuing to have a leader from the military and observing, "The men who inherit the mantle of Party power in Eastern Europe will have to be able to cope with societies that have grown increasingly sophisticated, not only in their demands for material goods but also in their political aspirations." Also right on point: "Gradually, very gradually, Eastern Europe is reasserting its Europeanness, a process that was encouraged initially by the increased contacts between East and West in the 1970s. There are still few illusions about what such a process can achieve . . . [but] the more Gorbachev tries to appeal to European sentiment in support of his foreign policy, the more he will encourage both the regimes and the peoples of Eastern Europe to search for their reference point in their European heritage rather than in their recent history."[13]

A year later, IISS analysts expanded their coverage of East-Central Europe, writing of a "new spirit abroad" that is "easily felt but difficult to define." At the state level, the IISS analysts felt, this meant "reform being put back solidly on the agenda—not just economic reform but political reform too." That coupling aroused "high expectations" but was "unfamiliar and dangerous ground." Gorbachev was seen as a man in a hurry, viewed with suspicion by communist party apparatchiks in the allied countries, but "there was the fact that the political leaderships were themselves ready for reform in three East European countries, and in a fourth (Czechoslovakia) resigned to it." As for the people, "In society at large Gorbachev has struck a responsive chord . . . surprisingly so for a Russian—he may actually be more popular there than at home." The IISS analysts wrote this about Gorbachev's thinking on East-Central Europe: "His views about its future have not yet matured into a policy." And the Western analysts drew the conclusion that the combination of Gorbachev's powers of persuasion, the awareness on the part of national party leaderships of the need to reform, the "burgeoning support for reform" among the people, and the evolving "economic breakdown" would mean "opposition to reform will be kept on the defensive and will gradually weaken," even though reformists seemed temporarily stymied.[14]

By the end of 1988, the analysts noted "mixed and extraordinary movement within the Eastern bloc . . . as some governments began to accept the implications of [Gorbachev's] preachings on reform, while others saw these as threatening stability or regime survival, and opposition to the possibilities of reform began to cohere." At this point the IISS analysts believed in the existence of two ad hoc factions among the bloc: a reforming troika of Russia, Poland, and Hungary, and a rejectionist front of East Germany, Czechoslovakia, Romania, and Bulgaria, the latter pronouncing its support for reform but doing nothing to enact them. Western observers aptly noted, "The reformers are hoping to control the changes they have set in motion, so as to avoid destabilizing their own positions, but even their caution cannot rule out the possibility that they are unleashing forces that will be difficult to control." The analysts also noted public remarks by Gorbachev during a visit to Yugoslavia in March 1988 that hinted at a repudiation of the Brezhnev doctrine, though he did not explicitly say so, and another hedge during a Gorbachev visit to Poland. The annual felt the most significant political development of the year was "the reappearance of pluralism as a serious issue" in Hungary and Czechoslovakia (which had been pictured as rejectionist a year earlier), though "signs of the beginning of a generational change in leadership" in East-Central Europe were also of great import.[15] In summary, the developments along the Soviet periphery were open and noticed.

What may have been dimly evident in London was blindingly apparent in Moscow. In December 1988 Gorbachev himself told the Politburo that unless Moscow was willing to assume the massive debts of the East-Central European countries, there was essentially nothing it could do. Historian Jacques Lévesque, author of the deepest inquiry into why Gorbachev abandoned the Brezhnev doctrine,[16] brought back from the archives of the former Soviet Union a series of three documents that reveal Moscow's insights with precision. All three were commissioned by the Soviet leadership based on advice in late 1988 and delivered in February 1989. One is a study from the Bogomolov Commission that commenced with general observations and then made specific forecasts for East-Central European nations. The paper opened with the frank statement that "Societies in Eastern European countries are beginning to change their character," with "an aggravation of contradictions and a growth of crisis developments," and "symptoms visible in all spheres of public life." Economic problems had leapt to the fore, but there was a "dramatic weakening of the positions of the ruling communist parties," complicated by dogmatic ideology whose "old forms block the renewal of the social system or provide a rationale for resistance to reform." Like the *Strategic Surveys*, this assessment grouped Poland and Hungary together and found ongoing reforms threatened by the fall in the living standards of substantial portions of the population. The most favorable scenario for Poland would be an accord at the roundtable talks, which would be "an unstable compromise" including a period of instability during a gradual transition to a mixed economy. The most probable scenario for Hungary was judged to be radical reforms with "step-by-step rebuilding of the parliamentary system on the foundation of party pluralism." For Czechoslovakia, "with a high degree of probability one can accept rapid escalation as soon as this coming spring or in the fall," that could be warded off only by "a decisive replacement of a considerable part of the current party-government leadership, removal of all publicly compromised people" and other measures. As for East Germany, the conservative nature of its leadership, even without any formal opposition, meant perestroika could not take hold without considerable Soviet prodding. "We face a choice," the paper bluntly declared, "to thwart the evolution described above or take it in stride and develop a policy accepting the probability and even the inevitability of this process." Thwarting the process—in effect enforcing the Brezhnev doctrine— "would be tantamount to fighting time itself, the objective course of history," a doomed prospect. The paper went on to reason that the nations affected would not necessarily drop out of the Warsaw Pact and that Moscow could content itself with some modicum of neutrality on its periphery on the lines of the careful neutrality maintained by Finland, or "Finlandization" in the idiom of the day.[17]

The International Department of the Central Committee secretariat compiled another review. This too observed that relations with the periphery had reached a critical stage and that, "having broken with the previous type of relations, we have not yet established a new type." As for East-Central Europe, in several lands "the process of rejection of existing political institutions and the ideological values by the societies is already underway." Further, "the ruling parties cannot rule in the old way any more, and the new 'rules of the game' . . . have not been worked out." The transitional period would be critical. The International Department proposed an eight-point program that sought to minimize intrusions into the local squabbles of the periphery, while preserving a role for the Soviet Union as a sort of Great Uncle to the struggling parties.[18] The Ministry of Foreign Affairs added its own analysis, warning that the Central Europeans, watching the Moscow-Washington ballet of negotiation, might well have concluded that the periphery had become secondary to the Soviets, and advocated work to ensure East-Central Europe remained on a socialist path and within the Warsaw Pact. But even the MFA advised that policy "should be distinguished by self-restraint and calm" and that the use of forceful methods "and especially the use of military force is completely excluded, even in the most extreme situation."[19] There exists one more report in this series, assembled by the KGB, but it has never been declassified. What is clear from all this is that by early 1989 expert opinion in Moscow was already discounting the loss of East-Central Europe.

Alexander Yakovlev, who supervised these studies, was a Politburo member and close adviser to Gorbachev. There should be no doubt the Soviet leader was informed of them. What impact the studies had on Gorbachev is impossible to say. But what *is* clear from a variety of transcripts of Politburo meetings and Gorbachev encounters with leaders of Hungary, Poland, Czechoslovakia, and East Germany over the months of 1989 is that Moscow's chief continued to counsel reform. For example, the Hungarian record of talks with Gorbachev on March 23–24 notes that the Moscow leader finished his session with Károly Grósz by saying, "Today we have to preclude the possibility of repeated foreign intervention into the internal affairs of socialist countries." This came after Grósz had opened the meeting by saying events in his country were "accelerating."[20] Here and elsewhere, including in public, Gorbachev began to speak of the necessity of preserving the "common European home" of the nations of the continent. Visiting East Berlin for the observance of the fortieth anniversary of the founding of the German Democratic Republic (GDR) in October, Gorbachev essentially declared Moscow would keep its hands off the local situation. At a meeting with Gorbachev a few weeks later, on November 1, East German leader Egon Krenz revealed not only that GDR economic reforms were a failure, but also that the state was running a balance-of-trade deficit of over $12 billion, had to borrow money just to pay interest on existing foreign debt, and could proceed only by lowering the standard of living of citizens, who were already fleeing the GDR by the thousands. East Germany was bankrupt. Gorbachev was stunned.[21]

Bush Administration Hesitation

London and Moscow could equally see what was happening. Washington could too, but where Gorbachev ran faster, President George H. W. Bush, who replaced Reagan on January 20, 1989, moved very slowly. He commissioned policy studies, called national security reviews (NSRs) in the Bush administration, on a range of issues. Of these, NSR-3 concerned Soviet-American relations, NSR-4 East-Central Europe, and NSR-5 Western Europe. President Bush then sat back to await the results, which were slow in coming. Concrete policy actions tarried even longer. One good explanation for Washington's torpor is that a dynamic response to the rapidly changing international situation required the United States to alter a long-standing Cold War strategy, specifically "containment."

Enshrined in U.S. foreign policy as early as 1947, containment postulated an aggressive Soviet Union that needed to be isolated by American actions to shore up anti-communist states and collective security arrangements that created a multilateral web of opposition, a sort of iron curtain in reverse. A sustained effort to prevent Soviet expansion, Truman administration officials hoped, might force the Soviets to recoil upon themselves or, at a minimum, forge an alliance sufficiently strong to defeat any Russian attempt to break out of isolation. Successive American presidents up through Reagan had followed this general policy, which led to success in the Berlin crises of the 1950s and the Cuban missile crisis of 1962. The détente of the 1970s can be viewed as an adjunct of containment or as a moderation of the old policy. In any case, some observers attribute the Soviet collapse of the 1980s to the steady implementation of the containment policy. George H. W. Bush, active in foreign affairs since the 1960s, was steeped in the tenets of containment and well versed in its corollaries.

The main problem in tracing the fall of the Soviet Union to the success of containment lies in the nature of that policy. At its core, containment was a stabilizing strategy viewed by some as passive or defensive, but nevertheless an approach of holding the main lines of confrontation in Europe while countering Soviet forays elsewhere. However one understands détente, it is nevertheless true that the 1970s changed the nature of containment. The development of greatly increased trade between East and West, magnified cultural contacts, and the interpenetration of the global economy diminished the security imperative. To the extent that containment remained the central U.S. strategy, its scope had widened beyond a simple security competition. It was Ronald Reagan who abandoned containment. The very essence of the claim that other presidents played to hold back the Soviets, whereas Reagan played to win, resides in the notion that President Reagan went beyond containment to assume an offensive posture of rolling back the Iron Curtain. But as discussed in several contexts thus far, the texture of the Cold War itself changed during the period after 1983, and accommodation rather than rollback became the strategy of the later Reagan administration. President Bush may have seen himself as restoring containment or as operating from a stance of "containment-plus," a mixed strategy of maintaining lines of containment while seeking further advantages that could accrue to the West.

Former Bush administration officials portray its actions in a different light. Secretary of State James A. Baker, for example, quotes President Bush saying, as early as February 1991, "We must take the offensive. We cannot just be seen as reacting to another Gorbachev move. We need to do it to keep the public behind the alliance. Maybe Eastern Europe is it—get in there in his end zone. Not to stir up revolution, but we're right on human rights, democracy, and freedom."[22] But Mr. Bush undertook no initiatives. His first public comment focused on the Soviet Union, not Europe per se, and came in a speech on May 10. Though President Bush spoke of moving beyond the old strategy of containment, he made no concrete proposals, instead challenging Gorbachev—who five months earlier had declared a unilateral withdrawal of hundreds of thousands of Soviet troops from the Warsaw Pact countries—to move beyond rhetoric. Bush chose Poland and Hungary for his first foray into East-Central Europe, visiting both in July 1989. Meeting with both Jaruzelski and Wałęsa in Poland, he offered only $100 million in assistance while Poles had been talking of $10 billion. In Hungary, the figure was $25 million. It cannot yet be established whether Washington calculated that the Pact countries were about to collapse—the records that will show Bush's true opinions remain secret—but the White House could not know Moscow's private views on enforcing the Brezhnev doctrine. Ensuring a hard landing for the East-Central European countries maximized the danger of Soviet military intervention, which risked wider conflict. The United States can thus take little credit for what happened.

Events moved swiftly toward an endgame. Poland proved the catalyst. The Polish government, implementing the roundtable agreements, legalized the Catholic Church and permitted a vote that returned a strong Solidarity majority within a limited electoral framework. Jaruzelski was induced—in part by the United States—to stand for president of a transitional government, and a Solidarity cabinet took office in August. In Hungary, the communist party transformed itself into a Socialist one, the nation adopted a new constitution in mid-October, and a month later voters approved an election. In Czechoslovakia, security forces first attempted to crack down, once more arresting Václav Havel and others, but dissidents quickly coalesced into a "Civic Forum," with which the government of Ladislav Adamec was obliged to open talks. Communist party leaders were forced to resign as the Czech "Velvet Revolution" took hold. Czech president Gustav Husak on December 10 swore in a majority noncommunist cabinet and then resigned. Václav Havel became the president of Czechoslovakia. Transformations also took place in Romania, Bulgaria, and eventually Yugoslavia.

For several years, the two Germanys had been circling around each other in a delicate dance. East Germany's Erich Honecker had made a first-ever visit by a GDR leader to West Germany in late 1987. The West Germans, encouraging rapprochement, made large loans to the GDR in 1983–84 and began giving the East small amounts of aid, in part fueled by GDR promises to permit a certain amount of emigration to the West. By 1989 the writing was on the wall for the GDR. That May, its state planning commission revealed the impending bankruptcy of the nation (anticipated to occur by 1991) to the Politburo. Conditions were such that thousands of citizens sought to leave through Czechoslovakia or Hungary. In September, Hungary, in return for West German credits, opened its border with Austria, encouraging an exodus that became the largest since the erection of the Berlin Wall. This undermined the GDR government. Protesters took to the streets, unheard of in the tightly controlled GDR. Honecker resigned on October 17 and was replaced by Egon Krenz. The entire cabinet resigned on November 7, the entire Politburo the next day. The new government adopted a law permitting travel between East and West Germany, and on November 10, as a result of a combination of tightly held information on the regulations, confusion, pressure from crowds demanding to be allowed to cross the Berlin Wall, and a minister's radio interview that seemed to approve immediate opening of the border, security forces lifted the barriers at The Wall. Crowds flowed both ways. Soon people began to tear down the Berlin Wall. In less than a month, the GDR government disintegrated. By

December 5, Honecker and other former communist officials were under arrest. The Soviet periphery, and the Cold War, had been transformed.

Great Ideas as Dynamic Forces

Before proceeding further, a brief pause is necessary because the human rights issue lies at the heart of one argument for how the Cold War ended. Some maintain that Ronald Reagan won the struggle by bashing the Soviets on human rights. Actually, the United States was slow to understand the implications of the Helsinki Act's Basket 3. The Ford administration accepted the provisions almost without a thought. It was President Jimmy Carter who first embraced human rights, and he pressed the issue against opposition from both conservatives *and* those concerned over Soviet-American relations. Neither group understood the deep international resonance of the issue. Conservatives lambasted Carter for a pie-in-the-sky policy, and arms controllers worried that Russian annoyance over Carter's championing of human rights would obstruct superpower negotiations.[23] But Carter's advocacy succeeded so well that by the time Mr. Reagan took office, it was no longer possible for an American president to ignore human rights.

What President Reagan mostly did was cloak old-style security actions in human rights rhetoric, for example, justifying secret wars in Nicaragua and Africa and a covert operation in Poland as fights for peoples' human rights, not elements of his anti-communist crusade. The only references to Hungary in the Reagan memoir are to its 1956 Uprising. On Czechoslovakia, he refers to the Prague Spring or speaks generically about free states versus oppressed ones. Reagan supported certain specific human rights cases in the Soviet Union, including those of Jewish emigration, in particular of Natan Sharansky; the case of some Pentecostalists who had taken refuge in the U.S. embassy in Moscow; and freedom for the imprisoned Russian dissident physicist Andrei Sakharov. He mentioned human rights at the summit meetings in Geneva and Reykjavik, the latter encounter just days after the spy swap deal that permitted Sharansky to leave Russia, but the transcripts show only talk, no substantive negotiation. By the time Mr. Reagan determined a more forthright stance, the floodgates were already creaking on the rush of events that would sweep away the Soviet empire. When President Reagan visited Berlin in June 1987 and in a speech challenged the Soviet Union to "tear down this Wall"— he claims to have said the same thing to Gorbachev privately shortly before—East Germany was already in extremis and the Berlin Wall had little more than a year left to it.[24]

The published version of President Reagan's diary refers once—and only to Hungary—as a "target" for "friendly efforts to woo them a little away from the Soviets."[25] That was in January 1985, and the friendly efforts were not American but British—Prime Minister Margaret Thatcher chose Hungary for her first visit to a land on the communist periphery for a few days in February 1984. Thatcher recalls, "In retrospect, my Hungarian visit was the first foray in what became a distinctive British diplomacy toward the captive nations of eastern Europe. The first step was to open greater economic and commercial links, making them less dependent upon the closed [Soviet] system. Later we were to put more stress on human rights."[26] The diplomacy was distinctive because Thatcher sought to go beyond what Reagan was doing. American triumphalists who seek to credit Ronald Reagan for changes in Central Europe are in effect stealing a British achievement. In addition, the leading edge of the British policy was to expand trade. Fighting for human rights only came later. The conclusion that the true movers of the tectonic changes that came in East-Central Europe were the people of those nations, not the policymakers in either London or Washington, is inescapable.

Actually, East-Central Europe was never Ronald Reagan's or George H. W. Bush's to win. It was, however, Mikhail Gorbachev's to lose. The Soviets had substantial interests in all the lands of the periphery and, more than that, had troops in garrisons everywhere except Romania and Bulgaria. And Moscow had a doctrine of intervention to prevent any change in the political status of these nations. The threat of a Soviet military move, with all it entailed for both East-Central Europe and the Cold War as a whole, was something that contributed to the potential danger of the 1980s. Refusing to invoke the Brezhnev doctrine required *two* choices from Gorbachev: a negative decision on military action plus an affirmative one to encourage democratization in the nations of the periphery. When that process led to the eclipse of communist leadership throughout East-Central Europe as political pluralization took hold, the pressures on the Soviet leader must have been enormous. Gorbachev's reasons may have been high-minded or self-interested, rank or lofty, depending upon the observer, but his course was certainly bold, and it led directly to one of the end points of the Cold War.

The importance of Great Ideas in history is nicely illustrated in how the Cold War ended. Ideas affect individuals. They know no boundaries, are difficult to suppress, and, as these stories show, can lead to the rise of mass movements, even multinational ones. Neither the nuclear freeze nor the demand for human rights was the product of a government initiative, but rather the outpouring of personal emotion and its coalescence into mass mobilization. Governments had to *respond* to the movements spawned by these ideas. However belated or halfhearted the responses may have been, however cynical may have been efforts to manipulate those movements affecting the Cold War adversary, the fact of these government actions on both sides of the Cold War demonstrates that the sides eventually recognized their importance.

Each of the movements sketched here primarily affected one side in the conflict. Neither of them ended the Cold War, but they did more than merely establish situational factors with which Washington and Moscow had to cope. The Reagan administration succeeded in outmaneuvering the nuclear freeze campaign and placing its new nuclear weapons in NATO countries, but the underlying reality was that Western European public opinion had wakened to the dangers of a superpower war. There would be no more free ride for United States defense programs vis-á-vis NATO. Publics in both Western Europe and the United States held governments increasingly accountable for lack of progress in halting the arms race, creating powerful forces to reduce tensions. These were enduring political forces that exerted their influence through the remaining years of the Cold War conflict. On the Soviet side, Moscow and its allies employed security measures to limit the sway of human rights norms in the East-Central European nations and Soviet Union itself, and in that sense they too outmaneuvered the power of the Idea. But the success was only on the surface. The real effect of human rights was to undermine whatever legitimacy remained for the governments of the communist satellite nations. This erosion of foundations goes far toward explaining the rapidity with which the communist governments were swept away once the lid came off. Beneath surface stability lay a seething cauldron of discontent. In combination with the structural factors that will be examined in the next chapter, the penetration of the Idea made the outcome inevitable. A powerful tool in exploring these kinds of multinational developments is international history.

International History as a Tool

One of the strongest contributions of recent years, at least in diplomatic history, has been in the field of international history. This new movement perhaps lacks a formal definition, but it essentially resides in the use of multinational research techniques. To illuminate a given subject, scholars use archives in different nations. The stories in this chapter, particularly those of the Soviet periphery, are good examples. More than that, the history of the Soviet Union and its East-Central European allies, as well as the domestic developments within the Central European states themselves, would be difficult to reconstruct without recourse to Soviet and Central European sources and, in the best case, their archives. What could be better than to discover the Soviet record of a meeting between Gorbachev and, say, a Hungarian leader, plus the Hungarian memorandum recording the same conversation? In the particular case of the peaceful revolutions along the Soviet periphery, there has been a special advantage with the demise of the Cold War since that resulted in a truth-telling that included the release of many records of the former communist governments. These lodes of fresh primary sources have enriched history, and it will be many years before they have been mined to capacity. The best situations are those where materials available in different places overlap, as in the Gorbachev example above, or where records of an event still secret in one country are open in another.

International historical research can be useful to shed light on an episode when the records of one player remain closed. For example, at this writing, the documents of the first Bush administration are closed at the fiat of the second and, beyond that, will still be classified for security reasons until scholars gradually open up the vaults. Records of the Reagan presidency are in a very preliminary stage of appearing. In these cases, documents from the former Soviet Union and the East-Central European states provide primary source material on many episodes in which Bush or Reagan were involved. On occasion, the records of the other side are the *only* ones currently in the public domain. Some practitioners refer to these international research techniques as furnishing a "back door" to history. That is, a bare-bones account assembled from assorted sources and supplemented by available interviews, memoirs, and periodical treatments—an amalgam that used to be considered sufficient to draw historical conclusions—can now be augmented by true primary sources, even if seen through the eyes of another nation.

There are two principal difficulties that apply to multinational documentary research. The historian must be wary of them. The obvious one is access and coverage. There remains wide variation in the availability of records in different nations. The former Soviet Union is possibly the boundary case. Archival statutes adopted in 1995 give Russian ministries a great deal of control over which of their records are even sent to archives, and regulations afford archivists considerable latitude in what records they may actually serve to a researcher. This system subjects the record to manipulation both from governments that wish to present a certain version of events and, more prosaically, from corrupt functionaries. East-Central European countries are less subject to these problems, but difficulties in terms of access to records remain. Possibly the closest to being fully open are the records of individuals and political parties, like Solidarity, because they have a heroic story to tell. Records of the former East Germany are also largely available because the German successor state opened all GDR records as a matter of law. Western European and Scandanavian archives are subject to their own secrecy rules but are generally open to the degree that accords with their standing procedures.

In any case, the researcher needs to be alert to the possibility that she or he is not being given the full picture. If that proves true, there is also historical value in examining why access is being denied and what purpose this serves.

A special word is in order regarding the efforts of the Cold War International History Project (CWIHP) of the Smithsonian Institution's Woodrow Wilson International Center. Created not long after the Cold War ended, the CWIHP has played a crucial role in the evolution of international history, supporting historians in many lands in gaining access to and using their archival records, encouraging nations to open their archival records, holding conferences that highlight insights gleaned from these records, widening the circle of those aware of the international historical sources, and also serving as a clearing house in the West for this wealth of material. The CWIHP's published working papers, *Bulletin*, and digitized virtual archive are hugely valuable as repositories for the available records.

A second problem nevertheless follows from the first. Spotty access to records results in a history that is one of snapshots or slides rather than motion pictures. A diplomatic historian researching a standard topic in U.S. foreign policy would seek records that establish the structural and political factors influencing the decision, the policy positions of the various departments involved in deliberations, the options actually proposed and why, the way these are interpreted by the president's staff, the proceedings of meetings where the policymaker airs the alternatives, the record of the decision made, and then records showing how this was implemented or reflected in policy. In international history so far, often only one or a few of these aspects are embodied in the available research material. This makes it difficult to draw definitive conclusions. Memoirs and interviews may be available to supplement the documentary record, the state of which makes these especially useful. Nevertheless historians need to proceed with caution in making generalizations from the material. And if snapshots are the best that is available, use them.

The central tasks in researching broad historical forces are to identify the factors at work and to determine what kinds of data are pertinent in establishing the mode and success of their operation. Neither is a simple task. Fundamental forces in history do not exist in a vacuum. Other factors can mask the one at issue or be as important. And trends are rarely uniform. Wise policies, suddenly discovered resources, serendipitous developments that draw everyone's attention away from essential trends, and Great Leaders, individually or together, can delay the evolution of a trend. Arguably, Mikhail Gorbachev hoped for exactly that when he gambled that perestroika could reverse the decay of the Soviet Union. The next chapter will examine other factors that made it exceedingly unlikely that Gorbachev could have succeeded. But if Soviet disintegration had been delayed, by five years, by ten, by some other number—an uptick in the prevailing trend lines—does that mean the broad historical factors were not determinant? That is an important judgment for the historian.

The narrative in this chapter began by designating three broad factors in the ending of the Cold War: fear of nuclear conflict, the captivating force of the idea of human rights, and economic developments. A key part of the work is simply to identify the factors. Memoirs can help. If a reading of numerous recollections of a given set of events keeps throwing up the same general observations as to constraints and limits, it is a fair supposition that a broad factor has been elicited. Conventional wisdom is often wrong but frequently draws on those factors generally assumed to be operating. And it may be correct. That too is a judgment call for the historian. Observation is another tool. The researcher will inevitably encounter an array of data in investigating the subject. Some of it will be quite striking. Patterns may emerge, and patterns across a range of subjects suggest a broad operating factor at work. In this chapter, the evolution of political opposition to the Euromissiles across a range of Western European nations and in the United States went through similar stages and relied upon the same arguments. Similarly the development of dissidence among the Central European states along the Soviet periphery evinced a pattern. And Soviet retrenchment had parallel effects on the range of choice for the communist governments of each of those states. There are good reasons to consider these as broad factors. Does this set of factors exhaust the full range of themes? Probably not. But that is another reason to conduct a multilevel analysis of the type that is attempted here.

Historical judgment also requires an evaluation as to relative importance of the variables. Which trend was the most important? If not, why not? If so, why is that? These are matters for individual observers with their specific cases. For the end of the Cold War, the issues of fear in the West and human rights in Central Europe are probably less important than the matters addressed in the next chapter. In logic, these themes would be necessary but not sufficient, or subordinate. Fear in the West, raising security concerns, put pressure on both the United States and Soviet Union to move toward accommodation on nuclear disarmament, while collateral effects of the NATO arms buildup put additional strains on the Soviet military economy. Those developments favored a break in the arms control impasse, on the one hand, and further complicated the overall Soviet problem, on the other. As for the impact of human rights, this led to upheaval along the Russian periphery and political sensitivity in the Soviet Union itself, which threatened communist power. Had Russia possessed greater resources, both challenges might have been overcome. This leads to the judgment that the economic factors were the most determinant, and that is where we shall turn next.

Data collection is by source, while structuring narrative history and drawing subsequent conclusions takes place subject by subject. Previous chapters have referred to various types of source material, and all of them can yield information on a range of topics. For example, a document that renders the transcript of a Warsaw Pact meeting on whether to intervene in Poland not only relates the positions taken by the leaders of various nations but also can provide information on the problems being faced by those countries, from military readiness to economic constraints. A memoir can furnish commentary on the social and cultural milieu in which the individual functions, as well as details of particular decisions in the way the author would like them to be remembered. A newspaper or television news tape can contain raw data on many topics, cultural and social information, even analyses. A report on U.S. policy toward a given country can yield information on military matters, trade, political issues, and foreign policy. A collection of statistics speaks to its particular subject but may also fit with other information to produce a wider picture. The historian must be creative in planning sources to consult and then be alert to the data specific to her or his cases. In diplomatic history, the range of appropriate source material may be especially broad and include data from multiple countries. In general, the best results flow from casting a wide net to see what comes in with the catch. On the matter of Moscow's economic problems and their role in the end of the Cold War, that catch is very interesting indeed.

CHAPTER 5

BLUE JEANS, BLUEGRASS, AND NATIONAL PRIDE

Economics, Politics, and Culture

EAST-CENTRAL EUROPE IN MANY WAYS PRESENTED a microcosm of trends at work on a grand scale within the Soviet Union. The evolution of those trends led to the Soviet collapse as surely as any other set of factors, while the steady weakening of Soviet power ensured the fall of the Iron Curtain could occur without application of the Brezhnev doctrine. Gorbachev's reforms began as an attempt to shake the Soviet Union out of its lethargy, gathered momentum as the Soviet leadership came to realize the task could not be accomplished without structural changes in economics and politics, and ended by undermining what had been traditional bases of the Soviet state. Simultaneously, long-standing but unresolved issues among the Soviet polity, an amalgam of Russians along with many other nationalities, acted as centrifugal forces tending toward disintegration of the union. Ethnic and social groups were encouraged by the apparent ability of the nations of the Soviet periphery to assert their independence and, in another collateral effect of the growing acceptance of human rights norms, moved to a higher level of demands. Russian society, demoralized by the economic stagnation of the state and the evident disparity in wealth between the party hierarchy and the masses, gave progressively less support to state efforts to stave off these effects. Over the 1980s, the Soviet Union became increasingly less stable.

At the same time, traditional foundations of Soviet power—the communist party, the security services, and the military—were beset by shrinking legitimacy. They were also restive under Gorbachev's perestroika, fearing the impact of society's democratization on their own power. The evolution of events in the Soviet Union soured them on Gorbachev's leadership and eventually led them to attempt the use of force to terminate it. At that point, the fact that the structural foundations of the state *had* changed acted to shift the ground beneath them. The coup d'etat failed. The Soviet Union was swept away.

Some argue that the Cold War ended with the fall of the Berlin Wall in 1989. Others date that moment to the demise of the Soviet state in 1991. As noted in chapter 1, there is at least one other plausible endpoint. Whichever date the observer chooses, it is evident that November 1989 sounded a death knell and that August 1991 marked an irreversible passage. Key factors in this evolution can be traced to systemic developments in the Soviet Union itself. These developments were internal to the USSR. They were not the product of U.S. foreign policy, relations with Western Europe, or upheaval along the Soviet periphery, yet they played a major role in ending the Cold War.

Soviet Economic Problems

Outlining this history is easier than laying out the details. A good point of departure is the work of historian Stephen Kotkin, who lived and traveled extensively in the Soviet Union beginning in 1984 and began his work from the vantage point of charting the decline of a steel town, one of the engines of Soviet industry. In his book *Armageddon Averted: The Soviet Collapse, 1970–2000* (2001), Kotkin maintains that, more than a totalitarian state and military behemoth, the Soviet Union existed as a "comprehensive experiment in non-capitalist modernity."[1] He argues that the Soviet Union, a major oil producer, encountered a cruel trick of history during the 1970s, when a prolonged spike in oil prices led to the illusion that this resource could furnish a new basis for the Russian economy. Energy exports accounted for 80 percent of Soviet hard currency earnings between 1972 and 1985 (a significant portion of the remainder came from foreign sales of gold, an important Soviet mining product), rising from $23 billion to $140 billion. Simultaneously with the windfall, Soviet successes in education and socialization also produced rising expectations among citizens. Comparisons with living standards in the United States found the Soviet Union wanting. Demands for consumer goods sharpened, but the economy remained overwhelmingly (70 percent) oriented to industry, transport, and construction. In addition, a great deal of that infrastructure dated from Stalin's era and was neither efficient nor capable of easy conversion to meet demand. Moscow had barely awakened to the problem at the point in the early 1980s that oil prices began declining, leaving the Soviets with rust-belt industries, allies clamoring for help, frustrated consumers, *and* dwindling budgetary resources. Full employment was an advantage of the Soviet economy, but workers had no reason to increase productivity and little to buy with their cash.

Regardless of the pace of change, Soviet society had been transformed by this late Cold War period. Kotkin's data shows that by the late 1970s two-thirds of Soviet citizens lived in cities or towns, most in apartments with kitchens and private baths, an advance over earlier times. Over 90 percent of families owned refrigerators, 60 percent washing machines, and 93 percent had televisions, triple the number of a decade before. Many families could also afford vacation homes (*dachas*). Data for 1978 showed that the number of people who took vacations within the Union (35 million) had more than doubled within that decade, while over a million traveled abroad, mostly to Eastern Europe. Ten percent of the population had completed college (compared to 3 percent in 1950), and 70 percent high school (40 percent in 1950). The government controlled information tightly, so citizens were mostly unaware of the disparities between their own standard of living and that in the West, and their own progress had been palpable. Soviet intellectuals were restive, we are told, for example, by the noted academician Georgi Arbatov, who writes, "There was a sour mood, combined with cynicism, among the intelligentsia."[2] The government took the edge off this dissent with a combination of offers of selective access plus the watchfulness of the KGB. But rising expectations went hand in hand with these social changes.[3]

Ideally, the Soviets' planned economy had the potential to meet social demands. But planners were burdened with the result of earlier industrial development and the rigidities of the system. The standard mechanism of creating five-year plans put a premium on long-range prediction in an environment where statistical measurements cloaked as much as they revealed. Kotkin offers the example of the Soviet steel industry: production of rolled steel was very high, and incentives were linked to raw production weight, meaning heavier steel counted more. There was a disincentive to change even as modern products required more refined metals. Much of the industrial infrastructure had been built in the 1930s and was not easily adaptable. Plants needing the refined products accepted the crude metal and tried either to barter it in a black-market, subterranean economy or to shave the steel to finer tolerances, work that counted toward production "norms" even though it produced no end products.[4] Meanwhile, military spending stayed off the table, accounting for a large fraction of output (20 to 30 percent of gross domestic product [GDP]) and, equally important, consuming a very high proportion of Soviet production of such sophisticated products as electronics and servomechanisms. Under the circumstances, annual GDP increases on the order of 2 percent amounted to stagnation even as consumer demand could not be met.

Another issue was the "nationalities problem." The Soviet Union was and remained an amalgam of many different peoples and ethnicities, not assimilated but largely kept in an isolation that favored the Russian group. The fifteen republics of the union each represented a major ethnicity, and within them, there were over a hundred smaller autonomous zones akin to the Bantustans of South Africa. Until the 1980s, individual nationalisms were largely masked by the slowly rising standard of living. It had long been a tenet of Western Cold War thinking that the nationalities problem could be exploited to the detriment of the USSR, and this era brought efforts in that direction similar to what the Reagan administration did in East-Central Europe. Contrary to the claims of triumphalists, however, Zbigniew Brzezinski during the Carter administration, not the Reaganites, launched the movement in this direction. Covert imports of miniature Bibles and reproductions of dissident literature (samizdat) were ramped up during the Reagan administration, but the program had already begun.

The structural weaknesses of the Soviet economy and the centrifugal forces of the nationalities problem were known factors, before the advent of Gorbachev and both inside and outside the USSR. Arbatov dates the period of final stagnation to 1982. At the time, the American journalist Robert Kaiser, a reporter for the *Washington Post* who had been an acute observer of Russia since the 1960s, was on assignment in Moscow. Of 1983 he noted, "Nearly every conversation I had in Russia that summer touched on some aspect of the economic failures that had come to haunt the Soviet system."[5] Yegor Ligachev, who became a senior official under Andropov and joined Gorbachev's Politburo, recalls that when Andropov rose to the leadership in 1983, "I, like many other provincial Party secretaries, was impatient for change, uncomfortably aware that the country was headed for social and economic disaster."[6] He attributes the national malaise to a model of socialism that put too many of the means of production in the hands of the state, particularly the collective farms, which were "unjustifiably equated to state property in many ways" and thus "held back the initiative of labor collectives." Combined with the dominance of the Soviet military-industrial complex, this "hampered the realization of major social programs and the development of the consumer sector of the economy." Meanwhile, "contradictions had arisen between the Center and the republics"—an elliptical reference to the nationalities problem—further complicating the situation. Ligachev finishes, "In short, it was becoming clear that social transformations were needed."[7] Gorbachev, writing of the end of Brezh-nev's reign, complains of the blind adherence to old dogma and the propensity of the leadership to overlook extensive developments in everything from science and technology to the life of the people. He recalls, "The prevailing mood was the expectation of far-reaching changes."[8] Gen. Dmitri Volkogonov, assessing the state of the union at the end of Chernenko's leadership, notes, "Many people sensed that the country had moved towards an invisible boundary, beyond which the desired changes might be possible."[9] Andropov set in motion a number of measures, but Gorbachev, at least, believed these "reforms" merely scratched at the surface of the malaise by focusing more on labor discipline and order than structural changes.[10] Chernenko essentially put the Soviet Union in a holding pat-tern. That left Gorbachev.

Pervasive Soviet secrecy hampered efforts to cope with the nation's problems. Even Politburo members did not learn the true costs of the Soviet military until 1985. The military devoured 16 percent of the state budget in the secret budget but 40 percent in reality. It ate up 80 percent of expenditures on science and technol-ogy. Military production accounted for 20 percent of GDP, not the 6 percent the generals asserted. Gorbachev notes he did not find out some things until the eve of his resignation as president, that is, in 1991. "Nonetheless," he writes, "I knew the greatest 'secret,' namely that our budget was full of holes. It was being continually replenished by the savings bank, in other words money was being drawn from the savings of the citizens and by raising the internal debt." In 1986 the budget deficit amounted to 80 billion rubles.[11] Economist Yegor Gaidar, who advised Gorbachev at the moment, a few years later, when the Soviet Union attempted to transition to a market economy and who would serve Boris Yeltsin's successor government as acting prime minister, compiled an extensive study of economic pressures on empires in general and the Soviet Union in particular.[12] Gaidar's data demonstrate with figures the sharpening contradictions. For one thing, he quantifies unmet con-sumer demand by studying Soviet citizens' rate of savings, showing this as flat over the decade of the 1970s, but mushrooming between 1980 and 1985, Gorbachev's first year as general secretary. The rate rose from 5 to 16 percent, the raw number of rubles doubled (to 60.9 billion), while as a proportion of the entire Soviet GDP, unmet demand leaped from 4.7 to 7.8 percent. Put another way, the (lower) level of GDP the military claimed they soaked up (6 percent) amounted to less than the unmet consumer demand.

Meanwhile, the Soviet Union became the world's largest importer of grain in 1980 and by 1985 was buying 70 percent more than Japan, the next largest importer. At that time, grain was being imported into Ukraine, long the breadbasket of the Soviet Union. The Soviet balance of trade for agricultural products increased sharply beginning in 1978, peaking from 1980 to 1982 (between $27 billion and $30 billion a year as measured in constant year 2000 dollars) and ameliorating somewhat only toward the end of the decade. The later improvement followed from growth in Soviet grain production, an important offset since world grain prices rose during this period. But the persistence of food supply problems also indicates that other agricultural products constituted the larger factor and that increased grain production could not solve the dilemma. Beyond the raw costs of products, the Soviet Union subsidized retail prices to consumers, assuming 51.5 percent of the burden for nine staples by 1989. In early 1987 the Politburo had already been told that in the absence of price increases, by 1990 the cost of subsidies would swell to over 100 billion rubles.

As basic problems festered, Soviet resources dwindled. Oil earnings dropped as world prices declined. Because Moscow had made basic decisions to pump oil at a very high rate in a desperate effort to fill its coffers and because investment in new pumping machinery was down, Soviet oil production fell just as prices collapsed, further complicating the equation. Oil sales brought in 30.9 billion rubles in 1984 but 22.5 two years later. Sales to Western Europe dropped by half. An oil industry that pumped 119 million tons of oil in 1980 and went to 624 million tons of oil in 1988 managed only 515.8 million tons four years later. Coal production tumbled by an almost identical 19 percent over the same period, an indication that lack of investment was a generalized problem not confined to the oil industry. With a few exceptions, such as Iraq, other foreign sales, in particular military equipment, went to nations that could not afford to pay and that were often given such favorable terms they contributed little to Soviet currency accounts.

Even reforms could have potential results unfavorable to the state. One of Gorbachev's efforts was a campaign against alcoholism designed to encourage higher worker productivity. Gorbachev maintains the program was not implemented as intended, and should have been phased in more gradually, with other revenue compensating for what was lost. Taxes on liquor sales accounted for 36.7 billion rubles in the Soviet state budget in 1984—an amount greater than the cost of Soviet aid to its allies. Over a quarter of that was gone in 1986. Combine the shortfall in revenues with unanticipated costs—such as higher prices for agricultural imports or the sudden huge burden of coping with the Chernobyl nuclear accident—and the dimensions of the Soviet economic problem begin to come into view.

Mikhail Gorbachev acquired much more information on the real status of the Soviet Union during the year of Chernenko's leadership, when the latter's declining health led him to skip Politburo meetings frequently. He asked Gorbachev to fill in as chairman, effectively making Gorbachev his understudy. The rising leader went beyond the party apparat, talking to Moscow and Leningrad residents, industrial and agricultural managers, scientists and economists. Existing plans were woefully out of date. "I felt that we could not succeed in implementing reforms in the economy," writes Gorbachev, "if we did not bring about fundamental restructuring of management structures and decentralization of management functions. Everyone enthusiastically agreed: without these no reforms would last."[13] The leadership summoned an All-Union plenum of the CPSU Central Committee. Gorbachev wanted a mandate for his policy, cloaked as a process of continuing forward motion, concretizing measures contemplated under Andropov that were intended to perfect socialism. This April 1985 plenum marks the beginning of perestroika.

Gorbachev observes in his memoir that in a totalitarian state a process of change could be initiated only from above, by the leadership. He then argues, "Past experience showed that if the spark of reform was not caught by the masses, it was doomed."[14] The subsequent history of the Soviet Union is the record of Gorbachev maneuvering among the varied power centers in an effort to advance his agenda. The Politburo he carried with him as its leader, but some members, more entrenched in the old ideology, increasingly resisted change. The party apparat, torn between its loyalty to the higher leadership and its traditional prerogatives, opposed change. Industrial managers were also torn, between the quest for a modern economy and the overhang of decades of investment in the old industrial structure. The military and KGB resisted change but paid lip service to the Gorbachev program, understanding their position depended on the vitality of the Soviet state. At Chernobyl, the military had been the first responders and had borne the brunt of the logistic and security aspects of disaster management, and they had failed. The tragedy had one positive aspect in that it stripped away the military's credibility, forcing it to take on a more positive attitude toward reform, if only to curry favor with the people. Gorbachev needed a mass mobilization to overcome these forces of inertia.

With a keen political sense General Secretary Gorbachev began reaching out, visiting many parts of the Soviet Union—from Leningrad and Ukraine to the Siberian oil cities—to connect with the people, demonstrate his direct concern, and popularize the reform agenda. The Soviet leader also sought to placate the military, initially allocating it new funds for technological improvements and the war in Afghanistan. These maneuvers took time. "I have to admit," Gorbachev recollects, "that we underestimated the odds against us. We were too long under the illusion that the problem was simply the difficulty of winning support for perestroika. We allowed the time-frame for structural transformation to be dragged out for three or four years and thus missed the most economically and politically favorable time for them in 1987–8. This was a strategic miscalculation."[15] Close aide Anatoly Chernyaev estimates that it was in late 1987 and early 1988, "as perestroika headed for a showdown with Stalin's legacy," that domestic politics entered a critical phase.[16]

Gorbachev's first big gambit would be the Twenty-seventh CPSU Congress held in early 1986. Here he unveiled a more extensive program of radical reforms, securing the party's formal adherence. This program included accelerated economic and social measures in a new five-year plan (the USSR's twelfth) plus a rejection of all-out struggle and military confrontation. After Chernobyl, another Central Committee plenum confirmed the new course. And in January 1987 a plenum met to review progress, becoming the starting point for glasnost, Gorbachev's liberalization of ideological controls, designed to bring along the citizenry. Party cadres continued to fight a rearguard action against reform. The rigidities in the Soviet state structure and the requirements for maintaining the necessary levels of imports were such that it was already becoming apparent that resources for transformation were quite limited. The leadership had to free up rubles committed to other purposes in order to be able to reinvest them.

The defense sector represented the most obvious place to obtain convertible resources. Defense was the only area where a set of specific measures could yield large results. In 1986 Gorbachev not only told the Soviet military to prepare for an end to the Afghan war but also sought to reinvigorate arms reduction negotiations with the United States. The INF Treaty would eliminate a whole category of nuclear weapons and thereby render unnecessary the full slice of defense industry devoted to intermediate-range missiles. Exchange of instruments of ratification of the treaty at a Moscow summit in June 1988 occasioned a moment of hope, especially in the United States but in Russia as well. One of the plants that formerly had produced SS-20 missiles would be converted to manufacture baby carriages. And the last Soviet troops left Afghanistan in February 1989.

But the swords-to-plowshares aspect of these measures should not be over-rated. The economic disparities in the Soviet Union further increased during the last half of the decade, precisely during the time Gorbachev was attempting his reforms. Oil prices were down, production was falling, and the gold reserves the Russians could sell for hard currency early in the 1980s were depleted. A contradiction also existed between the drive to market the Soviet Union's second largest export product—weapons—and the notion of production cutbacks, not to mention the nation's professed peaceful intentions. Defense reductions ultimately offered limited gains.

The Soviet rust-belt industries failed to produce quality merchandise, preventing Moscow from making up shortfalls by other exports. The economic reforms of perestroika raised expectations and themselves created dislocation that exacerbated the problem. Low productivity limited the availability of consumer goods. Imports were reduced, but given insufficient resources, with few offsetting investments in consumer production, citizens, who faced lengthening lines and even scarcer stocks in stores, became further frustrated. The budget deficit could not be solved simply by printing more money because this fueled inflation and worsened the situation across the board. Stephen Kotkin's analysis illuminates this point:

That a concerted, expert-advised reform had made matters worse came as a shock. Prior to 1985, the planned economy—greased with extensive black marketeering, choked by phenomenal waste, and increasingly dependent on foreign imports—had stagnated, but it had functioned. Compared with their parents and grandparents, the Soviet population was better fed, better clothed, and better educated. Comparisons, however, were made not with the Soviet past, or developing countries, but with the richest nations in the world, and both the leadership and population expressed increasing impatience. *To compete with advanced capitalism* the only recourse seemed to be going beyond partial reforms and introducing the very mechanisms, private property and the market, whose suppression constituted the essence of socialism [italics in original].[17]

Hesitant to go that far, well aware that the state's stability created the foundation for its security, Gorbachev grasped at every possible alternative.

This picture puts Soviet foreign policy, especially its foreign aid and subsidies, in an entirely different light. The empire on the Soviet periphery had been main-

tained by subsidies and aid. Moscow had cushioned the impact of the oil price
hikes for East-Central Europe by ensuring its supplies and offsetting much of the
cost for the fraternal nations. Cuba got its oil for free, though it sent much of its
sugar crop to the Soviet Union. Throughout the period, the tonnage of oil shipped
to the allies remained double what the Soviet Union sold to Western Europe and
Japan. That cost Moscow potential hard currency earnings. In addition, the Russians supplied their allies an annual average of $24 billion in direct aid, roughly
equal to Soviet imports of agricultural products or, by mid-decade, agricultural
and machinery imports combined. Terminating the subsidies and reducing foreign
aid became a matter of *Soviet* national security, largely accomplished by 1989. No
wonder that Gorbachev encouraged the Warsaw Pact allies along their own roads
to reform. And maintaining an empire on the periphery in the absence of Soviet
aid was not possible. At the same time, it was also impossible to redirect oil exports
to hard currency markets because of the existing world oil glut, while several of
the East-Central European currencies were not convertible, meaning that earnings
from that region were difficult to transmute into support for Moscow's budget.

The whole system needed retooling. Factional problems within the CPSU
obstructed progress. Ligachev, the chief ideologist, professed his commitment to
reform and spoke the rhetoric of perestroika but really represented the traditionalists. Ligachev was locked in battle with Alexander Yakovlev, an enthusiastic reformer. The Soviet leader wanted both on his side but could not manage it. Chernyaev
believes his boss, a trustful person who had to fight to overcome his own party past, was afflicted by a "dualism" that "was reflected in his unwillingness to
deal harshly with those in the apparat who were really perestroika's opponents."[18]
Avoiding personality clashes forced Gorbachev into even more radical approaches
to reform. Among the biggest would be his reorganization of the Soviet state,
which created a powerful presidency and a legislature, the Congress of People's
Deputies, and relegated the communist party to second place, reversing the long-
standing primacy of the CPSU. This became the product of the Nineteenth Party
Conference, held in June 1988. Soviet apparatchiks at a stroke were robbed of their
preeminence. That point was driven home a few months later, when Gorbachev
initiated a series of party commissions that kept the apparatchiks busy. As Kotkin
puts it, "Gorbachev *deliberately* broke the might of the apparat [italics in original]."[19]
But government officials had been so used to ceding authority to party bosses
that making and implementing decisions became much more difficult. Meanwhile,

the creation of a legislature and institution of real elections, which were a central feature of the reform process—and became a core element of glasnost—were arguably a bid to enlist the mass of Soviet citizenry as a counterweight to the rising dissatisfaction of the elite.

Elections for the Congress of People's Deputies took place in March 1989. Voting clearly showed the people's demand for change. Thirty-five local CPSU first secretaries, including those for both Moscow and Leningrad and some who had run unopposed, lost their election bids. The party boss for Lithuania was defeated by a nationalist figure. Boris Yeltsin, who had emerged as a Gorbachev opponent, won the largest constituency in Moscow itself. The newly enshrined legislature became a raucous place, far different from the rubber-stamp Supreme Soviet it replaced. The socialist republics of the Union also began to develop into power centers. The Russian republic in particular, where Yeltsin emerged as leader, would be first among equals, an entity without whose cooperation no All-Union measure could be successful. Political difficulties spiraled beyond a simple division between factions in the CPSU. A democratic opposition coalesced around Yeltsin, while hard-liners in the military and KGB wanted to restore the old Soviet system.

Price hikes on basic staples, a radical reform in the sense of overturning a long-standing subsidy policy, became inevitable. Arguments over price reform went on for months. Gorbachev tried to take the edge off this inflation with a campaign to convince citizens that they would remain unaffected, that their cash would be passed back in the form of wage increases. But inexperienced bureaucrats botched the campaign. The price hikes became a rallying cry for a developing opposition that grew steadily. Soviet citizenry became reluctant to follow Gorbachev's lead. This domestic political problem increasingly forced the Soviet leader to seek achievements in foreign policy in order to make a path forward.

Gorbachev's December 1988 UN speech declaring unilateral reductions in Soviet forces in the Warsaw Pact represented one of his extreme choices. And again, the move proved a double-edged sword because new bases had to be built and stocked in the USSR to accommodate the troops leaving East-Central Europe. Were it not for West German leader Helmut Kohl—in another example of critical actions by individuals in history—who championed a deal many Germans found questionable, under which the Germans financed much of the troop drawdown, the withdrawals might have been impossible to accomplish. Ironically, by vacating the Eastern European security zone for which Russians had fought so hard in World War II and by demanding changes to military doctrine, Gorbachev's decision soured his relations with military and security services leaders and heightened the danger of the kind of political intervention the Soviet military attempted in 1991.

Most ambitious of all the reforms would be the so-called 500 Day Plan. Conceived by economists Stanislav Shatalin and Grigory Yavlinsky, the program aimed at converting the Soviet Union from a planned to a market economy in the very short interval of a year and a half. This amounted to the very reform the communist leadership had resisted for so long. Incredibly ambitious, the market transition plan became the subject of intense arguments through the summer of 1990. The Union government developed a competing concept. Controversy raged into the fall. The Russian republic held out for the original plan. A modified version of the Union plan passed the legislature that October. As the debaters fiddled, the economy burned. A national coal miners' strike over wages began in the Ukraine and affected industrial output everywhere. The intense economic debate damaged support for the All-Union government and widened the cleavage between it and the Russian republic, ultimately President Gorbachev's most important constituency. It also created dissension in Gorbachev's inner circle. In the spring of 1991, official figures showed price increases of 22 percent over the previous year. Coal production had fallen by 11 percent, oil by 9 percent, and exports had declined 18.4 percent in a single quarter. Despite import reductions of a phenomenal 45.1 percent, the budget deficit, projected at 16.7 million rubles for the full year, already stood at 31.1 billion rubles. The entire gross national product was down by 8 percent, again in just one quarter. And price increases were set to go into effect on April 2, 1991.[20]

Gorbachev was not blind. Over the two years between 1989 and 1991, the Soviet leader made a series of concessions to hard-liners in an attempt to regain their confidence. Some measures were self-contradictory, as in February 1990, when Gorbachev pushed an initiative through a party plenum under which the CPSU accepted a multiparty system and abandoned its leading role, implemented in a way that preserved that primacy. He proposed a fresh reorganization of the All-Union presidential system, attempted at the eleventh hour to revert to centralized planning, watched as close ally Eduard Shevardnadze resigned, went through a succession of prime ministers, and endeavored to enlist the masses anew with a national referendum held in March 1991. Some charge the Soviet leader with lacking the determination to stick to the choices he made, abandoning difficult courses before they could succeed. Some view him as careening wildly between strategy and tactics. Others see Gorbachev as a complete opportunist, still others as a visionary. To bring the discussion full circle, the maneuvers impeded reform efforts like the 500 Day Plan and the new anticipated wage and price measures. Gorbachev's actions also put hard-liners in control of key positions just as circumstances ignited the restive minorities of the nationalities. The storm broke throughout the land.

The Soviet Nationalities

As a young foreign service officer, Jack F. Matlock Jr. accompanied a congressional delegation on a visit to Tajikistan in November 1961. Matlock was an acute observer of Soviet affairs, joined the Foreign Service, worked on Soviet matters on the Reagan NSC staff, and in 1987 became the U.S. ambassador to Moscow, there to witness the Gorbachev experiment through its last four years. Of his early experience in Tajikistan Matlock reflects, "It was obvious that I had witnessed a particular form of colonialism. . . . Economic and political decisions were made not in these republics by the people who lived there but by 'planners' in Moscow. People on the spot, whether carpetbagger or native, simply carried out orders from above."[21] Those observations succinctly describe a process of exploitation in which artificial (and subjective) measures for economic efficiency were imposed on the republics, but even Matlock fails to capture the full scope of the nationalities problem. Beyond ignoring the interests of the republics, the Soviet Union actively discouraged expressions of ethnic, religious, and nationalist sentiment, not in the service of some project to assimilate the populations and create a unified land, but to preserve a separate but unequal relationship that favored the Russian republic over all others. Because of historically low birthrates among the Russians and a shrinking life expectancy, combined with high birthrates in the republics, questions of the treatment of the nationalities only became more sensitive.

Autonomy for the republics existed in name only—and there Matlock strikes just the right tone with his use of "carpetbaggers"—for the Soviets sent Russians to manage and lead the nationalities and represent their interests before the state. In fact, communist personnel policy over the decades typically had party officials alternate assignments in Moscow with jobs in the republics. Joining and loyally serving the CPSU offered no guarantee of advancement to ethnic nationals. In 1966 some 57 percent of Central Committee members were Great Russians. By 1981 that proportion had grown to 68 percent. Virtually everyone on the Central Committee's secretariat was Russian. Six of the eleven Politburo members of 1966 were Russians—but ten of fourteen in 1981. Typically, in Uzbekistan, where Uzbeks made up 68.7 percent of the population in 1979, Russians constituted a majority in the republic's Party Bureau (the local equivalent of the USSR's Politburo) and on the secretariat of its Central Committee. In the history of Kazakhstan, only two of its seventeen party leaders had been Kazaks.[22]

Language training and use illustrates Soviet policy and shows the development of nationalist sentiment in microcosm. In 1979 almost 40 percent of the Union's non-Russian citizens could not speak that language. Yet when Marshal Akhromeyev reported to the Twenty-seventh CPSU Congress in 1986, he cited figures that showed that of those inducted into the army in 1984, the number who could not speak Russian was double what it had been a decade earlier. In 1986 in Belorussia (today Belarus), where 80 percent of the people declared Belorussian their first language (by the 1979 census), there was only one urban school that taught the language. Less than 5 percent of literary works published in Belorussia in 1984 were in the vernacular. Ukraine did a little better, with 16 percent of urban schools teaching its language (and a 73.6 percent ethnic Ukrainian population). Fully half of the republic's children attended Russian-language schools. Language became a particular source of unrest in the Baltic republics of Estonia, Latvia, and Lithuania, where efforts to force the use of Russian eventually backfired and led the republics to declare the primacy of their native languages. By 1986 this focus of controversy had already burst into the open. In 1987 a leading Estonian linguist charged that Soviet promotion of bilingualism actually amounted to disguised Russification. In Kirghizstan, a well-known writer complained that workers were afraid to speak their language, fearing the KGB might accuse them of nationalist excess. Jack Matlock tells the revealing story of trying to help a couple of American graduate students who wanted to study Uzbekistan and learn its language—the university refused to teach them even after the U.S. ambassador intervened.[23]

Mikhail Gorbachev, who hailed from the Caucasus, close to the Georgian republic and several smaller autonomous zones, and not far from Ukraine, had spent much of his party career there. Gorbachev could have been expected to be somewhat attentive to nationalities issues. Shevardnadze actually came from Georgia and could have sensitized his chief. A national who had attained high rank in the CPSU, Shevardnadze was exceptional among the ethnics. Gorbachev's efforts to mobilize the masses to support his reforms should have led him in the direction of conciliating the nationalities. Instead, for several years after he took power, First Secretary Gorbachev seemed indifferent to the nationalities problem, including only perfunctory comments reflecting hackneyed thinking in his various reports to party congresses, plenums, conferences, and Central Committee meetings. Chernyaev writes, "As it turned out, for a reformer of Gorbachev's magnitude it was a major, perhaps fatal mistake not to foresee what democratization might mean for national issues."[24]

In his memoir, Gorbachev recollects his experience in Stavropol and emphasizes his interactions with various religious and ethnic minorities. His wife, Raisa, came from Siberia and had even studied minorities in gathering data for her academic thesis on collective farms. Gorbachev drew the conclusion that repression was useless; the solution lay in simple cooperation, but he did not move from that to a realization that an affirmative policy, an explicit approach to modernization, or political concessions were required. Moscow's attitude remained reactive. "At first," Gorbachev concedes, "we based our policy on decades-old practice." He foresaw only "spontaneous outbreaks of nationalism" owing to "hangovers" from the past or outside forces, not real problems. Chernyaev remarks that Gorbachev recognized a nationalities problem in general but attributed it simply to the rigid bureaucracy and the center's disrespect for national differences. In fact, Gorbachev visited the Baltic republics only about a year before the nationalist surge there began to spiral out of control and did not see it coming. He returned to profess that the Baltic political situation was good—"The people feel at home in this enormous country of ours." He wanted to increase respect for national languages and to stop handling the republics "like pieces of sausage." When Gorbachev finally suggested a party plenum to focus specifically on the nationalities, it took over a year to organize, yet the plenum ended up as a hastily convened affair that occurred with the fat already in the fire.[25]

At the Twenty-seventh Party Congress, Yegor Ligachev suggested an exchange of cadres among the republics, code words for sending more Russian overseers.[26] In Uzbekistan, corruption charges led to a purge of the communist party: eighteen thousand members expelled, three thousand demoted, a hundred prosecuted for crimes, two sentenced to death. Uzbeks saw most of the posts thus opened taken up by outsiders, primarily Russians.

Alienation took different courses in the various republics and was long delayed by KGB disruption, suppression of dissidents, and active measures. The first undeniable incidents took place in Kazakhstan late in 1986, sparked by the dismissal of another ethnic exception, Dinmukhamed Kunayev, a Kazakh who had led the republic and the party there for almost two decades. For two days after the announcement of Kunayev's firing, as many as ten thousand Kazakh youths took to the streets in Almaty, the capital, shouting nationalist slogans. Security forces broke the demonstrators with water cannons and bullets. "The riots began among students and then spread to other groups," Gorbachev notes. "At some point the situation became quite dramatic. Force was used." Soviet reports of the incident minimized it; for example, Prime Minister Nikolai Ryzhkov, speaking in Helsinki, claimed that only a couple hundred persons had participated in the protests. Soviet press reports spoke of drunk and doped rioters provoked by Kunayev's associates. But other reports tallied a thousand arrests, two hundred seriously injured, and twenty killed, including seven policemen. More than a thousand students were expelled from the university. Matlock records the event as misunderstood by Soviet officials, who marked it down as local resistance to the anti-corruption drive that had ousted Kunayev. On December 25, 1986, the Politburo adopted a resolution that, as the Soviet leader writes, "was not so much an attempt to get a grip on what had occurred and learn a lesson from that, as to teach a lesson to Kazakhstan and the others."[27]

Chernobyl became a specific problem in Ukraine. That republic hosted much of the Soviet Union's nuclear power infrastructure. Weeks before the nuclear accident there, a Ukrainian journal had published an article that warned of safety problems at Chernobyl. Afterward, in March 1987, scientists met in Kiev to consider plans for two more atomic piles at the Chernobyl plant. Only two of sixty experts voted in favor of proceeding. Other ecological issues created dissatisfaction as well. Armenians complained of massive industrial pollution in the republic. The Central Asian republics were arid and faced water shortages, yet Moscow had a plan to divert Siberian rivers, which would have exacerbated the problem. Already, injudicious agricultural practices had resulted in the drying of much of the Aral Sea, which in turn changed the ecosystem and climate, shortening the growing season. Opposition from the republics finally forced cancellation of the river diversion scheme. Meanwhile, Kazakhstan was greatly affected by a natural disaster, a major earthquake in 1988. The Baltics had problems with Soviet plans for chemical and other plants that threatened to impact their own lands. A hydroelectric project in Latvia and oil drilling platforms off the Lithuanian coast were cancelled late in 1986.[28]

Another set of problems directly affected the Soviet armed forces. Given the language barriers, integration of minority recruits into the military posed difficulties. And hazing—which had long afflicted the Soviet military—was applied with extra relish to the minorities, especially Central Asians. At the same time, the Afghan War increased military manpower requirements, resulting in more minorities being inducted. Draft evasion became endemic, but evaders were hunted with greater determination in the republics than in Russia. The veterans of the war, soon called *afghantsy* throughout the Soviet Union, especially the wounded and injured, reminded the minorities that while the nation demanded much, it provided little in return. Only Soviet manpower utilization policy—where Central Asians were first sought for Afghan service *because* of their languages but later posted elsewhere for fear of susceptibility to mujahideen propaganda—served to ameliorate the situation.

Meanwhile, Crimean Tatars, long ago banished from their lands by Stalin, demonstrated outside the Kremlin for three days running during the summer of 1987, demanding a right of return. A government commission first announced that some would be allowed to go back, leading to more anguish, and then that all Tatars could return, creating problems in the Crimea, where land had been taken over by Russians and Ukrainians. Tajikistan coveted land in another republic that had belonged to it in the past. In Ukraine, Belorussia, and Moldova, intellectual ferment that began with the debates over the use and teaching of the languages led to the creation of dissident groups agitating for national causes.

The Caucasus became the locale for the next violent outbreaks, which took place in 1988. The national causes of Azerbaijan, Nagorno-Karabakh, Armenia, Ossetia, and Georgia (many of which are still playing out in the early twenty-first century) were all at issue in several of these events. Ethnics of each group lived in the other republics. Matlock, for one, believes that glasnost, by making citizens more confident in stating their grievances, contributed to the crisis. Nagorno-Karabakh wanted to join the Armenian republic. Armenians rioted against Azerbaijanis, whom they regarded as instigators. The KGB reported that these disruptions were encouraging other national tendencies, particularly in the Baltic republics. Violence against Armenians broke out. Soviet troops intervened. A diaspora carried Armenians out of Azerbaijan and Azeris home from Armenia. Demonstrations in Armenia grew to include hundreds of thousands of people. Gorbachev's Politburo grappled with these headaches for months.

A most disturbing incident occurred in the spring of 1989 in Tbilisi, Georgia. Though some details remain murky, available evidence strongly suggests an attempt by Soviet hard-liners to exploit the nationalities issue to turn Gorbachev back toward an authoritarian policy, or failing that, to embarrass him.[29] What became known as the Tbilisi Massacre began with protests, initially as part of Georgia's conflict with Abkhazia, but then taken over by activists who favored Georgia seceding from the USSR. There had been protests in Tbilisi a few months before.

On April 7 Georgian republic officials telephoned Moscow and sent messages asking for authority to put down the demonstrations. The news went to Viktor Chebrikov, chief of the Central Committee secretariat. This is where the story becomes strange.

At the time, President Gorbachev and Foreign Minister Shevardnadze were in London on a state visit. Gorbachev had not designated anyone to act in his stead. Chebrikov took the problem to Yegor Ligachev. With the reorganization of the Soviet state, Prime Minister Nikolai Ryzhkov and the Union's Interior Ministry should have handled this matter. Instead the action was kept entirely within CPSU channels. Ryzhkov eventually learned about these events by reading *Pravda*. Chebrikov until 1988 had been chairman of the KGB. Ligachev, of course, was the chief figure among Politburo conservatives who would have been most sympathetic to the Georgian party's demands for action. Earlier he had been considered Gorbachev's second, often chairing the Politburo in Gorbachev's absence, and he had headed a Central Committee working group. But factional bickering had distanced Ligachev from the Soviet leader, and his working group had not been active for a long time. In his own account, Ligachev notes the unusual approach from Chebrikov and defends himself by maintaining what he did—convening a group to assemble options for Gorbachev—was not out of the ordinary. The Soviet leader was due back from London that night. Ligachev also notes that Chebrikov refused to discuss the matter on the phone and that Chebrikov had apparently informed others of the Tbilisi problem before him. (As former head of the KGB, Chebrikov knew the dangers of wiretaps better than anyone.) Ligachev's group not only considered options, it authorized the movement of troops to Tbilisi. That evening Gorbachev's departure from London was delayed three times. When he finally arrived at Vnukovo Airport late that night, Gorbachev was met by Ligachev's working group and told of the emergency. Gorbachev emphasized the need for a peaceful resolution and ordered Shevardnadze to go to Tbilisi and resolve the situation. The latter, a Georgian, would have been capable of doing so.

Shevardnadze telephoned the Government House in Tbilisi only to be told the problem was in hand and his visit not necessary. He informed Gorbachev, who asked him to keep an eye on matters. In the morning, Chebrikov chaired another working group session, which Shevardnadze also attended. Ligachev had left for vacation and was not involved. The meeting received a dispatch from Tbilisi authorities repeating what Shevardnadze had been told on the phone. Shevardnadze recounts that he later learned that troops were deploying in Tbilisi as this occurred.

Meanwhile, at the Government House, Georgian party officials held their own deliberation and approved a program that included imposing a curfew, using the troops for a show of force, and sending representatives to meet with the protesters. No such meeting took place. Instead, officials decided to clear away the protesters before dawn.

Police, including special police of the OMON (Otryad Militsii Osobogo Naz-nacheniya) swat teams, gathered, and there were over 2,500 troops with fifteen armored vehicles. The military forces included airborne troops, motorized rifle units, and troops brought in from more than a thousand miles away (Perm, Gorki, and Moscow). Only one battalion of 650 men was from Tbilisi. Approximately ten thousand people were in the square when the police action began at 4:00 a.m. on April 9—officials had been told there would be just a couple of hundred protesters during early morning hours. Troops used CS and CN gas and a few grenades of a chemical agent, in violation of Defense Ministry regulations. Weather conditions impeded the dispersion of the gas. All but one of the nineteen people who died were killed by gas inhalation; 183 were hospitalized (and about 70 were sent home after treatment); and 1,000 people were treated at dispensaries over the next few days. Some thirty-seven government personnel were injured (twenty-two of them by security forces), and twenty-eight were victims of toxic substances.

Shevardnadze cancelled a trip to Berlin for negotiations on Germany to fly immediately to Tbilisi. Over the following days, he conducted his own inquiry. He concluded that at every stage information had either been censored or distorted: "News reaching the center was fabricated by the apparatus." Indeed, "the system went into its usual mode [of] fighting in order to win back the territory lost to perestroika." Moreover, the military actions taken "could not have been implemented without the sanction of the Ministry of Defense." Beyond that, the crowd had been large enough to preclude a force option, the troops had used "unacceptable means," the operational commander had violated specific orders to protect certain sites, and the people responsible for the use of chemical weapons had concealed that fact until confronted with incontrovertible evidence.[30] Shevardnadze presented his findings to the Politburo on April 20. Gorbachev observed, "Once again we see that we're going through a crisis of methods, in the broadest sense." He issued strict orders to Defense Minister Dmitri Yazov that the military was not to act in any civilian situation without explicit Politburo instructions.[31]

The Tbilisi Massacre is worth this detail for two reasons, both of consummate importance. First, the cabal that carried it out—for this was an action of "the

system," as Shevardnadze puts it, that is, the old regime—represents the first crys-
tallization of the forces of "order" that would attempt to reimpose the communist regime two years later. Gorbachev writes in his memoir that Marshal Yazov's
participation with the 1991 coup plotters stunned him, but Tbilisi shows Yazov
aligned with them from an early date. Second, the Georgian secession movement
demonstrates the momentum that centrifugal forces, driven here by the nationalities problem, had already attained. Gorbachev made his real complaints privately—
to Chernyaev, the day after the Politburo's discussion of Tbilisi. His aide drew the
proper conclusion, writing of the republics in his diary that night, "Gorbachev
faces a choice: Either occupation, which means reconstructing the 'empire,' or federation, which means confederation."[32]

Under federation, the units—the republics—would have states' rights, including the right to secede. And the Soviet Union had reached that point because of the
nationalities question. In his diary, Chernyaev had expressed himself as especially
struck because these events had occurred in Georgia, a republic with which Russians were close, a people alongside whom they had shed blood. The Georgians
were not like the Baltic peoples, "whose separatist desires have always been clear."[33]
Indeed separatism in the Baltic republics had grown swiftly, beginning with their
complaints about language. Until 1986 these seem to have sufficed as expressions
of autonomy, but after that, the spiral of hostility accelerated. An activist group
in Lithuania took the name of the partisan fighters who had resisted Russian occupation in the 1940s. In April 1987 the party committee of the Estonian capital
Tallinn decided to restrict the influx of Russians entering the republic to take up
new industrial jobs. Twelve months later, both Estonia and Latvia instituted fines
on industries for each Russian worker they hired. In the summer of 1988, activist
groups in all three Baltic states called for demonstrations to demand publication of
the secret protocols of the Molotov-Ribbentrop Pact, the deal between Hitler and
Stalin under which the Soviet Union had taken over the Baltic republics in 1940.
These protests became annual events. On the fiftieth anniversary of the signature
of the pact, August 23, 1989, almost a million Balts joined hands in a demonstration that formed a physical link between the capitals of all three states, a distance
of hundreds of miles. As an indicator of the connectivity between issues, note
that the Latvian human rights group Helsinki 86 was among those pressing this
avowedly nationalist issue. When Helsinki 86 sponsored a demonstration to honor
Latvians deported by the Soviets in 1940, authorities who had prohibited the protest—unlike in Tbilisi a couple of years later—did nothing. In the fall of 1987

Estonian experts previously regarded as pro-Russian came out in favor of making the republic a self-managing economic zone. While still KGB chief, Viktor Chebrikov in April 1988 attributed the unrest in the Baltics to the imperialist secret services. Within months activists in all the Baltic states were demanding full political and economic decentralization for the republics of the USSR.

At the Nineteenth Party Conference, the communist party leaders from the Baltics made speeches with themes not much different from the nationalists' demands. Gorbachev denounced nationalisms for undermining the union in a July 1988 speech, and in October the draft law designed to implement the reorganization he had unveiled at the party conference made republics' rights the prerogative of the legislature and added provisions favoring the Russian Federation. That seems to have been a tipping point. On November 16 the Estonian Supreme Soviet adopted a declaration of sovereignty and asserted a right to negate laws promulgated in Moscow. The USSR rejected the Estonian party's move. Then, shortly before the 1989 election, *Pravda* published the draft program for economic management in the republics, which accorded them only limited budget control and very little on economic planning. On May 18, 1989, Lithuania declared its sovereignty. Latvia followed two months later, a few days after the text of the Molotov-Ribbentrop Pact was finally released. Lithuania declared its full independence in March 1990. A widespread miners strike begun in Ukraine also threatened the national economy.

Through this succession of events, the nationalities question brought the Soviet Union to the brink of dissolution. The Russians did in fact note the play. A hundred thousand Russians—some estimated several times that number—marched through the streets of Moscow in February 1990. Several weeks later, another Moscow demonstration brought out fifty to a hundred thousand more. At the Mayday parade, protesters jeered Gorbachev atop Lenin's Mausoleum. Soon after Boris Yeltsin emerged as president of the Russian Federation, he too declared that its laws superceded those of the Soviet Union. The federation soon fought the Union leadership over budget allocations, the composition of the Politburo, and the 500 Day Plan, one of whose authors had become Russia's deputy prime minister. Shortages heightened the anxieties of citizens. In the summer, there were riots in several cities, including Moscow and Leningrad, sparked by a shortage of cigarettes. That September, bread was briefly unavailable in Moscow. Leningrad authorities began to ration food before the end of the year. Each episode increased Russian impressions, accurate or not, of being shortchanged by the union, strengthening Yeltsin's hand. By July, when the Twenty-eighth CPSU Congress met, he felt confident

enough to demand that party delegates mind their actions lest someday they be in-
dicted for damaging the state. When Gorbachev modified the federation proposal
to incorporate features of a competing plan developed by his colleague Ryzhkov,
Yeltsin announced the Russian Federation would implement the original scheme.

The Soviet leadership could not govern without Russia. Its possible secession
was the fatal danger that lurked behind the republics' striving for a greater share
of power. The Baltic republics' actions first raised that specter. In January 1990
Gorbachev went to Vilnius, the Lithuanian capital, to begin negotiations on the
relationship with the union. This opened the door. The independence declaration would be a ploy, "suspended" by the Lithuanians in June, but hanging over
Moscow's head. By the summer, all the republics had made similar declarations of
sovereignty as talks on a Treaty of the Union dragged on. Gorbachev's program,
in which he pushed through the legislature a repeal of the constitutional provision
ensuring the primacy of the CPSU and later reorganized the government as a presidency with a national council composed of the heads of the federated republics,
aimed at accommodating the nationalists. But Gorbachev had become increasingly
isolated, to the degree that, having secured powers to rule by decree during the period of the 500 Day Plan, he was forced to order industries to fulfill their contracts
for delivery of raw materials and precursor products. The draft treaty would be
revealed in November.

Such developments shook Soviet hard-liners. That mattered because these
people controlled the military and the security services. In September, military
maneuvers near Moscow created suspicions that the hard-liners were preparing
to intervene in politics. Defense Minister Yazov denied any such intent, but the
move remained ominous. On November 13 Gorbachev promised to guard the
integrity of the military and preserve the union, warning of a bloodbath if the
state collapsed. Two weeks later, he decreed that Soviet troops could use force if
attacked or harassed by the people. A reformist interior minister was fired on December 2 and replaced by hard-liner Boris Pugo, seconded by Gen. Boris Gromov,
the last commander of Soviet troops in Afghanistan. Increasingly disillusioned by
these and other measures, Eduard Shevardnadze resigned. His last act was a speech
to the legislature on December 22 warning that "a dictatorship is approaching."[34]
Gorbachev sought to quiet fears of a creeping military coup, telling the Congress
of People's Deputies that he agreed perestroika needed to be defended but dis-
agreed with Shevardnadze's thesis: "The president does not have information . . .
that someone, somewhere is preparing a junta or some similar dictatorship."[35]

That confidence could not have lasted long. On January 2, 1991, the Interior Ministry's OMON troops seized the press plant of Latvia's main newspaper. Gorbachev insists he had every intention of seeking a peaceful resolution of problems with the Baltics, but a few days later, he refused to assure the Lithuanian prime minister that there would be no recourse to force in her republic. On January 9 the KGB's elite Alpha Detachment surrounded a Lithuanian television transmitter, and four days later, "Bloody Sunday," Alpha took down the television facility, while paratroops with armored vehicles and Interior Ministry forces occupied the printing plant in Vilnius and closed the airport and railroad station. Firing live ammunition, the troops killed fourteen citizens and wounded many more. Furious, Gorbachev, who had issued no directive for such action, tried to find out what had happened. Minister Pugo reported he had no idea where the instructions had come from. Minister Yazov imagined that local commanders had given the order.

This amounted to a replay of the Tbilisi Massacre, with one exception: the Soviet leader's own position is much more ambiguous in Bloody Sunday. The incident brought an outpouring of protests—many aimed at Gorbachev—including a crowd of 300,000 who marched in the snow in Moscow to demand, for the first time, Gorbachev's resignation. There were more marches, manifestos, and accusations throughout the USSR, including the Russian Federation. Among the participants were Gorbachev associates such as Stanislav Shatalin of the 500 Day Plan. Anatoly Chernyaev would have resigned save that his secretary sequestered his resignation letter until the moment passed and Chernyaev had second thoughts. In any case, according to Chernyaev, Gorbachev failed to denounce the security forces' excesses or even present a clear position on the matter, and he spoke of a reimposition of controls on the media, which had been highly critical. Pugo and Yazov were completely evasive in speaking before the legislature, and Gorbachev failed to intervene there either. Barely a week later, a further incident occurred in Latvia, where OMON units actually attacked the republic's Interior Ministry, killing four more civilians. This time, Yazov told the Soviet leader that he had rejected three late-night requests from the Latvian prime minister's office to send in the military, and the OMON troops were Pugo's. In his memoir, Gorbachev writes, "there was something strange about the whole business," but his account of these events is disingenuous, depicting Latvian bystanders as "republican forces"—troops rather than civilians.[36] Andrei Grachev, another associate and the leader's last spokesman, notes, "Gorbachev strangely appeared to be either a genuine supporter of the conservatives or perhaps their impotent hostage."[37]

On January 24 Gorbachev saw American ambassador Matlock to receive a letter from George Bush. He asked for Matlock's impressions. The American warned
the Soviet leader that it was becoming difficult to maintain his previous view that
Gorbachev was genuinely seeking fundamental reform. "We are on the brink of
civil war," Matlock recounts Gorbachev replying. "My main task is to prevent it."
That, said Gorbachev, made necessary a period of "zigs and zags."[38] On January
26 Gorbachev issued a decree giving KGB and Interior Ministry personnel the
right to inspect factories and offices. Late in January, Pugo and Yazov came up
with the idea of mounting patrols of combined military–Interior Ministry troops
in the cities. The republics simply banned them. On March 28 a show of force in
Moscow that included armored vehicles failed to deter protesters from making a
banned march into Red Square. Unknown to Gorbachev, hard-liners were already
developing drafts of a decree to impose martial law. In June Prime Minister Valentin Pavlov, supported by Pugo, Yazov, and KGB chairman Vladimir Kryuchkov,
asked the legislature for the same emergency powers Gorbachev already enjoyed.
The request was rejected. Several days later, the mayor of Moscow warned Ambassador Matlock that hard-liners were planning a coup, specifically naming Pavlov,
Yazov, and Kryuchkov. All three of them would be participants in the actual coup
attempt. Matlock passed the warning to Gorbachev. President Bush reiterated it
to Gorbachev and told Yeltsin, who was at that moment visiting Washington. Another aide, a former KGB officer, also warned Gorbachev not to put excessive
trust in his KGB security detail. Gorbachev later chided the source of this report
for "telling tales to the Americans." Matlock observes that Gorbachev "acted like a
somnambulist, wandering around oblivious to his surroundings."[39]

The last act on the nationalities question took place against this backdrop of
intense anxiety. The original draft union treaty had been widely rejected. Gorbachev
then submitted the concept of a union treaty to referendum, and it was approved
by 76 percent of the electorate on March 17. Gorbachev began a round of negotiations with the republics on finalizing language for a new agreement. Whatever else
it accomplished, Bloody Sunday ended any prospect of the Baltics adhering to the
union. When talks opened, only nine republics, not including any of the Baltics,
attended. Yeltsin and Gorbachev submerged their differences long enough to ham-
mer out the accord. They came to final agreement at the end of July. Gorbachev
announced that the Treaty of Union would be formally signed on August 20.

The treaty ceremony gave the hard-line conspirators a deadline. Meeting at a
KGB bathhouse in Moscow, they determined to press ahead. The group included

Gennady Yanayev, vice president of the USSR; Interior Minister Pugo; Gen. Valentin Varennikov, Yazov's deputy; the chairman of the Supreme Soviet; Gorbachev's chief of staff; plus two senior members of the Central Committee staff in addition to the individuals named previously. The top officials constituted themselves as the State Committee on the State of Emergency. A delegation of the conspirators went to visit Gorbachev, then on vacation in the Crimea, to demand his agreement. Failing that, they demanded his resignation. Gorbachev refused. His KGB bodyguards cut off his telephones and effectively imprisoned him. Late into the night of August 18, some of the conspirators crafted an order imposing a state of emergency on the country. This was issued in Moscow at 5:30 a.m. on August 19. Kryuchkov put the KGB on alert, summoned officers from leave, doubled their pay, and emptied Lefortovo Prison to receive those arrested. Four parliamentary deputies were detained and held on a military base. The action began to unravel almost from the beginning. American spy satellites and communications intercepts revealed the plotters had made few preparations for their attempt, dubbed Operation Grom.

President Yeltsin of the Russian Federation learned of the conspiracy, returned to Moscow, and closeted himself in the White House with other Federation officials, using fax machines to alert the world and call out Russian citizens. Yeltsin denounced the "state of emergency" as a criminal act. Prime Minister Pavlov resigned from the plotters' "state commission." The White House, seat of the federation parliament, became a fortress against the plotters, protected by citizens. Too late, Marshal Yazov summoned a tank division, a motorized rifle division, and airborne troops to Moscow. Some were detained by impromptu barricades erected by Muscovites. The KGB Alpha and Vympel detachments, the Interior Ministry's OMON troops, and militia were also involved.

When troops did surround the White House, their shaky morale became evident. Some defected to Yeltsin's side. The civilian members of Kryuchkov's state commission held a press conference to announce and defend their actions, but he, Yazov, and Pugo all stayed away. Those who appeared were clearly as shaky as the coup forces. On the afternoon of August 20, leaders ordered an attack on the White House for that night. Troop commanders tried to convince the leaders that an assault would be impossible without bloodshed. About an hour before the expected attack, several Muscovites were killed as they attempted to delay the movement of coup forces. The shock stopped everything. The putsch failed. The troops were sent back to base. A new delegation headed by Kryuchkov himself again traveled to the Crimea to commiserate with Gorbachev, who refused to see them. They were arrested at the airport when they returned to Moscow. Boris Pugo and his wife committed suicide. In the wake of the failed coup, the CPSU was outlawed. Gorbachev resigned as general secretary on August 24. On December 25 he resigned his post as president of the USSR, which ceased to exist.

Perestroika

Did Mikhail Gorbachev destroy the Soviet Union with his effort to implant perestroika? Did the coup plotters destroy it with their misguided conspiracy? Did the fall of the Soviet Union end the Cold War? None of the above, says television and movie actor David Hasselhoff. *He* ended the Cold War with his 1989 song "Looking for Freedom" (actually a cover of a 1970s-era German tune) and a concert given at the Berlin Wall some weeks after the upheaval of November 10.[40] Hasselhoff is not the only claimant to that mantle. The American rock group Pink Floyd did something similar. A Czech rock group helped break down barriers in that land—and, in fact, one of the events that energized Václav Havel was his coming out in support of those rockers when the government attempted to suppress them. In Hungary, there were fights over which classical music compositions were suitable for performance in a communist state. Yuri Andropov in the Soviet Union was a devotee of American jazz and would listen to his extensive collection at home at night. In Romania, the American television show *Dallas* was permitted to be broadcast on government-controlled TV and the contrast between this display of American opulence and the pervasive poverty in the nation helped mobilize Romanians to overthrow Nicolae Ceauşescu.

Then there were the Beatles. The British rock group was defunct by the 1980s, but its gripping music lived on and penetrated the barriers erected to exclude Western cultural influences. Their song "Back in the USSR" inevitably touched Russians but was only the leading edge. Many garage bands and performance artists, not only in the Soviet Union but even more so in East-Central Europe, drew their inspiration from the West and got started by surreptitiously—or openly—bringing Western music and drama to communist society. The Beatles, active or not, were quintessential Western cultural ambassadors. The music of more contemporary bands such as U2 flowed into the East through channels opened by the Beatles. Not insignificant in this broadening of passages were the broadcasts of Radio Free Europe and Radio Liberty, beaming music and news into the East. The youth culture never quite bought into the communist system and wore T-shirts and listened to rock music as a badge of nonconformity. One need go no further than to visit any of these countries and be bombarded with offers to buy the visitors' shoes, blue jeans, even the shirt off one's back, to perceive the hunger for things Western in the Soviet Union and elsewhere. Parents, struggling to obtain Western electronics and other consumer goods as symbols of affluence, merely broadened this trend.

And communist governments sought the masses' favor by loosening cultural controls. Official youth groups, such as the Soviet Komsomol, became major actors in this evolution. Stephen Kotkin again captures this flavor well:

> Tape recorders, owned by about one-third of the population, as well as cheap X-ray plates (pressed as LPs) facilitated the circulation of forbidden Soviet popular ballads as well as smuggled rock and roll. In 1968, ostensibly to combat worrisome trends in youth culture, Komsomol officials gathered at a retreat to watch the officially banned film *Easy Rider*. Soon, almost every Soviet high school and factory acquired its own rock-and-roll band, which the Komsomol hired to perform at official events. By the late Brezhnev era, Soviet public spaces were decorated not just with official slogans but also with graffiti about sports teams, rock music, sex, and the merits of punk music versus heavy metal. School children "ranked" each other by their jeans, with Western brands being the highest.[41]

We still lack the systematically collected evidence, as well as the detailed historical analysis, to weight cultural transformation as a factor in the end of communism, but there should be no doubt its role was significant. Youth had an *incentive* to break down the Berlin Wall and bring down the Soviet Union, if only to topple the barriers that impeded their access to Western culture.[42]

There is one area where the evidence base is deeper and the picture can be viewed with some confidence. Because Gorbachev sought to mobilize public support through glasnost, there is considerable source material on the struggle to open up the Soviet media to commentaries and information on *Soviet* politics, economics, and social conditions. It is even possible to recount some of the inner struggles among the leadership. There is no space to cover this issue in any great detail, but the broad outlines of developments can be sketched briefly.

A few months after becoming top leader in Moscow, Gorbachev replaced the chief of the Department of Propaganda. "But for the entire enormous ideological machine of the Party," he notes, "it was business as usual. The system could be altered only by opening up 'windows,' one by one, in this system of total secrecy, and only the General Secretary had the means of doing this." He adopted a new, more impromptu personal approach to interviews and took steps to encourage media discussion of social and political issues. The Chernyaev memoir and, even more, his diaries are replete with accounts of conversations with Gorbachev and others on specific articles that had appeared in Soviet newspapers or magazines in which the leader took an active part in commenting on content, philosophical thrust, political importance of the material, or counters and follow-ups. Gorbachev soon found that the pent-up energy of Soviet writers generated a "criticism fever," which in turn led to opposition from the apparatchiks. Party staff, even on the Central Committee, unaccustomed to their actions being examined, complained. Typically, Ligachev writes of the "so-called radical press."[43] According to him, media questions arose at almost every Politburo meeting. More and more, initiatives were blocked in what Gorbachev terms the "vertical structure" of the party bureaucracy. One example, drawn from the debates on nationalities, would be the question of language instruction in the republics, which was championed vociferously by the writers' unions of the various nationalities and was knocked down hard in official organs such as *Pravda*.

Cultural figures could help change the social context in which political affairs occurred, and the media could keep up pressure on party hacks. Gorbachev saw perestroika gaining "an increasingly broad social base" as a result of "truly committed people at the newspapers and television and radio stations," and he adds, "It is difficult to overestimate the importance of this." Yet Gorbachev felt torn between protecting glasnost and holding the cultural mavens accountable, in this case with a press law. "I myself began to see that some of them were going too far: criticism began to be insulting and vicious; frankly libelous materials based on the distortion of facts were being published." Or again, "Glasnost broke out of the limits that we had initially tried to frame and became a process that was beyond anybody's control." He says he began to think of such a law as early as 1986. Not until an October 1990 plenum did Gorbachev put regulations for mass media on a party agenda. Chernyaev reports that Gorbachev *joked* about a press law—then suddenly became serious when he was in dire straits early in 1991. In between, a great deal happened.[44]

At the beginning, the Soviet leader did not accord glasnost the scope he ultimately gave it. Chernyaev believes his boss followed Leninist tenets and intended what would have amounted to a propaganda campaign. But he found party outlets unsatisfactory, for they held to a multitude of taboos: no criticisms of party higher-ups, the military, foreign trade, scientific-technological development, statistics in general, the security services, and so on. Because of corruption and the black markets, keeping those subjects off the table took away the ability to progress. Gorbachev determined to break the logjam by inserting handpicked editors into key positions in publishing. He started by bringing Alexander Yakovlev back from Canada, where he had been ambassador, to manage the mass media. Ligachev, who would become a main enemy, supported Yakovlev's appointment as a matter of giving the new general secretary the team he wanted. Ligachev blames Yakovlev for the "radical" editors appointed to many newspapers and magazines, except for *Ogonyok*, where he participated in the selection. All editors had to be approved by the party, and so did any change in the format, size, or coverage of the periodicals. A party organ called Glavlit monitored content, recommending punishments for authors and editors of articles deemed too critical or subversive. Yakovlev and Ligachev spent a great deal of time meeting editors who appealed Glavlit's actions.

Ligachev claims that Yakovlev rarely reported back on his activities and that Yakovlev, who became very close to Gorbachev, surrounded the Moscow leader with a cloud of his own people. Where Ligachev wanted a disciplined press, as in the old days, Yakovlev espoused the argument that the media functioned as a mirror of society. By 1988, when Glavlit lost its primacy, the forces of glasnost had won out, but the debate continued until the fall of the USSR and persisted after Ligachev retired. Independent periodicals began to appear. In any case, Ligachev saw his role as restraining the vigor of this movement: "The radicalism embodied by Yakovlev at the highest level of the Soviet leadership threatened to disrupt the tempo of perestroika and accelerate the pace of transformation without taking reality into account."[45]

Gorbachev held periodic meetings with editors of the top-ranked magazines and newspapers. He would also telephone them whenever he wanted. At the meetings, usually attended by Ligachev and Yakovlev, Gorbachev did most of the talking. He cajoled, criticized, or encouraged by turns. According to Ligachev, who maintains he spoke to the general secretary several times about the uselessness of these events, no one paid the slightest attention to what Gorbachev said. When he brought it up, the boss would order the party ideologists to get involved, but without effect. Ligachev writes, "I think Gorbachev at first underestimated the social consequences of the destructive work of press, television, and radio. But the role of the media in the destabilization of the Baltics was very clear, as in the popular front press Lithuania, Latvia, and Estonia became battering rams, shaking the pillars of socialism and the Union."[46]

Beyond the mass media stood the world of books and films. The various creative workers' unions existed in the party milieu, were equally dedicated to preserving privilege, and were only slightly less concerned with tradition, including traditional interpretations. Offending works were denied an audience. Glasnost challenged the suppression of dissident and émigré works, and increases in the numbers of young artists in the unions challenged the authority of senior members. Two key test cases occurred relatively early. The first was Anatoly Rybakov's novel *Children of the Arbat*. A child at the time of the Russian Revolution, Rybakov had lived through the Stalin era, and *Children of the Arbat* was his look back, a searing work that depicted the life of families, even prominent members of the nomenklatura, their very lives hostage at any moment to Stalin's whims. The book had been written in the 1960s and circulated quietly in samizdat form. Twice, most recently in 1978, it had actually been accepted for publication but cancelled by party ideologists at the last moment. Now the question arose anew. Chernyaev sent the manuscript to Yakovlev in the summer of 1985. The latter, who professed never to have heard of this work of Rybakov's and not to recall such abuses from Stalin, opposed publication. Gorbachev, however, appreciated Rybakov's evocation of the atmosphere of those days. Ironically, Ligachev supported him. *Children of the Arbat* was published in 1987. Gorbachev writes, "The publication of Rybakov's novel helped to conquer the fear that many people still had of the consequences of unmasking totalitarianism."[47]

Release of the film *Repentance* created the other major dispute. Georgian filmmaker Tengiz Abuladze conceived this visual re-creation of Soviet horror in Stalin's era. In the film, the dictatorial mayor of a small town purges with abandon and at once evokes Mussolini, Hitler, Stalin, and Beria. One day he dies and is buried, but the body is mysteriously exhumed and left in the mayor's son's front yard. This happens repeatedly, until the audience eventually discovers the village conscience, an old woman who refuses to let the man rest in peace. Moscow ideologists tried to prevent *Repentance* from being completed, but Eduard Shevardnadze, then first secretary of the Georgian communist party, protected Abuladze's project, which was finished in 1984. When Shevardnadze went to Moscow to work with Gorbachev, party hacks renewed their effort to suppress the movie, ordering destruction of the only copy. Abuladze made a videotape of it. Those who helped him make the copy were arrested. The movie garnered a few screenings restricted to nomenklatura as a result of a private understanding between Abuladze and Yakovlev, but the ideologists demanded the Politburo approve any general release. Shevardnadze went to the general secretary and insisted he view the film. Gorbachev considered it a bombshell and avoided a fight by leaving the decision to the cinematographers' and artists' unions. No problem there. Ligachev opposed letting *Repentance* be entered at the Cannes Film Festival. He failed. It won the Jury's Special Grand Prize at Cannes in 1987 and a Soviet film award, and in 1988 Abuladze received the Lenin Prize.[48]

Gorbachev sympathized with the aims of the Young Turks among artistic circles, but their fights over privileges and positions frustrated him, and he saw Soviet art, film, and literature of the glasnost era as failing to produce major new works. At the same time, he thought little of the elders. Gorbachev once groused to Chernyaev, "Those talentless old fools! They praise themselves, give themselves awards and titles. But if you did exhibit their work . . . nobody would come!"[49] He believed the Soviet intelligentsia to have been the part of society most challenged by perestroika because it forced them to shift long-set ways of thinking. But Gorbachev had other, political uses for the intelligentsia too. Using the wedge of the new thinking as a catapult for his political program was Gorbachev's real aim in unleashing glasnost, and there he had considerable success.

In the summer of 1986, shortly before the annual writers' conference, the KGB reported that Western intelligence services were influencing Soviet writers to oppose communist traditions. Rybakov was among those singled out. Gorbachev should have been pleased, though he allowed the report to go to the Politburo. Yakovlev objected that if every offending writer was ejected from the country, there would be no one left. Ligachev complained that the KGB was wasting its time following writers and had better things to do. Gorbachev's program was working. A week after the Reykjavik summit, Gorbachev spent half a day in discussion on the environment, the nuclear threat, and questions of morality in politics. The subjects were not new in that year of Chernobyl, but the participants were unusual: they were not nuclear experts but cultural figures, including Westerners such as the actor Peter Ustinov, authors Arthur Miller and Alvin Toffler, and others. The group had been convened by the Kyrgyz writer Chingiz Aitmatov, one of the nation's best authors, the winner of the 1963 Lenin Prize. A couple of years later, Aitmatov nominated Mikhail Gorbachev for chairman of the Congress of People's Deputies. Glasnost did indeed produce a modicum of social mobilization.

By far the most notorious episode in the glasnost wars was the so-called Nina Andreyevna affair. This concerned a letter to the editor of *Sovetskaya Rossiya* from Andreyevna, an instructor at Leningrad Chemistry-Technology Institute. The paper's editor, aligned with Ligachev, published Andreyevna's full-page article, titled "I Cannot Betray My Principles," on March 13, 1988. The piece amounted to a cry in the wilderness from the nomenklatura, who were increasingly confused by perestroika, adrift in a new world where old elements of communist ideology were being ignored or, worse, reversed. Andreyevna objected to the extra-party political groups springing up everywhere and demanded a rededication to class warfare. It was, according to Gorbachev, "a frontal assault on the reform process."[50]

The general secretary left on a trip to Yugoslavia on the day the article appeared, and he discovered it while reading the papers on the plane. While Gorbachev was away, Soviet officials dealt with the question of further circulation of the piece, whether to reprint it in other journals and so on. Andreyevna's article served as a sort of litmus test, since those who liked it were perestroika's opponents, while reformists loathed the thrust of the piece, which was to turn the clock back to lockstep authoritarianism. The battle was joined when Gorbachev returned. A question immediately arose over the provenance of the article. Ligachev writes that he "became familiar with" the Andreyevna article only when, like Gorbachev, he read it in the paper, but he admitted to the Politburo that he had seen the newspaper editor prior to publication to consider how to proceed. Yakovlev told Chernyaev (and the latter recorded this in his diary on March 26) that Andreyevna had written a mere half-page-long letter and that it was on Ligachev's orders that a team from *Sovetskaya Rossiya* went to Leningrad to rework the letter into an article. Ligachev asserts, to the contrary, that the original had been a thirty-page typescript, virtually a monograph.

At one of the editors' conferences with CPSU bosses, Yakovlev recounted, Ligachev had held up a copy of the published article and declared that it represented the party line. Ligachev insists that he had nothing to do with the publication, admits the editorial meeting, but says he simply recommended to those present that they read the piece: "what was attractive in this letter was precisely what interested me during that time—the refusal to accept the outright slander, the careless censure of the past." Two Politburo meetings discussed the article and issued a censure—some of those who had praised it, like Gromyko, suddenly took a dim view. And *Pravda* carried a refutation a few weeks later.

The Nina Andreyevna affair accelerated the isolation of Yegor Ligachev and temporarily silenced perestroika's critics. Gorbachev even came to believe it had been useful to get that point of view out in public and deal with it. But the effect proved temporary and not entirely benign. At a certain level, what the affair accomplished was to derail the moderate opponents of reform, who would ultimately have remained on Gorbachev's side, and leave the field to the hard-liners. And, of course, the sharpening nationalities question was at hand to energize them. The whole incident illustrates how cultural developments can assume political importance. Ultimately, glasnost, as a factor in this history, played a real role, but a contributory one. It did not rise to the level of an independent variable.

More Structural Factors

In summary, by the early 1980s, independently of any Cold War developments, the internal situation in the Soviet Union had attained a crisis level. Large forces contributed to that, among them the rise of human rights norms detailed in the last chapter, but two others more so: the structural rigidities of the Soviet economy and the nationalities question. Andropov recognized there were problems, but Gorbachev attempted to solve them. He did this through perestroika. Unfortunately for the Soviet Union—and for Gorbachev—international economic conditions were such as to limit his options, the scale of the problem remained poorly understood, and the economic aspect was only one part of the challenge the Soviet Union faced. International conditions militated against the resolution of Soviet problems because oil prices fell, reducing Soviet hard currency earnings and, consequently, investment capital. American policies of trade sanctions and embargoes on high-technology exports to the Soviet Union affected this situation only at the margin and were much less important than Moscow's basic resource position. The Soviets' other exports, many in noncash transactions or subsidized deliveries, were also of only marginal importance.

The scale of the Soviets' challenge remained poorly understood because of serious deficiencies in the exchange of information. Closely guarded statistics and a complete paucity of knowledge in some areas left the leadership unaware of the existence of actual budget deficits—supposedly impossible in a planned economy—and disguised the degree to which the Soviet military dominated industrial production and scientific development. Independent of any other factors, the drive for Soviet economic retrenchment required cutbacks in both military spending and foreign aid. Certain Soviet actions that were interpreted in the West as consequences of Cold War policies were instead, given the necessity for retrenchment, inevitable. These were dictated by structural factors and would have occurred whether or not there was a Cold War. The only matter of choice for Moscow leaders was where to cut on their menu of options.

Nationalities questions constitute a second structural element afflicting the Soviet Union. These created centrifugal forces moving toward dissolution of the Union. Gorbachev and other senior leaders were late to appreciate the dimensions of this problem and slow to react to it. They continued to posit small solutions, increasingly inadequate against the backdrop of deepening cleavage. Autonomy, sensitivity to cultural differences, and recognition of national languages might have sufficed to heal the divisions in the mid-1980s but had little potential as solutions by the end of the decade.

One judgment made in the previous chapter needs to be modified in light of what has been described here. Had the Soviet Union possessed greater resources, went that proposition, it might have resolved its problems on human rights and with the allied countries on the Soviet periphery. But the account here shows that the Soviets were insensitive to the problems of the nationalities—which involved human rights—suggesting that the same propensity to respond too late and with inadequate proposals for accommodation would have applied to the periphery also. That argues against the possibility that with the mind-sets they had, Soviet leaders, including Gorbachev, could have turned the tides of change in East-Central Europe. At the same time, the account here of the Soviet economy indicates that its shortcomings were so deep and ranged so far that no solution on these grounds was possible. Moscow would have found it extremely difficult to spare the resources to shore up the periphery when the center teetered on the brink of the abyss. Consequently, I think it fair to judge that the Warsaw Pact alliance would have been lost regardless of whether the Soviet Union was saved.

Communist party officials, the nomenklatura, the military, and other hard-liners had an interest in preserving the old ways. In the Soviet Union built-in inertia against change grew into increasing resistance to reform. Gorbachev initiated glasnost to break this reflexive opposition. He achieved some success in this endeavor, but without stronger measures against anti-reform elements, particularly hard-liners, the cultural reforms had a limited impact. Instead, the situation evolved into a polarized confrontation of extremes, in which Gorbachev made concessions to the hard-liners in an effort to preserve his political control. He was unable to restrain those hard-liners when they took actions against the nationalities, most importantly in the Baltics. These had the effect of ensuring the dissolution of the Soviet Union. At the same time, in August 1991, when hard-liners tried to restore authoritarian rule by force, centrifugal forces and the economic collapse had all but guaranteed they would have no popular support for their initiative. The failed coup marked the effective end of the Soviet Union, although it formally passed into history in December.

Data Collection and Historical Narrative

Economic history is a well-established subfield of history, and social history the most exciting development in the field over the past two decades or so. Probably not too much needs to be said in regard to these two areas. A few points on data collection will be made below. But the more interesting theme to take up here is the idea of synergism. With more details and figures, the end of the Soviet Union could be told as a purely economic story. Similarly, it could be told as the cultural story of the failed nationalities policy. Either could be retailed as a unique expla-nation for the Soviet downfall, although both would require a dollop of political history, since Gorbachev's perestroika was an avowed attempt to solve one of these problems, and as a reform effort, it had obvious implications for the second. But there are also clear interrelationships between the different factors. Nuclear plants were in Ukraine, poisonous chemical factories in Latvia. Conversely, a concentra-tion of Soviet industrial investment in the Russian republic stunted growth in the other national states. And Soviet politics cut across all the economic and cultural divides, most notably in that glasnost constituted a national initiative not limited to any of the parts of the USSR. The different tracks here have a *synergism* in ex-plaining the Soviet collapse, a value greater than the weight of the parts, as they also do in explaining how the Cold War ended. Historical inquiry has increasingly become a search for multi-causal explanations, and the observer should be alert to synergisms. There are times when "causes" evolve independently and culminate in an event, but there are also cases where the different tracks intersect and influence each other along the way to the nexus. The end of the Cold War is such a case. It cannot be reasonably explained without including the Soviet collapse, and the latter is itself a multi-causal sequence of events.

As a matter of constructing a historical narrative, there is another point to touch. The historian as writer is obligated to *tell a story*, not simply to relate facts or items of detail construed as facts or determined by diligent analysis to be facts. This is important not only from the standpoint of creating a successful work but also in order *to communicate historical judgment,* and even the facts themselves. The object of the exercise is to educate the reader on a subject the historian considers important. For that it is necessary to gain and hold the reader's interest. A reader immersed in the story will come away with much more—both judgments and facts—than one who must struggle through the material. Creativity in telling the story requires the historian to make a different set of judgments: choices on what themes to press, what to include or exclude, at what length, in what depth. Those choices should be related to the historian's analysis of the causes and sequence of events. Doing this actually simplifies the writing since the author thus provides her/himself with benchmarks that show the way forward. Structuring the narrative becomes a process of laying out those details and intermediate analyses that illuminate the causes and events, at each stage returning to themes central to the account, on the path to reaching ultimate conclusions.

Data collection is intimately related to subject, and subjects are specific to times, places, and the author's aims. Independent of the subject, it is not easy to establish general rules. I will offer only two rules of thumb. First, be alert to the credibility and comprehensiveness of data. Undependable sources may in fact contain useful data but should be used with care and corroborated with other sources wherever possible. If such data *is* used, the author should clearly indicate this and may want to include a discussion of why the material seems plausible or why using it became necessary. Undependable data should be restricted to the narrowest use possible and should not be relied upon as the basis for drawing broad conclusions on an overall subject.

Comprehensive data is a good check on other source material. Of course, this material may be compromised too—witness the Soviet official budget figures that Gorbachev found so unreliable—so comprehensiveness in itself is no guarantee of accuracy. But a broad collection of material is the best safeguard against sources that may individually be inaccurate. Broad collection offers the best opportunity to uncover material that permits comparison with other sources, as well as the opportunity to find data that might have been overlooked on the first pass. Sets of statistics are obviously relevant in economic history, but qualitative discussions, particularly of how, when, and why statistics were compiled, are important in understanding what the data shows, where it might be weak, and what has been left out. In social and cultural history, a wide range of data may be relevant to the inquiry, and as yet the field lacks general agreement on what standards to apply.

A second rule of thumb is to collect more data than you can use. This is not wasted effort. Casting a wide net maximizes opportunity to acquire comprehensive data. The *n*th source may be the one that yields the crucial insight that makes the analysis or the piece of data that confirms or disproves some other material. There is a problem in deciding when to *stop* collecting—a project is useless if it can never be finished—but as a general proposition, the historian should always be alert to the potential of new sources. At the analysis and writing stage, having too much material enables the author to choose among the best data in presenting the case. In addition, narrative that works to the limit of the sources is risky—the historian makes a bid for the definitive and stands in danger of falling short. Of course, the narrative may *be* the definitive account, but since the universe of source materials is constantly evolving, the bid is a reach. Conversely, a very narrow range of source material is one indication that a subject is not ripe for a full historical analysis. Essays and "research notes" are often employed to draw attention to fresh source materials and may be more appropriate when an issue is significant and merits treatment but the resource base is yet to be fully developed.

To return to our substantive subject, another layer must be added. Some observers of how the Cold War ended attribute success to manipulation. Western intelligence services, primarily but not exclusively the CIA, and related government actions drove the Soviet Union to distraction. The KGB is portrayed as less effective. These contributions are sometimes construed as the primary factor in the outcome. It is important to explore this facet of the history.

CHAPTER 6

THE SHADOW COLD WAR

DIPLOMACY, TRADE, ECONOMIC AND CULTURAL INTERACTIONS, military buildups, even the rise of human rights norms—all took place in the open, but all had submerged elements that in effect made up a shadow Cold War that took place beyond the event horizon. This centered on the intelligence arena, the one key area left to review. Glimpsed briefly in the War Scare of 1983, the bulk of the intelligence story has hardly been touched so far. The interactions among intelligence work and political-military strategy, diplomacy, and economics are important to study. Cold War triumphalists hold that the conflict was won essentially by manipulation, most of it within this arena. In the triumphalist view, the United States, acting primarily through the CIA but also by means of certain trade measures and the Reagan arms buildup, bankrupted the Soviet Union and forced its dissolution. This narrative has already presented several streams of evidence that supply more convincing explanations for the evolution, but the triumphalist school presents an argument that contains a certain plausibility and should be engaged directly.

As a point of departure, it must be noted that this school *agrees* that the fall of the Soviet Union was fundamentally a crisis of resources.[1] Analysts of this stripe proceed to argue that the Reagan administration understood the weakness of the Soviet Union and adopted a conscious policy to complicate Moscow's situation, "a series of actions designed to throw sand in the gears of the Soviet economy."[2] The policy had both overt and covert components. In the open, the administration began a military buildup that supposedly forced a Soviet response, an embargo on high-technology exports, and trade sanctions designed to prevent the Soviets from completing critical development projects, such as the Siberian natural gas pipeline, which Moscow intended to use for exports to Western Europe. Reagan then flummoxed the Soviets with his Strategic Defense Initiative, which presented Moscow with an insuperable challenge.

On the covert side, the CIA carried out a variety of secret operations intended to deepen Moscow's problems. These included activities in East-Central Europe—discussed briefly in chapter 2—in the Soviet Union itself, in Africa, and in Central America. The centerpiece of the covert effort was the secret war against the Russians in Afghanistan.

Several other aspects of the record are germane to considering the contributions of intelligence to the end of the Cold War. The most obvious is the strong controversy that developed regarding whether the CIA had "missed" the disintegration of the Soviet Union, one of several issues of intelligence analysis that came to the fore during the 1980s. Another set of issues concerns the role of spies during these Cold War years. On the Soviet side, there is the question of the KGB's so-called active measures and what role they did or did not play in the Euromissile political movement. All these subjects will be considered in evaluating the part intelligence played in the upheavals of the decade.

The Victory Thesis and the Strategic Balance

Fundamental to the triumphalist argument is the proposition that Ronald Reagan and his colleagues understood Soviet weakness and appreciated that this offered the opportunity to meddle in ways that would count. Other presidents, it is argued, worked to offset Cold War developments while Ronald Reagan was the first who played to win. This is an attractive and succinct reduction of a complex set of factors into a bold assertion of judgment. The first question is how that judgment comports with real-world events, starting with Mr. Reagan's election and continuing through his administration.

There can be no doubt that Ronald Reagan arrived at the White House committed to challenging Soviet power. Rhetoric about supposed Soviet gains in Africa, Asia, and Latin America had dominated Republican discussions of foreign policy in the election. Reagan himself declared the Soviets to be authors of "all the unrest that is going on" across the globe.[3] The situation in Poland—about which the CIA had briefed Mr. Reagan during the campaign—was white hot. Days after entering office, President Reagan denounced détente as a one-way street. Reagan thought communist ideology to be morally bankrupt, and he was alert to signs of its fiscal distress. Intelligence officer Robert M. Gates notes that Reagan, "rudimentary, even primitive" as his understanding of the Soviet economy might be, was very receptive to CIA reporting on Soviet economic malaise, and Gates writes, "Ronald Reagan probably was alone in truly believing that these trends [of U.S. inadequacy] could be reversed while he was President *and* that the Soviet Union itself could be defeated."[4]

President Reagan wanted to lead a global campaign for democracy, and he steadfastly denounced opponents of his edgy military-diplomatic policies as naysayers who would condemn the United States to military inferiority, implying that his own course was reversing that existing condition. But Mr. Reagan's choice of "democrats" to support—oligarchs in El Salvador and Honduras, military dictators in Panama, cold-blooded killers in Nicaragua and Angola, white separatists in South Africa—put the president's understanding of the concept of democracy in question. In his 1982 speech to the British parliament, Reagan asserted that a push for democracy was possible because of a revolutionary crisis of communism, but the sense was more one of ideological, not economic, poverty, and the president assumed his democrats were above reproach. Famously, President Reagan once compared the Nicaraguan *contras* to America's Founding Fathers. Reagan continued enunciating his formula into the spring of 1983, when he declared the USSR to be an "evil empire." But at every stage, Reagan warned of Moscow's power, not its bankruptcy. This president believed in peace through strength, and said so, but a wide gulf separates that from the claim that Mr. Reagan adopted a conscious strategy of defunding the Soviet Union. Reagan wanted armaments in order to reverse what he saw as Soviet military superiority.

President Reagan's acolytes were of the same stripe. Former members of the Committee on the Present Danger dominated the upper reaches of the administration, and that group tirelessly pressed the view that the Soviets were seeking strategic superiority, if they had not already obtained it. Conservative defense intellectuals spoke of the "window of vulnerability" (about which more in a moment) and alleged the Soviets had a doctrine of "assured survivability"—by which they meant that through a combination of powerful nuclear forces; measures to protect the leadership with deep, fortified command centers; antiballistic missiles; and civil and industrial defense, the USSR sought victory in nuclear war. Members of the CPD opposed the SALT II treaty as it prevented the United States from regaining parity, charged that Moscow had outstripped the United States in military spending, and maintained that U.S. conventional forces were hopelessly inadequate. These people *became* the Reagan administration. The Defense and State departments as well as the National Security Council staff were populated by former CPD members and like-minded figures.

From their perspective, the ramp-up of U.S. military budgets, starting with a $1.5 trillion add-on (to a budget request President Carter had already increased), was an effort to restore the military balance, not ruin Moscow.

Triumphalists point to three Reagan decisions, expressed in national security decision directives (NSDDs), as forming the core of his secret strategy to trigger Soviet collapse. It is reasonable to ask how Washington's sense of Soviet power was expressed in these orders. The first is NSDD-32, which President Reagan approved in May 1982. It set basic U.S. policy for defense and foreign affairs. Four of the eleven central objectives cited in NSDD-32 concern the Soviet Union. One does indeed refer to weakening "the Soviet alliance system by forcing the USSR to bear the brunt of its economic shortcomings, and to encourage long-term liberalizing and nationalist tendencies," but that text and others contain multiple references to "Soviet adventurism," Soviet efforts to increase influence, a need "to contain and reverse the expansion of Soviet control and military presence throughout the world" as well as "opportunities for Soviet expansion." A reference to "increasing pressure on [the Soviet] economy and the growing vulnerabilities of its empire" is paired with the expectation that the Soviet military would "continue to expand and modernize." Thus the NSDD contained conflicting visions, a mind-boggling concept of a weakening enemy capable of conquering the world. Moreover, the language on U.S. objectives in the document is not linked to any specific program, *and* the document *explicitly* concedes "the loss of U.S. strategic superiority."[5]

The second key directive is NSDD-66, which President Reagan approved on November 29, 1982. This also refers to "the military or strategic advantage and capabilities of the USSR." The Western alliance, it states, generally understands it should refrain from actions that help the Soviets, including purchase of Soviet natural gas during an interim period, and will reach a common accord on treating technology exports and loans to Moscow. But the NSDD further notes that the alliance does *not* intend "to engage in economic warfare against the Soviet Union," and the main programmatic feature of the directive is President Reagan's *revoking* the trade sanctions he had previously imposed on the Soviets, which were hurting the Western allies.[6]

The third of these seminal documents was NSDD-75, issued on January 17, 1983. This was a specific directive on U.S.-Soviet relations and envisioned an effort to promote "the process of change in the Soviet Union toward a more pluralistic political and economic system," by means "within the narrow limits available to us." Elsewhere the NSDD anticipated that change in the USSR would be "evolutionary." Among programmatic elements were the goals of ensuring that East-West economic relations "do not facilitate the Soviet military buildup" or subsidize the Soviet economy; "loosening" the Soviet hold over East-Central Europe, especially Poland, including by promoting human rights; keeping up "maximum pressure on Moscow for withdrawal from Afghanistan"—and ensuring the costs of the Soviet war there remained high; and taking a variety of measures in the third world, especially against Soviet-Cuban activities.[7]

There is smoke here, but no clear fire. These records do not support the contention that President Reagan declared economic war on Russia or sought the collapse of the USSR. Even in their obscure language, the bureaucratic directives imply that Washington proved unable to enlist its allies in a full-blown effort of that sort. Soviet economic weaknesses are noted, but their exploitation is viewed as instrumental to lesser purposes than compelling the disintegration of the USSR. And there is no clarion call for a secret war, only a bid to integrate diplomatic, economic, and military policies so that they have a gradual impact on Moscow. The documents refer to policy elements that did affect the Soviets adversely, but they anticipate evolutionary change and base many trade and technology restrictions on the premise of blunting Soviet strategic superiority.

The texture of actual Reagan administration defense programs adds to this impression. From the administration's perspective, the ramp-up of U.S. military budgets, starting with a $1.5 trillion add-on (to a budget request President Carter had already increased), was about restoring the military balance, not ruining Moscow. Among the more expensive efforts would be a command-and-control initiative that sought to install means of communication and leadership protection that could operate in a nuclear war environment. Improving missile silo survivability was another aspect. The resurrection of the B-1 bomber, as aircraft were considered to be highly survivable, also contributed to this goal; but Carter had cancelled it because the B-2 "stealth" aircraft was considered a superior system. In fact, delays in B-2 production resulted from budget limitations that were partly created by the B-1's resurrection and greatly increased the price of the aircraft, ultimately shrinking procurement to only a handful of planes. The major strategic debate of the era, over where and how to deploy the Peacekeeper ICBM, intimately involved survivability questions. One can argue over whether the Reaganites really believed their own rhetoric or actually harbored secret ambitions of sealing American nuclear advantages in stone, but it is not accurate to maintain that the declaratory and implemented Reagan strategy was based on an appreciation of American strength and Soviet weakness.

Virtually sub rosa, the administration also pursued a retooling of U.S. nuclear weapons that furnished both land-based and sea-based missiles with doubly powerful warheads. In addition, technological improvements in guidance systems made Soviet missile silos highly vulnerable to U.S. strikes. These guidance-yield combinations were deployed on all U.S. ICBMs and on the Trident II D-5 submarine missile, creating a potential first-strike capability. In fact the Russians considered the SDI program so threatening precisely because it could give the United States the capability to mount a first strike, the riposte to which might be blunted by ballistic missile defenses. The defense guidance that underlay President Reagan's directives on nuclear war fighting leaked in May 1982, revealing that planners had been ordered to construct forces capable of "prevailing" in war, in part by "decapitating" (destroying) the Soviet leadership (thus Moscow's fear of the Pershing II had a basis in U.S. nuclear war planning).[8]

American intelligence had a first contribution to make in assessing the state of the nuclear balance. All U.S. agencies participated in the elaboration of national intelligence estimates (NIEs), which represented the considered opinions, and predictions, of intelligence on the key questions of the day. The NIE 11 series dealt with the Soviet Union, and one of its biggest components was the NIE 11-3/8 reports, which contained several volumes covering Soviet offensive and defensive nuclear forces.[9] In the late 1970s conservatives had mounted a concerted attack on the NIEs, saying they represented a myopically optimistic view of the USSR. This began with an experiment in so-called competitive analysis in 1976, in which a group of outsiders—many of whom went on to become founders of the Committee on the Present Danger—were empaneled to critique the Soviet estimates. This group, called Team B, had filed an ambitious critique of the NIEs, targeting everything from the CIA's vision of Moscow's intentions to projections of Soviet military spending to Russian capabilities in antisubmarine warfare or ballistic missile defense.[10]

The Team B exercise became the origin of the window of vulnerability. This abstruse bit of nuclear arcana started from Team B's gripe that there was no reason to suppose that the CIA's estimates of Soviet ICBM accuracy were correct and that under specified conditions of technological improvement, accuracy could be much higher, high enough to make U.S. land-based missiles vulnerable in their silos.[11] Under this argument, a Soviet nuclear attack could disarm the U.S. ICBM force using only a fraction of Russia's land-based missiles, then rely upon the reserve force plus submarine missiles and bombers to threaten the destruction of the rest of the country, compelling the United States to surrender rather than retaliate. The counterargument that U.S. missiles could be launched with the initial attack in progress, thus not "lost," was dismissed as a dangerous invitation to accidental war. The more significant counter that loss of ICBMs left the United States with thousands of capable weapons on submarine-launched missiles and bombers got little traction. This was the window of vulnerability. What made it a window was the possibility that military expansion could right the situation by some time in the 1980s. The CIA estimates, by accepting higher projections of Soviet missile accuracy, produced NIEs that seemed to confirm the threat.[12]

In the last year of the Carter administration, the director of central intelligence, Adm. Stansfield Turner, acquiesced in an NIE containing a maximalist depiction of the threat, in hopes of warding off continuing attacks on U.S. intelligence reporting about the Soviets. He rued this act later, as the Reaganites simply pocketed the concessions and demanded even more extreme projections of the Soviet threat.[13] William J. Casey, President Reagan's campaign director and Turner's successor, intervened very actively in the NIE process. In the case of the Soviet estimates, Casey delayed *any* follow-on report until he felt confident he had control of the process. The 1981 Soviet estimate was not written until the spring of 1983, and then it continued to project a somber view of the Soviet threat. By then, the national intelligence officer managing NIEs on strategic forces, Lawrence K. Gershwin, was projecting that Moscow could have huge numbers of nuclear weapons of every kind, including nuclear warheads on missiles even within the constraints of arms agreements. Until 1986, while Robert Gates remained deputy director for intelligence, these estimates encountered no objections from higher-ups. Douglas MacEachin headed the Office for Soviet Analysis (SOVA), and he objected to the outsized Soviet force projections, complaining to Gates's successor, Richard J. Kerr, that even at the low end, NIE projections of Soviet force increases would require Moscow to spend resources on nuclear forces greater than the Soviet spending peak of the 1960s (11 percent versus 10). MacEachin ordered a massive internal study, which was completed in 1988. He believed that estimators were simply asking analysts to calculate the maximum possible production rate for Soviet weapons, then stapling together the results without regard for Moscow's defense planning or resource base.[14] The study eventually found that the NIEs had predicted a Soviet force mainly (over 90 percent) equipped with brand new missiles (the real proportion at that point was slightly over 50 percent). Equally important, the date of deployment for Soviet weapons systems had been expected sooner than it happened for ten of seventeen systems. Predictions were accurate for only six. The national estimates had overestimated Soviet numbers in the majority of cases. The NIEs of the late 1970s had actually been *wrong* on numbers of specific weapons but *correct* on overall numbers of Soviet nuclear warheads because analysts had made offsetting errors.[15]

In the meantime, the window of vulnerability closed, not owing to any American buildup but because it had never existed. A particular type of Soviet ICBM, which the CIA called the SS-19 (the Soviet designation was UR-100), with the warheads and the accuracy attributed to it, had been considered the main threat to U.S. missile silos. In the war-game scenarios used to assess vulnerability, the SS-19 force had sufficed to destroy the U.S. land-based missile component, enabling hypothetical Soviet war planners to reserve the remainder of their nuclear forces. But as the CIA watched Soviet ICBM tests, the SS-19 failed to perform as predicted. By 1985 the conclusion became inescapable that the SS-19 threat was a myth. That year's NIE reduced its accuracy estimate for this weapon, ending the theoretical vulnerability of U.S. ICBMs.[16] In 1988 the CIA observed the Soviets beginning to dismantle their SS-19s to substitute a follow-on system Moscow had begun to develop only in the early 1980s.[17]

The elephant in the room in all of this was the *American* threat to *Soviet* nuclear forces, excluded from the NIEs because the CIA was not permitted to do "net assessment" and war-gaming nuclear exchanges went both ways. American forces with the improved warheads and guidance systems deployed in the 1980s posed a high-order threat to Soviet missile forces, a window of vulnerability in reverse. The real status of the nuclear balance at the time was that land-based forces on both sides were becoming endangered as a result of the existence of highly capable missile forces that could be retargeted on a near-real-time basis.

A second issue with the CIA's contribution to Reagan administration perceptions of the Soviet Union involved the NIEs on the Soviet economy and Moscow's military spending. Starting with the Defense Intelligence Agency in the early 1970s, then the Team B critique, analyses of Soviet defense spending had come under fierce attack. By 1975 the CIA was already estimating that Moscow spent more on its military than the United States spent on its. In May 1976 the CIA had revised sharply upward its projections of Soviet military spending even while continuing to assess that Moscow had serious economic problems. In 1977 the CIA warned of serious strains to the Soviet economy over the next decade. Nevertheless, the agency had expected Soviet defense spending to increase at a rate of 4 to 5 percent annually, with military investment consuming 10–15 percent of the USSR's gross national product. The agency remained under intense pressure on these reports, making it extremely difficult to cast an estimate that reduced the dimension of the threat.[18] This was evidence for a Soviet Union on the march.

Doubts grew, and major CIA reviews of the data began. Soviet analyst Kay Oliver had noted consumer discontent for Carter administration superiors as early as 1979. During Reagan's first year, agency experts had theorized that the Soviet pattern was similar in many ways to those of less-developed countries, an awful commentary, and pointed directly to the Soviet fixation on heavy industry and its rigid planning-budgeting system as an obstacle, again raising the question of a frustrated population. In June 1982 the CIA studied the USSR's ability to shift resources from military production to civilian purposes, anticipating Moscow's leaders might feel driven to such a choice. That paper reiterated the 4 to 5 percent growth estimate for military expenditures at least through 1985, predicted that a cutback of perhaps 20 percent could result in real gains for the overall economy, noted the Soviet military could be expected to object, and judged, "We believe such an abrupt shift is highly unlikely in the short run." Economic manipulation of the type considered by the Reagan administration was specifically evaluated as raising the cost to Moscow of maintaining its then-current allocation of resources but was not viewed as a decisive weapon. Soviet leaders, the CIA believed, "are convinced—and we concur that some growth remains to be squeezed from the present resource-allocation scheme."[19]

Robert Gates takes pains to point to early CIA information on Soviet problems, but that was not the major thrust of the agency's reporting.[20] In August 1982 economic analysts felt it necessary to publish a paper simply defending the CIA models used to project Soviet defense spending.[21] A year later, when the CIA published a major review that concluded that the rate of Soviet spending for defense procurement had hardly changed since 1976 (while increases in overall military spending had slowed), the work was not deemed credible without massive background studies. According to one of the agency's primary analysts of the Soviet economy, the estimates "encountered a great deal of resistance in the upper levels of CIA and in the Department of Defense." A further report that attempted to explain the shift was written but could not get approval by higher-ups.[22] It finally circulated only two years later, in 1985.

The issue of economic reporting on the Soviets is particularly important, not only because it bears on the later controversy over whether the CIA missed the fall of the Soviet Union, but also more directly for its immediate impact on President Reagan. Shortly after the inauguration, according to Peter Schweizer, Director Casey personally delivered a report on the Soviet economy to Reagan. The supposed report pointed to economic weaknesses and suggested the Soviets were overextended—and led to the deliberately manipulative program triumphalists believe was adopted almost immediately. Thereafter Reagan would periodically be supplied with similar material. This was "opportunity intelligence" of the type that Casey acolyte Herbert Meyer specialized in producing (an example is in the documentary appendix). Donald Regan, who became White House chief of staff in 1986, later told Schweizer that the president "loved that stuff. He would take the big stack and read them one by one over the weekend." But both Casey and Gates were reluctant to promulgate CIA reports that rejected a view that Moscow harbored aggressive intentions or concluded that the Soviet giant might have feet of clay. These criteria applied to the CIA's economic reporting. Given Schweizer's thesis, the agency should have been rushing to supply visions of Soviet weakness, but it was not. This casts doubt on the original proposition. By the time Don Regan arrived at the White House, the reporting had turned more pessimistic, *and* Casey had relented on suppressing it. The triumphalist account does not square with facts that can be established.[23]

"What I realized only years later," Gates recollects, "was that Bill Casey came to CIA primarily to wage war against the Soviet Union." Something of a bully, Gates observes, Casey was interested in the intelligence that furthered his purposes and quite willing to intervene in intelligence analyses, though not current reporting. A tough analyst could push through a point of view by sticking to his guns, but more often than not, analysts were reluctant to incur Casey's wrath.[24] In the early Reagan period, Casey established his control over the NIEs by fighting for his particular views in estimates on Soviet use of chemical weapons in Afghanistan and Cambodia, alleged Soviet support for terrorism, and the attempted assassination of Pope John Paul II. The CIA's analysts of Soviet activity faced not only Casey's jaundiced eye, but that of Gates as well. Melvin A. Goodman, a senior Soviet analyst who later resigned over the pressures on CIA intelligence, observes that "the systematic politicization of intelligence collection and analysis became institutionalized during Casey's tenure. . . . Gates knew how the intelligence process worked and how to ensure its responsiveness to Casey's policy interests." According to Goodman, Gates used reorganization and personnel transfers "to bolster reporting that emphasized the Soviet threat and to inhibit analysis that emphasized Moscow's serious economic problems and worsening international position."[25] At a 1993 panel discussion on the CIA's Soviet economic reporting, Goodman made an example of gross overestimates of Soviet oil production in the mid-1980s: seeking a report, Gates went to the CIA Office of Global Issues (OGI) for figures and found them lower than he wanted, then ordered the analysts to write their report in conjunction with the Defense Intelligence Agency (DIA), knowing this would upwardly bias the final projection.

One final point should be made on the CIA economic estimates concerning Soviet military spending. Throughout the period, intelligence analysts looking at Moscow's defense budgets, applying their sophisticated models that "costed" Soviet expenditures based on observables of military equipment produced, ended up with a *steady* projection. Analysts argued over the rate of increase in Soviet spending, over whether the CIA's rate findings were too low or not—the DIA's William T. Lee was a notable proponent of the low-ball charges—but the trend line remained steady. That was still true in the late 1980s, when re-analysis of data led the CIA to conclude it had *overestimated* Soviet defense spending and underestimated the burden of defense on the Soviet economy. In one way, these findings were not surprising—Moscow stuck to its five-year plans, except in 1985, when Gorbachev became the top leader and threw money at defense as part of his first measures, an action that was probably political as well as military-technical. But the real meaning of the steady trend line is that *Moscow never responded to the Reagan buildup by altering its plans for committing resources to defense*—not initially, not after SDI, not ever. The triumphalist notion that Reagan's military programs forced the Soviet Union into a disastrous spending competition does not correspond to empirical evidence. Soviet military spending had its own logic built from the momentum of defense programs and Moscow's decisions thereon. Moreover, the assertion that CIA economic warfare ordered by Reagan bankrupted Soviet foreign currency accounts does not correspond to the agency's own economic reporting—an exhaustive joint study by the CIA and DIA published shortly before the fall of the Soviet Union finds that Soviet capital accounts remained in the black until 1987, and then returned to profitability, including during the crisis years of 1988 through 1990, when the Union truly stood at the edge of the abyss.[26]

In summary, it is not received history that President Reagan understood American strength *or* Soviet weakness, and U.S. intelligence was manipulated in ways that made any recognition of Soviet difficulties harder. The record is plain that Reagan assumed office with the impression that *U.S.* debility required certain actions of him and that he was in some kind of dire straits with respect to Soviet nuclear forces in particular. The overwhelming perception among Reagan officials was that the Soviets were on the march, not that they were on the verge of collapse. If the president himself believed otherwise, that was important, but its importance would be limited among the constellation of policy entrepreneurs. Trade measures were intended to impede a perceived Soviet advantage, that is, they were *defensive,* not offensive, in nature. The idea that the United States manipulated oil or gold prices to hurt the Russians is fantasy. The Reagan military buildup was adopted not with the goal of bankrupting the Soviet Union but with the aim of closing an alleged—and in fact ephemeral—*American* window of vulnerability, and seeking U.S. strategic superiority. The Soviets did not, in fact, respond to the Reagan programs. The technology controls Reagan adopted were to help limit Soviet force improvements, not to reduce Moscow to tears. The sanctions hurt Western European allies as much as, if not more than, the Soviets. The Reagan military buildup did not deploy *any* weapons system not previously planned by the Carter administration with the exception of the B-1 bomber. In short, it is a myth that the overt side of Reagan policy was cleverly designed to defeat the Soviet Union, and a construction that is only possible in hindsight, that is, by means of post hoc analysis.

CIA Covert Operations

Not long after taking office, President Reagan ordered CIA Director Casey to expand and reenergize programs for direct action. Under State Department auspices, Reagan also created new propaganda efforts christened as "public diplomacy." And outside the government, the broadcasting efforts of Radio Free Europe and Radio Liberty—once CIA projects but now independently run, acted in concert with U.S. policy. President Reagan declared his support for "freedom fighters" everywhere. The Carter administration had already begun a number of CIA covert action projects, including some targeted against the USSR at home and in Afghanistan. Director Casey expanded those and added projects aimed at Nicaragua, Cuba, Angola, Mozambique, Libya, Mauritania, and others. Between 1981 and 1984, U.S. intelligence budgets expanded by about a quarter while the CIA's slice of that pie doubled. By 1984 covert action consumed the majority of the CIA budget.[27]

Director Casey wanted to fight Russians. Many of his CIA projects were cloaked in anti-Soviet rhetoric, but only a few had much direct impact on the Soviet Union. Moscow's stakes in Nicaragua, Angola, and Mozambique were so small relative to the overall dimensions of the Cold War that success or failure hardly mattered—except in the Nicaraguan case, where the shaky politics of the covert operation threatened the United States more than Russia. The Nicaraguan adventure, conducted against increasing public opposition, ultimately damaged Reagan's presidency and thus his ability to act on Soviet-American bilateral issues, by no means Casey's objectives. Some of Casey's operations affected Cuba, which followed its own course of forward defense against "Yanqui imperialism" by supporting revolutionary forces in much the same way as Moscow. The Reagan administration had a special focus against Cuba, but again Moscow's stake remained limited. Even had successful U.S. covert operations raised Moscow's costs in the third world manyfold, this would still not have compared even to the price of the Soviets' Warsaw Pact alliance. Thus most of these covert activities should be noted but then set aside.

Activities in East-Central Europe more directly implicated core Cold War interests. The CIA's role in support of Solidarity has previously been briefly discussed in our account of the lengthy Polish political crisis. The administration policy set in January 1981 focused on political and economic measures, effectively on incentives against a Soviet invasion or martial law. The possibility of a CIA operation was discussed in March, but Casey preferred to avoid this unless the Soviets intervened. The CIA director held conversations with Pope John Paul II about this time and found the pope in favor of attempting to calm Solidarity. Little could be accomplished in Poland if the Catholic Church was opposed. General Jaruzelski's imposition of martial law that December changed the playing board, and funding for a CIA project reportedly followed a few months later, but swung into higher gear in the summer of 1982, when the White House demanded options. Casey asked William Clark, national security adviser, to schedule a specific meeting to discuss a CIA operation that September. "Once the covert operation was underway," Gates records, "Casey paid little attention to it."[28] By contrast, National Security Council staffer Richard Pipes maintains that no formal intelligence action was taken—Casey worked privately, off the books, with a handful of trusted CIA operatives, because "it was feared it would leak."[29] If accurate, this foreshadowed the events of the Iran-contra affair. A covert operation undertaken without a "presidential finding," or memorandum of notification to the congressional oversight committees, is not legal in the U.S. system.[30]

The CIA mostly worked through third parties to avoid being linked directly to Solidarity. It did place a communications interception detachment at the U.S. embassy in Warsaw. Frankfurt, Germany, became the forward base for the Polish activity. Israeli intelligence became an important source of information from Jewish immigrants and those living in Poland, according to Schweizer. When the Mossad did not produce, Casey complained to Israeli officials. French intelligence exfiltrated out of Poland certain activists who could then be contacted in the West. Sweden served as a conduit for computers, fax and photocopying machines, newsprint, and radio equipment. These materials fed a growing Polish underground press and broadcast network. When Swedish customs caught wind of suspicious smuggling—the CIA's supply efforts—Casey intervened with Swedish officials to call off the hounds. Human rights groups, labor organizations such as the AFL-CIO, and religious groups had their own programs to help Solidarity, with agendas compatible enough to the American one that little CIA guidance seemed necessary. The operation was reorganized in 1983 to function through Brussels, where the CIA liaised with international labor supporters for Solidarity. It reportedly involved only a few million dollars a year. In 1985 the Soviets obtained some evidence of Solidarity's international connections when a courier was arrested and found with letters from the outside. The U.S. military attaché was expelled from Poland, and some American diplomats in Krakow were roughed up. The Polish government tried to shut down the flow of support to the dissidents and had some success developing an agent in Sweden with knowledge of shipments, but in 1986 the Swedes, with CIA help, identified the agent, who was transferred to a harmless post. Meanwhile, the CIA widened the circle of recipients of its aid to include Czech dissidents.

In 1983, for the first time in almost two decades, U.S. intelligence compiled an NIE on the reliability of the non-Soviet forces within the Warsaw Pact, in effect assessing Moscow's view of its peripheral allies at that time. The NIE furnishes a mirror for the fears of Soviet leaders and an indirect measurement of the effectiveness of CIA covert action. The estimate concluded, "The Soviet Union is concerned about the military reliability of its Warsaw Pact allies in the event of a conflict with NATO." Its most loyal allies were seen as Bulgaria and East Germany. Czechoslovakia was pictured as resigned to Soviet control and politically stable but probably a source of concern. Poland was accorded the most extensive discussion, its economic problems were noted, the Solidarity crisis was discussed in some detail, but most U.S. intelligence agencies concluded that although "the extent of current Soviet confidence is in question . . . the Polish armed forces would carry out initial Pact wartime orders." The sole holdout was U.S. Army intelligence, which argued, "Soviet confidence in the Polish armed forces will not be restored until the party regains preeminence and Solidarity is no longer a major factor." Ironically, Russia's least reliable allies were assessed as Hungary and Romania, where there were no CIA covert action programs.[31]

Scattered evidence reveals few CIA covert operations directly targeting the Soviet economy. Early in the administration, technical studies at both the CIA and the Pentagon indicated the importance of Western gas and oil technology to Soviet production and distribution systems. The Soviets depended on their oil exports and had high hopes for a gas pipeline they were building to the Czech border for deliveries into Western Europe. In fact, one of the differences between the Reagan directives NSDD-66 and NSDD-75 shows that between the fall of 1982 and the following spring, Washington was forced to abandon hope of getting the Europeans to refuse Soviet natural gas, substituting a fallback that the allies would not buy more Soviet gas than they had already contracted from the first pipeline. Moscow had a second "strand" of this pipeline under construction. Indications of a CIA operation suggest that the United States turned elsewhere to obstruct deliveries. According to former secretary of the Air Force Thomas C. Reed, the activity began at the suggestion of an NSC staffer who learned that the Soviets were seeking computer software to control the pipeline from a Canadian manufacturer. Computer experts were hired to write code that would cause the software to malfunction once it had been placed in operation and had worked for a certain amount of time. Reed describes the malfunctions as changing "pump speeds and valve settings to produce pressures far beyond those acceptable to the pipeline joints and welds." The result, he writes, was "the most monumental non-nuclear explosion and fire ever seen from space." According to Peter Schweizer again, after several years, Soviet technicians were still working to delete the flaws that had been worked into critical software. Other actions affected Soviet chemical plants, tractor factories, and computer chips.[32]

Aside from economic sabotage, there were political actions. Among these was one connected to the 1985 Geneva summit, when the CIA bent its efforts to foster simultaneous anti-Soviet protests in Geneva. Just before departing for the summit, President Reagan had received a CIA briefing at the White House that focused on Soviet internal problems. Gates records telling Reagan that the CIA did not think Gorbachev would be able to solve Moscow's economic problems and that the

Soviet leader needed to control defense spending to have any chance at all. Avoiding an arms control agreement would maximize Soviet defense requirements. From the standpoint of Casey's policy interests—and the CIA director had also sent Reagan a paper arguing against any deal on the SDI—fomenting protests in Geneva might further sour the pot for the negotiations. Had Gorbachev taken enough umbrage, this CIA project might have delayed or disrupted the understanding between the two leaders that was about to emerge.[33]

Among the longest enduring political actions was the effort to insert publications into the Soviet Union and its periphery. This had both overt and covert aspects, much like Radio Free Europe/Radio Liberty, and began during those early years, specifically in 1956. Zbigniew Brzezinski ordered intensification of the CIA effort during the Carter administration, and both Reagan officials and French intelligence chief Alexandre de Marenches have claimed prowess in placing this material. The overt side of the program circulated Western books, not just propaganda but almost any literature requested by an Eastern national. Poland was the best customer. Yet the overt effort peaked in 1968 at 328,000 items. In 1970 the CIA reported it had moved 2.5 million items by its secret channels. There is as yet no data available for the 1980s, although it is fair to expect that this will eventually show the project had some impact, particularly on the strengthening of human rights norms in East-Central Europe.[34]

At this point it is worth pausing to reflect for a moment on the Cold War as a historical phenomenon. There are observers who argue that perceiving the conflict as an East-West affair distorts our vision. The "North-South" dimension—the relationship between the industrial and underdeveloped worlds—in this view is equally or more crucial. Odd Arne Westad's important work on the international history of the Cold War expounds this view most forcefully.[35] But the problem is to differentiate ends from means. The Cold War, to the degree that it was a "war," raged between the industrialized West—the "first world"—particularly the United States, and the Soviet Union and its camp—the "second world"—also industrialized but along different principles with different norms. That conflict would have existed regardless of what happened in the underdeveloped world, the "third world." Meanwhile, there was a *separate* conflict in the third world, one that involved the struggle for independence and autonomy for peoples who had been colonized decades or centuries before by first world nations. That struggle is known to history as decolonization, and it would have occurred whether or not there was a Cold War. In the idiom of political science, both the Cold War and decolonization were independent variables. The importance of the third world in the Cold War was to furnish a series of stages upon which the superpowers and their allies competed for international support and engaged their proxies.

There is also a temporal dimension to East-West versus North-South visions of the era. While detailed exposition is beyond the scope of this work, the third world assumed its biggest role in the Cold War between about 1955 and 1980, that is, in the period between the Bandung Conference of Asian and African states and the Iran hostage crisis, during which a nonaligned movement of third world nations began emerging and acquired increasing importance. Decolonization proper began at least a decade earlier and by 1980 had about run its course. Thus in the Cold War's last decade—the subject of this inquiry—the cockpit of conflict returned to the East-West axis. From Moscow's perspective, its economic assistance to Cuba, by far the largest of its third world programs, was a greater burden than all other third world endeavors combined—and there was no secret war in Cuba at this time. This study has argued that the program of CIA covert operations of the 1980s, even had they all been successful (which they were not), would have had little impact on the main conflict. Moreover, the Casey secret war project in Nicaragua ended by potentially damaging the United States much more than it could ever have affected the Soviet Union. Reagan triumphalists are not correct when they argue that U.S. covert operations were a key factor in the end of the Cold War. The boundary case is Afghanistan.

Afghanistan

By far the biggest covert operation—and the one for which the most claims have been made—was the effort to counter the Soviet war in Afghanistan. Like so much else, this began under Carter but expanded greatly in both scope and expense during the Reagan years. This was a real secret war, a paramilitary operation with associated psychological, political, and diplomatic strategies, not simply a political action, as in Poland, or an economic sabotage action, like the effort inside the USSR. Estimates of the total amount the CIA spent on the Afghan War range up to $9 billion.[36] Since U.S. spending was mostly matched by Saudi Arabian allies and small additional amounts were spent on Afghan covert operations by Pakistan, the United Kingdom, France, the People's Republic of China, and Muslim civilians throughout the region, the total cost of this secret war may have been in excess of $20 billion. On the Soviet side, admitted casualties are 19,000 dead, but actual numbers may be higher. Western officials estimated 35,000 dead, unofficial estimates are in the 40,000–50,000 range, with some Soviet journalists claiming up to 280,000 killed, a likely exaggeration. Budgetary outlays were between about $25 billion and $70 billion. Some observers believe the Afghan War, by itself, caused the destruction of the Soviet Union.[37]

The CIA, acting through Pakistani intermediaries who trained and supported Afghan tribes, armed a whole resistance movement. But for the CIA, for a very long time, the war in Afghanistan would be a spoiling operation. The Soviets had had a relationship with the Afghan government in the 1970s. A communist faction had overthrown that government and sparked the tribal revolt, then sought an even closer alliance with Moscow. That faction had proved incompetent and another Afghan communist faction had enlisted Moscow's full support. The coup at the end of 1979 and simultaneous Soviet intervention were to perfect the fight against the rebellion. The CIA threw its weight onto the other side of the scale—at first under Carter, then Reagan—preventing an Afghan communist victory. For years, the aim was to bloody the Russians, not defeat them, and the tribes did well enough at that. And Washington's perception was not that the Soviets were defeated—as late as 1983, U.S. officials still worried that the Russians would move past Afghanistan to invade Pakistan. The classic assumption made was that Moscow sought a warm-water port on the Indian Ocean littoral.[38]

The CIA appreciated the increasing military capability of the Afghan rebels, but analysts refused to credit them with the capability to defeat the Russians. In both 1983 and 1985, CIA studies concluded that the rebels could not win militarily. The 1985 study, of Afghanistan five years into the war, the most ambitious made to that point, depicted the war as a stalemate. Laying out data for severe Soviet losses, the CIA nevertheless found the Russian forces holding their own. Despite numerous Afghan successes—including rocket attacks into Kabul, the bombing of the highway tunnel that was the main route for Soviet supplies entering the country, and even rebel raids into the adjoining Soviet republics—the Soviets retained the ability to mount major offensives. In 1985 they attacked rebel forces in the strategic Panjshir Valley and separately engaged the Afghan rebel bases in the mountains along the Pakistani border. The CIA projected several possible levels of Soviet reinforcement of its forces and concluded that no sustainable troop level would win the war for Moscow, even though the rebels could not attain victory either.

The Soviets made the same calculation. When Gorbachev came to power, he ordered a final push for victory but warned the Russian generals that if they did not succeed within two years, he was going to withdraw. The Russians sent their best field commander, the general who had previously headed Soviet forces in East Germany. He changed tactics, relying to an increasing degree on air strikes, attacks by gunship helicopters, and operations by Soviet special forces, fully one-third of which were sent into battle. The escalation pressed hard on the rebels.

Bill Casey held the Afghan CIA operation close, essentially acting as its military theater commander. He followed events from Washington and made annual visits to the frontline nation of Pakistan, stopping along the way to consult the Saudi allies. As the big boss, however, Casey demonstrated *no* clear determination to press for victory in the Afghan War. The CIA's station chief in Pakistan and its task force leader for this operation during these early years were both objects of strong political attacks from those who wanted the Afghan operation to seek a Soviet defeat. The central theme of the movie and book *Charlie Wilson's War* is precisely this struggle over the American objective. It is fair to say that this debate over CIA goals dominated American strategy for the Afghan operation until April 1985. It was only at that point, after President Reagan had approved NSDD-166 in March, that a Soviet defeat became the CIA's aim in Afghanistan. It was under the provisions of the new strategy that Stinger shoulder-fired antiaircraft missiles were given to the Afghan rebels. A year passed before these reached the front in numbers and rebels were trained to use them. In late 1986 Stingers scored significant successes against Soviet gunships and began to inhibit Moscow's military operations.

By then, General Secretary Gorbachev had reached the end of his tether with respect to Afghanistan. Anatoly Chernyaev observes that it took only about a year for Gorbachev to decide that the new approach had not worked. Gorbachev told the Twenty-seventh Party Congress that Afghanistan had become a "bleeding wound." He made public the intention to withdraw. In July 1986 he ordered token withdrawals of some units. At the Politburo on November 13, 1986, the Soviet leadership made the collective decision to alter the *Soviet* objective in Afghanistan from ensuring the survival of a friendly ally to one of preserving Afghanistan as a neutral nation. The Russian generals were given one or at most two years to secure that objective. In 1987, when they had still failed to make progress, Gorbachev made his final decision for a pullout. Moscow negotiated through the United Nations to create an international framework protecting its withdrawal, which was eventually completed in February 1989.

Ultimately, CIA covert operations did not win the shadow Cold War. In Afghanistan the Soviet decision to change direction *preceded* the advent of the CIA's newly rearmed Afghan rebels. Withdrawal was already implicit in Moscow's revised course. Moreover, Washington's debate over the goals to be sought in Afghanistan vitiates the triumphalist proposition that the CIA operation formed part of any supposed secret strategy to bring about the collapse of the Soviet Union. In truth, the CIA operation went through a process of "mission creep" and took its final form only as Moscow modified its own strategy. As for Poland, the CIA project there assisted the underground and Solidarity, but it was not the determinant factor. By the CIA's own estimate, the allies in whom Moscow could have the least confidence were those in which the CIA was not actively fomenting resistance. The CIA remained an active player in the shadow Cold War, but its intervention would not be decisive.

Soviet Intelligence Operations

Soviet intelligence services would also not be key to the massive upheavals to come. In Poland, the Soviet security service was very active and had close relations with— and, some would say, command authority over—the Polish internal security and foreign intelligence services. In the first months of the Solidarity crisis, Andropov, while he remained chief of the KGB, had already brought the Polish interior minister to Moscow for "consultations." The Polish party and government were surveilled by the secret police, including by use of telephone taps. After martial law began, there were several successive sweeps of Solidarity and other activists fueled by Soviet concerns and the Jaruzelski government's fears. Wałęsa's imprisonment has been mentioned in our discussion of his role, but many of his close associates, and several thousand Poles in all, joined him in prison. An effort to discredit Wałęsa included leaking the fact that he had served as a secret police informant during the 1970s. Polish security supplied the KGB with statistics showing that more than 10,000 individuals were arrested by the end of 1982, with 400 demonstrations broken up, 1,200 pieces of printing equipment seized, and 12 underground radio stations closed.[39] The KGB also concerned itself with the activities of foreign journalists in Poland and used its own undercover agents to monitor the steadfastness of Jaruzelski's regime. There were also efforts to discover and shut down the CIA's channels for aid to Solidarity. For all the intense activity, security measures failed to halt the spread of opposition in Poland.

When an assassination attempt was made against the "Polish pope," John Paul II, on May 13, 1981, suspicion quickly fell on the KGB, which certainly had an interest in John Paul's activities because they directly affected Poland. CIA Director Casey tried to force the issue, commissioning a special national intelligence estimate

(SNIE) to examine the KGB role and demanding a rewrite when the SNIE failed to find significant KGB involvement. Various researchers made charges against the KGB, and testimony at the trial of the assassin uncovered links to a Bulgarian intelligence officer, which fueled intense speculation. But no KGB connection was ever demonstrated. There is an extensive record of Soviet and Polish intelligence efforts to build an intelligence net to report on Pope John Paul II but none on connections to the attempted murder. British historian Christopher Andrew, using former KGB officer Vasili Mitrokhin's data, writes, "If the Pope had died the KGB would doubtless have been overjoyed. But there is no evidence in any of the files . . . that it was involved in the attempt on his life."[40]

In Afghanistan, the KGB was central to several of the assassinations and coups that occurred, including the murder of a U.S. ambassador; maintained a stable of hundreds of agents and informants; and tried to undermine the resistance through the use of special units that pretended to be Afghan rebels. The KGB also had primary authority for the creation and operation of an Afghan communist intelligence service, one of whose chiefs, Mohammad Najibullah, became the last communist ruler of Afghanistan. Mitrokhin compiled an extensive study of KGB activities through 1983, and his account reveals numerous KGB maneuvers that, taken together, failed to derail the resistance and contributed significantly to internal divisions among Afghan communist factions. In this way, the KGB may have had a negative impact on the Soviet war in Afghanistan. At a minimum, it succeeded in arousing the suspicions of both the Afghan party and the Soviet military with respect to its own activities.[41]

The 1980s hard-liners in the West claimed that the KGB was behind the Euromissile protests. More specifically, Soviet disinformation ("active measures") had misled what protesters there were who were not actually beholden to Moscow, and the latter were often held to include not just communists, such as the French and Italian communist parties, but the World Peace Council, British labor unions, the Campaign for Nuclear Disarmament, and the Women's International League for Peace and Freedom. In one formulation, John Barron, an author who had been given privileged access to CIA materials for a book about the KGB, wrote that "Soviet fronts helped assemble throngs" for demonstrations. He cited the presence of a KGB officer at a 1981 conference to build the protest movement; a KGB officer, who had been in contact with the Dutch peace movement in his guise as a journalist, expelled from the Netherlands; and a Danish writer arrested for KGB contacts. He also claims active operations to build Euromissile protest movements by the East German intelligence service HVA (Hauptverwaltung Aufklärung, a part of the Stasi).[42] Similarly, the conservative British journalist Chapman Pincher wrote of Soviet propaganda "echoed by the peace movements and the 'willies' [willing], [and that] charged Reagan with 'threatening world peace.'" Or again, "while CND claims to be independent, taking no money from Soviet sources and needing none, it is as sensitive as any other 'peace' movement to the political initiatives concocted by the Politburo."[43]

What remains lacking is evidence that the KGB exercised any controlling role in the antinuclear movement, that Moscow directed the protests. When the Rand Corporation studied the Soviet campaign against the Euromissiles on behalf of the U.S. Air Force in 1985, its analyst decided Moscow had adopted a two-track strategy with a "campaign from above" and one from "below." The latter was the popular campaign, and the Rand study indeed pointed to Soviet front organizations. Rand's analyst, Alexander Alexiev, decided the KGB had a "direct and important, albeit less well-known role" and pointed to Soviet disinformation as the vehicle and to the presence of five hundred KGB and Eastern European intelligence officers and 2,300 HVA agents in West Germany. But charges of "manipulation" of the antinuclear movement were characterized as "allegations."[44] On the eve of deployment, the CIA itself reported on the Soviets and the Euromissiles. Its paper mentioned no specific KGB directive role, and as for Soviet authority in general, that was embodied in instructions from the International Department of the CPSU to Western European communist parties, not the KGB. The CIA report found that "intense pressure" had been put on visiting officials of the Italian Communist Party during a 1981 visit to Moscow.[45] It is suggestive that Vasili Mitrokhin, in his extensive archive on the KGB, produced nothing at all on KGB operations with respect to the antinuclear opposition.[46] More tellingly, the archives of the Stasi, including those of the HVA, were opened after the end of the Cold War and contain an extensive record of East German *intelligence reporting* on the Euromissile opposition, but no indication of an effort to control and direct the movement.[47] The most reasonable conclusion is that the KGB kept informed on antinuclear activities in Western Europe but that Moscow kept its political direction in communist party channels. Whatever actions Moscow in fact took, the KGB did not succeed in preventing deployment of the Euromissiles, leaving the USSR under the threat of the highly capable Pershing IIs.

One hometown KGB operation should also be mentioned. For decades the Soviet service tried to penetrate the U.S. embassy in Moscow. In the 1980s these activities involved both spy operations and technical surveillance. There was a certain amount of controversy over KGB use of a "spy dust" to track Americans moving around Moscow, and more over taping interior conversations by bouncing laser beams off windows. But even more controversy followed in 1984, when the Soviets tried to recruit Clayton Lonetree and other U.S. Marine guards at the embassy. Lonetree would have served to afford the KGB access to the building that could have been used to plant bugs or other devices, but he admitted the recruitment attempt and was sent home. This morphed into concerns that the embassy communications room had already been bugged. No bugs are reported to have been found. More serious by far was the KGB operation to saturate with bugs a new embassy under construction in the Soviet capital. Defector Vladimir Sheymov warned of this activity, and the United States confirmed it in 1982 and 1983. Construction of the building was halted two years later amid a welter of technical surveys and investigations. It resumed only five years later, and the embassy's top floors were destroyed, to be completely replaced by redesigned construction completed under high security.[48] Most serious of all, the *French* embassy actually did find a bugged communications device in 1983, and Paris concluded that the KGB had had access to all its secret communications with the embassy for a period of seven years.[49] The KGB's secret information likely provided the Politburo with useful tidbits but not much more, if only because recent diplomatic practice has increasingly excluded embassies from the most sensitive areas.

One final subject needs mention. Moscow's resource equation could have been affected by KGB technology theft from the West, especially the United States. The Soviet Union had a committee that collected requirements for foreign technology across a dozen ministries and assigned the work to Soviet intelligence. Although Soviet military intelligence actually filled more requirements than the KGB (its officers were more technically knowledgeable, on average, than the KGB's), the spy agency had a full unit of its scientific and technical directorate, Directorate T, and a dedicated network of field agents, Line X, laboring full-time on technology acquisition. Western technology the Soviets acquired enabled the USSR to copy devices or components and could reduce Moscow's expenditures for research and development. This issue had become important in the United States during the Carter administration, and Reagan carried on and amplified technology denial efforts—another instance of an element of the supposed Reagan victory plan actually predating his tenure.

Until 1981 the United States had only a general sense of Soviet technology operations. Moscow was known to be after hardware and documents on computers, lasers, guidance and navigation systems, communications, propulsion systems, sensors, and manufacturing processes and materials. At some point in about 1980, French intelligence recruited a KGB walk-in agent, Col. Vladimir Vetrov, an engineer with Directorate T whose specific task was to evaluate the Soviets' purloined technical secrets. For more than a year, Vetrov, code-named "Farewell," fed the French a series of KGB technology documents, more than four thousand in all. French Socialist president François Mitterrand decided to alert the Americans to this threat. At an economic summit in Ottawa in the summer of 1981, Mitterrand saw Reagan privately and informed him of the Farewell material. The chief of the French internal security service later visited Washington to share particulars of the Farewell file. Vetrov himself was lost—arrested in February 1982 after he knifed a KGB colleague who interrupted Vetrov and his mistress, also wounded, who had been making out in Vetrov's car. The KGB discovered Vetrov's espionage while he was in prison for murder. Farewell was executed in 1985, but the United States, with more detailed leads, was able to trace Soviet technology theft more accurately.[50]

In the summer of 1985 CIA analysts did a detailed survey of the Soviet program, which the Pentagon released as a pamphlet that September. The study claimed that as many as five thousand Soviet programs benefited from technology theft. In the early 1980s the Soviet interministerial committee was issuing requirements at a rate of 3,500 a year, and the Russians had collected something on the order of 30,000 pieces of hardware and 400,000 documents—90 percent of them unclassified—either by theft or simple purchase. Almost two-thirds of the acquisitions were from the United States. Half of the hardware and a substantial portion of the documents went directly to Soviet military research and development. The estimate of Moscow's cost savings from 1976 to 1986 was $700 million.[51]

While the numbers appear huge, the result seems underwhelming. Senior Soviet officials admitted their technology was five to seven years behind the United States. The Soviet targets for theft matched the older technology. Where the United States was embarked on a frenzy of microminiaturization and capacity surge, Soviet targeting focused on more traditional manufacturers. Only three of the nine top corporate targets for Soviet technology theft were electronics manufacturers.[52] Computers are a good example. Russia's mainframe machine was a reverse-engineered variant of the IBM 360 series, current in the United States from the mid-1960s. There were many fewer of them, and they had no equivalent in modern U.S. technology. The highest capacity Soviet machines were equivalent to models superceded in the United States a decade earlier. The most widely distributed Soviet desktop computer ran from paper tapes, not disc drives, and plugged into the television set for a monitor. Core memory in most machines was thirty-two kilobytes of data, where the U.S. standard already stood at 256 K. A clone of the Apple II was produced, but, too expensive, it was discontinued. Scientists and top officials preferred personal computers from IBM or Yamaha. The Soviets were estimated to have produced more than fifty thousand home computers. But the United States alone had manufactured more than 25 million.[53] On the bottom line, if Soviet savings were $700 million over the decade, or even that amount *in a year*, KGB operations were reducing Moscow's burdens by only a tiny fraction. Overall, KGB activity was not capable of turning the course of the Cold War.

Espionage

In the United States, 1985 became known as the "Year of the Spy" for the number of espionage cases that broke into the open at that time. It is appropriate to consider the role of espionage in the end of the Cold War. Did spies give either side a decisive advantage in the events of the 1980s? Is an answer to that question even possible? To take the second question first, while our inquiry cannot be definitive, it can suffice to approach the larger issue. Two decades out, the broad outlines of the spy wars are at least visible and the major agents known. There are undoubtedly spies from the era who remain unknown, but it is highly unlikely at this remove that an agent of central importance would remain completely hidden. Moreover, there are no major policy choices or diplomatic maneuvers by the superpowers that are not accounted for by what *is* known. Thus there is some reason for confidence in our analysis.

There were legions of spies on both sides. An exhaustive treatment is not possible given the scope of this study. And some of the key figures in the shadow war have been mentioned at one point or another in the narrative. Some more will be added here. On the CIA side, Ryszard Kuklinski must take pride of place. Not only did he furnish top secret Soviet and Warsaw Pact data over a very long time, Kuklinski provided key information on Soviet and Polish government intentions in the Solidarity crisis on which the Carter and Reagan administrations based specific diplomatic choices. One spy whose existence, but not identity, is known was (presumably) a senior officer on the Soviet general staff who furnished the

CIA with information on Politburo decisions and Soviet defense policy during Gorbachev's first year. The British gave the CIA access to the critical reports of spy Oleg Gordievsky, whose intelligence proved crucial in the War Scare of 1983. At an important but less critical level was the spy Adolf Tolkachev, who provided inside information on Soviet aircraft and missile programs until his arrest in June 1985. Lesser spies provided information on Soviet naval activities and Warsaw Pact military forces. Through France, the CIA obtained information from Vladimir Vetrov that opened eyes on the whole area of Soviet technological theft. In the sense of logic, the sum of this human intelligence was necessary but not sufficient. A spy may have prevented nuclear war in 1983, and another enabled the United States to tailor its policy on Poland in a way that minimized the chance of an outbreak of war while discouraging a Soviet invasion. Beyond that, CIA spies did not win the Cold War.

Soviet spies were even less successful in terms of the big picture. The KGB gathered very important information, but it never penetrated the president's inner circle, the NSC staff, the State Department, or the Pentagon. The agents of the Year of the Spy were led by the Walker ring, a network of two brothers, John and Arthur Walker, and a friend, Jerry Whitworth, who gave the Soviets access to naval communications from 1967 to 1984. They gave the Soviets a window on U.S. naval operations and order of battle information but had no access to policy information. Ronald Pelton, an employee of the National Security Agency, gave the KGB data on U.S. code-breaking efforts, in particular a penetration of Soviet military communications channels. Two other spies uncovered that year were not KGB agents at all, but worked for Israel and China respectively. By far the KGB's most valuable agents were Aldrich Ames in the CIA and Robert Hanssen of the FBI. Ames began spying in 1985 and Hanssen in 1979. Both remained active into the 1990s—Hanssen in fact until 2001. There were also lesser fry, including the CIA's Edward Howard, who defected in 1983 while still an officer in training, and Karl F. Koecher, a contract officer who worked for the Czechs and whose information was reported to Moscow.

Some observers argue that spies have no larger importance—that their information merely fuels the shadow wars and eliminates spies for the other side. There is some value to this view. The Soviets' CIA, NSA, and FBI spies were indeed mostly useful for data on the adversary's spying. But like the CIA with Gordievsky and Vetrov, some of the KGB's best information came from allies, in this case, the East Germans, whose penetrations in West Germany included senior officials, among them government ministers, senior aides, and at least one general. The Soviets also had at least one penetration in Norway, an agent who worked for NATO at times and could pass information from that source. But the poverty of the KGB's sources is suggested by the fact that in several years of intense concentration, their Operation RYAN never could fulfill its collection requirements. And, beyond policy, the most important U.S. military secrets were those associated with a new generation of weapons, inter-netted with data links that the United States saw as "force multipliers," equipped with precision guidance and so-called stealth technology, plus military doctrines to govern them. The KGB achieved little discernible success against these targets either, although it never stopped trying.

To the overarching question posed here, the answer must be that espionage did not convey decisive advantage to either side. The CIA achieved a position of relative superiority in obtaining vital intelligence, but that did not translate into a major policy leverage, and the advantage disappeared in 1985 with the wholesale destruction of the CIA's agent networks in the wake of betrayal by Ames and Hanssen. For half a decade until the Cold War's end, espionage proved essentially a null factor in the evolution of events.

Predicting the Collapse of the Soviet Union

The CIA could have made good use of a well-placed spy in the last throes of the Cold War. Ever since, there has persisted a dispute over whether the CIA "missed" the end of the conflict, whether the Cold War's end represented a CIA intelligence failure. This is the last great debate over the shadow war, and a study of how the Cold War ended would not be complete without considering this question. There are multiple parts to the problem, and each will be discussed briefly. One question, prefigured early in this chapter, is how far pressures on the CIA militated against a timely prediction of the Soviet collapse. There is also the matter of whether different parts of the agency (the Offices of Soviet Analysis or Global Issues and the National Intelligence Council—that is, analysts versus estimators) shared the same views on the USSR. And there is the normative question of the degree to which accurate forecasts were obstructed by conceptual factors. In addition, there is the "light at the end of the tunnel" question: at what point did the Soviet collapse begin to come into view? Finally, we get to the actual CIA reporting and the associated, policy-oriented matter of whether the CIA gave warning of the Moscow coup d'etat. The existence of an intelligence failure in the Soviet case has almost been assumed. Is that conventional wisdom correct?

Pressures on the CIA certainly existed from the beginning of the Reagan administration. As related, the administration, in particular its policy entrepreneurs, were wedded to a certain view of the Soviet threat. Intelligence analyses pointing to Soviet disintegration had a hard road to follow and making them could be career-threatening for analysts. These conditions did not persist throughout the period, however; the character of external pressures changed. President Reagan moved toward accommodation between about 1985 and 1988. Under President George H. W. Bush, the climate changed again. During Bush's first year, the administration reverted to a more pessimistic view of the Soviets, but that was the year of the fall of the Berlin Wall and disappearance of the Soviet client states. After the December 1989 Malta summit, Bush moved quickly to a position quite supportive of Gorbachev, almost a condominium between the superpowers. As far as CIA analyses are concerned, pressures on the agency then favored *optimistic* reporting on Gorbachev, creating a new obstacle to accurate appreciation of the Soviet collapse. To some degree, a window opened between about 1985 and 1988, during which time the CIA's reporting was least likely to bump up against policy predispositions. But this point can be overdone. In January 1987 Secretary of State George Shultz complained so vociferously about the CIA's manipulating him with its reporting that Robert Gates met with him in an effort to still the waters.[54] Both before and after that, the situation was even more complicated.

Differences also existed within the CIA. Management of analysts posed one problem. At the top level of management was Robert Gates, first as deputy director for intelligence, then as deputy director for central intelligence, the number two job in the U.S. intelligence community. In the former role, Gates had final approval authority on papers from the line analytical units, the Office of Soviet Analysis and the Office of Global Issues. In both jobs, Gates had a supervisory role over the officers of the National Intelligence Council (NIC), responsible for the estimates. Gates writes, "I believe to this day that my skepticism in early 1986 that [Gorbachev] intended to revolutionize both foreign and domestic policy was justified by his actions."[55] In their 1987 encounter, Gates told Shultz that NIC officers had strong views and were inclined to venture beyond their "legitimate intelligence role." He needed to "rein them in."[56] Differences between analysts and estimators also existed. Papers from units like SOVA and OGI went through an editing process in which office chiefs could force revisions, make analysts redo their sums, demand more evidence for an assertion, and so on. These devices could improve the product, but they could also be used to suppress unwanted views. Gates appointed those office chiefs and had a say on the hiring of NIC officers too. Kay Oliver was the chief at OGI. The chiefs at SOVA from 1984 through 1992 were George Kolt and Douglas MacEachin. Senior analyst Mel Goodman, a branch chief at SOVA through this period, describes both as "intelligence hawks."[57] They also served as national intelligence officers for the Soviet Union on the NIC, a post Gates himself held early in the decade. Noncomforming views on the USSR had to jump a high hurdle.

Beyond personal difficulties lay the conceptual issues. One set of these concerned purely technical matters. Problems with estimating the Soviet economy have already been mentioned. Economists—and not just with the CIA—had a hard enough time with Western economies, where government budgets, corporate earnings, profits, personal income, agricultural production, market trends, and currency exchange rates were all publicly available data, and both official and private sector sources made it their business to collect that data and present it. For the Soviet Union, the data was just not there, much of it considered national security secrets; budget figures disguised more than they revealed, currency values were not available because the ruble did not trade in international exchange markets, and the five-year plans conveyed an impression of stability we now know to have been inaccurate. Political information was equally sketchy. Reaganite Kenneth Adelman, complaining later of the intelligence, remarked that the CIA did not even know whether Andropov had a wife until she appeared in mourning at his funeral. That was just an example, but it was true that perfectly acceptable tradecraft included scanning photographs of senior Soviet leaders atop Lenin's Tomb for clues to who had primacy in the Politburo. A generation of "Kremlinologists" cut their teeth reading the tea leaves of pictures, the meaning behind the speeches the Soviets chose to publicize, and the statistics they chose to release. Beyond the data problems lay the dimensions of the upheaval at issue in the Soviet collapse. To predict that a superpower—an authoritarian state at that, known for its internal controls, with a history seven decades long—would simply be swept away? *That* required special analytical acumen. In the face of bureaucratic obstacles, administration predispositions, and conceptual problems, *expecting* the CIA to successfully predict revolutionary change in the Soviet Union should more properly be seen as having been unrealistic.

For all these obstacles, U.S. intelligence did a good job of remaining alert to the possibilities. Over time, the sense of a Soviet economy in peril hardened into a definite understanding of Moscow in extremis. Within months of the advent of

Gorbachev, SOVA warned that his "attempt to bolster popular support for the regime carries political risk. . . . [It] could generate concern within key bureaucracies that they are being circumvented, and generate popular expectations that he may not be able to satisfy."[58] CIA analysis found the Soviet industrial base antiquated, the energy sector stagnant, technology lagging, agriculture inefficient, and the bureaucracy hidebound. Soviet economic growth was written down to a historic low of 1.4 percent for the four years until 1982. Kay Oliver's paper, the one briefed to Reagan before the Geneva summit, was repeated as an NIE in November 1985. It found "growing tension between popular aspirations and the system's ability to satisfy them."[59] By 1986 the CIA was telling the Joint Economic Committee (JEC) of Congress that refurbishing the Soviet industrial base was certain to involve conflict with the defense sector, an assessment based on another SOVA paper. After the Soviets' Twenty-seventh Party Congress, the CIA predicted that tensions within "the Gorbachev camp" over the pace of change would be a key indicator.[60] In February 1987 SOVA predicted that Gorbachev's "cautious changes" would fall short of his goals.[61] By April 1988 the CIA view presented to the JEC held that "too few economic resources [are] chasing too many needs" and that Gorbachev's goals were themselves overambitious.[62] Two months later, SOVA observed that "meager progress" in industrial modernization "creates powerful incentives for at least a short-term reduction in military procurement."[63] In September 1988 SOVA warned that whatever Gorbachev's successes, they had alienated elites and created the possibility of a leadership crisis.[64] All these CIA reports identified trends actually at work in the USSR, ones that led to the collapse.

The CIA's observations on the conflict between economic revitalization and military development in the Soviet Union were accentuated within months when Gorbachev appeared at the United Nations to declare his unilateral withdrawals of Soviet troops from the Warsaw Pact countries. Coincidentally, that same day, a CIA team led by Douglas MacEachin and Robert Blackwell, the national intelligence officer for the Soviet Union, was briefing the Senate Intelligence Committee. Blackwell told the senators that Gorbachev's moves to revamp the party bureaucracy had effectively neutered the CPSU Central Committee, were an extremely sensitive move, and would not have been expected even six months earlier. MacEachin's deputy told the group that Gorbachev seemed to have decided on a course of even more radical economic reforms; that the economy had performed poorly, with plans for 1989 that were even more inflationary; and that the Soviet budget deficit "is coming home to roost." Several of the intelligence officers noted disputes within the community over Soviet economic problems and their impact on military forces, and were resistant to predicting force cuts of even twenty thousand to fifty thousand troops. MacEachin said, "In all honesty, had we said a week ago that Gorbachev might come to the UN and offer a unilateral cut of 500,000 in the military, we would have been told we were crazy."[65] Indeed that was true.

At what point did it become possible to forecast revolutionary upheaval in Russia? This was the moment. Within a few short months from December 7, 1988, Gorbachev would slice Soviet military forces, pull Russian troops out of Afghanistan, cast off party controls, witness Estonia assert autonomy by demanding that Russians learn its language, suffer the effects of the Russian military's shot across the bow—its crushing of the demonstration at Tbilisi—and see Solidarity legalized in Poland and the beginning of roundtable talks. Until that time, it is not reasonable to have expected a forecast of Soviet collapse. Until late 1988, analysts could argue over the success of reforms but the context remained that of a stable USSR. Some had an inkling—Robert Blackwell told the group that day in December 1988:

> The revolution we're talking about in the Soviet Union—I really think it is, Gorbachev describes it that way—it is really part of—it's a global communist revolution. All of those systems in one way or another are coming up to the natural limits of the Stalinist order. The problem for every one of them has essentially been they've adopted some form of Stalinist mechanism for running and controlling their country and they have come up against the revision of the superstructure. . . . It simply is not working in this environment.[66]

Surprisingly, this vision was closer to what Robert Gates was saying at the time, and further from the vision of the director of central intelligence, by then William H. Webster. In an October 1988 speech, Gates had expressed pessimism that Gorbachev could succeed, whereas on December 12 Webster told the Council on Foreign Relations that Gorbachev was "a highly skilled politician," adding that he had "brought new life and dynamism to Soviet politics" and that "we cannot rule out the possibility that he . . . can, ultimately, pull off a revolution from above."[67] The revolution Webster anticipated was the success of perestroika.

This is where the CIA missed its opportunity for prescience. Its contribution to the incoming Bush administration's policy review on the Soviet Union was hedged and bureaucratic. Condoleezza Rice, at the time the NSC staffer responsible for Soviet affairs, would dismiss it as not "presidential." As Rice put it, the

CIA report "wasn't in any sense of that word forward-leaning. It wasn't operational. It got the moniker 'status-quo plus.'"[68] The CIA was pulled between leaders who held different views on the potential of Soviet reforms and an administration at first suspicious of Gorbachev, then his cheerleader. That made the alternatives either the Soviet leader or a hard-line successor regime, not a new country. Analysts confronted this issue in September 1989, in a report that actually used the phrase "centrifugal trends" referring to Soviet problems but pictured them as applying only to Gorbachev or a successor. Written by Grey Hodnett, a SOVA officer, the paper argued that implementation of market reforms would likely delay economic recovery indefinitely, that the fragmentation of political power would continue, but that Gorbachev was unlikely to use force or impose martial law.[69] President Bush remarks, "I found the CIA experts particularly helpful, if pessimistic."[70] At this time, Robert Gates, by then in the White House as deputy national security adviser, quietly set up an interagency group to consider actions to take in the event of a Soviet collapse.

A pair of national intelligence estimates frame the most authoritative judgments offered by U.S. intelligence during this period. An NIE published just ahead of the Malta summit looked at the Soviet system in crisis and found its problems so large they were expected to endure beyond the two-year period of the analysis. Estimators projected the economy would progress very little or even decline. But the prediction for Gorbachev was sanguine, his position viewed as "relatively" secure, his power significantly enhanced. Measures were expected to curb the press and rein in the nationalities. A less likely scenario depicted Gorbachev using "massive force to hold the country together and save the regime." Buried in the text of the NIE as one of several "far less likely" outcomes—seemingly to ensure all bases were covered—was a scenario in which Gorbachev lost control of the situation when ethnic violence and separatist demands led to "social revolution." The analysis hardly measured up to the opinion Robert Blackwell, the manager responsible for its drafting, had expressed a year earlier. In fact, SOVA inserted a dissent in the estimate, insisting that neither the existing Soviet system nor the one Gorbachev aimed for could cope with the crisis and that the more probable end state would be a chaotic but increasingly pluralistic nation. It added that a military intervention would most likely be led by traditionalist leaders who had outmaneuvered Gorbachev.[71] Director Webster told Congress in March 1990, describing this NIE, that Gorbachev's removal would lead to a neo-Stalinist leadership, but one not inclined to reverse Soviet reforms.[72] It needs to be said that by this time it had become almost a parlor game in Washington to guess how long Gorbachev had left—I participated in it myself—so the CIA would have been on exceedingly precarious ground in finding his leadership secure. But the question remains whether a Soviet leadership change or a collapse was foreseen.

By November 1990, with the Soviet republics clearly restive and the economy a shambles, U.S. intelligence cast a new estimate but considered the situation so volatile that it refused to make any prediction covering more than one year. This NIE found the situation fragile and a strong probability that the Soviet crisis would worsen, perhaps greatly. Responding to policymaker demands, the CIA framed estimates with more explicit probability ratings, and this NIE forecast a 50-50 chance the Soviet situation would deepen but retain its texture and a 20 percent or less chance of any of three other scenarios: anarchy, a military coup, or a breakthrough to Gorbachev's goal of a democratic market-driven society. But for the case of the military intervention—the scenario that actually occurred—the NIE predicted a probability "much lower" than the 1 in 5 generic rating given these scenarios. In fact, "Community analysts believe a coup—either by the military acting alone or in conjunction with the security services and CPSU traditionalists—to be the least likely variant." And the NIE projected a better than even chance that a USSR comprising certain of the republics, including the Russian Federation, would survive. Analysts made no prediction as to Gorbachev's hold on power, but they accurately viewed Yeltsin as having superior political strength.[73]

In-house CIA defenders claim to have successfully predicted the end of the Cold War, largely based on the presence of the coup scenario and on one other paper, a more tactical sort of warning issued in April 1991. This SOVA paper, "The Soviet Cauldron," baldly opened by declaring the Soviet empire and system of governance were breaking down. After citing indications for that point and observing that Gorbachev had been forced into expedient measures by the traditionalists, the paper found that "explosive events have become increasingly possible," pointing to "preparations for a broad use of force in the political process" by military and KGB leaders. The CIA correctly noted that Gorbachev, while he might not wish such an intervention, was "increasing the chance of it through his personnel appointments" and "estrangement" from the reformers. Analysts also predicted that an effort at intervention would begin in Moscow, by targeting Yeltsin. Finally, the CIA anticipated the putsch would fail and that reformers would make it an opportunity for a "strategic breakthrough" to democracy.[74]

When the anti-Gorbachev plotters made their move, the Bush administration, alerted by this CIA analysis and warned by Moscow mayor Gavriil Popov's private approach to Ambassador Matlock, was surprised only by the specific timing and incidentals. But this does not get the CIA off the hook for intelligence failure in the collapse of the Soviet Union. As often happens, the story is more complicated than that. In this case, the CIA operated under numerous political, institutional, and conceptual constraints. Despite those obstacles, U.S. intelligence managed to track the broad outlines of Soviet decline pretty well. It maintained a healthy skepticism regarding Gorbachev's reforms and even had an inkling of revolution when the end began to come into view. Yet the CIA failed to make the last step. Revolutionary change in the USSR was appreciated as a theoretical possibility but a very low-order probability, in large part because of a failure of imagination—how could a superpower simply disintegrate?—and because to some degree U.S. intelligence was seduced by the "Gorby-mania" that pervaded the Bush administration. Predicting revolutionary change is inherently difficult, and in the final analysis the CIA did not quite manage to do it.

The Impact of Defense Programs and Intelligence Activities

Many national security designs and defense programs dominated U.S. policy during the final decade of the Cold War. Intelligence activities operated underneath the surface, and intelligence analysts helped leaders understand the meaning of what happened in the open. The same was true in the Soviet Union. The narrative has discussed various aspects of this shadow conflict. The interactions between defense programs and intelligence, the operations of the CIA and KGB, the activities of spies, and the contribution of the CIA to predicting the Soviet collapse have all been considered. A number of observations are pertinent.

First, the triumphalist narrative of the outcome is importantly flawed. It imputes a degree of perspicacity to American leaders that did not exist or existed only as an inchoate belief in the future. The notion of the secret plan endows coherence and purposefulness to many actions that were actually undertaken for other reasons. These were judgments made after the fact, *post hoc* as in the term of art. Intervening developments (changes in the energy market or the actions of the Polish government vis-á-vis Solidarity, for example) are attributed to the operation of the plan without serious attention to other explanations in this kind of post hoc analysis. Equally important, the narrative *telescopes time* by assuming that the final outcome of the Cold War was visible to Reagan administration officials engaging in their very preliminary battles at the beginning of the decade. Even had a secret plan existed *and* postulating that Reagan officials had had the *strategic goal* of winning the Cold War, the state of play in 1981 was such that the measures adopted could do no more than advance the ball on the field. Victory was not an option at that time. As for the Soviets, there is no evidence that they had equivalent intentions.

Defense policies and intelligence programs, more importantly, did not affect the overall Cold War situation the way triumphalists would like to believe. Military developments in general, defense spending, weapons technology, arms racing, and the associated elements of the superpower strategic balance were measures of hostility in the Cold War. They were not a structural element in themselves and were not capable of ending the Cold War, except in one case: that where the Cold War might have turned hot and ended in a world-altering military engagement. Moscow's fear that the United States might attain an overwhelming nuclear superiority could have activated that possibility, which makes it especially disturbing that Reagan administration officials did not go out of their way to be especially alert for evidence of the kinds of Soviet concerns manifest in the Able Archer 83 episode. The triumphalist argument that U.S. defense spending bankrupted Moscow falls before the evidence that *Soviet* defense investment followed its own course and never responded to American, except in the most general way. Conversely, the adherents of this view avoid dealing with the extent to which the swollen defense budgets the administration introduced contributed to the Reagan recession of the early 1980s or to the evidence that the additional U.S. defense spending actually resulted in few new weapons entering the American arsenal.

Intelligence operations, meanwhile, affected the Cold War competition only at the margin. Reagan-era covert operations in Europe had an indeterminate impact, dwarfed by the penetration of the iron curtain by the simple idea of human rights norms. In the third world in general, U.S. covert operations had little effect. In Afghanistan, these operations had a greater specific effect on the Soviets, but in a context in which the Afghan War as a whole was a minor element in the overall constellation of Moscow's problems. Meanwhile, Soviet covert operations, largely aimed at influencing the popular movement against the Euromissiles in the West, also conveyed limited discernible advantages. On both sides, such operations had significant potential for negative impact on the perpetrators, whether the weakening of a Euromissile opposition was discovered to have been manipulated by Moscow or an American president was caught in activities of questionable legality by a CIA covert operation. Covert operations were a double-edged sword. The overall impact of secret services on both sides was marginal in the evolution of events.

Intelligence analysis should have served as a mechanism for reducing tensions. Better understanding of the perceptions and fears of the adversary could have enabled leaders to avoid those actions most likely to exacerbate tensions *if the leaders' intent had been to prevent conflict.* Moscow was largely denied that opportunity owing to the weakness of its apparatus for analyzing intelligence. Washington's ability to rely upon this tool was limited deliberately—by CIA and Pentagon officials intent upon waging their anti-Soviet campaign—who combined to ensure that intelligence reporting would avoid the kinds of judgments that challenged their action plans.

The Reagan administration assumed office with a sense that the Soviet Union was on the move and that the United States was vulnerable to Soviet attack. It made a very conscious effort to reverse that perception with respect to strategic nuclear forces. But the administration worked with and profited politically from conservative attacks on U.S. intelligence that served to inhibit any CIA judgment that the Soviets were, in fact, inferior. That good judgments emerged nonetheless was a result of diligent, even heroic, efforts by CIA analysts. Meanwhile, in its operational role, the CIA engaged in a variety of covert actions that complicated Soviet policies but did not destroy the USSR. Similarly, the KGB engaged in a series of activities of its own that had some impact but fell short of seriously affecting U.S. or NATO policies. The sides also scored some notable successes in espionage, but again the shadow war did not determine the Cold War. Finally, the CIA tracked the decline of the Soviet Union but in the last analysis failed to predict the Soviet collapse. Intelligence activities of all kinds figure enough in how the Cold War ended that no substantive study can be considered complete without accounting for them, but by themselves the spies did not win (or lose) the Cold War.

Thesis and Conclusions

Now a few points on doing history. The most vital concerns perspective. This is really a discussion on the role of "objectivity." The triumphalist narrative is important here in another way. The present study has shown how, in various ways on a number of levels, the triumphalist narrative distorts or ignores elements of the story of the Cold War's final years. These distortions or lacunae did not happen by accident. Emphasizing certain elements and minimizing or suppressing others is *necessary* to create an account that leads to a certain conclusion. "Ronald Reagan won the Cold War" became the point of departure in structuring that narrative, and facts plus standards for inclusion had then to be chosen to substantiate that thesis. This is a danger that every historian should avoid.

Before going any further, it is crucial to note that a thesis *is* necessary in any historical study. The analyst organizes ideas and alerts her/himself to relevant data by elaborating a thesis and then specifying the range of information required to examine what has been postulated. In addition, the thesis is the first step toward creating a conclusion (about which more in a moment). The conclusion is the space where the historian takes the information and analyses developed through the narrative and applies them to the thesis. The triumphalists do nothing wrong in having a thesis.

Other historians may differ, but I am not going to argue that the fault was one of "objectivity." Instead, I would make the observation that every historian has a point of view and brings that to the material. A value-neutral stance would be very useful, but few are capable of achieving that level of perfection. What *is* possible, however, is objectivity with respect to information, facts, the historical record. The historian gathers the relevant data, performs such intermediate analyses as may be necessary, and constructs a narrative that relates the data to the thesis. Material that belongs in a deliberation of the thesis should be included irrespective of whether the author's point of view is supported thereby. What is possible is to be objective with respect to the presentation of information. The skill of the historian goes into explaining how data demonstrates the thesis, even more so into showing how or why discrepant information does not derail it. Another element of practical objectivity is the historian's responsibility to modify the thesis or acknowledge when the facts fail to support it. Triumphalism falls short in meeting these tests. The historian herself is the first judge of satisfaction, but be sure that readers and peers will uphold standards if the author failed to do so.

A few words on conclusions will be offered here since I will present the conclusion of this text without any section on working in history. On a depressingly frequent basis, I encounter studies that consist of narrative—sometimes massive amounts of narrative—and little or no conclusion, almost as if the author has run out of steam in reaching this point and wants to do nothing more than exit the project. This is a mistake, one not difficult to avoid, and it is no simple matter of space devoted to a final chapter. Long conclusions that say little are also objectionable. Rather, the conclusion is a moment of unparalleled opportunity. Here the author, having established facts and debated intermediate points, has created the basis to drive home the historical argument.

With a properly designed research project, the historian has a thesis and the data that bear on it, either confirming or refuting the original proposition. (The conclusion is not the place to introduce new data, which should be done in earlier sections, though an exception can be made for theoretical or methodological considerations that bear on the concluding argument.) There are also the themes the author has selected and brought back into the narrative at various stages in its progression. And there is the question of implications that can be drawn from either thesis or themes. Discussion of these points provides meat for the conclusion. Here the historian should bring back the themes of the narrative, comment on how what was found following each of these lines of inquiry contributes to the overall subject, summarize the contributions of any data not already covered, reintroduce the thesis, and discuss the validity of that proposition in the light of the other material. Finally, the author should draw out the implications of thesis and themes. Do these things, and you will have executed a successful historical inquiry. Having said all that we ask again, how did the Cold War end?

CHAPTER 7

HOW THE COLD WAR ENDED

A NUANCED ARTICULATION OF THE END OF THE COLD WAR is now possible. Having layered a series of discussions of many different sets of factors upon our initial, bare-bones presentation of this history, the narrative changes in important respects.

The Reagan administration took office in 1981 with the intention of reversing what it viewed as adverse trends in international relations that favored the Soviet Union. There was determination to fight the Soviets, and officials undertook a number of measures designed to retard Soviet economic progress or technological improvements or to contend with Moscow over specific Cold War battlefields. The actual status of the military balance, as opposed to the officials' impression or their public descriptions of it, especially with respect to strategic nuclear forces, was much more favorable to the United States. Increased defense spending by the Reagan administration preserved existing trends and accentuated U.S. nuclear superiority. The administration's reluctance to negotiate equitable arms reduction agreements, its aggressive rhetorical stance, its combativeness on Cold War battlefronts, and its evident military investments all contributed to a widespread impression—a global one, not merely in Moscow—that the United States sought to heat up the Cold War confrontation.

Beneath its outward appearance and superpower trappings, the Soviet Union had entered a phase of stagnation. Long-standing educational programs and a modicum of economic development had produced a better-educated Soviet polity with increasingly sophisticated tastes and a standard of living higher than that of previous generations. But growth in the Soviet command economy, driven by planners in a series of multiyear programs, favored heavy industry and military production, leading to an accumulation of unfulfilled consumer demand and to increasing public frustration. Inefficiencies in the industrial system and rigidities in standing practices further constrained the system's ability to cope with these problems. The philosophical and ideological tenets of Soviet communism increasingly failed to overcome the public's ennui. Security measures were also unable to curb an increasingly disaffected and vocal intelligentsia. Soviet leaders further complicated their situation by disguising shortfalls and by filling budget deficits through drawing on the public's savings.

Dynamic global forces operated to the detriment of the Soviet Union. The oil boom of the 1970s proved to be a Trojan horse for Moscow. Initially, very favorable prices led Soviet leaders to believe they could solve their problems with trade, stocking stores with foreign consumer goods and taking the pressures off allies by subsidizing their energy costs. Moscow made a fateful decision to maximize output by pumping more oil rather than investing in production technology, which resulted in a crash landing in the mid-1980s, when production had peaked in existing old fields, new ones had not been developed, and world oil prices had declined. At that point, the Soviet Union had overcommitted its available resources in a climate of diminishing foreign income.

The rise of nationalism and ethnic politics across the globe affected the Soviet Union very specifically. Moscow was well aware of its nationalities problem and had had policies in this area since the nation's beginnings. But to be aware was not to solve, and for decades Soviet leaders had discounted the problem, running the Union for the benefit of the Russian ethnic group. Leaders continued to minimize the problem into the 1980s, a moment when ethnic activism surged, at first demanding language training, then increased autonomy, and finally independence. The nationalities' agitation created centrifugal forces that pushed apart the republics of the USSR. The ethnic movements proved far too strong to be suppressed by security measures. Political accommodation opened the door to concessions that weakened central control from Moscow.

The ethnic movements were assisted by the rise of another global trend, the increasing acceptance of human rights norms. Acknowledging group and individual expression, the human rights movement also encouraged nationalism in the states of the Soviet periphery, which had been kept in the empire by the collective security embodied in the Warsaw Pact, by foreign aid and trade subsidies, and by ideological control. But the same phenomena of rising expectations, rigid economies, and declining export income that affected the USSR devastated the nations of East-Central Europe. Soviet leverage declined as the allied states faced the vagaries of domestic discontent and the challenge of economic failure. The allies' measures to solve their own problems weakened the Soviet empire and eventually forced Moscow to choose between military intervention and acquiescence in the demise of the Warsaw Pact.

Poland's Solidarity crisis posed the first test case for Moscow's control of the periphery. Ronald Reagan came to office when the Polish crisis was already well under way, at a moment when the Soviets had already been dissuaded from an initial intervention. President Reagan's efforts to sustain Polish dissidents, and CIA programs to assist them, were marginal to the main lines of development of the Polish transformation. Economic problems forced the Polish government to retrench, with measures that could be successful only if given popular support, forcing government concessions to the dissidents. Moscow's intervention to preserve the client state would have required the expenditure of such resources to prop up the regime that the option was effectively foreclosed. Variants of this scenario were enacted in each of the countries of East-Central Europe.

Dynamic forces structured the problem, but individual agency played a key role in these and other events of the decade. Labor leader Wałęsa for the Polish dissidents, Prime Minister Jaruzelski for the government, and Pope John Paul II for the Catholic Polish polity all made moves that converted sharp crisis to political evolution and ultimately to roundtable talks that resulted in transition to a democratic noncommunist government. In effect, individual agency became crucial to *peaceful* transition. The same would be true in Hungary, Czechoslovakia, Bulgaria, and East Germany. And Mikhail Gorbachev's role would be paramount, a point to which we shall return shortly.

To some degree in the East, to a greater extent in the United States, and with considerable political power throughout Western Europe, fear of nuclear war operated as a dynamic force. Fears focused on the Euromissiles. The publics in several countries were roused to such intensity that deployment of the U.S. missile forces incurred huge political costs. Despite the strong efforts of Reagan administration policy entrepreneurs, Euromissile deployment would be a pyrrhic victory. On the Soviet side, top leaders condemned the military for creating a major headache for Soviet diplomacy. On the U.S. side, the NATO alliance was strained by the pressures exerted to compel allied cooperation in the deployment. At a certain level, the political forces manifest in the Euromissile opposition helped convince a conservative West German government to improve its trade and relations with the Soviet

Union and ultimately to assist in the country's reunification by defraying Soviet costs for withdrawal from East Germany.

Also manifest in the missile deployment, at least of the Pershing IIs, was the extreme military threat to the Soviet Union. This prospect crystallized Moscow's fears, immanent since 1981 and expressed in the KGB's Operation RYAN special collection program, and led to the War Scare of 1983. That moment could have been the end of history had one more spark lit the kindling, but instead it galvanized one of the major individual actors, Ronald Reagan. From the beginning of 1984, the president rose above his policy entrepreneurs, rejecting their counsel in favor of reaching out to Moscow. Between the Geneva and Reykjavik summits, Reagan and Gorbachev put in place a framework for negotiation that began to move the superpowers toward agreements on reducing nuclear arms. Never again would the Cold War be so dark, never again would the nuclear factor drive confrontation. A leader had stared into the abyss and backed away from it.

Individual agency did not exercise a uniform effect. On the U.S. side many of the policy entrepreneurs worked to sharpen the Cold War conflict. President Reagan's vision and rhetoric initially sustained these entrepreneurs, and his management methods gave them virtually free rein to implement aggressive policies. Collectively, the entrepreneurs' efforts helped create the situation that made nuclear war a possibility in 1983. Later, at Reykjavik, they collaborated to torpedo a presidential negotiating initiative. President Reagan gained great credit for turning away from the trend toward confrontation. This, rather than his initial approach, may have been his greatest contribution to ending the Cold War. Meanwhile, Moscow had its own difficulties with entrepreneurs. The "traditionalists," as they became known to U.S. intelligence officers, did a great deal to obstruct and delay Soviet reforms, intervened against the republics, and ended by mounting a coup d'etat that became the catalyst for the Soviet Union's disintegration. Whatever chances there had been for Soviet reform, success was critically dependent on rapid action, so the traditionalists' obstruction and foot-dragging had both indirect and direct impact on the Soviet collapse. For every Reagan there was a Yazov. At both the top and at institutional levels, individual agency retains its importance in the Cold War narrative.

The preeminent Great Leader of this tale has to be Mikhail Gorbachev. His predecessors had begun to recognize the Soviet malaise. Andropov took steps to search for a solution, but it was Gorbachev who did something about it. Political acumen and agility enabled Gorbachev to find a way forward when, time after time, his reform measures bumped into obstructions or stalled in the face of the dimensions of the USSR's difficulties. Gorbachev's willingness to confront problems head-on permitted him to attempt reforms in the first place, and his determination to transform the Soviet Union gave him the will not to give up. But his tendency to hesitate cost the loss of the key moment when mere reform might still have been possible. His problem-solving attitude enabled him to see accommodation with the West as a tool for reforming the USSR, and realism enabled him to relinquish Moscow's hold on the empire of the periphery once the cost of maintaining it became too high. But Gorbachev's weaknesses also lay at the center of the union's demise—his propensity to change course at the first crosswind denied some reform efforts the time necessary to take effect. Pragmatism led Gorbachev to dismantle the rule of the Communist Party of the Soviet Union in the course of trying to save the nation and at a time when the institutions of Union government were inadequate to substitute for the old forms of leadership. Gorbachev's unwillingness to recognize the severity of the nationalities problem precluded early action that might have prevented centrifugal forces from spiraling out of control. And his feud with Boris Yeltsin robbed the union of its best source of potential support, while his predilection for tactical compromises afforded the anti-perestroika traditionalists the opening needed for their plot against him. The impacts of Gorbachev's human dimension on the Soviet Union—both positive and negative—show beyond doubt that despite the operation of global forces the individual continues to have a primary role in the evolution of historical events.

As the foregoing discussion suggests, my analysis is that the main lines of development in the end of the Cold War resulted from the forces and factors that figured in the Soviet Union's gamble for survival. The West was not simply a bystander. European bank credits, technology exports, and other trade, such as they were, helped Soviet leaders to a certain degree, and a greater flow might have afforded Gorbachev some leeway in his reform efforts. The same is true of American trade. But Reagan administration efforts in these and other areas, however purposeful, had an impact only at the margins of the Soviet crisis. And traditional strategies of containment, left behind by Reagan, restored to a degree by Bush, did not worsen the Soviet problem so much as slow the development of policies that might have fostered a degree of cooperation—assisting the Soviet Union with the aim of maintaining international stability.

The Reagan defense buildup did not force an offsetting Soviet military investment. The CIA's political actions in East-Central Europe were not determinative

in the creation or growth of dissidence in the empire and did not measurably accelerate the process of transformation along the Soviet periphery. The forces that
accomplished this were global in nature and already in play. The Berlin Wall fell
and the Soviet empire disappeared because the governments of Moscow's allies
were overcome by permanently operating factors—worldwide economic trends
and normative changes with which, given their structural rigidities, the Soviets were
unable to cope. This was not a result of U.S. policy action. The CIA's war in Afghanistan, however serious a problem it posed for the Soviet military, was a relatively small feature on the menu of the USSR's problems. In fact, the available data
indicates that the costs of the Afghan War, Soviet foreign aid, and Soviet imports
(including grain *and* technology), added together, did not amount to as much as
Moscow's annual budget deficit. The War Scare of 1983 *did* produce pressures for
conciliation (on both sides), but given that the Reagan administration was hardly
aware of this event at the time—and not convinced of it afterward—the crisis
cannot be accounted a part of Washington's plan for the Cold War. If the United
States *had* contrived this crisis in order to produce a Cold War breakthrough, that
would not be very comforting either—nuclear brinkmanship in an era of vulnerable land-based missile forces postured on hair-trigger alert would have been no
act of statesmanship. Ronald Reagan bears some responsibility for managing institutions and entrepreneurs in a fashion that made excess possible, although he
deserves credit for altering course in the wake of it. In the end, U.S. actions had
only a marginal effect on the outcome, and Soviet internal contradictions had a
fundamental one.

Though President Reagan changed course during the latter part of his administration, the first President Bush resumed a policy of seeking U.S. advantage
through a process of diplomatic engagement with Moscow. This poses the alternative questions of, first, whether the American turning would even have happened had George H. W. Bush been the U.S. leader in the early 1980s, and, second,
whether a cooperative stance unveiled earlier might have yielded a different result.
The hypotheticals are unanswerable, of course, except for speculation. On the
first, a Bush administration, sensing its advantage, might have pressed Moscow in
such a way as to push the Soviets into initiating war. This was still the period of
Andropov, after all, and the Soviet fears were intense. On the second hypothetical,
global forces were not to be denied. Continued Western imports and credit would
have softened the hard edge of the Soviet crisis, but its dimensions were enormous.
Owing to the proclivity that existed in the Soviet system for disguising problems

and reporting inaccurate information, the leadership was unaware of the true state of affairs. Chernobyl demonstrates that temptations for misreporting persisted through at least 1986. Corruption remained endemic and would no doubt have siphoned off a proportion of foreign capital and commodities, however derived. The "soft-landing" scenario, had it come about, would more likely have merely delayed the Soviet collapse.

One question that remains open is whether there actually was a chance for successful reform of the Soviet system by the time Gorbachev came to primacy in 1985. Indeed, that opportunity may have dissipated even before Ronald Reagan took office in January 1981. A deeper and more systematic investigation of both the prevailing dynamics and the structural factors that affected the Soviet state, and a closer relation of those problems to the action potential of Soviet institutions, would be necessary to approach that issue. But the matching hypothetical—what might have been the result had Gorbachev succeeded Brezhnev as early as 1982—helps bring that question into focus. With his reformist bent, the greater resources still available to Moscow at that time, and his ability to charm the Western Europeans at least, Gorbachev's program might have acquired momentum before inertia built so heavily against it. Critical issues would have been how successfully Gorbachev could have brought Soviet institutions into line behind him, how quickly he could have modified the ongoing five-year plan, and how well he could have compelled the Soviet bureaucracy to provide accurate information. Gorbachev's early misstep with his campaign against alcoholism suggests that he too had a learning curve to negotiate. So this possibility might not have made much of a difference. Assuming the opposite, however, had the Gorbachev reforms been successful—given that his initial goal was to reform the *Soviet* system—the net result could have been to *prolong* the Cold War.

While this hypothetical is a complete construct, it does suggest one feature of the historical situation that really existed: actions by Moscow were more important to the final outcome than those taken in Washington.

A different hypothetical is also interesting: What if Moscow had moved very early to an accommodation with the ethnic minorities? Until 1988 their dissatisfaction had yet to aim at extrication from the USSR. Gorbachev might have been able to contrive a union of republics under these circumstances, arriving at the soft landing that some observers talked about. But even in 1988 Gorbachev was not yet thinking in terms of a "union treaty" at all—a fresh commentary on the role of individuals in history. This is illuminating because the scenario with the better potential outcome involved Soviet, not Western, action, which goes again to the relative value of Russia-centric versus U.S.-centric explanations for the end of the Cold War.

———————

When did the Cold War end? In chapter 1, a series of terminal dates were mentioned. Lacking the layers of the history that have been supplied by intervening chapters, we were not then well positioned to consider this matter. Now the subject should be engaged. There were five potential end dates proposed: mid-1988, at the moment of ratification of the INF Treaty; December 1988, when Gorbachev appeared before the United Nations General Assembly to announce unilateral Soviet withdrawals; November 1989, with the disappearance of the communist states of East-Central Europe and the fall of the Berlin Wall; August 1990, the time that the Soviet government for the first time acted in condominium with the United States in opposing Saddam Hussein's conquest of Kuwait; and August 1991, when the Soviet conservatives launched their abortive attempt to overthrow the government of the USSR. By far the best known of these end points are the 1989 fall of the Berlin Wall and the 1991 coup, but each of the alternatives will be considered briefly here.

Ronald Reagan popularized the mid-1988 date, declaring at the Moscow summit that the Cold War was over. It reflected his achievement in negotiating the INF Treaty, which indeed marked a lowering of East-West tensions, as well as the newly regained momentum of a long-stalled arms control process. But it was Reagan himself, in Berlin twelve months earlier, who had challenged the Soviets to "tear down this Wall." Residual hostilities endured. The Soviets were as yet unwilling to relinquish their empire of the periphery, though Gorbachev had already begun reassessing his policies for East-Central Europe and encouraging reforms there to match what he was doing in the USSR. This date seems premature. Reagan's enthusiasm at the summit related more to his immediate sense of achievement than to any true resolution of the global conflict.

The second alternative date is December 7, 1988. The Cold War had always been about the Soviet threat to the West, in particular Western Europe, and, in its most virulent form, a direct conquest by application of force by the Soviet Union and the Warsaw Pact. Gorbachev's moves during the second half of 1988, culminating in his United Nations speech, represented a huge departure from Moscow's Cold War policies. In terms of the periphery, by December 1988 Gorbachev, though he had not quite decided to abandon East-Central Europe, had passed the midpoint in his reassessment. The conversion of the Soviet military to an assertedly defensive doctrine had real meaning, though its primary importance was atmospheric, signaling a less aggressive Soviet attitude. But unilateral withdrawal of a significant fraction of Russian troops from the Warsaw Pact countries was both real and concrete. Absent those forces, a Soviet attack on NATO became problematic from a strictly military point of view, an option that went from a much-discussed, and much-feared, possibility that imperiled the NATO countries to an alternative force posture that NATO could face with equanimity. The threat of war diminished and with it the threat to the West. To the extent the Cold War was about that threat, it suddenly receded. In addition, during those last months of 1988, the Soviets reached an accord with China on disputed borderlands, reducing tensions in another way, and began in earnest its withdrawal from Afghanistan. Gorbachev also consolidated his position in Moscow with the retirement of President Andrei Gromyko. Finally, the November 1988 Estonian declaration of sovereignty showed that the Soviet nationalities problem had assumed its final form, beginning to push the Soviet republics apart. If one has to choose a single date for the end of the Cold War, December 7, 1988, would be my candidate.

The November 9–10, 1989, date of the fall of the Berlin Wall probably has pride of place as a Cold War end point. It catalyzed the fall of the Soviet allied states on the periphery, which disappeared with such rapidity that before the end of the year all of them were gone, replaced by successor governments that increasingly adopted the trappings of democracy and pro-Western policies to boot. These were all huge developments, and if the Cold War was symbolized by the existence of an "iron curtain," the fall of the Wall certainly heralded its end. But a Soviet resort to intervention remained possible, and short of that, Moscow could still have confected a new relationship with the periphery. And war remained possible between the superpowers. In my view, November 1989 denotes the moment that Cold War developments became irreversible, not the actual end of the conflict, and it betokened the progress toward reducing Cold War tensions that Gorbachev had signaled at the United Nations almost a year earlier.

Soviet-American cooperation at the onset of the Gulf War in August 1990 is another possible choice. The ability of the United States to move most of its NATO-committed military forces out of Europe in order to conduct the Gulf War attests to the reduction of Cold War tensions in Germany. That moment also marked the advance of the "four-plus-two" negotiations on Germany that would end with German reunification and with Soviet acquiescence to the unified Germany as a member of NATO, an outcome unimaginable for a USSR contesting the Cold War. This end date is popular with veterans of the first Bush administration, who found themselves interacting freely and easily with Soviet officials—former adversaries, now collaborators. But the image of condominium falls in the face of the Bush administration's own continued effort to extract advantages from the Soviet Union and the shallowness of Soviet cooperation on the Gulf War, which turned into something different when the United States actually began moving toward military action.

The final possibility is August 1991 and after, when the Soviet Union shuddered under the impact of the conservative coup and then disappeared as an international legal entity. It is certainly true that the disappearance of the USSR rendered continuation of the Cold War physically impossible. This would be my default selection, but for the analytical reasons proposed earlier, I prefer the December 1988 date to mark the end of the conflict.

Who won the Cold War? It is interesting that this question has virtually disappeared in recent years, for assertions of America's victory were a favorite refrain of the triumphalists. Measuring "victory" is a particular problem. The Cold War was an extended episode in international relations, not a clash of arms in which one combatant completes the action by occupying the enemy's capital or driving his armies from the field. No territory changed hands, no defeated enemy ended by paying reparations, no treaties were signed to mark the conflict's end. American diplomats continued to live and work in Moscow, for indeed in all the long years of the Cold War, there had never been a rupture in relations. Nor did the United States leave NATO, the Western alliance it had joined to pursue the long conflict, and in fact, NATO today is a major participant in a fresh war in Afghanistan that has been under way since 2001.

One measure of victory might be the drawdown of military budgets bloated by years of conflict. There *was* discussion in the United States of a "peace dividend," but that is difficult to find in U.S. budget data. In current dollars, U.S. military spending dipped briefly in 1991 but thereafter returned to the levels of fiscal years 1989 and 1990 and would again reach the 1991 spending rate in fiscal 1995, not so long after the end of the conflict—and *all* those levels were more than $100 billion a year higher than the U.S. military budget for 1981. A slightly different metric, "total obligational authority," measured in constant (1998) dollars, shows reductions of 8 or 9 percent annually beginning in 1992, with spending returning to the 1981 level in 1995 and thereafter remaining relatively constant. Put differently, the peace dividend simply returned U.S. military spending to what it had been prior to the Reagan defense buildup, a time of high Cold War tension. Defense planners established a "base force" concept of military manpower. Some 2.1 million Americans served in the military in 1981. Ten years later, the number was slightly over 2 million. The peace dividend cut manpower by about 100,000 a year until 1995, when the number stabilized above 1.5 million.[1] Most of the U.S. troops stationed in Europe to fight a NATO war against the Warsaw Pact countries stayed and were there in 2000 to be deployed to the Middle East for the Iraq War.

In short, the United States replaced its Cold War standard for military spending and personnel with a post–Cold War superpower standard virtually as high and distributed in similar fashion. Russian military forces really did decline—precipitously—in line with the contraction of Moscow's economy, so the American military was not maintaining these forces against any threat from that quarter. Soon all manner of former Soviet military equipment was to be had for a pittance from mail-order catalogues, Army-Navy stores, secondhand stores, and the like. If victory is to be measured in removal of the burden of military effort, the United States did not achieve it.

Another aspect is bound up in those figures for the Reagan military buildup. This effort was not costless. Instead, the Reagan administration built up a huge U.S. budget deficit that had no detectable effect on Soviet military spending and marginal impact on the military balance. The deficit spending continued at a lesser rate under the first Bush administration and the deficit itself would be bequeathed to President William J. Clinton. It took both of Clinton's terms in office to eliminate that deficit. Americans were still paying for the Cold War a decade after it had ended.

The most concrete "victory" of the last Cold War decade clearly was that of the Afghan resistance against the Soviet occupation of their country, a CIA covert operation. But the CIA did not create the Afghan rebellion, it merely took advantage of a burgeoning resistance that had already pushed the Soviets into an increasingly desperate intervention. The CIA operation furnished the rebels with sophisticated weapons that the United States then worked for years to recover, and it energized and mobilized Islamic fighters who became cadres for the terrorist wars against the West of the twenty-first century. Given that the Afghan success was overblown in the first place, from this remove it no longer seems to be the victory that was advertised.

Some American commentators during the Cold War spoke of victory as "convergence," that is, success would be confirmed if the Soviet Union came around to Western ways—capitalism and free-market societies. By that measure, there was a victory in the Cold War. But at this writing, with the U.S. government meeting its own economic crisis by effectively nationalizing banks and corporations and with the failed Republican contenders in the 2008 elections accusing opponents of somehow being "socialists," it could be argued (facetiously) that Russia and the United States actually traded places. This is a lesson in the pitfalls of history. In the last analysis, *no one* won the Cold War, or perhaps everyone did—for we are still here to tell the tale and to learn from it. But the losers in the Cold War are the people—everywhere—who found themselves crushed under the weight of a misbegotten conflict that followed a dangerous path to an ignominious but remarkable end.

APPENDIX OF
DOCUMENTS

1. Report from Colonel Kuklinski ("Jack Strong"), September 15, 1981

Source: Document no. 5034F049-96B6-175C-95588F05194A1694, Cold War International History Project (CWIHP) Virtual Archive, www.CWIHP.org. Reprinted by permission of the Woodrow Wilson International Center for Scholars.

At an extraordinary session of the [National Defense Committee] took place on [September 13], which [Polish Workers Party chief Stanisław] Kania attended for the first time, no final decision was made about the imposition of martial law. Almost all of the participants supported it. It seems that the tenor of the meeting surprised Kania. Although he did not question that such a development was inevitable, he reportedly said, in these precise words, that "a confrontation with the class enemy is unavoidable. This involves first a struggle using political means, but if that should fail, repression may be adopted." Note-taking was forbidden. . . . [Gen. Czesław] Kiszczak declared that Solidarity knew the details of our plans, including . . . its secret codename. . . . Since this morning we have been working . . . on a unified plan of command for the surprise introduction of martial law. . . . In brief, martial law will be introduced at night, either between Friday and a work-free Saturday or between Saturday and Sunday, when industrial plants will be closed. Arrests will begin around midnight, six hours before an announcement of martial law is broadcast over radio and television. Roughly 600 people will be arrested in Warsaw, which will require the use of around 1,000 police in unmarked cars. That same night, the army will seal off the most important areas of Warsaw and other major cities. . . .

Please treat with caution the information I am conveying to you, since it appears that my mission is coming to an end. The nature of the information makes it quite easy to detect the source. I do not object to, and indeed welcome, having the information I have conveyed serve those who fight for the freedom of Poland with their heads raised high. I am prepared to make the ultimate sacrifice. . . .

2. Transcript of Meeting of the Politburo of the Communist Party of the Soviet Union, December 10, 1981

Source: Document no. 3B3F5A3C-0813-9003-E61F6E745757D4FB, CWIHP Virtual Archive, www.CWIHP.org. Reprinted by permission of the Woodrow Wilson International Center for Scholars.

On the Question of the Situation in Poland

BREZHNEV: This question is not listed on the agenda. But I think that the session of the Politburo should begin with this matter since we have specially dispatched [officials] . . . to meet with the Polish comrades and go over certain matters of the utmost urgency. . . .

K. V. RUSAKOV: . . . No one knows what will happen over the next few days. There was a conversation about Operation "X." At first [the Poles] said it would be on the night of 11–12 December, and then this was changed to the night of the 12th and 13th. And now they're already saying it won't be until around the 20th. What is envisaged is that the chairman of the State Council, Jablonski, will appear on radio and television and declare the introduction of martial law. At the same time, Jaruzelski said that the law on the introduction of martial law can be implemented only after it is considered by the Sejm [legislature]. . . . Thus, everything has become very complicated. The agenda of the Sejm has already been published, and it makes no mention of the introduction of martial law. But even if the [Polish] government does intend to introduce martial law, Solidarity knows this very well. . . .

Jaruzelski intends to keep in close touch about this matter with his allies. He says that if the Polish forces are unable to cope with the resistance put up by Solidarity, the Polish comrades hope to receive assistance from other countries, up to and including the introduction of armed forces. . . .

If we consider what is going on in the provinces, one must candidly say that the strength of the party organizations there has been completely dissipated. To a certain degree the administrative apparatus there is still functioning, but in effect all power has now been transferred to the hands of Solidarity. In his recent statements, Jaruzelski is apparently trying to pull the wool over our eyes, because his words fail to reflect a proper analysis. If the Polish comrades don't quickly get organized . . . and resist the onslaught of Solidarity, they will have no success at all in improving the situation in Poland.

Yu. V. ANDROPOV: From the discussions with Jaruzelski it is clear that they have not yet reached a firm consensus. . . . The extremists in Solidarity are attacking the Polish leadership by the throat. The Church in recent days has also expressed its position, which in essence is now completely supportive of Solidarity.

Of course in these circumstances the Polish comrades must act swiftly in launching "Operation X" and carrying it out. . . . It would seem that either Jaruzelski is concealing from his comrades the plan of concrete action, or he is simply abandoning the idea of carrying out this step.

I'd now like to mention that Jaruzelski has been more than persistent in setting forth economic demands [for] us and has made the implementation of "Operation X" contingent on our willingness to offer economic assistance, and I would say even more than that, he is raising the question, albeit indirectly, of receiving military assistance as well. . . .

As far as economic assistance is concerned, it will of course be difficult for us to undertake anything of the scale and nature of what has been proposed. No doubt, something will have to give. . . . We do not intend to introduce troops into Poland. That is the proper position, and we must adhere to it until the end. I don't know how things will turn out in Poland, but even if Poland falls under the control of Solidarity, that's the way it will be. . . .

A. A. GROMYKO: . . . I fully agree with what has already been said here. . . . We can say to the Poles that we view the Polish events with understanding. There is no basis whatsoever for us to alter this measured formulation in any way. At the same time we must somehow try to dispel the notions that Jaruzelski and other leaders in Poland have about the introduction of troops. There cannot be any introduction of troops into Poland. I think we can give instructions about this to our ambassador. . . .

D. F. USTINOV: . . . The situation is worsening day by day . . . and now all hopes are riding on Jaruzelski. . . . The Poles themselves requested us not to introduce troops. . . .

M. A. SUSLOV: I believe, as is evident from the other comrades' speeches, that we all have the same view of the situation in Poland. . . . If troops are introduced that will be a catastrophe. I think we have reached a unanimous view here on this matter, and there can be no consideration at all of introducing troops. . . .

V. V. GRISHIN: . . . There can be no talk at all of introducing troops. . . .

K .U. CHERNENKO: I fully agree with what the comrades have said here. . . .

3. CPSU Central Committee Information Cable, December 13, 1981

Source: Document no. 503500E3-96B6-175C-9E5521183A621780, CWIHP Virtual Archive, www.CWIHP.org. Reprinted by permission of the Woodrow Wilson International Center for Scholars.

. . . "As our friends know, the Polish leadership has introduced martial law into the country, announced the formation of a Military Council of National Salvation, and detained the most extremist elements of 'Solidarity,' the 'Confederation for an Independent Poland,' and other anti-socialist groups.

"A good impression has been created by W. Jaruzelski's address to the people, in which, in our view, all the basic questions were given appropriate emphasis. In particular, what is especially important is that the address reaffirmed the leading role of the [Polish Worker's Party] and the commitment of the [Polish People's Republic] to the socialist obligations stipulated by the Warsaw Pact.

"To ensure the success of the operation, the Polish comrades observed strict secrecy. Only a narrow circle around Jaruzelski knew about the action. Thanks to this our friends have succeeded in catching the enemy completely unawares, and the operation so far has been implemented satisfactorily.

"On the very eve of implementation of the projected operation, W. Jaruzelski communicated about it to Moscow. We informed him that the Soviet leadership looked with understanding upon the decision of the Polish comrades. In so doing we ensured that the Polish comrades would resolve these matters solely by internal means.

"In our preliminary evaluation, the measures taken by the Polish friends are an active step to repulse counterrevolution, and in this sense they correspond with the general line of all the fraternal countries. . . ."

4. Impact of Credit Restrictions on Soviet Trade and the Soviet Economy, May 1982

Source: CIA, Intelligence Memorandum, SOV-82-10070, CIA Electronic Reading Room, http://www.foia.cia.gov/browse_docs_full.asp.

Overview

One of the most difficult problems for the Soviet leadership in the 1980s will be how to deal with a severe scarcity of hard currency at a time when the economy is slowing sharply. Although the slowdown results from the interplay of many forces, and the overall weight of hard currency imports in the economy is small, these imports play an important role in easing food shortages, raising energy production, sustaining technology and productivity, and making up for unexpected shortfalls of key products.

But while the Soviet need for Western goods and technology is rising, during the 1980s the purchasing power of Moscow's hard currency earnings is likely to decline:

- The volume of oil exports will be steadily squeezed between rising oil consumption and oil production that is now constant and will fall later.
- Soft oil markets probably will keep real oil prices from rising for several years.
- Gas exports will increase substantially if the gas export pipeline is built, but not enough to offset the drop in oil exports.
- Hard currency earnings from arms sales are unlikely to increase because LDC [less developed country] clients will be less able to pay.
- Other exports suffer from production problems (wood products, metals), or an inability to compete on a large scale in Western markets (machinery, chemicals).

The Soviet hard currency position is still relatively strong; the debt-service ratio is only about 17 percent. Nonetheless, prospective stagnation in the volume of exports means that any attempt to achieve a substantial increase in imports will quickly push up hard currency debt to an unacceptable level. Indeed, a large inflow of Western capital would be required just to maintain the current level of real imports and would result in a doubling of debt by 1985 and a quadrupling by 1990.

The debt-service ratio would approach 30 percent by 1985—a level high enough to cause concern in financial circles—and reach dangerous proportions (45 percent) by 1990.

In this tight situation, a Western credit policy of restricting the volume and hardening the terms of government-guaranteed credits can play an important role in:

- Avoiding overexposure by private banks, as has already occurred in Eastern Europe, and the potentially costly claims on Western budgets if guarantees have to be made good.
- Putting added pressure on the Soviet authorities to reexamine their priorities.
  . . .

Even moderate declines in hard currency imports can greatly complicate Soviet economic problems and make allocation decisions more painful. Large agricultural imports are essential to the growth of meat consumption even in normal crop years. Expansion of gas production and exports requires massive purchases of Western large-diameter pipe. Large imports of metals and chemicals are an integral part of Soviet economic plans. Orders of Western machinery and equipment have already been sharply curtailed; further cuts would certainly impinge on priority programs in steel, transportation, agriculture, and heavy machine building.

It is unlikely that Soviet military and foreign policy programs would go unscathed if sizeable cuts in allocations of foreign exchange had to be imposed. The economy is so taut—indeed, it is already rent with widespread shortages—that the repercussions of any substantial cuts are bound to spread widely, even to military industries with their traditional immunity. Moreover, such programs as aid to Cuba or third world countries, which directly or indirectly use up foreign currency and are already unpopular within the USSR, would encounter greater opposition.

5. Excerpts Regarding Poland from KGB's 1981 Annual Report, April 13, 1982

Source: Document no. 3B55A9CB-F043-9C87-F67C880605DACA5B, CWIHP Virtual Archive, www.CWIHP.org. Reprinted by permission of the Woodrow Wilson International Center for Scholars.

Of Special Importance
Special Dossier
Committee on State Security of the USSR
13.04.82
No. 728-A/OV To Comrade L. I. Brezhnev
Moscow

. . . The foreign intelligence service has sought to thwart the crude interference by the USA and other NATO countries and their special services in the internal affairs of Poland and to ward off their encroachments on the foundations of socialism in the [Polish People's Republic]. The foreign intelligence service had also sought to discredit the counterrevolutionary forces in that country. . . .

More than 30 anti-Soviet and other politically hostile groups were uncovered. Attempts to form nationalist groups in Ukraine, the Baltic republics, Armenia, and certain other republics were crushed. . . .

More than 70 Solidarity activists, who were inciting strikes among Polish workers employed at construction sites in the Soviet Union, were discovered and expelled from the USSR. A provocative strike action in Estonia, instigated from abroad, was broken up.

Chekist [internal security] agencies provided active help to party organs and administrative bodies to prevent conflicts from growing in labor collectives, including a number of defense enterprises. . . .

Mass subversive ideological actions, aimed at the personnel of Soviet military units in Poland and Afghanistan, were disrupted. A number of attempts to form groups of servicemen around politically hostile aims were thwarted. . . .

6. National Security Decision Directive 32, "U.S. National Security Strategy," May 20, 1982

Source: Ronald Reagan Papers, White House Staff and Office Files, Executive Secretariat, NSC, box 91311, fol. NSDD-32, Ronald Reagan Library.

. . . The national security policy of the United States shall be guided by the following global objectives:

*   To deter military attack by the USSR and its allies against the U.S., its allies, and other important countries across the spectrum of conflict; and to defeat such an attack should deterrence fail.

- To strengthen the influence of the U.S. throughout the world by strengthening existing alliances. . . .
- To contain and reverse the expansion of Soviet control and military presence throughout the world, and to increase the costs of Soviet support and use of proxy, terrorist, and subversive forces.
- To neutralize the efforts of the USSR to increase its influence through its use of diplomacy, arms transfers, economic pressure, political action, propaganda, and disinformation.
- To foster, if possible in concert with our allies, restraint in Soviet military spending, discourage Soviet adventurism, and weaken the Soviet alliance system by forcing the USSR to bear the brunt of its economic shortcomings, and to encourage long-term liberalizing and nationalist tendencies within the Soviet Union and allied countries.
- To limit Soviet military capabilities by strengthening the U.S. military, by pursuing equitable and verifiable arms control agreements, and by preventing the flow of militarily significant technologies and resources to the Soviet Union. . . .

The key military threats to U.S. security during the 1980s will continue to be posed by the Soviet Union and its allies and clients. Despite increasing pressures on its economy and the growing vulnerabilities of its empire, the Soviet military will continue to expand and modernize. . . .

A war with a Soviet client arising from regional tensions is more likely than a direct conflict with the USSR. . . .

Given the loss of U.S. strategic superiority and the overwhelming growth of Soviet conventional forces capabilities, together with the increased political and economic strength of the industrial democracies and the heightened importance of Third World resources, the United States must increasingly draw upon the resources and cooperation of allies. . . .

The modernization of our strategic nuclear forces and the achievement of parity with the Soviet Union shall receive first priority. . . .

The United States will enhance its strategic nuclear deterrent by developing a capability to sustain protracted nuclear conflict. . . .

With the growing vulnerability of our strategic deterrent, we must enhance the survivability of our offensive forces, and complement those efforts with effective programs to provide for continuity of government, strategic connectivity, and civil defense. . . .

7. *Whence the Threat to Peace,* 1982

Source: Official statement by the USSR Ministry of Defense (Moscow: Military Publishing House, 1982).

. . . . The present US Administration . . . [has] set out to upset the military-strategic equilibrium shaped during the past decade between the USSR and the USA, between the Warsaw Treaty Organization and the North Atlantic bloc. To justify their line of securing military superiority over the Soviet Union and the Warsaw Treaty, the myth of a "Soviet war threat" fabricated years ago is being backed up by claims that the USA and NATO as a whole have "fallen behind" in the military field and "windows of vulnerability" have appeared in the US war machine. . . .

As for the Soviet Union, it initiated no new types of weapons throughout postwar history. In building its armed forces, it only reacted to dangers created [by U.S. development of novel weapons]. The USSR has never aspired to positions of military superiority, and has always confined itself to measures that sufficed to ensure dependable security for itself and its allies. This has been repeatedly and officially stated by Soviet leaders at the highest level. . . . Leonid Brezhnev said, "We are not seeking military superiority over the West, we do not need it. All we need is reliable security." . . .

Soviet military doctrine is of a strictly defensive nature. This has been stated at the highest level. The Declaration of the Warsaw Treaty member countries of May 15, 1980, says in so many words: "We have not, never had, and never will have any strategic doctrine other than a defensive one."

Soviet military doctrine has been and is based on the principle of retaliatory, that is, defensive actions. The strategic nuclear forces of the USSR have never been called "strategic **offensive** forces," as is the case in the United States of America.

The Soviet Union considers any nuclear attack a capital crime against humanity. This has been reasserted by Leonid Brezhnev in October 1981, when he said that to count on victory in a nuclear war is dangerous madness. "Anybody's decision to start a nuclear war in the hope of winning it," he said, "is tantamount to suicide."

Soviet military strategy reposes on the principle that the Soviet Union will not be the first to use nuclear weapons. In fact, it is opposed to the use of any weapons of mass destruction. . . .

The logic of war and the nature of modern armaments would, if nuclear war broke out in Europe or anywhere else, inexorably make it worldwide. None but completely irresponsible people can maintain that a nuclear war can be fought according to previously established rules. . . .

Peace "from a position of strength" is what the men in Washington would like to have. These days, they are not concerned about the equality and equal security of the sides, and are bent on developing new, increasingly more destructive weapons of mass annihilation, on securing military superiority over the Soviet Union, and establishing hegemony and direct domination over other countries and nations.

8. National Security Decision Directive 66, "East-West Economic Relations and Poland-Related Sanctions," November 29, 1982

Source: Ronald Reagan Papers, White House Staff and Office Files, Executive Secretariat, NSC, box 91286, fol. NSDD-66, Ronald Reagan Library.

I have reviewed the . . . consultations with our Allies conducted by Secretary Shultz. . . . This framework agreement establishes the security-minded principles that will govern East-West economic relations for the remainder of this decade and beyond. In putting these principles into practice, the Allies have committed themselves to immediate actions on the key elements of East-West trade including: agreement not to sign or approve any new contracts for the purchase of Soviet gas during the urgent study of Western energy alternatives; agreement to strengthen the effectiveness of controls on high technology transfer to the USSR, including examination of the necessity of multilateral controls on critical oil and gas equipment and technology; and agreement to harmonize export credit policies. It is my goal that firm allied commitments emerge from the studies in each of these major categories and that the resulting common policies will be substantially agreed by . . . May 1983. . . .

Poland-related Sanctions

On the expectation of firm allied commitments . . . reflecting U.S. policy objectives emerging from the work program . . . I approved the cancellation of the December 30 sanctions on oil and gas equipment and technology to the Soviet Union and the June 22 amendment extending those controls to U.S. subsidiaries and licensees abroad. In addition I have approved the resumption of case-by-case licensing for commodities under national security controls. Sanctions imposed against the USSR following the invasion of Afghanistan remain in effect. . . .

9. Soviet Strategy to Derail US INF Deployment, February 1983

Source: CIA, Intelligence Assessment, SOV 83-10025X, Princeton Collection.

In attempting to forestall US deployments of intermediate-range nuclear forces (INF) in Europe, scheduled to begin late this year, the Soviets will continue a complex strategy of inducements and threats designed to influence NATO governments, particularly West Germany before its March elections. With time growing short, their near-term objective evidently is to pressure NATO to delay the deployments and to move from its zero-option proposals.

Moscow has begun an intensive effort to brief West European governments on the new Soviet proposal for a subceiling on missile launchers in Europe. The subceiling would result in substantial reductions in the number of Soviet medium-range ballistic missile launchers opposite NATO but would be linked to the number of French and British ballistic missile launchers and would preclude the deployment in Europe of US INF missiles. The Soviets have argued that their new proposal demonstrates "flexibility," in sharp contrast to US "intractability" in adhering to its zero option proposal. They have also hinted in vague terms to West European governments of certain "concessions" they might adopt at INF negotiations in return for greater US flexibility.

At the same time, Moscow has warned NATO of the serious consequences should the US position remain unchanged . . . and the United States proceed with its deployments. Such consequences probably include: the lifting of their unilateral SS-20 moratorium, deployment of additional SS-20s in Europe, and the development of new cruise and ballistic missiles for deployment opposite NATO. Thus Moscow is trying to persuade the Europeans that their security would be better served by its proposal for a missile subceiling than by US INF deployments followed by corresponding Soviet countermeasures.

Along with these diplomatic moves, the Soviets have actively promoted the European "peace movement" through aggressive propaganda and covert activities. They have focused their efforts primarily on those scheduled to base the new NATO missiles with the chief emphasis on West Germany. Their campaign covers a wide spectrum of activities—from overt efforts to create a fear of nuclear war to covert measures, including forgeries and disinformation to put NATO governments in the worst possible light. . . .

Nevertheless the Soviets realize that their overt "peace" campaign in Western Europe has been their most effective tactic. They also recognize that the peace movement there has indigenous roots and has acquired a momentum of its own. They will do what they can to nurture it without appearing too heavy handed.

10. National Security Decision Directive 75, "U.S. Relations with the USSR," January 17, 1983

Source: Ronald Reagan Papers, White House Staff and Office Files, Executive Secretariat, NSC, box 91286, fol. NSDD-75, Ronald Reagan Library.

U.S. policy toward the Soviet Union will consist of three elements: external resistance to Soviet imperialism; internal pressure on the USSR to weaken the sources of Soviet imperialism; and negotiations to eliminate, on the basis of strict reciprocity, outstanding disagreements. Specifically U.S. tasks are:

1. To contain and over time reverse Soviet expansionism by competing effectively on a sustained basis with the Soviet Union in all international arenas—particularly in the overall military balance and in geographical regions of priority concern to the United States. This will remain the primary focus of U.S. policy toward the USSR.
2. To promote, within the narrow limits available to us, the process of change in the Soviet Union toward a more pluralistic political and economic system in which the power of the privileged ruling elite is gradually reduced. The U.S. recognizes that Soviet aggressiveness has deep roots in the internal system, and that relations with the USSR should therefore take into account whether or not they help to strengthen this system and its capacity to engage in aggression.
3. To engage the Soviet Union in negotiations to attempt to reach agreements which protect and enhance U.S. interests and which are consistent with the principle of strict reciprocity and mutual interest. This is important when the Soviet Union is in the midst of a process of political succession. . . .

A. Functional

1. *Military Strategy*: The U.S. must modernize its military forces—both nuclear and conventional—so that Soviet leaders perceive that the U.S. is determined never

to accept a second place or a deteriorating military posture. Soviet calculations of possible war outcomes under any contingency must always result in outcomes so unfavorable to the USSR that there would be no incentive for Soviet leaders to initiate an attack. The future strength of U.S. military capabilities must be assured. U.S. military technology advances must be exploited, while controls over the transfer of military related/dual-use technology, products, and services must be tightened. . . .

2. *Economic Policy*: U.S. policy on economic relations with the USSR must serve strategic and foreign policy goals as well as economic interests. In this context, U.S. objectives are:

- Above all, to ensure that East-West economic relations do not facilitate the Soviet military buildup. This requires prevention of the transfer of technology and equipment that would make a substantial contribution directly or indirectly to Soviet military power.
- To avoid subsidizing the Soviet economy or unduly easing the burden of Soviet resource allocation decisions, so as not to dilute pressures for structural change in the Soviet system.
- To seek to minimize the potential for Soviet exercise of reverse leverage on Western countries based on trade, energy supply, and financial relationships.
- To permit mutual beneficial trade—without Western subsidization or the creation of Western dependence—with the USSR in non-strategic areas, such as grains. . . .

3. *Political Action*: U.S. policy must have an ideological thrust which clearly affirms the superiority of U.S. and Western values of individual dignity and freedom, a free press, free trade unions, free enterprise, and political democracy over the repressive features of Soviet Communism. We need to review and significantly strengthen U.S. instruments of political action. . . . The U.S. should:

- Expose at all available fora the double standards employed by the Soviet Union in dealing with difficulties within its own domain and the outside ("capitalist") world (e.g., treatment of labor, policies toward ethnic nationalities, use of chemical weapons, etc.).
- Prevent the Soviet propaganda machine from seizing the semantic high ground in the battle of ideas through the appropriation of such terms as "peace." . . .

B. Geopolitical . . .

3. *The Soviet Empire.* There are a number of important weaknesses and vulnerabilities within the Soviet empire which the U.S. should exploit. U.S. policies should
seek wherever possible to encourage Soviet allies to distance themselves from Moscow in foreign policy and to move toward democratization domestically.

(a) *Eastern Europe.* The primary U.S. objective in Eastern Europe is to loosen
     Moscow's hold on the region while promoting the cause of human rights
     in individual East European countries. The U.S. can advance this objective
     by carefully discriminating in favor of countries that show relative inde-
     pendence from Moscow in their foreign policy, or show a greater degree
     of internal liberalization. U.S. policies must also make clear that East Eu-
     ropean countries which reverse movements of liberalization, or drift away
     from an independent stance in foreign policy, will incur significant costs
     in their relations with the U.S.

(b) *Afghanistan.* The U.S. objective is to keep maximum pressure on Moscow
     for withdrawal and to ensure that the Soviets' political, military, and other
     costs remain high while the occupation continues. . . .

11. Ethnic Balance in the Soviet Military in a Decade of Manpower Shortage, April 1983

Source: CIA, Intelligence Assessment, SOV 83-10062, Princeton Collection.

The Soviet military faces a demographic dilemma in the 1980s. While military
planners, accustomed to 20 years of abundant manpower, wrestle with a smaller supply, they must also manage an influx of ethnic groups traditionally viewed
by the military as of relatively lower "quality" than Slavic conscripts. The ethnic
"problem" is not new. The shifts in ethnic composition of the draft pool began in
the 1970s and will continue beyond 1990. The proportion of non-Slavic minorities
among 18-year-olds will rise steadily from 25 percent in 1970 to nearly 40 percent
by 1990.

New estimates of the size and ethnic composition of certain noncombat units
indicate that they absorb most of the minority conscripts, thereby preserving Slavic
dominance in the combat services. We define the Soviet national security or "combat" force to include those elements of the military that perform missions of na-

tional defense similar to those of the US military. This includes all military personnel except those of the Construction, Railroad, Internal Security, and Civil Defense Troops. Two-thirds of the personnel in [those branches] are minority conscripts. In this sense, these three services act as an ethnic "sponge." Currently, this assignment policy holds down the minority share of conscripts in the national security force to about one-fifth compared with one-third of the draft-age population. The non-Slavic share of the officer corps is even less, presently estimated at only 10 percent.

Part of the explanation for the ethnic pattern of conscript assignment is the lower educational and Russian-language fluency levels of some minority groups. However, this alone cannot explain the persistence over time of the very high proportion of minorities in noncombat service, since minority educational and linguistic achievements improved substantially in the 1970s. A major element is probably longstanding ethnic distrust. . . .

12. Commentary by Soviet General Staff Chief Marshal Nikolai N. V. Ogarkov, May 9, 1984

Source: Interview in *Krasnaya Zvezda*, May 9, 1984.

. . . . A paradox arises: on the one hand, it would seem, a process of steadily increasing potential for the nuclear powers to destroy the enemy is taking place, while on the other hand there is an equally steady and, I would say, even steeper reduction in the potential for an aggressor to inflict a so-called "disarming strike" on his main enemy. The point is that with the quantity and diversity of nuclear missiles already achieved, it becomes impossible to destroy the enemy's systems with a single strike. A crushing retaliatory strike against the aggressor even with the limited quantity of nuclear charges remaining to the defender—a strike inflicting unacceptable damage—becomes inevitable in present conditions. The calculation . . . on the possibility of waging a so-called "limited" nuclear war, now has no foundation whatever. . . . That is the terrible logic of war.

13. A Space-Based Anti-Missile System with Directed Energy Weapons: Strategic, Legal and Political Implications, 1984

Source: Study on the SDI by the Committee of Soviet Scientists for Peace Against the Nuclear Threat (Moscow: USSR Academy of Sciences, 1984).

Government circles and the public at large in the USA recently have been discussing a great deal the Reagan Administration's plans to set up a large-scale "defense" against nuclear missiles. The system is expected to consist of several layers deployed in outer space and using various types of directed-energy weapons. . . .

Recent Western studies indicate that technical prerequisites for developing systems for directed-energy transfer over dozens of thousands of kilometers are not available. . . . The specific features of directed-energy weapons are first of all linked with the very rapid propagation of destructive factors (electromagnetic waves or high-energy particles) close to the maximum possible velocity in nature—the velocity of light. . . . Various systems, now being considered in the USA as possible components of directed-energy weapons, are at very different stages of technical development. . . .

Western estimates putting the cost of a multi-layer space anti-missile system at $1.5 or $2 trillion appear to be justified. . . .

The enormous technological problems posed by the space-based anti-missile weapons and their unprecedented costs call into question the entire strategic logic of those who advocate this system. But even if we assume that it would be possible to clear many of its scientific and technological bottlenecks through the concentration of huge resources, [and] the super-effort of researchers and engineers, it will appear nevertheless that the [space-based anti-missile system] is very vulnerable to various means of countermeasures. . . .

Argumentation in favor of the stabilizing role of a large-scale anti-missile system might have . . . sense only if the Reagan Administration, simultaneously with taking a decision on its development . . . renounced the buildup and improvement of nuclear offensive forces. However, what is happening is just the opposite—the nuclear strategic offensive and tactical weapons are being formed and developed all along. As a result, the creation of an anti-missile system would only complicate to a large extent the task of deterrence. It will make this task even more uncertain because survival and limited damage in a nuclear war would come to depend even more heavily on performing just the first strike—in order to protect oneself against the retaliatory strike by the victim of aggression with the aid of [space-based anti-missile systems]. Besides that, there will be a greater incentive for delivering a pre-emptive strike. . . .

14. Memorandum of Conversation between President Ronald Reagan and Prime Minister Margaret Thatcher, Camp David, December 22, 1984

Source: Ronald Reagan Papers, National Security Files, Records of European and Soviet Affairs Directorate, box 90902, Ronald Reagan Library.

Private Meeting, Aspen Lodge

. . . Turning to Gorbachev's visit to the UK, **Mrs. Thatcher** said he was an unusual Russian in that he was much less constrained, more charming, open to discussion and debate, and did not stick to prepared notes. . . . **Mrs. Thatcher** contrasted Gorbachev with Gromyko, whom she observed would have sharply replied [to British points regarding the difficulty of emigration from the USSR] that emigration was an internal matter and not open for discussion. Gorbachev was not willing to debate the point, but he did allow her to discuss it without cutting her off. He also avoided the usual Soviet reaction of citing [a] lengthy position of principle. . . . She had also emphasized to Gorbachev that the President is an honorable man who sincerely wants to improve relations with the Soviet Union. . . . **Mrs. Thatcher** noted that Gorbachev had implied that returning to [the arms talks in] Geneva was not an easy decision for the Soviets. He also indicated the Soviets would come to Geneva with serious proposals. The President replied "we hope so." She continued that she had emphasized to Gorbachev that Britain supports the U.S. SDI program and told him it was not linked to a first strike strategy. . . . Gorbachev had told her "tell your friend the President not to go ahead with space weapons." He suggested if you develop SDI the Russians either would develop their own, or more probably, develop new offensive systems superior to SDI. . . .

Expanded Meeting, Laurel Lodge

. . . **Mrs. Thatcher** again underlined that Britain backed the U.S. research program. She said she understood that we will not know for some time if a strategic defense system is truly feasible. If we reached the stage where production looked possible we would have some serious and difficult decisions to take. There are ABM and Outer Space [weapons] treaties. Future technological developments and possible countering strategies must also be considered. . . . It was her impression from her talks with Gorbachev that the Soviets were following the same line of reasoning. They clearly fear U.S. technological prowess . . . [but we] do not want our objective of increased security, opined the **Prime Minister**, to result in increased Soviet nuclear weapons. . . . **Mrs. Thatcher** said these comments reflect real concerns. We have some real worries, especially about SDI's impact on deterrence. . . .

Mrs. Thatcher noted that the President said earlier that initial indications are that an SDI program is feasible. Mrs. Thatcher said she must admit that personally she has some doubts. In the past, scientific genius had always developed a counter system. . . . She emphasized her concern with any implication of dropping our successful nuclear deterrent strategy and stressed that it is important that we work out privately what we will say publicly about SDI. She said that several points appear pertinent. We must emphasize that SDI is only a research program; and that our objective is both to maintain a military balance and to enhance, not weaken deterrence.

The President said we need to address the points Mrs. Thatcher has raised and to reach agreement on SDI, a program he called worth pursuing. He noted that the experts continue to tell him that research is promising and SDI may be feasible. . . . We cannot and should not, however, continued the President, have to go on living under the threat of nuclear destruction. We must eliminate the threat posed by strategic nuclear weapons. My ultimate goal is to eliminate nuclear weapons. The Soviets are now beginning to echo this same view. . . . They must also be concerned about our economic strength. It will be especially difficult for them to keep spending such vast sums on defense. Such spending is in neither of our interests. . . . We must deal with the Soviets from a position of strength. But we also know that in a nuclear war there would be no winners. . . .

Mrs. Thatcher replied that it is correct to emphasize military balance, not superiority. Balance gives us security. Making a specific reference to SDI, she said research contributes towards maintaining a military balance. We need to explain to our publics that SDI is only a research program, that it does not contravene any existing treaties and if we get to the development stage, many alternative factors will have to be considered at that time. For example, the ABM Treaty may have to be renegotiated.

Secretary Shultz stressed, our concern is that the current situation is not balanced. The Soviets have many more offensive nuclear systems than foreseen under SALT I. . . . The Soviets have positioned themselves to break out from under the conditions imposed by the treaties. Their emphasis on defensive systems puts us in an unequal position. Our view is that there is an imbalance. . . .

Saying she didn't wish to debate strategic theory, **Mrs. Thatcher** noted that some claim SDI would be an incentive for the Soviets to produce more offensive systems and could encourage the Soviets to launch a preemptive first strike. From our point of view, said Mrs. Thatcher, deterrence remains our fundamental objective. . . .

Secretary Shultz interjected that we cannot just sit back and let the Soviets build up a significant advantage in defensive systems. . . . At the President's request, **National Security Advisor McFarlane** expanded on the U.S. SDI program. Calling Mrs. Thatcher's questions thoughtful and well-reasoned, McFarlane underscored that her remarks are based on the assumption that offensive deterrence in its present form can and will endure. This may not be true. In recent years the character of Soviet offensive systems has changed dramatically. . . . **McFarlane** continued that our dilemma has been what to do to restore the strategic balance. . . . **McFarlane** observed that our current dilemma—one over which the President expressed concern several years ago—is our inability to match the Soviet offensive buildup. This is why the President asked us to explore other alternatives. . . .

Saying SDI as she understood it seemed to suggest inherent U.S. superiority, **Mrs. Thatcher** added she was not convinced of the need to deploy such a system, particularly if it could be knocked out by other technological advances. . . .

15. Memorandum of Conversation between President Ronald Reagan and General Secretary Mikhail Gorbachev, Geneva Summit, November 20, 1985

Source: Ronald Reagan Papers, National Security Files, Jack Matlock Files, box 92137, Ronald Reagan Library.

. . . Reiterating that he did not wish to dramatize differences in the two sides' approach[es], Gorbachev that the Soviet Union truly desired a serious search for mutually acceptable proposals. . . . There were elements in the U.S. proposal, however, which clearly departed from the January 1985 U.S.-Soviet understanding on the goals and subjects of the Geneva talks. On the one hand, the President and his colleagues asserted that the U.S. had not departed from this understanding, that the U.S. was in favor of radical reductions in defensive [?] nuclear weapons and in favor of preventing an arms race in space.

The President's Strategic Defense Initiative (SDI) was regarded by the U.S. as consistent with the January understanding. This was a "revelation" to the Soviets. No matter under what flag the U.S. chose to cover it, SDI amounted to placing weapons in space, to spreading the arms race to space. This view devalued the remaining elements of the U.S. proposals. What purpose could be served by radical reductions if the U.S. contemplated deploying weapons in space—with all the attendant consequences.

When the Soviets had proposed that the two sides agree to close the door to deployments of weapons in space, it was consistent with both the U.S. and USSR's security interests. Gorbachev noted that the U.S. had claimed the Soviet Union was ahead in scientific research on space questions; if so, the U.S. should want to stop the process now. As the U.S. did not, Soviet superiority in space research did not appear to be the problem.

Gorbachev felt he had to say that he did not know what lay at the bottom of the U.S. position. How the U.S. had come to its position was not important. . . . What was important to him was the position itself. Gorbachev was concerned that [it] . . . was fed by an illusion that the U.S. was ahead in the technology and information transfer systems on which space systems could be based, and that a possibility therefore existed to obtain military superiority. . . . The U.S. might even consider it possible to obtain a first-strike capability, or, under certain circumstances, to launch a first strike. The Soviet Union needed to consider worst cases in developing its policies. . . .

With mounting urgency, Gorbachev said he must return to the problem of SDI, even at the risk of injecting some tension into the discussion. He did not want to do this. But he could not ignore the importance of the problem. . . . If the U.S. departed from the [January understanding] road, Gorbachev did not know when it would be possible for the two countries to meet on it again. Everything at the Geneva . . . talks would come to a halt. For its part, the Soviet Union remained committed to the goals of the . . . understanding, and was prepared to do everything possible to achieve them. . . .

The President underscored that SDI was not a weapons system or a plan for conducting war in space. It was an effort to find a more civilized means of deterring war than reliance on thousands of nuclear missiles which, if used, would kill millions on both sides. Never before in history had the possibility existed of a war which would bring about the end of civilization. . . . The U.S. did not see in SDI a means of obtaining military advantage over the Soviet Union. The benefits of SDI would be for the USSR as well as the U.S. . . . . The U.S. objective was that whoever developed a feasible defensive system would share it, so that any threat to the other side would be eliminated. . . .

Gorbachev replied that he understood the President's arguments but found them unconvincing. They contained many emotional elements, elements which were part of one man's dream. Gorbachev did not wish to suggest that the United States did not want peace. But the fact was that SDI would result in the appearance of weapons in space. They might be built as anti-missile weapons but they would have the capability of striking earth. The USSR could never know for sure. The Soviets had agreed on 50 percent reductions in nuclear weapons. But the President was advocating a whole new class of weapons. Describing these weapons as a shield was only packaging. They would open a new arms race in space. . . . Gorbachev said there were dreams of peace and there were realities. . . .

Gorbachev asked the President with some emotion why he would not believe him when he said that the Soviet Union would never attack. Before the President could respond, Gorbachev repeated the question. He again interrupted the President to insist on a response.

The President stated that no individual could say to the U.S. people that they should rely on his personal faith rather than on a sound defense. Gorbachev questioned the sincerity of the President's willingness to share SDI research, pointing out the U.S. did not share its most advanced technology even with its allies. . . .

The President again asked Gorbachev to consider whether he could not accept the idea of a shield.

16. Memorandum of Conversation between President Ronald Reagan and General Secretary Mikhail Gorbachev, Reykjavik Summit, October 11, 1986

Source: National Security Archive Electronic Briefing Book no. 203, document 9.

Larger Meeting

The President agreed to listen to Gorbachev's proposals.

Gorbachev indicated that in the basic exchange of opinions on bilateral relations, he had recognized an admission of the mutual ultimate aim of total elimination of nuclear weapons. This stemmed from what had been agreed in Geneva, i.e., that a nuclear war must never be fought. On January 15 [1985] the Soviet side had proposed a plan for the complete elimination of nuclear weapons. The US side had also made various proposals. Gorbachev wished to confirm that the US side should understand that during the movement towards complete elimination of nuclear weapons, it was expected that there would be equality and equal security for both sides at all stages of this process. Neither side should attempt to strive to achieve superiority.

Gorbachev said that he wanted to begin with the area of strategic offensive weapons. In Geneva the Soviet side had proposed a reduction of these weapons by 50 percent . . . but now he wished to say that the Soviet side is interested in radical reductions of strategic offensive arms by 50 percent and no less. . . . [U]nlike previous Soviet proposals, wherein the 50 percent covered all weapons reaching the territory of the other side, the present one concerns only strategic weapons, without including medium-range missiles or forward-based systems. This takes into account the US viewpoint and is a concession.

Gorbachev continued that . . . in reducing these forces by 50 percent, the Soviet side would be prepared to have a considerable reduction of heavy missiles, in answer to US concerns. He wished to stress that this would be considerable, and not just cosmetic. However, he would expect the US side to have the same regard for the Soviet side's concerns. One example of this would be the fact that there are now 6500 nuclear warheads on American submarines. . . . The Soviet side knows the great precision of US missiles, both submarine-based and land-based. Therefore each side would need to meet the concerns of the other one, and not try to back it into a corner.

Gorbachev continued that . . . taking into account the situation in Western Europe . . . the Soviet side was proposing to have a complete elimination of US and Soviet medium-range nuclear forces in Europe. In doing so, the Soviet side made the concession not to count English and French nuclear forces. . . . In Asia the US should take back its demands about these missiles or give instructions to both sides to negotiate this issue. . . . With regard to missiles of less than 1000 kilometer range, the Soviet side proposed a freeze. . . .

Gorbachev continued that the third item was the question of the ABM Treaty and nuclear testing. He thought that for both sides to have greater confidence . . . it would be important to set a specific period for non-withdrawal, . . . a sufficiently long period of time, but not less than ten years, followed by a 3–5 year period for negotiations on how to proceed. . . . [A]nother issue connected with . . . adherence by both sides to the ABM Treaty would [be] the prohibition of anti-satellite weapons. . . . The Soviet side was proposing to arrive at a mutually acceptable agreement on this score. . . .

The President replied that the General Secretary's proposals were very encouraging, although there were some differences vis-à-vis the US position. The first one concerned INF. The zero proposal in Europe was acceptable, but the missiles in Asia should also be reduced. . . . After consultation with Secretary Shultz, the President said that instead of the zero option, there could be a maximum of 100 warheads on each side [author's note: which would have permitted deployment of virtually the entire planned Pershing II force (108 missiles)]. . . . But the main issue was strategic arms. The US side also wants to reduce them to zero. But there is a problem with the question of the ABM provisions. SDI was born as an idea which would give a chance to all of us to completely eliminate strategic weapons. . . .

17. Memorandum of Conversation between President Ronald Reagan and General Secretary Mikhail Gorbachev, Reykjavik Summit, October 12, 1986

Source: Ronald Reagan Papers, National Security Files, Executive Secretariat, NSC, Records System File, box 8690725, Ronald Reagan Library.

. . . In introducing his counterproposal, Gorbachev began by saying that it incorporated the positions of the U.S. and Soviet sides and also strengthened the ABM Treaty, while drastically reducing nuclear arms.

The USSR and United States undertake for ten years not to exercise their existing right of withdrawal from the ABM Treaty, which is of unlimited duration, and during that period strictly to observe all its provisions. The testing in space of all space components of anti-ballistic missile defense is prohibited, except research and testing conducted in laboratories. Within the first five years of the ten-year period (and thus by the end of 1991), the strategic offensive arms of the two sides shall be reduced by 50 percent. During the following five years of that period the remaining 50 percent of the two sides' strategic offensive arms shall be reduced. Thus, by the end of 1996, the strategic offensive arms of the USSR and the United States will have been totally eliminated. . . .

The President said he had the following proposal[:]

[Author's note: In the source document this actually appears as an "introductory explanation" at the head of the text.] Both sides would agree to confine themselves to research, development and testing which is permitted by the ABM Treaty for a period of five years, through 1991, during which time a 50% reduction in strategic offensive arsenals would be achieved. This being done, both sides will continue the pace of reductions with respect to all remaining offensive ballistic missiles with the goal of the total elimination of all offensive ballistic missiles by the end of the second five-year period. As long as these reductions continue at the appropriate pace, the same restrictions will continue to apply. At the end of the ten-year period, with all offensive ballistic missiles eliminated, either side would be free to introduce defenses. . . .

Gorbachev again asked that the President look at the Soviet proposal, which, he said, incorporated both the U.S. and the Soviet point of view. If it were acceptable, the Soviet side would be prepared to sign off on it. . . .

The President replied that if both sides had completely eliminated nuclear weapons and there was no longer any threat, why would there be any concern if one side built a safeguard, a defensive system against non-existent weapons. . . .

Gorbachev replied that without that there was no package. . . . [Following some additional discussion, a break ensued from 4:30 to 5:30 p.m. After the break, President Reagan read an amended proposal that used the Soviet language in general but the U.S. preference for permissible SDI activities and a second-stage reduction of ballistic missiles only.]

Gorbachev asked again whether the language on laboratory testing had been omitted on purpose. He was trying to clarify the U.S. proposal.

The President confirmed it had been left out on purpose.

Gorbachev continued that his next question was that the first part of the proposal talks about strategic offensive weapons, and the second part about ballistic missiles. He asks why there is this difference in approach.

The President said he had received the message while he was upstairs [with his advisers] that the Soviets were mainly interested in ballistic missiles. He had thought earlier that they were thinking of everything nuclear, and then he had heard it was ballistic missiles.

Gorbachev said no, they had in mind strategic offensive weapons. . . . [H]e could confirm that the Soviets are for reducing strategic offensive weapons. Other agreements could cover other weapons, for instance medium-range weapons. . . .

The President said we had proposed reducing all ballistic missiles on land and sea, but he was ready to include all the nuclear weapons we can.

Gorbachev said we should use the whole triad. . . .

The President agreed this could be sorted out. He asked whether Gorbachev was saying that beginning in the first five-year period and then going on in the second we would be reducing all nuclear weapons—cruise missiles, battlefield weapons, sub-launched and the like. It would be fine with him if we eliminated all nuclear weapons.

Gorbachev said we can do that.

The Secretary said, "Let's do it." . . .

The President said if they could agree to eliminate all nuclear weapons, he thought they could turn it over to their Geneva people with that understanding, for them to draft up that agreement, and Gorbachev could come to the U.S. and sign it.

Gorbachev agreed. He continued that now we want to turn to the ABM Treaty. He was apprehensive about this. . . .

The President said he would not destroy the possibility of proceeding with SDI. He could not confine work to the laboratory. . . .

Gorbachev said he understood this was the President's final position. . . .

The President said he could not give in.

Gorbachev asked if that was the last word.

The President said yes. . . .

18. National Intelligence Estimate, "Soviet Policy Toward Eastern Europe under Gorbachev," May 1988

Source: NIE 11/12-9-88, reprinted in *At Cold War's End: US Intelligence on the Soviet Union and Eastern Europe, 1989–1991*, ed. Benjamin B. Fischer (Reston, VA: Central Intelligence Agency, 1999).

KEY JUDGMENTS

General Secretary Gorbachev's policies have increased the potential for instability in Eastern Europe. But they have also expanded the scope for diversity and experimentation, affording new possibilities for evolutionary reform in the region.
. . .

Soviet policy under Gorbachev has sought to balance the competing objectives of encouraging change and promoting stability. Although Gorbachev has avoided a high-risk strategy of forcing change on these fragile political systems, continuing Soviet pressure, as well as the example of the Soviet reform program, has introduced new tensions. . . .

At best, Gorbachev's approach can achieve only evolutionary progress toward political rejuvenation and improved economic performance in Eastern Europe. Continued, and probably heightened, Soviet pressure will lead to sharper conflicts, both within Eastern European societies and between Moscow and its allies. . . .

DISCUSSION [Paragraph numbers omitted]

Outlook: Growing Diversity, Sharper Conflict

Soviet policy toward Eastern Europe is likely to continue along the lines already established under Gorbachev. Its key elements will be:

- Within the framework of firm party control, *sanctioning of diversity and experimentation* as the keys to economic and political viability.
- Continued *pressure for reform* without dictating specific measures to demanding slavish emulation of Soviet practices.
- Insistence on *foreign policy coordination*, whereby the East Europeans are afforded greater room for tactical maneuver but are expected to hew closely to the broad lines set in Moscow.
- Mounting pressure for *improved East European economic performance* and increased cooperation in high-technology areas.
- Longer-term efforts toward *strengthened institutional ties*, coupled with alliance management techniques that facilitate Soviet control and influence through a more participatory system of give-and-take. . . .

Popular Upheaval. Several of the usual instability indicators—discontent over living standards, weak and divided leadership, social unrest—are evident in several countries, and all face pressures emanating from Moscow. New shocks—severe austerity measures, the death or ouster of a top party leader, or the emergence of an organized and emboldened opposition—could bring about instability almost anywhere, with Poland, Romania, and Hungary the most likely candidates for trouble:

- The likelihood of multiple, simultaneous upheavals is higher than it has been in more than 30 years. In the late 1980s and into the early 1990s virtually all the Eastern European countries face analogous sets of problems: stagnant economies, leadership successions, and reformist pressures from Moscow.

- As in the past, however, possible scenarios would be highly country-specific. Only in Romania is there a significant possibility of widespread violence; elsewhere the greater likelihood would be a broad-based, organized challenge to regime authority. (In Poland, however, this latter scenario could also lead to a cycle of repression and violence.)

For Gorbachev, a possible upheaval in Eastern Europe constitutes the greatest external threat to the Soviet reform program and his own continued tenure. Despite the greater tolerance he has shown for experimentation, he will expect his allies to take swift, decisive action to end any political violence or major unrest. Indeed, the Eastern European leaderships are at least as aware as Gorbachev is of the need for vigilance, and they have at their disposal large security forces that have been effective thus far. . . . Should events overwhelm the capacity of local leaders, there is no reason to doubt that he would take whatever action was required, including military intervention, to preserve party rule and Soviet authority. . . .

Sweeping Reform. Gorbachev has expanded the limits of acceptable reform. In Hungary and Poland particularly, reform blueprints are being circulated that go well beyond anything now on the agenda in Moscow. And now the Hungarians have put in place a leadership team containing radical reformers, such as Imre Pozsgay, head of Hungary's Patriotic People's Front. . . . Given the fate of previous reform movements, there would be strong elite and popular inhibitions against direct challenges to party supremacy and the Soviet alliance system. If Eastern Europe's past is any guide, however, a genuine reform movement in Hungary or elsewhere would tend inevitably toward national self-determination and autonomy. . . .

19. Gorbachev's Growing Confrontation with the KGB: A Coming Showdown? June 1988

Source: CIA, Intelligence Assessment, SOV 88-10045X, Princeton Collection.

Despite evidence of significant KGB support for Gorbachev's bid for party leadership in 1985, there now appears to be a growing rift between the General Secretary and the KGB, including its chairman, Viktor Chebrikov. This relationship began to change as Gorbachev's domestic reforms were increasingly perceived by elements in the KGB as threatening their interests. Now, Gorbachev apparently wants to curb the power and influence of the KGB itself. There is evidence that some in the KGB are starting to fight back. . . .

Differences between Gorbachev and Chebrikov came out in the open last September, when the KGB chief criticized aspects of the General Secretary's reform agenda for harming the country's security. Chebrikov and other senior KGB officers apparently fear that *glasnost*, greater toleration of dissent, and reforms in the legal system sharply reduce their ability to guarantee the stability of Soviet society. Senior security officials also apparently believe that, over the long run, Gorbachev wants a reduced role for the KGB, and they are concerned this will threaten their jobs and privileged positions.

Chebrikov is now siding with more cautious members of the Politburo who are trying to slow the General Secretary's program. Recent rumors of Chebrikov's opposition to *perestroyka*, reports that he was "Second Secretary" Ligachev's only supporter at a heated Politburo meeting over reform, and unconfirmed stories, leaked to Western reporters and diplomats, of the replacement or augmentation of Gorbachev's KGB bodyguards with military troops suggest that Chebrikov is increasingly perceived as taking a greater role in leadership politics on the side of the conservatives.

The KGB, which has become involved in party politics at several critical junctures since Stalin's death, can be a dangerous adversary. Although the KGB has never acted on its own, it has been on the winning side in party power struggles in 1957, 1964, 1982, and 1985. Short of a political showdown, members of the KGB could use connections at home or abroad to spread rumors to damage the General Secretary, use information in their confidential files to discredit his supporters, or even provoke incidents to embarrass him.

Gorbachev needs a loyal KGB more than ever to monitor elite compliance with policies that are unpopular at lower levels as well as to monitor political attitudes. Thus far, however, the KGB has been largely untouched by Gorbachev's restructuring of Soviet agencies responsible for national security. This stability increasingly appears to be more a reflection of his difficulty in asserting control over the KGB than his high regard for its performance.

The revival of ethnic unrest in the Caucasus has posed a serious political challenge that may force the General Secretary to accede temporarily to the demands of Politburo conservatives. However, while in the short run Gorbachev may be forced to make a tactical retreat, we believe that political reconciliation appears unlikely.

The General Secretary will need to gain control of the security service to further his reforms and to preclude its becoming involved in plotting against him by more conservative party leaders. Gorbachev already has increased party oversight of KGB activities by naming a personal ally to a position in the Central Committee Secretariat to supervise legal reform, the police, and the KGB. This action may have bought him some time but to achieve his goals he will ultimately have to replace Chebrikov. . . .

20. SDI: Technology, Survivability, and Software, May 1988

Source: U.S. Congress, Office of Technology Assessment, OTA-ISC-353 (Washington, DC: U.S. Government Printing Office, May 1988).

Finding 1: After 30 years of BMD [ballistic missile defense] research, including the first few years of the Strategic Defense Initiative (SDI) . . . questions remain about the feasibility of meeting the goals of SDI. . . .

Finding 2: Given optimistic assumptions . . . the kind of first-phase system that SDIO [the Strategic Defense Initiative Organization] is considering might be technically deployable in the 1995–2000 period. . . . Depending on [an array of specified factors] such a system might destroy anywhere from a few up to a modest fraction of attacking Soviet intercontinental ballistic missile (ICBM) warheads. . . . Additional defense capabilities would soon be needed to sustain this level of defense against either increased or more advanced, but clearly feasible, Soviet offenses.

Finding 3: A rational commitment to a "phase-one" development and deployment . . . would imply: a) belief that the outstanding technical issues will be favorably resolved later; b) willingness to settle for interim BMD capabilities that would decline as Soviet offenses improved; or c) belief that U.S. efforts will persuade the Soviets to join in reducing offensive forces. . . .

Finding 4: The precise degree of BMD system survivability is hard to anticipate . . .

Finding 5: There has been little analysis of any kind of space-based threats to BMD system survivability. . . . In particular, SDIO and its contractors have conducted no serious study of the situation in which the United States and the Soviet Union both occupy space with comparable BMD systems. Such a situation could place a high premium on striking first at the other side's defenses. The technical (as well as the political) feasibility of an arms control agreement to avoid such mutual vulnerability remains uncertain.

Finding 6: The survivability of BMD systems now under consideration implies unilateral U.S. control of certain sectors of space. . . .

Finding 7: The nature of software and experience with large, complex software systems indicate that there may always be irresolvable questions about how dependable BMD software would be and about the confidence the United States could place in [effectiveness] estimates. . . .

Finding 8: No adequate models for the development, production, test, and maintenance of software for full-scale BMD systems exist. . . .

Finding 9: There is broad agreement in the technical community that significant parts of the research being carried out under SDI are in the national interest. There is disagreement about whether this research is best carried out within a program that is strongly oriented toward an early 1990s BMD deployment decision, and that includes system development as well as research elements. . . .

21. Solidarity Memorandum "On Starting the Roundtable Talks," September 4, 1988

Source: Document no. 5034D242-96B6-175C-992FABF9B73B5B13, CWIHP Virtual Archive, www.CWIHP.org. Reprinted by permission of the Woodrow Wilson International Center for Scholars.

Right now we can begin to discuss the topics for negotiations, which I presented in my statement of 26 August. I think that in the beginning of next week talks should be concerned with two questions:

1. implementation of the promise made by the authorities that there would be no repression toward striking workers, and that those [repressive measures which] have been applied will be annulled.
2. union pluralism and within its framework the legalization of NSZZ 60 "Solidarity," consistent with the [demands] of the striking crews.

I think that the first stage of implementing the principle of the "Roundtable" process should be a factual discussion of the above topics and preliminary decisions. The composition of the meeting should initially be trilateral [including the Church], as was our meeting on 31 August. I am going to present personal proposals separately.

A positive consideration of the above mentioned questions will allow for a broader debate on economic and political reforms in our country.

Lech Wałęsa

Gdansk, 4 September 1988

22. General Mikhail S. Gorbachev Address to 43rd UN General Assembly Session, December 7, 1988

Source: UN General Assembly, Provisional Verbatim Record of 72nd Meeting, New York.

. . . The history of past centuries and millennia has been a history of almost ubiquitous wars and sometimes desperate battles, leading to mutual destruction. They occurred in the clash of social and political interests and national hostility, be it from ideological or religious incompatibility. All that was the case, and even now many still claim that this past—which has not been overcome—is an immutable pattern. However, parallel with the process of wars, hostility, and alienation of peoples and countries, another process, just as objectively conditioned, was in motion and gaining force: The process of the emergence of a mutually connected and integral world.

Further world progress is now possible only through the search for a consensus of all mankind, in movement toward a new world order. We have arrived at a frontier at which controlled spontaneity leads to a dead end. The world community must learn to shape and direct the process in such a way as to preserve civilization, to make it safe for all and more pleasant for normal life. . . . It is evident, for example, that force and the threat of force can no longer be, and should not be instruments of foreign policy. . . .

Today I can inform you of the following: The Soviet Union has made a decision on reducing its armed forces. In the next two years, their numerical strength will be reduced by 500,000 persons, and the volume of conventional arms will also be cut considerably. These reductions will be made on a unilateral basis, unconnected with negotiations on the mandate of the Vienna meeting [on Mutual Balanced Force Reduction (MBFR) in Europe]. By agreement with our allies in the Warsaw Pact, we have made the decision to withdraw six tank divisions from the GDR [East Germany], Czechoslovakia, and Hungary, and to disband them by 1991. Assault landing formations and units, and a number of others, including assault river-crossing forces, with their armaments and combat equipment, will also be withdrawn from the groups of Soviet forces in those countries. The Soviet forces situated in those countries will be cut by 50,000 persons, and their arms by 5,000 tanks. All remaining Soviet divisions on the territory of our allies will be reorganized. They will be given a different structure from today's which will become unambiguously defensive, after the removal of a large number of their tanks. . . .

The inheritance of inertia of the past are continuing to operate. Profound contradictions and the roots of many conflicts have not disappeared. The fundamental fact remains that the formation of the peaceful period will take place in conditions of the existence and rivalry of various socioeconomic and political systems. However, the meaning of our international efforts, and one of the key tenets of the new thinking, is precisely to impart to this rivalry the quality of sensible competition in conditions of respect for freedom of choice and a balance of interests. In this case it will even become useful and productive from the viewpoint of general world development; otherwise, if the main component remains the arms race, as it has been until now, rivalry will be fatal. . . .

23. Diary of Anatoly S. Chernyaev, December 17, 1988

Source: National Security Archive Electronic Briefing Book no. 250, trans. Anna Melyakova and ed. Svetlana Savranskaya (Washington, DC: National Security Archive, May 23, 2008), http://www.gwu.edu/~nsarchiv/NSAEBB/NSAEBB250/Chernyaev_Diary_1988.pdf.

. . . . Meanwhile, I can record what happened at the UN. . . . In the hallway groups of officials met [Mikhail Gorbachev—"M.S."] with applause. . . . For over an hour [during the speech] nobody stirred. And then the audience erupted in ovations, and they would not let M.S. go for a long time. He even had to get up and bow as if he were on stage.

24. Report of the Bogomolov Commission on the Soviet Union and East-Central Europe, February 1989

Source: Donation of Professor Jacques Levesque, National Security Archive.

Societies in Eastern European countries are beginning to change their character. Attempts to build socialism with Stalinist and neo-Stalinist methods, the spread of which occurred in the region not without the active involvement of the Soviet side, ended up in a stalemate. The situation was expressed in an aggravation of contradictions and a growth of crisis developments. The degree and scale of conflicts vary: from the more or less hidden tension, fraught with sudden explosions, to chronic crisis without any visible ways out, signaling the beginning of disintegration of the social-political system not excluding cataclysms as well. Such processes are irreversible; they are the result of the long-term evolution of the regime, and in a majority of countries they accompany a transition to a new model of socialism but can also lead to a collapse of the socialist idea. In the last year or year and a half the development of events in Eastern Europe has sharply accelerated and has acquired elements of unpredictability. . . .

In the political sphere the crisis manifests itself first of all in the dramatic weakening of the positions of the ruling communist parties, in some cases so dramatic that one can speak about a crisis of confidence in them. Some of these parties undergo an internal crisis: their membership is decreasing since rank-and-file members do not want to bear responsibility for decisions which they could never influence. The old social basis is eroding. . . . Under pressure from multiplying and intensifying alternative political structures . . . the [Hungarian Socialist Workers' Party] and the [Polish United Workers' Party] have become so weak that they have to share power and accept a coalition form of government, agree to a transition to a genuine multi-party system, and to the legalization of dissenting opposition forces. . . .

A degradation of common ties is taking place in various forms. Interest in present forms of integration is visibly weakening as well as hopes to substantially increase its effectiveness through direct ties and cooperation in technology. Due to profound structural problems and flaws in the mechanism of trade cooperation, bilateral trade with the USSR is decreasing, which produces very negative consequences for the national economies of our partners and creates additional obstacles in the path of economic reforms. . . .

Possible practical steps of the USSR . . .

- Working out a strategic program to develop our relations with Eastern European socialist countries in the framework of a new model of socialism and a proportional reflection of this program in official documents and speeches.
- Advancement of our proposals to reform the Warsaw Treaty Organization, stipulating a larger role for the fraternal countries. . . .

- A further gradual reduction of our military presence in Eastern Europe taken at our own initiative and by agreement with the host countries. . . .
- Development of bilateral consultations on mutually beneficial measures permitting an alleviation of the consequences of restructuring in the countries of Eastern Europe. . . .
- In case appropriate proposals are made, we should agree to some form of continuous and periodic consultations with West European countries and the US on the issue of the prevention of upheavals in one or another country of Central and Eastern Europe.
- Introducing the practice of genuine consultation on the issues of foreign policy with our allies instead of informing them about decisions that have already been made. . . .

Overcoming the crisis process in the countries of Eastern Europe presupposes outright de-Stalinization. This should encompass both their internal life as well as their relations with the Soviet Union. The model of economic and political development imposed on these countries after 1948 has clearly exhausted its capabilities. . . . To a certain degree one can speak about the end of the postwar era. . . .

From the viewpoint of the world socialist perspective any attempt to stop this evolution by force could have the gravest consequences. . . .

25. Memorandum to Alexander Yakovlev from CPSU Central Committee International Department, February 1, 1989

Source: Donation of Professor Jacques Levesque, National Security Archive.

THE STRATEGY OF RELATIONS WITH EUROPEAN SOCIALIST COUNTRIES

Our relations with socialist countries, including the allies of the Warsaw Treaty Organization, entered a difficult, critical stage. The transition to the principle of equal and mutual responsibility, which began in April 1985 and was affirmed during the Working Meeting in Moscow in 1986, gave us an opportunity to remove many layers and eliminate perceptions of our conservatism. *Perestroika*, the development of democratization, [and] *glasnost*, confirmed the role of the Soviet Union as the leader in the process of socialist renewal. More and more we are influencing our friends by our own example, by political means. . . .

In the present circumstance we could formulate the following "minimum program" for our relations with socialist countries in the transitional period:

First of all, we should have a balanced and unprejudiced analysis of the development of socialist countries, of their relations, and we should prepare scenarios of our reaction to possible complications or sharp turns in their policies ahead of time, at the same time decisively rejecting the old stereotypes, and avoiding willful improvisations which did us great harm in the past. . . .

Second, we should keep in mind that the significance of our contacts with the party and state leadership of the socialist countries is preserved and even increases in significance, especially because in the existing situation our friends could develop a "complex of abandonment." . . .

Third, in explaining the essence of *perestroika* policy, we should try to avoid any artificial transfer of our experience to the context of other countries. . . .

Fourth, by strictly adhering to our obligations, we should preserve the existing ties that link the socialist countries to the USSR and try to ensure that the inevitable, and, for the common interests, to a certain extent beneficial process of integrating the socialist economies with the West develops in a balanced, coordinated way. . . .

Fifth, taking into account the key role of the armed forces in the case of the possible deterioration of the situation, it is important to maintain genuine partnership between the armies of the socialist countries both on a bilateral basis and in the framework of the Warsaw Pact. . . .

Sixth, we should continue our policy of decreasing our military presence in the socialist countries, including the future possibility of a complete withdrawal of our troops from Hungary and Czechoslovakia. . . .

Seventh, it is certainly in our interest that the changes that are ready to happen in the socialist countries, with all the possible variations, develop as much as possible inherently without unnecessary shocks and crises, within the framework of socialist solutions. . . .

Eighth. By making use of the favorable opportunities created by *perestroika* which overturned the stereotypes of "Moscow conservatism," we should actively seek channels for contacts with all the forces in the socialist countries which compete for participation in acquiring power. Contacts [with] churches are becoming more important because the church's influence is obviously on the rise in the socialist countries.

In general, at this stage it is particularly important to reject the old stereotypes in our approaches, which have outlived themselves. . . .

26. The Political Processes in the European Socialist Countries and the Proposals for Our Practical Steps Considering the Situation Which Has Arisen in Them, February 24, 1989

Source: Memorandum by the Soviet Ministry of Foreign Affairs, donation of Professor Jacques Levesque, National Security Archive.

The socialist community is experiencing the most difficult period in its development in the entire postwar period. An extremely complex situation has arisen in Eastern Europe. We are talking about the fate of socialism in a number of countries of this region, the future of the Warsaw Pact, [and] the fundamental interests of the Soviet Union.

The serious difficulties which the European socialist countries have encountered are chiefly connected with a crisis of the administrative command model of socialism. This model has entered into obvious contradiction with the requirements of the development of society, has become a brake on the path of socioeconomic and scientific-technical progress, and has created a real threat of a growing gap between the socialist world and the West. . . .

In some countries—Hungary, Poland, and Yugoslavia—the leadership is carrying out political and economic reforms extremely decisively, in others—Romania, the German Democratic Republic, Czechoslovakia, and Bulgaria—[the leadership] actually remains a follower of the administrative command system. . . .

The surmounting of a negative legacy and the renewal of socialism are occurring with difficulty and conflict. The ruling parties of a majority of countries have delayed carrying out reforms and several of them have lost the confidence [of] the public and are now losing control over the course of events. This chiefly concerns Poland and Hungary. . . .

As a whole, a growth of nationalism in all East European countries, and a strengthening of centrifugal tendencies in their policies has been observed. . . .

27. Record of Conversation between President Mikhail Gorbachev and Prime Minister Miklós Németh of Hungary, March 3, 1989

Source: Document no. 5034D3D8-96B6-175C-9FD704945B3E213D, CWIHP Virtual Archive, www.CWIHP.org. Reprinted by permission of the Woodrow Wilson International Center for Scholars.

. . . NÉMETH: In the days when Lenin was at the helm, there were endless debates and a clear political line was formed all the same.

GORBACHEV: Yes, because there were entirely different conditions both in the Party and in the country. Now we are opening the way towards socialist pluralism. The multiplicity of opinions is not a tragedy for the society; on the contrary, it is a real advantage. Of course, there are some who want to exhibit democracy for their own selfish objectives, but it can be dealt with, it is merely a question of struggle. . . .

NÉMETH: Yes, the conditions are changing. . . . Every socialist country is developing in its idiosyncratic way, and their leaders are above all accountable to their own people. Whether it be one party or more—life will show which solution is more effective. Within our conditions, state and party have become the same. This affected the development of the country in a most unfavorable way. [But] we should not eradicate everything with one stroke, because what we achieved is worth noting.

GORBACHEV: I believe that Pozsgay's statements are quite extremist in this respect. The events of 1956 indeed started with the dissatisfaction of the people. Later, however, the events escalated into a counterrevolution and bloodshed. This cannot be overlooked.

NÉMETH: Most important of all, these questions should not cause division in the society. Some say that we need to look at history in the same way, because otherwise there will be no unity in society at all. In reality, however, unity in interpreting the past does not exist. The main thing is that we have unity with regard to the present situation and in the policy to follow.

GORBACHEV: Indeed, every generation is responsible for the present, first and foremost.

NÉMETH: I am convinced that the organic interrelation and conformity of the economy and politics in fundamental issues is indispensable. A principal question is that of pace. We Hungarians started economic reform long ago, while leaving political institutions intact. Since last May, we have witnessed a rapid development and transformation of the political system. A new election system, the reorganization of parliament, and other measures followed one another in such a rapid succession, the wheels of the machine are turning with such dizzying speed that it could pose a potential danger to society if this process interrupted economic development.

Nobody actually doubts that a democratic constitutional state is unavoidable for a successful people's economy to function. Having only that, though, without a productive economy, then political transformation will happen in a void, *l'art pour l'art.* Pozsgay says that there is nothing wrong with politics superseding the economy. We, on the contrary, think that harmonization of the two is needed. We support and develop economic institutions, in parallel with changes in the political sphere. We will act with responsibility.

GORBACHEV: You have touched upon an important issue. The process of renewal is gradually spreading over the entire socialist bloc, and adds to the political culture and historical experiences of all these countries according to the local conditions. The most important for all of them, however, is turning toward the people and revitalizing the socialist system. . . .

28. Hungarian Government Agreement on National Roundtable Talks, June 10, 1989

Source: Document no. 5034D4F1-96B6-175C-9C42FB1EAF1BEB05, CWIHP Virtual Archive, www.CWIHP.org. Reprinted by permission of the Woodrow Wilson International Center for Scholars.

AGREEMENT

About the Commencement of Substantial Political Negotiations between the Hungarian Socialist Workers' Party, the Members of the Opposition Roundtable and the Organizations of the Third Side, 10 June 1989

I.

The necessity to help the nation out of a serious political and economic crisis, and the democratic transformation of the conditions of power [make] appropriate the dialogue between all the political circles that feel responsible for the future. Handling the crisis and creating a multiparty system is only possible with the agreement of the democratic forces. It presupposes that mutual objectives and aims are taken into account, that all participants are willing to make an agreement, and it necessitates trust and self-restraint.

The fate of the nation can be improved by respecting the requirements of the constitution and firmly rejecting violence. It is in our mutual interest that social conflicts are solved according to the generally agreed norms of European political culture: with public consent. The transition from a single-party system to representational democracy and constitutional government can only be realized by free elections. Well-functioning representative bodies and a firm consistent government that is trusted by the people are needed to stop the worsening social and economic crisis. The peaceful political transition and the relief of aggravated economic and social tension can only be realized by mutual agreement. An array of historical examples warn us that common problems can only be solved with consensus. All civil organizations and movements have to take part side by side in the hard and contradictory process of transition. . . .

The equal negotiators accept the following governing principles for the talks:

- the basis of power is the sovereignty of the people; none of the political forces can monopolize it and declare themselves the sole repository of the people's will, and none can aspire to unconstitutionally curtail political rights;
- the will of the people has to be expressed without preceding limitations, in the course of free elections, the result of which is binding for everyone, and from which no political organization that complies with the requirements of the constitution can be excluded;
- handling the crisis, ensuring a democratic transition and resolving political conflicts is only possible in a peaceful way, avoiding violence; none of the civil organizations can have direct control over military forces;
- an important condition of the successful and constructive political negotiations is that the nation and [the parties'] interests are considered and respected; a further condition is mutual and anticipatory confidence;
- only mutually acceptable conditions can be the basis for cooperation and agreement;
- when determining the participants of negotiations and their legal standing, exclusion of a political nature is unacceptable, although the functioning of the negotiation process must be considered;
- the objective of negotiations is the formation of political agreements that can be accompanied by the necessary government measures and bills, together with the deadline for their realization; the negotiations themselves, however, do not directly exercise the functions of constitutional law;
- during the course of the negotiations the parties refrain from all unilateral steps that would obliterate the goal of negotiations; legislation cannot precede political agreement;
- all negotiating partners will have the political agreements accepted in their own organizations, and represent them in public as well, while assisting in the enforcement of the agreements by every possible political means. . . .

29. Memorandum of Telephone Conversation between Chancellor Helmut Kohl and President George H. W. Bush, October 23, 1989

Source: *"George Bush–Helmut Kohl Telcon, 10/23/89 re: Eastern Europe,"* Selected Documents from the Archives, George H. W. Bush Library, http://bushlibrary. tamu.edu/research/pdfs/telcon6-23-89.pdf.

CHANCELLOR KOHL: I wanted to tell you briefly how I see events in Hungary, Poland, and the GDR [East Germany]. In Hungary, things are going the best. The people are incredibly courageous, and very determined. The present government is taking an enormous risk: the changes have their origin within the reform movement in the Communist Party, but it is not at all certain that the reformers will be able to get credit in the course of the election. It is quite possible that the Party will come in only second, and there might be a coalition. We have supported the Hungarians quite vigorously. . . .

I will go to Budapest and perhaps also to a second city, but that is not certain. The economic situation is relatively good there. They can make it, though the next two years will be decisive. On November 9 I will go to Poland. . . . Our negotiations have been essentially concluded. I will do all I can to support the new government. . . . There is a lot of good will and many good ideas but the Poles do not know how to put them into practice. They have to introduce currency reforms, a new banking system, and other steps to open up a new market-oriented economy. . . . My feeling is that our Western friends and partners should be doing more. There is a difference between words and deeds. I also want to enter into a new phase with the Poles. . . .

In the GDR, changes are quite dramatic. None of us can give a prognosis. It is not clear whether the new man will have the determination and the strength to carry out reform. Gorbachev told me that he had encouraged reform during his visit, but I am not sure how courageous he [new GDR party leader Egon Krenz] is. There is an enormous unrest among the population. Things will become incalculable if there are no reforms. My interest is not to see so many flee the GDR, because the consequences there would be catastrophic. Our estimates are that by Christmas we will have reached a total of 150,000 refugees. . . .

PRESIDENT BUSH: . . . I know your position and I think I know the heartbeat of Germany. The strength of NATO has made possible these changes in

Eastern Europe. . . . We are trying to react very cautiously and carefully to change in the GDR.

30. Soviet Record of Conversation between President Mikhail S. Gorbachev and Egon Krenz, General Secretary of the Socialist Unity Party (SED) of the German Democratic Republic, November 1, 1989

Source: Document no. 5034D721 96B6-175C-96E82D14FAB9B625, CWIHP Virtual Archive, www.CWIHP.org. Reprinted by permission of the Woodrow Wilson International Center for Scholars.

. . . GORBACHEV: . . . I cannot tell you that we have already "broken in the horse of perestroika," which turned out to be quite restless. In any case, we have not completely tamed it yet. Sometimes it even tries to throw the rider off. But we have gained very valuable experience.

KRENZ: . . . At the [Socialist Unity Party] Politburo we came to the conclusion that the crisis has not emerged [just] in the last several months. Many problems have accumulated over the years.

But the main mistake was probably that we did not make serious conclusions based on the new processes of social development, which began in the Soviet Union, other socialist countries, and which were ripe in the GDR [East Germany] itself. . . .

GORBACHEV: From the political point of view, the situation is clear, but from a simply human standpoint—[it is] dramatic. I was also concerned about this. In general I had good relations with [your predecessor] Honecker, but it seemed recently as if he had lost his vision. If he had been willing to make the necessary changes in policy on his own initiative 2 or 3 years ago, everything would have been different now. But apparently, he had undergone some kind of a shift, he ceased to see real processes in the world and in his own country. It was a personal drama, but because Honecker occupied a very high position, it grew into a political drama.

KRENZ: Yes, you are right, it is a drama, and for me too, because Honecker brought me up, he was my political mentor. . . . For Honecker the turn probably occurred in 1985, when you were elected General Secretary of the [CPSU Central Committee]. In you he saw a threat to his authority, because he considered himself the most dynamic political leader. He lost all touch with reality, and did not rely on the Politburo collective. . . .

GORBACHEV: This is a familiar picture. Some time ago, when I already was a [Soviet] Politburo member, I practically did not know our budget. Once when we were working with Nikolai Ryzhkov on some request of Andropov's having to do with budgetary issues, and we, naturally, decided we should learn about them. But Andropov said: Do not get in there, it is not your business. Now we know why he said so. It was not a budget, but hell knows what. . . .

Yesterday Alexander N. Yakovlev received [former U.S. national security adviser] Zbigniew Brzezinski, who, as you know, has a head with "global brains." And he said: If today the events turned out in such a way that unification of Germany became a reality, it would mean a collapse of many things. I think so far we have held the correct line: stood firmly in favor of the coexistence of two German states, and as a result, came to a wide international recognition of the GDR, achieved the Moscow Treaty, gave a boost to the Helsinki Process. Therefore we should confidently follow the same course.

You must know: all serious political figures—Thatcher, Mitterrand, Andreotti, Jaruzelski, even the Americans—though their position has recently exhibited some nuances—are not looking forward to German unification. Moreover, in today's situation it would probably have an explosive character. The majority of Western leaders do not want to see the dissolution of NATO and of the Warsaw Treaty Organization. Serious politicians understand that they are factors of a necessary equilibrium. However, Mitterrand feels like he has to mention his sympathy for the idea of German unification. The Americans are also speaking about such sympathies for the Germans' pull toward unification. But I think they do it as a favor to Bonn, and also because to some extent, they are anxious about too much rapprochement between [West Germany] and the USSR. Therefore, I repeat, the best course of action now is to continue the same line. . . .

I am convinced we should coordinate our relations with [West Germany] better, although Honecker tried to avoid it. We know about your relations with [them], and you know about our relations. . . .

The situation in Hungary and Poland today is such that they have nowhere else to go, as they say, because they have drowned in financial dependence on the West. Today some people criticize us: they say, what is the Soviet Union doing—allowing Poland and Hungary to "sail" to the West[?] But we cannot take Poland on our balance. [Former Polish leaders] accumulated $48 billion dollars of debt. Poland has already paid off $49 billion, and it still owes almost $49 billion. As far as Hungary is concerned, the International Monetary Fund has dictated its harsh ultimatum already under the late Hungarian leader János Kádár.

KRENZ [whose GDR had concealed from the Soviets its $40 billion budget deficit]: This is not our way.

GORBACHEV: You need to take this into account in your relations with [West Germany]. . . .

We need to think through all of this, and to find formulas that would allow people to realize their human needs. Otherwise we will be forced to accept all kinds of ultimatums. . . . Clearly, your constructive steps should be accompanied with demands for certain obligations from the other side. Chancellor Helmut Kohl keeps in touch with me and with you. We need to influence him. Once under the pressure of the opposition he found himself on the horse of nationalism. The right wing starts to present their demands for the unification of Germany to the Soviet Union and appeals to the US. The logic is simple—all the peoples are united, why do we Germans not have this right?

KRENZ: We have already taken a number of steps. First of all, we gave orders to the border troops not to use weapons at the border, except in the cases of direct attacks on the soldiers. Second, we adopted a draft of Law on Foreign Travel at the Politburo. . . .

31. Press Conference with SED Politburo Member Günter Schabowski at East German Press Center, November 9, 1989

Source: Document no. 5034D7FF-96B6-175C 98E17DFE653CFD6F, CWIHP Virtual Archive, www.CWIHP.org. Reprinted by permission of the Woodrow Wilson International Center for Scholars.

Question: . . . Mr. Schbowski, you spoke about mistakes. Don't you believe that it was a big mistake to introduce this travel law several days ago?

SCHABOWSKI: No, I don't believe so. . . .

There are a series of steps, and the chance, through expanding travel possibilities . . . the chance, through making it easier to leave, to free people from a (um) let us say, psychological pressure. . . .

So we want . . . through a number of changes, including the travel law, to [create] the chance, the sovereign decision of the citizens to travel wherever they want. (um) We are naturally (um) concerned that the possibilities of this travel regulation—it is still not in effect, it's only a draft.

A decision was made today, as far as I know. . . . A recommendation from the Politburo was taken up that we take a passage from the travel regulation and put it into effect, that (um)—as it is called, for better or worse. . . . Since we find it (um) unacceptable that this movement is taking place (um) across the territory of an allied state (um), which is not an easy burden for that country to bear. Therefore (um), we have decided today (um) to implement a regulation that allows every citizen of the German Democratic Republic (um) to (um) leave the GDR through any of the border crossings.

Question: (Many voices) When does that go into effect? . . . Without a passport? Without a passport? (No, no)—When is that in effect? . . . (Confusion, voices) At what point does the regulation take effect?

SCHABOWSKI: (Scratches his head) You see, comrades, I was informed today (puts on his glasses as he speaks further), that such an announcement had been (um) distributed earlier today [his information was erroneous]. You should actually have it already. So (reading very quickly from the paper) . . .

"Permanent exit is possible via all GDR border crossings to [West Germany]. These changes replace the temporary practice of using [travel] authorizations through GDR consulates and permanent exit with a GDR personal identity card via third countries." . . .

Question: When does it come into effect?

SCHABOWSKI: (Looks through his papers) That comes into effect, according to my information, immediately, without delay. . . .

Question: Does this also apply for West Berlin? You only mentioned [West Germany].

SCHABOWSKI: (Shrugs shoulders, frowns, looks at his papers) So . . . (pause), um hmmm (reads aloud): "Permanent exit can take place via all border crossings from the GDR to [West Germany] and West Berlin, respectively." . . .

32. Verbal Message from Mikhail Gorbachev to Helmut Kohl, November 10, 1989

Source: Document no. 5034D81E-96B6-175C-91B61A4AD7C985AB, CWIHP Virtual Archive, www.CWIHP.org. Reprinted by permission of the Woodrow Wilson International Center for Scholars.

As you, of course, know, the GDR [East German] leadership made the decision to allow the citizens of East Germany unrestricted travel to West Berlin and

[West Germany]. It is understandable, that this decision was not an easy one for the new leadership of the GDR. At the same time, the decision underlines the fact that deep and fundamental changes are taking place in East Germany. The leadership is acting in a concerted and dynamic manner in the interests of the people, and they are opening a dialogue with various groups and levels of society. . . .

With the current situation of de facto open borders and huge numbers of people moving in both directions, a chaotic situation could easily develop that might have unforeseen consequences.

In light of the time pressure and the seriousness of the situation, I thought it necessary to ask you, in the spirit of openness and realism, to take the extremely pressing steps necessary to prevent a complication and destabilization of the situation.

33. Verbal Message from Mikhail Gorbachev to François Mitterrand, Margaret Thatcher, and George Bush, November 10, 1989

Source: Document no. 5034D85C-96B6-175C-9031C41CF38BF698, CWIHP Virtual Archive, www.CWIHP.org. Reprinted by permission of the Woodrow Wilson International Center for Scholars.

In light of the rather extreme situation currently taking place in the GDR [East Germany], its capital city, and in West Berlin, and in reference to what I consider the correct and forward-looking decision by the new East German leadership, I have just sent a verbal message to Chancellor Kohl. I consider it necessary to inform you of the contents of the message as well. . . .

I have appealed to Chancellor Kohl to take the extremely pressing steps necessary to prevent a complication and destabilization of the situation.

Our ambassador in Berlin was instructed to contact the representatives of the governments of the three Allied powers in West Berlin. I hope that you will also contact your representatives so that the events do not take an undesirable turn.

In general, I would like to emphasize that deep and fundamental changes are currently taking place in East Germany. If statements are made in [West Germany], however, that seek to generate emotional denials of the postwar realities, meaning the existence of two German states, the appearance of such political extremism cannot be viewed as anything other than attempts to destabilize the situation in the

GDR and subvert the ongoing processes of democratization and the renewal of all areas of society. Looking forward, this would bring about not only the destabilization of the situation in Central Europe, but also in other parts of the world.

I would like to express my hope that you receive this news with understanding.

34. Memorandum of Telephone Conversation between Chancellor Helmut Kohl and President George H. W. Bush, November 10, 1989

Source: *"George Bush–Helmut Kohl Telcon, 11/10/89 re: Eastern Europe,"* Selected Documents from the Archives, George H. W. Bush Library, http://bushlibrary. tamu.edu/research/pdfs/telcon11-10-89.pdf.

CHANCELLOR KOHL: . . . I've just arrived from Berlin. It is like witnessing an enormous fair. It has the atmosphere of a festival. The frontiers are absolutely open. At certain points they are literally taking down the wall and building new checkpoints. At Checkpoint Charlie, thousands of people are crossing both ways. There are many young people who are coming over for a visit and enjoying our open way of life. I expect they will go home tonight. I would cautiously tell you that it appears that the opening has not led to a dramatic increase in the movement of refugees. . . . Krenz will carry out reforms but there are limits. . . . I could imagine that this will continue for a few weeks—that for a few weeks people will wait to see if the reforms come and if there is no light at the end of the tunnel they will run away from the GDR [East Germany] in great numbers. This would be a catastrophe for economic development. The figures this year—230,000 have come. . . .This is a dramatic thing; an historic hour. Let me repeat. There were two major manifestations [political gatherings] in Berlin. One was in front of the Berlin Town Hall. . . . The second was at the Kurfurstendamm. . . . The estimates are that there were 120,000–200,000 people. . . . There have been no conflicts, even though in East Berlin, Leipzig and Dresden hundreds of thousands have been in the streets. . . .

35. Diary of Anatoly S. Chernyaev, November 10, 1989

Source: National Security Archive Electronic Briefing Book no. 275.

The Berlin Wall has collapsed. An entire era in the history of the "socialist system" has come to an end.

Honecker fell[,] . . . today we got a message that [Bulgarian leader Todor] Zhivkov is "leaving." Only our "best friends" are left: Castro, Ceausescu, and Kim Il-Sung, who hate our guts.

The most important, however, is the GDR and the Berlin Wall. This is no longer a matter of socialism, but of a change in the world balance of powers, the end of Yalta, the end of Stalin's legacy and the defeat of Nazi Germany in the Great War.

This is what Gorbachev has done! He is truly a great man because he sensed the footsteps of history and helped it to follow its natural course.

A meeting with Bush is approaching. Will we witness a historic conversation? There are two main ideas in the instructions M.S. gave me to prepare materials: the role of two superpowers in leading the world to a civilized state and the balance of interests. But Bush might disregard our arguments. . . . We do not really have anything to show except for our past a the fear that we could return to totalitarianism.

36. Record of Telephone Conversation between President Mikhail Gorbachev and Chancellor Helmut Kohl, November 11, 1989

Source: Document no. 5034D8AB-96B6-175C-9AAA2B8D0F493693, CWIHP Virtual Archive, www.CWIHP.org. Reprinted by permission of the Woodrow Wilson International Center for Scholars.

The conversation took place . . .on the Chancellor's initiative.

The Chancellor said he wanted to respond to the verbal message from Mikhail Gorbachev, which he received at the beginning of the meeting in West Berlin the previous day.

Helmut Kohl stated that [West Germany] welcomed the beginning of reforms in the GDR [East Germany] and hoped they could be carried out in a calm atmosphere. He said: "I reject any radicalization and do not wish to see any destabilization of the situation in the GDR." . . .

Mikhail Gorbachev emphasized that the current profound changes in the world would take different forms and occur with varying shape and intensity in different countries. It was necessary for all sides to maintain stability and to take a balanced approach. . . .

37. Memorandum of Telephone Conversation between Chancellor Helmut Kohl and President George H. W. Bush, February 13, 1990

Source: *"George Bush–Helmut Kohl Telcon, 2/13/90 re: German Unification,"* Selected Documents from the Archives, George H. W. Bush Library, http://bushlibrary. tamu.edu/research/pdfs/telcon2-13-90.pdf.

CHANCELLOR KOHL: . . . The situation continues to be dramatic. Between the 1st of January and today, 80,000 have come from the GDR [East Germany] to the Federal Republic. That is why I suggested a monetary union and an economic community. We will have to urge the [GDR] government . . . to go through with these. . . .

Let me say a few words about my [recent] talks in Moscow. Gorbachev was very relaxed. He has just had a difficult week in the Central Committee, but he was confident that at the Party Congress he would see things through. But the problems he faces are enormous—nationalities, the food supply situation—and I do not see a light at the end of the tunnel yet. . . .

I told Gorbachev again that the neutralization of Germany is out of the question for me.

PRESIDENT BUSH: Did he acquiesce or just listen? How did he react?

CHANCELLOR KOHL: My impression is that this is a subject about which they want to negotiate, but that we can win that point in negotiations. The modalities will be important, but I do believe we can find a solution.

38. The Illegal Economy under Gorbachev: Growth and Implications, April 1990

Source: CIA, Intelligence Assessment, SOV 90-10020, Princeton Collection.

Impact of the Growth in the Shadow Economy

There has been much debate in the Soviet press over the size of the shadow economy. Both Soviet and Western experts agree that it is difficult to measure accurately, and estimates of its size vary greatly. [The report cites four estimates between August 1989 and December 1990 that range from 70–90 billion rubles to as many as 500 billion.] State Planning Commission (Gosplan) economist Tatyana

Koryagina, who has published the most scholarly Soviet studies of the shadow economy, believes that many recent unofficial estimates are inflated for political reasons—the growth of the shadow economy has become a cause for party traditionalists. Koryagina estimates that the value of goods and services produced or distributed by the shadow economy now amounts to 70–90 billion rubles (Soviet GNP is about 875 billion rubles). By her estimate, about 30 million Soviet citizens—as compared with a state labor force of 130 million—are involved in the shadow economy. Many of these individuals have full-time jobs in the state sector and engage in illegal economic activities either after hours or during work. According to official Soviet statistics published for the first time this year, in 1989 the illegal income of Soviet citizens reached—at a minimum—60 billion rubles, including 23 billion from the illegal production and sale of alcohol, 15 billion from under-the-counter dealings by workers in trade, public dining, and health and personal services, and 10 billion from the sale of stolen construction materials, automobiles, spare parts, and gasoline.

Whatever the shadow economy's value, it is undeniably large, and the surge generated by the current crisis in the consumer sector has alarmed Soviet leaders. According to [Minister of Internal Affairs Vadim] Bakatin, the shadow economy is the most dangerous criminal threat to Soviet society. Its growth is threatening to the Gorbachev regime in several important respects. . . .

39. Chancellor Helmut Kohl Statement to the German Bundestag on the Occasion of the Parliamentary Vote on Reunification of Germany, August 23, 1990

Source: *Documents d'actualité internationale*, November 15, 1990, no. 22, 411–14, available at Centre Virtuel de la Connaissance sur l'Europe, European Navigator, http://www.ena.lu (author's translation from the French).

Today is a day of joy for all Germans. Wednesday, October 3, 1990, will be the day of reunification. This will be a great day in the history of our people. . . . A little more than a year and a half ago [East German leader] M. Honecker said that The Wall would still exist a hundred years from now. Ten months later it fell. We must not forget, amid the enormous number of images and reports in which we have been submerged each day, the profound nature of the changes in the past ten months. . . . The rhythm of developments was determined by our compatriots of the GDR [East Germany], their desires for liberty and unity. After crying together, "We are the People!" they felt it well to ascend to "We are one people!" . . . This is why today we must thank, first, our compatriots of the GDR because it is thanks to them that we will achieve in a few weeks the liberty and unity of Germany. Their courage and moderation but above all their love of liberty have shown how to surmount despotism in a peaceful manner. Their action will remain forever one of the most remarkable chapters in German history. . . .

We must also thank our Western friends and partners, and especially the three Allies who have exercised particular responsibility concerning Berlin and Germany as a whole . . . and permit me to mention our American friends especially, starting with President George Bush, who, above all in the past few months, has shown himself a loyal friend of the Germans. And also [French] President Mitterand, who last February 14 declared, "Who cannot understand the hopes for unity of a people so long divided?" . . .

40. Beyond *Perestroika:* The Soviet Economy in Crisis, June 1991

Source: Intelligence Study, DDB-1900-164-91, CIA Electronic Reading Room, http://www.foia.cia.gov/browse_docs_full.asp.

Summary

Six years after Mikhail Gorbachev launched the policies and reforms that have come to be known as *perestroyka,* the Soviet economy is in crisis. Output is declining at an accelerating rate, inflation threatens to rage out of control, interregional trade has broken down, and the center and the republics are engaged in a fierce political struggle over the future of the multinational state. Since last fall, rather than responding to these problems with reforms, union authorities have attempted to reassert central control over the economy and politics with counterproductive results. Although a recent accord between the center and the republics may impart new momentum to reform, previous agreements of this sort have proven fragile. Even if reform proceeds anew, tough economic times are in store for the Soviets. If meaningful reform is not carried out, the economic future will be totally bleak.

Economy in Turmoil

The accelerating deterioration of the Soviet economy goes beyond declining output and rising inflation. Worsening imbalances between supply and demand have contributed to a breakdown of the distribution system, which has been aggravated by the efforts of regional authorities to insulate factories and consumers on their territories from the effects of shortages. The USSR's economic relations with the rest of the world also are suffering. Hard currency imports exceeded exports in 1990 for the second straight year, while the combination of a rising hard currency debt and a backlog of late payments to Western suppliers brought a credit crunch.

The economy's deterioration results largely from the central planning system's chronic weaknesses, which have been compounded by partial and ad hoc reforms, excessive growth in the money supply, and regional protectionism. The Soviet economy's traditional discipline—of central planners setting output targets for most products and allocating the supplies needed to produce at these levels—has eroded drastically under *perestroyka* but has not been replaced by the discipline of the marketplace. Moreover, rapid growth in the money supply—fueled by large budget deficits—has led to a scramble for goods, rising inflation, and acute shortages. As shortages have worsened, republic and local authorities have banned shipments of goods outside their borders, disrupting longstanding trade patterns and denying badly needed supplies to producers.

The Soviet economic decline also reflects the impact of policy mistakes and mismanagement. The budget deficits that brought monetary expansion and rising inflation were a serious blunder. In addition, the leadership's policy of shifting resources from investment and defense to consumption, although long overdue, has been mismanaged. Inadequate investment in basic materials and transportation has contributed to declining output and shortages of these vital goods and services, and increases in the defense industry's output of civilian goods have fallen short of overly ambitious targets. Also, efforts to step up imports to improve supplies of consumer goods quickly have left the USSR with a rising hard currency debt.

Mounting political and social tensions have exacerbated Soviet economic difficulties. Continuing center-republic clashes have contributed to a worsening confusion of economic authority, and ethnic disputes have brought a variety of conflicts—many of them violent—between and within republics. Strikes remain a growing problem, and popular concern over the environment has forced plant closures that have made a substantial dent in output.

Advances and Halts on Reform
Gorbachev's economic program, which the Soviet legislature approved in October, calls for replacing Marxist with market economics and, if strictly imple-

mented, would deregulate most prices, sell off a substantial portion of state assets, and introduce an element of genuine competition to an economy long dominated by monopolies. Like the failed reform programs of the past, however, it places much of the responsibility for implementation on the central government bureaucracy—the very institution that stands to lose the most from the dismantling of the old system. Moreover, the program's vague provisions and timetables have made it subject to selective implementation and delay by the political leadership. Indeed, in the several months that followed the legislature's approval of the program, Gorbachev's implementing decrees gave a clear priority to stabilization, to be accomplished largely by administrative measures and a new reliance on the police and Committee for State Security (KGB) to enforce the center's economic decrees. . . .

Grim Economic Outlook

There is no doubt that 1991 will be a worse year for the Soviet economy than 1990, and it is likely to be radically worse. The center's recent policy of seeking to stabilize the economy through primarily administrative means and the republics' accompanying refusal to comply with the center's orders already have led to a sharp drop in production. If this standoff continues, real gross national product (GNP) most likely would decline 10 to 15 percent and the annual inflation rate could easily exceed 100 percent. . . .

The message all of these scenarios have in common is that the Soviets, including the defense sector, will face hard times in the next few years regardless of which path they choose. The crucial question is not whether continued austerity will be required but when the end will be in sight. If reform acquires new momentum, the Soviets at least will have embarked on a path with the potential to lead to economic recovery. If economic reform continues to be postponed, the Soviets will face a future of seemingly endless and worsening crises.

41. The Soviet Cauldron, April 25, 1991

Source: Intelligence Report, reprinted in *At Cold War's End: US Intelligence on the Soviet Union and Eastern Europe, 1989–1991*, ed. Benjamin B. Fischer (Reston, VA: Central Intelligence Agency, 1999).

[Paragraph numbers omitted.] Economic crisis, independence aspirations, and anti-communist forces are breaking down the Soviet empire and system of governance. . . .

In the midst of this chaos, Gorbachev has gone from ardent reformer to consolidator. A stream of intelligence reporting and his public declarations indicate that Gorbachev has chosen this course both because of his own political credo and because of pressures on him by other traditionalists, who would like him to use much tougher repressive measures. His attempts to preserve the essence of a center-dominated union, Communist Party rule, and a centrally planned economy without the broad use of force, however, have driven him to tactical expedients that are not solving basic problems and are hindering but not preventing the development of a new system. . . .

Gorbachev has truly been faced with terrible choices in his effort to move the USSR away from the failed, rigid old system. His expedients have so far kept him in office and changed that system irretrievably, but have also prolonged and complicated the agony of transition to a new system and meant a political stalemate in the overall power equation. . . .

In this situation of growing chaos, explosive events have become increasingly possible. . . .

Of all these possible explosions a premeditated, organized attempt to restore a full-fledged dictatorship would be the most fateful in that it would try to roll back newly acquired freedoms and be inherently destabilizing in the long term. Unfortunately, preparations for dictatorial rule have begun in two ways:

- Gorbachev may not want this turn of events but is increasing the chances of it through his personnel appointments; through his estrangement from the reformers and consequent reliance on the traditionalists whom he thereby strengthens; and through his attempted rule by decree, which does not work but invites dictatorship to make it work.

- More ominously, military, [Interior Ministry], and KGB leaders are making preparations for a broad use of force in the political process. . . .

- A campaign to retire democratically inclined officers or at least move them out of key positions has been going on for some time. More recently a sensitive source reported that [Defense Minister] Yazov had ordered the Western Group of Forces (based in Germany) to form units of particularly reliable troops to do whatever was necessary to preserve the union. Although we lack direct evidence, it is highly likely that similar activity is going on in the military districts within the USSR.

- The deployment into Moscow on 28 March of some 50,000 troops from the Army and the [Interior Ministry], with KGB participation, went smoothly, indicating that a command structure for such an operation has been set up.

It is probably the totality of these psychological and actual preparations for the use of force that moved Shevardnadze to reiterate his warning that "dictatorship is coming." . . .

Any attempt to restore full-fledged dictatorship would start in Moscow with the arrest or assassination of Yel'tsin and other democratic leaders . . . the seizure of all media and restoration of full censorship; and the banning of all gatherings enforced by an intimidating display of force. A committee of national salvation— probably under a less sullied name—would be set up and proclaim its intent to save the fatherland through tough but temporary measures that would pave the way for democracy and economic reforms.

The long-term prospects of such an enterprise are poor, and even short-term success is far from assured:

- The number of troops that can be counted on to enforce repression is limited.
- The cohesion of the participating forces would be hard to sustain if, as is likely, the democrats refused to fade away.
- Any action against Yel'tsin would spark activity in other places, and security and military forces would be spread thin in any attempt to establish control over other Russian cities.

Even if the putsch works in Russia, a number of other republics would make use of the turmoil for their own ends. If it did not collapse rapidly, the attempted authoritarian restoration would fail over the next few years. Its putative leaders lack any constructive program and would not have the economic resources, nor most likely the political savvy, necessary to make dictatorship stick. It would probably run its course much as martial law did in Poland, with the added element of secessions, but almost certainly would entail more bloodshed and economic damage along the way.

Even a putsch is not likely to prevent the pluralistic forces from emerging in a dominant position before the end of this decade. They are blunting the center's drive against them and consolidating their own regional holds on power, while the traditionalist forces, which still control the government and other central institutions, increasingly discredit themselves because they lack a viable, forward-looking program. . . .

42. National Intelligence Estimate, "Implications of Alternative Soviet Futures," June 1991

Source: NIE 11-18-91, reprinted in *At Cold War's End: U.S. Intelligence on the Soviet Union and Eastern Europe, 1989–1991*, ed. Benjamin B. Fischer (Reston, VA: Central Intelligence Agency, 1999).

The USSR is in the midst of a revolution that will probably sweep the Communist Party from power and reshape the country within the five-year time frame of this Estimate. The outcome of this revolution will be affected by a number of factors, including the following:

- A sharply declining economy and standard of living that will get worse for the next few years no matter what economic program is adopted.
- The difficulties in implementing a market reform program and sustaining it against a popular backlash.
- Continued devolution of power to republic and local governments at the expense of the central government.
- The rising claim of nationalism on defining the state and legitimizing its policies.
- The increasing importance of popular expectations and aspirations, and the government's abilities to meet them, on a wide range of issues—including living standards and personal freedom.

No one can know what the duration or ultimate outcome of the revolution will be—particularly in a society where repression and centralized control have been the rule, and the culture has been resistant to change, but where recently, democratic aspirations appear to have become widespread.

Of the many conceivable outcomes, we believe four scenarios span the range of possibilities: a continuation of the current "chronic crisis" with no political resolution; a relatively peaceful "system change" into a smaller, more pluralistic and voluntary union in which the central government relinquishes substantial power; a chaotic and violent "fragmentation" of the country resulting in many new states with widely varying political and economic systems; and a "regression" through renewed repression into an authoritarian state run by a combination of hardliners in the military, security services, and Communist Party.

This Estimate's focus is on the content and implications rather than on the relative probabilities of such scenarios. The USSR could pass through any or all of these scenarios during the next five years. Nevertheless, we believe that, on the basis of current trends and our assessment of the critical variables—particularly the bleak prospects for the economy—the country is much more likely to be in a "system change" or "fragmentation" scenario five years from now than to remain where it is today in "chronic crisis." In our view, an attempt to impose the hardline regime of the "regression" scenario becomes more likely as the country verges on "system change" or "fragmentation," but, of the four scenarios, this is the least likely to be a lasting outcome. In any event, we believe that the USSR in its present form will not exist five years from now. . . .

Regression

This scenario assumes traditionalist forces seize control in order to break the back of the democratic reform movement and halt the republics' move toward sovereignty and independence. Although Gorbachev could lead such a move, it is more likely he would be compelled to go along or be forced from office. The security services and the military, who spearhead this course, use force on a large scale to reassert central control. Widespread arrests of leading opponents, including Yel'tsin, occur. The new leaders attempt to reinstitute centralized control over the economy. Although this averts collapse of the command economy for awhile, it does little to halt the economy's continuing sharp decline.

Implications for the USSR

This scenario would involve a series of harsh measures that succeed in reestablishing a measure of central control. The use of force could produce political "stability" for a few years, given the organizational weakness of the democratic forces and the lack of unity among the republics bent on secession. This course might also appeal to a significant portion of the Slavic–Central Asian publics tired of political debate and seeking political order and economic stability. Such popular support would prove short-lived, however, if the new government failed to deliver. Eventually renewed political opposition and civil disorder would probably develop.

The new leaders would find it difficult to gain popular legitimacy for their rule. The draconian step of reintroducing the command-administrative economic system, largely discredited under Gorbachev, would not be able to rebuild the center-republic economic ties disrupted by the independence movements. As workers saw their economic status continuing to deteriorate, they would become less reluctant to engage in passive and active resistance to the center's power.

The new government would also lack an ideological basis to justify its actions, since Marxism-Leninism has been totally discredited, along with the Communist Party. An appeal to Russian nationalism by the conservative leadership would be possible—and could take the form of a national salvation committee—but such a step would further antagonize the restive republics. It could provide the basis for an authoritarian regime in Russia, however, that follows a "Russia first" policy at the expense of the rest of the union.

The biggest problem for the leadership would be maintaining unionwide control. The use of force to hold the union together would almost certainly lead to open civil conflict within several republics, particularly those having their own paramilitary forces, such as Georgia and Armenia. Controlling such unrest would severely tax security and military forces; prolonged conflict would threaten the internal cohesion and discipline of the troops, particularly if they had to be used against Slavic groups.

This scenario could unravel quickly if the center were unable to quash the democratic resistance, if Yel'tsin or another popular leader were able to escape the center's dragnet and rally popular resistance, or if the military proved unreliable. Even so, reform and republic leaders might not survive even a short-lived repression, leaving a political vacuum at the center and in many republics. Such widespread unrest could also exacerbate the ethnic, political, and generational splits within the armed forces and security services.

If repression failed, the result would probably be anarchy and a chaotic disintegration of the union; that is, the "fragmentation" scenario. In that event, most republics would break away from the center. This breakup of the union would be most likely to be accompanied by civil war. . . .

NOTES

Introduction

1. The earliest and still the most prolific exponent of this view is Peter Schweizer. See his *Victory: The Reagan Administration's Secret Strategy That Hastened the Collapse of the Soviet Union* (New York: Atlantic Monthly Press, 1994); and also *Reagan's War: The Epic Story of His Forty-Year Struggle and Final Triumph over Communism* (New York: Doubleday, 2002). Schweizer's writings in conjunction with Caspar Weinberger are not materially different. For another exposition, see Jay Winik, *On the Brink: The Dramatic, Behind-the-Scenes Saga of the Reagan Era and the Men and Women Who Won the Cold War* (New York: Simon & Schuster, 1996).

2. The most recent statement of this view is in James Mann, *The Rebellion of Ronald Reagan: A History of the End of the Cold War* (New York: Viking, 2009).

3. Representative of this view are John Lewis Gaddis, *The Cold War: A New History* (New York: Penguin Press, 2005), and his earlier *The United States and the End of the Cold War: Implications, Reconsiderations, Provocations* (New York: Oxford University Press, 1992), which actually attributed an even greater share of the credit to Reagan alone. A similar view is that of Melvyn P. Leffler in his *For the Soul of Mankind: The United States, the Soviet Union, and the Cold War* (New York: Hill & Wang, 2007).

4. For varying interpretations of these kinds see Odd Arne Westad, *The Global Cold War: Third World Interventions and the Making of Our Times* (New York: Cambridge University Press, 2007), the most influential presentation of the role of the third world, and, on some of the other factors, Dick Combs, *Inside the*

Soviet Alternate Universe: The Cold War's End and the Soviet Union's Fall Reappraised (University Park: Pennsylvania State University Press, 2008).

Chapter 2: Players, Programs, and Plots

1. Lady Thatcher reportedly said this at the Aspen Institute in 1992, but it is not possible to verify since no records of the institute's sessions are available. Private information.
2. Margaret Thatcher, *The Downing Street Years* (New York: HarperCollins, 1993), 157.
3. Ronald Reagan, *An American Life* (New York: Simon & Schuster, 1990), 205.
4. Accessible sources on these events include Timothy G. Ash, *The Polish Revolution: Solidarity* (New York: Vintage Books, 1985); and Nicolas G. Andrews, *Poland 1980–81: Solidarity versus the Party* (Washington, DC: National Defense University Press, 1985).
5. Mark Kramer, "'In Case Military Assistance Is Provided to Poland': Soviet Preparations for Military Contingencies, August 1980" *Cold War International History Project Bulletin*, no. 11 (Winter 1998): 102. The discussion here of the Soviet side relies upon this and other materials made available by the Cold War International History Project (CWIHP) of the Smithsonian Institution's Woodrow Wilson International Center for Scholars, as well as the Volkogonov and Chernyaev collections of the National Security Archive. Kramer, a fine historian and master of the Russian sources, has sparkplugged much of the CWIHP's work in this field, as Svetlana Savranskaya has done for the National Security Archive. The CWIHP's materials also include Polish and Eastern European documents gathered by scholars in their respective countries. This material is compelling. References to CWIHP elsewhere in this narrative will be to its *Bulletin* or to its holdings of original documents in translation. Again, Kramer and Savranskaya are responsible for much of that translation work. Their contributions and those of other scholars who have participated in this endeavor should be commended.
6. "Stenographic Minutes of the Meeting of Leading Representatives of the Warsaw Pact Countries, Moscow, December 5, 1980," *CWIHP Bulletin*, no. 11 (Winter 1998): 110–20.
7. Douglas J. MacEachin, *US Intelligence and the Polish Crisis, 1980–1981* (Washington, DC: Center for the Study of Intelligence, 2000), 55–59.
8. In general see Paul Lettow, *Ronald Reagan and His Quest to Abolish Nuclear Weapons* (New York: Random House, 2005). Martin Anderson, a member of Rea-

gan's "Kitchen Cabinet" of private advisers, tells the story of accompanying the future president to a briefing at the North American Air Defense Command (NORAD) after which Mr. Reagan mused that some defense had to be found against nuclear weapons (Anderson, *Revolution* [New York: Harcourt Brace Jovanovich, 1988]).

9. Quoted in Richard Reeves, *President Reagan: The Triumph of Imagination* (New York: Simon & Schuster, 2005), 378.

10. Anatoliy Dobrynin, *In Confidence: Moscow's Ambassador to America's Six Cold War Presidents (1962–1986)* (New York: Times Books, 1995), 477.

11. Reagan, *American Life*, 297.

12. See, for example, Edward N. Luttwak, *The Grand Strategy of the Soviet Union* (New York: St. Martin's Press, 1983), a conscious evocation of Luttwak's earlier book *The Grand Strategy of the Roman Empire from the First Century AD to the Third* (Baltimore: Johns Hopkins University Press, 1976).

13. Ronald Reagan, *The Reagan Diaries*, ed. Douglas Brinkley (New York: Harper-Collins, 2007), 212.

14. Edmund Morris, *Dutch: A Memoir of Ronald Reagan* (New York: Random House, 1999), 662.

15. Lou Cannon, *Reagan* (New York: Putnam, 1982); and *President Reagan: The Role of a Lifetime* (New York: Public Affairs Press, 2000).

16. Reeves, *President Reagan*.

17. Schweizer, *Reagan's War*, 281–82.

18. Paul Kengor, *The Crusader: Ronald Reagan and the Fall of Communism*. (New York: Regan Books, 2006).

19. Joseph Shattan, *Architects of Victory: Six Heroes of the Cold War* (Washington, DC: Heritage Foundation, 1999), 246.

20. Quoted in Don Oberdorfer, *From the Cold War to a New Era: The United States and the Soviet Union, 1983–1991*, updated ed. (Baltimore: Johns Hopkins University Press, 1998), 61.

21. For detail on Karol Wojtyła see George Weigel, *Witness to Hope: The Biography of John Paul II* (New York: Cliff Street Books, 1999); and Carl Bernstein and Marco Politi, *His Holiness: John Paul II and the Hidden History of Our Time* (New York: Doubleday, 1996).

22. Quoted in Shattan, *Architects of Victory*, 203.

23. John O'Sullivan, *The President, the Pope, and the Prime Minister: Three Who Changed the World* (Washington, DC: Regnery Publishing, 2006), 182.

24. Accusations of Soviet complicity sparked a major intelligence dispute in the United States, where CIA Director William J. Casey, one of the policy entrepreneurs, made strong efforts to force agency analysts to the conclusion that the murder attempt had flowed from a KGB plot. Casey had some success in his effort, with a special national intelligence estimate drawing his preferred conclusion, but two years later, a CIA internal review decided the evidence had been much too ambiguous to support such a conclusion. The episode is one of those that led many to observe that CIA intelligence in the early 1980s had been politicized by the Reagan administration. The "bible" on the KGB's activities is the so-called Mitrokhin Archive, an enormous collection of notes from KGB records secretly copied by officer Vasili Mitrokhin, who later defected to the West. The materials have been summarized and presented by British intelligence historian Christopher M. Andrew and Mitrokhin in *The Sword and the Shield: The Mitrokhin Archive and the Secret History of the KGB* (New York: Basic Books, 1999). On the John Paul II assassination, that study comments, "There is no evidence in any of the files examined by Mitrokhin that it [the KGB] was involved in the attempt on his life" (p. 522).

25. Soviet regions were generally known as *oblasts*, but Stavropol and Krasnodar had the special status of being termed *krays*. (I am indebted to Svetlana Savranskaya for this information.)

26. Andrei Gromyko, *Memoirs*, trans. Harold Shukman (New York: Doubleday, 1989), 341–42.

27. Vladislav M. Zubok, *A Failed Empire: The Soviet Union in the Cold War from Stalin to Gorbachev* (Chapel Hill: University of North Carolina Press, 2007), 278.

28. Dmitri Volkogonov, *Autopsy for an Empire: The Seven Leaders Who Built the Soviet Regime*, ed. and trans. Harold Shukman) (New York: Free Press, 1998), 446.

29. Georgi Arbatov, *The System: An Insider's Life in Soviet Politics* (New York: Times Books, 1992), 276.

30. Zubok, *Failed Empire*, 282.

31. Pavel Palazchenko, *My Years with Gorbachev and Shevardnadze: The Memoir of a Soviet Interpreter* (University Park: Pennsylvania State University Press, 1997), 42–45. Gorbachev quoted on p. 43.

32. Mann, *Rebellion of Ronald Reagan*, 346.

33. Leffler, *For the Soul of Mankind*, 466.

34. Gaddis, *Cold War*, 238.

Chapter 3: Alice in Wonderland

1. Richard E. Neustadt, *Presidential Power: The Politics of Leadership from FDR to Carter* (New York: Wiley, 1980).

2. The following account relies primarily on Strobe Talbott, *Deadly Gambits: The Reagan Administration and the Stalemate in Nuclear Arms Control* (New York: Knopf, 1984); and Raymond L. Garthoff, *The Great Transition: American-Soviet Relations and the End of the Cold War* (Washington, DC: Brookings Institution, 1994).

3. Thomas Graham Jr., *Disarmament Sketches: Three Decades of Arms Control and International Law* (Seattle: University of Washington Press, 2002), 107.

4. Reagan, *American Life*, 551. Reagan wrote, "The Soviets saw [the Zero Option] as an attempt by us to reduce the immense Soviet imbalance of nuclear power in Europe—which it was." Throughout his account, Mr. Reagan conflates the Zero Option with the later "zero-zero" formula without explanation. The latter terminology did not come into use until the "Walk in the Woods" episode.

5. Lawrence Wittner, "The Surprising Effect of the Nuclear Freeze Movement on the Administration of Ronald Reagan," History News Network, November 13, 2003, http://hnn.us/articles/1797.html.

6. Reagan, *American Life*, 296–97.

7. George P. Shultz, *Turmoil and Triumph: My Years as Secretary of State* (New York: Scribner, 1993), 120.

8. Quoted in Graham, *Disarmament Sketches*, 115.

9. Shultz, *Turmoil and Triumph*, 120.

10. For a good general summary see John Prados, "The War Scare of 1983," in *The Cold War: A Military History*, ed. Robert Cowley (New York: Random House, 2005), 438–54. For a CIA view of these events see Benjamin B. Fischer, *A Cold War Conundrum: The 1983 Soviet War Scare* (Washington, DC: CIA, Center for the Study of Intelligence, 1997).

11. Peter V. Pry, *War Scare: Russia and America on the Nuclear Brink* (Westport, CT: Praeger, 1999), 37.

12. Alexander Dallin, *Black Box: KAL 007 and the Superpowers* (Berkeley: University of California Press, 1985). Post–Cold War revelations, such as interviews with the Soviet interceptor pilot involved in the incident, only further confirm the conclusion that the basic problem was command rigidity. For an analysis much more clearly focused on U.S. exploitation of the incident—and an interpretation that delves into how the Russians could have perceived the airliner as a

U.S. spy plane—see Seymour M. Hersh, *"The Target Is Destroyed": What Really Happened to Flight 007 and What America Knew about It* (New York: Random House, 1986).

13. Martin Walker, *The Cold War: A History* (New York: H. Holt, 1994), 276.

14. Quoted in Oberdorfer, *From the Cold War to a New Era*, 69.

15. Don Oberdorfer's journal entry, September 8, 1983, quoted in Don Oberdorfer, "The Cold War (1975–91) as a Journalist Saw It," in *From Détente to the Soviet Collapse: The Cold War from 1975 to 1991*, ed. Malcolm Muir Jr. (Lexington: Virginia Military Institute, 2006), 165.

16. Dobrynin, *In Confidence*, 522–25.

17. Author's notes, Vladislav Zubok talk, "A Failed Empire," Cold War International History Project, September 17, 2008.

18. Don Oberdorfer's journal entry, September 20, 1983, quoted in Oberdorfer, "The Cold War (1975–91)," 169.

19. For Gordievsky's role see Christopher Andrew and Oleg Gordievsky, *KGB: The Inside Story of Its Foreign Operations from Lenin to Gorbachev* (New York: HarperCollins, 1990), 588, 598–600. Andrew and Gordievsky subsequently published a selection of KGB documents that included general instructions for Operation RYAN and the mid-crisis special alert. Andrew and Gordievsky, eds., *Instructions from the Centre: Top Secret Files on KGB Foreign Operations, 1975–1985* (London: Hodder & Stoughton, 1991).

20. John Prados, "The War Scare of 1983," in *The Cold War: A Military History*, ed. Robert Cowley (New York: Random House, 2005), 451.

21. Reagan, *Reagan Diaries*, 199.

22. Reagan, *American Life*, 588. The speech itself is quoted on p. 590.

23. Victor Israelyan, *On the Battlefields of the Cold War: A Soviet Ambassador's Confession*, trans. and ed. Stephen Pearl (University Park: Pennsylvania State University Press, 2003), 348–51.

24. Dobrynin, *In Confidence*, 546.

25. USSR Ministry of Defense, *Whence the Threat to Peace?* (Moscow: Military Publishing House, 1982).

26. This is an important point in understanding the Soviets' great and continued fears of SDI as they emerged in the succession of arms control talks held through the 1980s. These arguments were underappreciated in the West, at least outside a narrow circle of technical experts. However, assuming that the difficulties of pointing and aiming energy beams, atmospheric attenuation,

and power generation could be solved, the use of directed-energy weapons to strike the earth's surface was much less technically demanding than in an SDI role, wherein target discrimination, computer software, and battle management issues constituted equal or more demanding obstacles to a practical system. For an excellent discussion of Soviet concerns see Peter J. Westwick, "'Space-Strike Weapons' and the Soviet Response to SDI," *Diplomatic History* 32, no. 5 (November 2008): 955–79.

27. Garthoff, *Great Transition*, 163–64, fn. 66.

28. Melvin A. Goodman, *Failure of Intelligence: The Decline and Fall of the CIA* (Lanham, MD: Rowman & Littlefield, 2008), 152.

29. Robert M. Gates, *From the Shadows: The Ultimate Insider's Story of Five Presidents and How They Won the Cold War* (New York: Simon & Schuster, 1996), 272.

30. Beth A. Fischer, *The Reagan Reversal: Foreign Policy and the End of the Cold War* (Columbia: University of Missouri Press, 1997).

31. Even David S. Sullivan, in a later incarnation as a conservative policy advocate, had some inkling of this. In a 1979 paper, Sullivan wrote, "If . . . Dr. Kissinger *did know* of the [missile's] large size in May 1972 . . . then Kissinger's 1972 and 1975 statements suggest that he not only misled Congress by incorrectly implying that the U.S. unilateral definition of a heavy ICBM would bind the Soviets, but he also knew in 1972 that the Soviets would violate the U.S. definition." Sullivan, *Soviet SALT Deception* (Boston, VA: Coalition for Peace Through Strength, 1979), 1–2. The ICBM in question, which the CIA knew as the SS-19, had been prefigured in the arms talks by various Soviet statements that they intended to continue modernizing their forces. An extensive and explicit conversation on this matter, following up on negotiations at Helsinki and talks directly between President Nixon and General Secretary Brezhnev, took place between Kissinger and Soviet diplomats in Moscow on May 25, 1972. The record of conversation specifically shows that the missile silo dimension issue was aired at length and that the Soviets rejected any definition of "significantly" larger missiles because it would inhibit their modernization program. Both U.S. and Soviet memoranda recounting this meeting confirm this point (U.S. Department of State, *Soviet-American Relations: The Détente Years, 1969–1972* [Washington, DC: Government Printing Office, 2007], 904–11). As for the U.S. definition, that was contained in a unilateral statement concocted precisely because the Soviets had rejected any such provision. That had no force in international law and did not bind the Soviets. Consequently Kissinger

misled Congress about whether or not he knew the size of the anticipated new Soviet rockets—and the sudden last-minute U.S. push for size constraints certainly suggests that he did. The best available negotiating history of the SALT I agreement remains that by the U.S. delegation chief, Gerard C. Smith, *Doubletalk: The Story of the First Strategic Arms Limitation Talks* (Garden City, NY: Doubleday, 1980).

32. This dispute is highly arcane and involves the content of specific definitions, paragraphs, and agreed statements that formed parts of the ABM Treaty, and it should not detain the main text here. Suffice it to say that the treaty did indeed prohibit the development, testing, and deployment of a system that could accomplish the *function* of missile defense, including future components that might substitute for the types current when the treaty was signed. Perle and his allies in this debate maintained that none of that was true so long as the weapons were based on different physical principles. See Raymond L. Garthoff, *Policy versus the Law: The Reinterpretation of the ABM Treaty* (Washington, DC: Brookings Institution, 1987). After Garthoff demolished the broad interpretation argument in this monograph, the State Department counselor, Judge Abraham Sofaer, threatened legal action against Garthoff and Brookings, but at a lunch with Garthoff and a senior Brookings official, he proved unable to demonstrate even one example of error in the analysis. Sofaer's threat evaporated. Raymond L. Garthoff, *A Journey Through the Cold War: A Memoir of Containment and Coexistence* (Washington, DC: Brookings Institution Press, 2001), 358.

33. For a detailed, more technical account of the reactor accident see Grigori Medvedev, *The Truth About Chernobyl*, trans. Evelyn Rossiter (New York: Basic Books, 1991).

34. Mikhail S. Gorbachev, *Memoirs*, trans. Wolf J. Seidler (New York: Doubleday, 1996), 190.

35. In a typical observation on the nature of Soviet society, diplomat Vadim Chulitsky once told American negotiator Thomas Graham, who was complaining to him of the Russians' obstinacy in talks, "You Americans do not understand. If one of us displeases his superior, not only does he lose his job but his wife loses hers, he loses his apartment, his car, and the children are dismissed from school. Naturally, people are very careful." Graham, *Disarmament Sketches*, 73.

36. Gorbachev, *Memoirs*, 191, 193.

37. Palazchenko, *My Years with Gorbachev and Shevardnadze*, 49.

38. Anatoly S. Chernyaev, *My Six Years with Gorbachev*, trans. and ed. Robert D.

English and Elizabeth Tucker (University Park: Pennsylvania State University Press, 2000), 65.

39. Palazchenko, *My Years with Gorbachev and Shevnardnadze*, 49.

40. Gorbachev, *Memoirs*, 402.

41. Israelyan, *On the Battlefields of the Cold War*, 365.

42. This and the following discussion draw on Carolyn M. Ekedahl and Melvin A. Goodman, *The Wars of Eduard Shevardnadze* (University Park: Pennsylvania State University Press, 1997), 71–82; and Eduard Shevardnadze, *The Future Belongs to Freedom*, trans. Catherine A. Fitzpatrick (New York: Free Press, 1991), 41–59.

43. Congressional Research Service, *Soviet Diplomacy and Negotiating Behavior, 1979– 1988: New Tests for U.S. Diplomacy* (Washington, DC: Government Printing Office, 1988), 600. One of a three-volume series on Soviet diplomacy during the Cold War, this contains the most exhaustive study imaginable on the MFA reorganization (see pp. 587–617).

44. "USSR CC CPSU Politburo Session on Preparations for Reykjavik," October 8, 1986, trans. Anna Melyakova and Svetlana Savranskaya, in *The Reykjavik File: Previously Secret U.S. and Soviet Documents on the 1986 Reagan-Gorbachev Summit* (National Security Archive Electronic Briefing Book no. 203), ed. Svetlana Savranskaya and Thomas Blanton (Washington, DC: National Security Archive, October 13, 2006), http://www.gwu.edu/~nsarchiv/NSAEBB/ NSAEBB203/Document08.pdf.

45. Gorbachev, *Memoirs*, 415.

46. "Russian Transcript of Negotiations in the Working Group on Military Issues," October 11–12, 1986, in *The Reykjavik File*, http://www.gwu.edu/~nsarchiv/ NSAEBB/NSAEBB203/Document17.pdf.

47. Palazchenko, *My Years with Gorbachev and Shevardnadze*, 57.

48. The records are in *The Reykjavik File*, http://www.gwu.edu/~nsarchiv/ NSAEBB/NSAEBB203/index.htm.

49. Reagan, *Reagan Diaries*, 444.

50. For example, Paul Lettow's most recent formulation, following the argument in his book *Ronald Reagan and His Quest to Abolish Nuclear Weapons*, is that Reykjavik "was largely shaped by Reagan's nuclear abolitionism and his conviction that that goal was close at hand. . . . After a day and a half of haggling . . . Reagan proposed that they abolish all nuclear weapons. Gorbachev agreed" (Lettow, "Reagan's Strategic Vision," in *From Détente to the Soviet Collapse*, 24).

In the very first of the Reykjavik negotiating sessions (*not* after a day and a half), Mr. Gorbachev declared, "I would like to precisely, firmly and clearly announce that we are in favor of such a solution to the problem which would ultimately provide for complete liquidation of nuclear weapons and would ensure equality and equal security of the USA and Soviet Union at all stages of movement toward this goal" (Soviet text, p. 2). This statement is missing from the U.S. record of the conversation. Where President Reagan refers to nuclear abolition, he links it to SDI by saying missile defense will *make possible* the abolition of these weapons (U.S. text, p. 7). At the second session, the president restricted himself to strategic ballistic missiles—clearly suggesting he had been taken in hand by the policy entrepreneurs, while Gorbachev renewed his bid to start with a 50 percent reduction in *all* strategic weapons (and accepted the zero option for Euromissiles). During the third session—even by the U.S. text—Secretary Shultz commented that both leaders had begun speaking of elimination of nuclear weapons and asked Gorbachev a question on the nature of the Soviet abolition proposal (U.S. text, p. 9; the Soviet text [p. 3] indicates that Shultz *did not* include Mr. Reagan in his remarks). Both Reagan and Shultz made statements attempting to define the terrain as a conversation about ballistic missiles only, and Mr. Gorbachev repeatedly reiterated his scope as including all strategic weapons. At the final session—which took place following the day and a half of haggling—Mr. Shultz read the text of a U.S. proposal that again reduced the scope of the negotiation to "offensive ballistic missiles" (U.S. text, p. 1). General Secretary Gorbachev, before Mr. Reagan spoke at this session, countered with the proposal that within a framework of observance of the ABM Treaty, during "the first five years of the ten-year period [and thus by the end of 1991], the strategic offensive arms of the two sides shall be reduced by 50 percent. During the following five years of that period, the remaining 50 percent of the two sides' strategic offensive arms shall be reduced" (U.S. text, p. 2). Later he referred to the "unique historical task of eliminating nuclear forces" (U.S. text, p. 3). President Reagan first referred to abolition when he asked, "If both sides had completely eliminated nuclear weapons and there was no longer any threat, why would there be any concern if one side built a safeguard?" (U.S. text, p. 5) Once a written text had been drafted, Mr. Shultz once more tried to reduce the scope to ballistic missiles alone (p. 8), and after a break, Reagan himself read a revised U.S. draft that provided a ten-year framework in which half of the "strategic offensive arms" would be dismantled during the first period and "all remaining offensive ballistic missiles" eliminated during the second. When Gorbachev began to explore what this meant, he discovered the language had been inserted deliberately. Reagan explicitly said his subordinates had told him the *Soviets* were primarily interested in reducing *missiles*, not *weapons* (U.S. text, p. 9). Gorbachev again affirmed all nuclear weapons would be included. In terms of testing and development of the SDI under the ABM Treaty, however, it became apparent that President Reagan intended to proceed full steam ahead. He would agree not to abrogate the treaty for the ten-year period, but refused to confine development work to the laboratory (U.S. text, pp. 9-16). Over this the negotiation foundered. This record shows that General Secretary Gorbachev did not reject a *Reagan* proposal to abolish all nuclear weapons. It is abundantly clear that policy entrepreneurs repeatedly brought President Reagan back to their agenda of seeking advantage by restricting ballistic missiles only, that Mr. Reagan eventually *did* respond to his desire to abolish all nuclear weapons in provisionally accepting the Soviet proposal, but that the president's infatuation with SDI led to the collapse of the summit. (All quotations are from the official records reproduced in documents 9–16 of *The Reykjavik File*, http://www.gwu.edu/~nsarchiv/NSAEBB/NSAEBB203/index.htm.)

51. A good example is the Congressional Research Service monograph *Soviet Diplomacy and Negotiating Behavior*, which contains nearly a hundred pages on the Geneva summit (pp. 237–336) but just six paragraphs on the summit at Reykjavik (pp. 655–58).

Chapter 4: "The Most Dangerous Decade in Human History"

1. The following discussion relies heavily upon the seminal work of Lawrence S. Wittner in his *The Struggle Against the Bomb*, vol. 3: *Toward Nuclear Abolition: A History of the World Nuclear Disarmament Movement, 1971 to the Present* (Stanford: Stanford University Press, 2003).

2. For a summary analysis of the development of the missile systems involved here and the background of the 1979 NATO initiatives see Leopoldo Nuti, "The Origins of the 1979 Dual Track Decision—A Survey," in *The Crisis of Détente in Europe: From Helsinki to Gorbachev, 1975–1985*, ed. Leopoldo Nuti (London: Routledge, 2009), 57–71.

3. David Cortright, *Peace Works: The Citizen's Role in Ending the Cold War* (Boulder, CO: Westview Press, 1993), 51–53. Reagan quoted on p. 92. Cortright, with

inside knowledge stemming from his leadership role in SANE, is, in general, the best source on public protests against nuclear war by Americans during this period.

4. Maarten Huygen, "Dateline Holland: NATO's Pyrrhic Victory," *Foreign Policy*, no. 62 (Spring 1986): 173.

5. Vincent Dujardin, "From Helsinki to the Missiles Question: A Minor Role for Small Countries? The Case of Belgium (1973–1985)," in *Crisis of Détente in Europe*, 72–85.

6. This debate is explored in detail in Giovanni Mario Ceci, "The Italian Catholic World and the Christian Democratic Party Facing the Dilemma of the Euromissiles, 1979–1983" (paper presented at Peace Movements in the Cold War and Beyond: An International Conference, London School of Economics, February 1–2, 2008). A copy of the manuscript is in the author's possession.

7. Jeffrey Herf, *War by Other Means: Soviet Power, West German Resistance, and the Battle of the Euromissiles* (New York: Free Press, 1991), passim.

8. Cortright, *Peace Works*, 174–75.

9. James A. Baker III with Thomas M. DeFrank, *The Politics of Diplomacy: Revolution, War, and Peace, 1989–1992* (New York: Putnam, 1995), 91.

10. Daniel C. Thomas, *The Helsinki Effect: International Norms, Human Rights, and the Demise of Communism* (Princeton, NJ: Princeton University Press, 2001), 215.

11. Schweizer, *Victory*, 226–27.

12. Document No. 4, Polish Government Report, "A Synthesis of the Domestic Situation and the West's Activity," August 28, 1987, in Paweł Machcewicz, "Poland 1986–1989: From 'Cooptation' to 'Negotiated Revolution,'" *CWIHP Bulletin*, no. 12/13 (Fall–Winter 2001): 98.

13. International Institute for Strategic Studies (IISS), *Strategic Survey, 1986–1987* (London: IISS, 1987), 111–113.

14. IISS, *Strategic Survey, 1987–1988* (London: IISS, 1988), 106–12.

15. IISS, *Strategic Survey, 1988–1989* (London: IISS, 1989), 88–95.

16. Jacques Lévesque, *The Enigma of 1989: The USSR and the Liberation of Eastern Europe* (Berkeley: University of California Press, 1997).

17. Document No. 1, Memorandum to Alexander Yakovlev from the Bogomolov Commission (Marina Slyvanskaya), February 1989, in Jacques Lévesque, "Soviet Approaches to Eastern Europe at the Beginning of 1989," *CWIHP Bulletin*, no. 12/13 (Fall–Winter 2001): 52–61.

18. Document No. 2, Memorandum from the International Department of the

Central Committee of the CPSU to Alexander Yakovlev, February 1989, in ibid., 62–68.

19. Document No. 3, Memorandum from the Ministry of Foreign Affairs, "The Political Processes in the European Socialist Countries and the Proposals for Our Practical Steps Considering the Situation Which Has Arisen in Them," February 24, 1989, in ibid., 68–72.

20. Quoted in Document No. 3, Memorandum of Conversation between M. S. Gorbachev and HSWP General Secretary Károly Grósz, Moscow, March 23–24, 1989, in Csaba Békés and Melinda Kalmár, "The Political Transition in Hungary, 1989–90," *CWIHP*, no. 12/13 (Fall–Winter 2001): 78.

21. Document No. 1, Memorandum of Conversation Between Egon Krenz, Secretary General of the Socialist Union Party (SED), and Mikhail S. Gorbachev, Secretary General of the Communist Party of the Soviet Union (CPSU)," November 1, 1989, in Hans-Hermann Hertle, "The Fall of the Wall: The Unintended Self-Dissolution of East Germany's Ruling Regime," *CWIHP Bulletin*, no. 12/13 (Fall–Winter 2001): 144.

22. Quoted in Baker, *Politics of Diplomacy*, 86.

23. Joshua Muravchik, *The Uncertain Crusade: Jimmy Carter and the Dilemmas of Human Rights Policy* (Lanham, MD: Hamilton Press, 1986). This is an extended exegesis on articles Muravchik began writing during the Carter administration, when he worked with the conservative Coalition for a Democratic Majority.

24. Reagan, *American Life*, 706.

25. Reagan, *Reagan Diaries*, 363.

26. Thatcher, *Downing Street Years*, 457.

Chapter 5: Blue Jeans, Bluegrass, and National Pride

1. Stephen Kotkin, *Armageddon Averted: The Soviet Collapse, 1970–2000* (Oxford: Oxford University Press, 2001), 6.

2. Arbatov, *System*, 235.

3. Kotkin, *Armageddon Averted*, 28, 40–48.

4. Ibid., 64.

5. Robert G. Kaiser, *Why Gorbachev Happened: His Triumphs and His Failure* (New York: Simon & Schuster, 1991), 67.

6. Yegor Ligachev, *Inside Gorbachev's Kremlin: The Memoirs of Yegor Ligachev*, trans. Catherine A. Fitzpatrick, Michele A. Berdy, Dobrochna Dyrcz-Freeman, and Marian Schwartz (Boulder, CO: Westview Press, 1996), 16.

7. Ibid., 356.

8. Gorbachev, *Memoirs*, 138.

9. Volkogonov, *Autopsy for an Empire*, 425.

10. Ibid., 147, 153.

11. Ibid., 215, 229. Gorbachev quoted on p. 147.

12. Yegor Gaidar, *Collapse of an Empire: Lessons for Modern Russia*, trans. Antonina W. Bouis (Washington, DC: Brookings Institution Press, 2007). The statistics that follow are drawn primarily from Gaidar's work.

13. Gorbachev, *Memoirs*, 172.

14. Ibid., 175.

15. Ibid., 236.

16. Chernyaev, *My Six Years with Gorbachev*, 150.

17. Kotkin, *Armageddon Averted*, 66–67.

18. Chernyaev, *My Six Years with Gorbachev*, 150.

19. Kotkin, *Armageddon Averted*, 77.

20. Jack F. Matlock Jr., *Autopsy on an Empire: The American Ambasador's Account of the Collapse of the Soviet Union* (New York: Random House, 1995), 501.

21. Ibid., 21.

22. Bohdan Nahaylo and Victor Swoboda, *Soviet Disunion: A History of the Nationalities Problem in the USSR* (New York: Free Press, 1990), 207, 235. The following discussion makes considerable use of this source.

23. Ibid., 207, 250–51, 266–67, 272; and Matlock, *Autopsy on an Empire*, 164–65.

24. Chernyaev, *My Six Years with Gorbachev*, 108.

25. Quoted in ibid., 107; and Gorbachev, *Memoirs*, 326–331.

26. Nahaylo and Swoboda, *Soviet Disunion*, 224–25.

27. Matlock, *Autopsy on an Empire*, 157–163; Gorbachev, *Memoirs*, 331. Gorbachev notes that the dismissal of Kunayev followed complaints to him from both Russian and Kazakh members of the republic's Central Committee secretariat and that Kunayev resigned when Gorbachev suggested that the charges be brought up before a Politburo meeting to which Kazakh party officials would be invited. Matlock, who interviewed Kunayev after the fall of the USSR, gives more weight to Kunayev's claim he was being undermined by an ambitious protégé, Nursultan Nazarbayev, the source of some of the complaints to Gorbachev, who in fact emerged as Kunayev's successor.

28. Nahaylo and Swoboda, *Soviet Disunion*, 241–44, 267–69.

29. The following account is based upon the report of the Commission of the

USSR Congress of People's Deputies (Sobchak commission), which was created to investigate these events; secret messages sent at the time (both of which sets of evidence are translated and appear in the *CWIHP Bulletin*, no. 12/13 [Fall–Winter 2001]); and memoir accounts, including Ligachev, *Inside Gorbachev's Kremlin*, 146–70; Chernyaev, *My Six Years with Gorbachev*, 218–20; and Shevardnadze, *Future Belongs to Freedom*, 192–97. In his own memoir, Gorbachev avoids the subject, I think deliberately, relegating the Tbilisi Massacre to a brief mention in a footnote and providing no substantive treatment whatsoever. This compares to the full pages he lavishes on the protests at Almaty.

30. Shevardnadze, *Future Belongs to Freedom*, 194.

31. Chernyaev, *My Six Years with Gorbachev*, 220. Gorbachev quoted on p. 219.

32. Quoted in ibid., 220.

33. Ibid.

34. Shevardnadze disputes that his resignation statement said anything about dictatorship (*Future Belongs to Freedom*, 196), but his extemporaneous speech is undeniable. It is quoted in Kaiser, *Why Gorbachev Happened*, 385.

35. Quoted in Kaiser, *Why Gorbachev Happened*, 386.

36. Gorbachev, *Memoirs*, 580–81. Gorbachev also quotes himself saying on TV on January 22 that "what had happened was contrary to my policy" and "the use of armed forces for the solution of political problems was inadmissible." Participants and close observers recall that Gorbachev avoided such a clear-cut position.

37. Andrei Grachev, *Gorbachev's Gamble: Soviet Foreign Policy and the End of the Cold War* (Cambridge, UK: Polity, 2008), 199. Also see Chernyaev, *My Six Years with Gorbachev*, 317–30.

38. Matlock, *Autopsy on an Empire*, 469–471. Gorbachev quoted on p. 471.

39. Ibid., 539–46. Gorbachev quoted on p. 545. Matlock believes the mayor accurately reported on a plan the execution of which the conspirators postponed for some weeks.

40. "Did David Hasselhoff Really Help End the Cold War?" BBC News, February 6, 2004. http://news.bbc.co.uk/nolpda/ukfs_news/hi/newsid_3465000/3465001.stm (accessed July 24, 2008).

41. Kotkin, *Armageddon Averted*, 42–43.

42. Cultural histories available for the period so far tend to focus on the United States, not the USSR, and to concentrate on the earlier period up until the 1960s. Possibly the most comprehensive is Stephen J. Whitfield's *The Culture of*

the Cold War, 2nd ed. (Baltimore: Johns Hopkins University Press, 1996). On film see Tony Shaw, *Hollywood's Cold War* (Amherst: University of Massachusetts Press, 2007). For an example closer to home, an excellent monograph on a (noncommunist) East-Central European nation, see Reinhold Wagnleitner, *Coca-Colonization and the Cold War: The Cultural Mission of the United States in Austria after the Second World War*, trans. Diana M. Wolf (Chapel Hill: University of North Carolina Press, 1994). For exchange programs see Yale Richmond, *Cultural Exchange and the Cold War: Raising the Iron Curtain* (University Park: Penn State University Press, 2003), abstracted in "Cultural Exchange and the Cold War: How the Arts Influenced Policy," *Journal of Arts Management, Law, and Society* 39, no. 2 (Fall 2005): 239–45. Also see "Culture, the Soviet Union, and the Cold War," ed. Musya Glants and Pamela Kachurin, special issue, *Journal of Cold War Studies* 4, no. 1 (Winter 2002). Useful articles include Donna Harsch, review of *Jazz, Rock, and Rebels: Cold War Politics and American Culture in a Divided Germany*, by Uta G. Poiger, *Journal of Social History* 35, no. 3 (Spring 2002): 750–53; Vessela Misheva, "The Beatles, the Beatles Generation, and the End of the Cold War," *Public Voices: Music and Civic Space* 9, no. 1 (2007): 13–43; Visnja Cogan, "Love and Peace or Else: U2 and the Development of Consciousness Inside and Outside the Framework of Rock," *Public Voices: Music and Civic Space* 9, no. 1 (2007): 44–57; Nick Gillespie and Matt Welch, "How 'Dallas' Won the Cold War," *Washington Post*, April 27, 2008; James G. Hershberg, "The Reagan Effect," *Washington Post*, June 28, 2004.

43. Ligachev, *Inside Gorbachev's Kremlin*, 93.
44. Gorbachev, *Memoirs*, 202–3, 210; Chernyaev, *My Six Years with Gorbachev*, 325, 335.
45. Ligachev, *Inside Gorbachev's Kremlin*, 109.
46. Ibid., 100.
47. Gorbachev, *Memoirs*, 206.
48. Shevardnadze, *Future Belongs to Freedom*, 32, 171–73.
49. Quoted in Chernyaev, *My Six Years with Gorbachev*, 73.
50. Gorbachev, *Memoirs*, 252. The following account also relies upon Anatoly S. Chernyaev, *The Diary of Anatoly S. Chernyaev: 1987–1988* (National Security Archive Electronic Briefing Book no. 250), trans. Anna Melyakova and ed. Svetlana Savranskaya (Washington, DC: National Security Archive, May 23, 2008), http://www.gwu.edu/~nsarchiv/NSAEBB/NSAEBB250/Chernyaev_Diary_1988.pdf; Chernyaev, *My Six Years with Gorbachev*, 151–56; Ligachev, *Inside*

Gorbachev's Kremlin, 298–311; and Michael Dobbs, *Down with Big Brother: The Fall of the Soviet Empire* (New York: Alfred A. Knopf, 1997), 202–9.

Chapter 6: The Shadow Cold War

1. Schweizer, *Victory*, xi–xii. Schweizer was the first analyst to present this case in detail, and he was given extraordinary access to former Reagan administration officials and documents. He renewed the argument later in a biography of Ronald Reagan and in writings in conjunction with former defense secretary Caspar Weinberger. Schweizer's work can be considered the progenitor of the triumphalist school, and *Victory* remains the most sophisticated vehicle for this construction of the history. It will be taken as such here.

2. Ibid., xiii.

3. Quoted in Garthoff, *Great Transition*, 20.

4. Gates, *From the Shadows*, 194.

5. "U.S. National Security Strategy," May 20, 1982 (declassified February 26, 1996), in Ronald Reagan Papers, White House Staff and Office Files, Executive Secretariat, NSC, box 91311, fol. NSDD-32, Ronald Reagan Library. Peter Schweizer (*Victory*, pp. 76–77) describes NSDD-32 as a document "outlining American objectives and goals in Eastern Europe" and providing for covert support of dissident movements, intensified psychological warfare operations, and "trade to wean away the regimes' heavy reliance on Moscow." He quotes Edwin Meese to the effect that the administration was effectively declaring the 1945 Yalta agreement to be irrelevant. None of this appears in the declassified document. However, one paragraph, which may (or may not) concern Eastern Europe has been deleted from the declassified NSDD.

6. "East-West Economic Relations and Poland-Related Sanctions," November 29, 1982 (declassified October 3, 1996), in Ronald Reagan Papers, White House Staff and Office Files, Executive Secretariat, NSC, box 91286, fol. NSDD-66, Ronald Reagan Library. In this case, Schweizer (*Victory*, p. 126) quotes NSC staffer Roger Robinson saying the directive was "tantamount to a secret declaration of economic war on the Soviet Union."

7. "U.S. Relations with the USSR," January 17, 1983 (declassified July 16, 1994), Ronald Reagan Papers, White House Staff and Office Files, Executive Secretariat, NSC, box 91286, fol. NSDD-75, Ronald Reagan Library. Here Schweizer (*Victory*, p. 131) quotes a key drafter of NSDD-75. Richard Pipes, another NSC staffer, said the directive was "the first document which said that what

mattered was not only Soviet behavior but the nature of the Soviet system. NSDD-75 said our goal was no longer to coexist with the Soviet Union but to change the Soviet system. At its root was the belief that we had it in our power to alter the Soviet system through the use of external pressure." The reader may judge for herself whether too much has been claimed for these Reagan presidential directives, but note that this succession of assertions forms the very heart of the triumphalist argument.

8. Richard Halloran, "Pentagon Draws Up First Strategy for Fighting a Long Nuclear War," *New York Times,* May 30, 1982.

9. In general see John Prados, *The Soviet Estimate: U.S. Intelligence Analysis and Soviet Strategic Forces,* rev. ed. (Princeton, NJ: Princeton University Press, 1986).

10. Anne Hessing Cahn, *Killing Détente: The Right Attacks the CIA.* University Park: Pennsylvania State University Press, 1998.

11. In technical analysis, the survivability of an ICBM silo was defined by calculations of the "expected damage" from a given attack pattern. Damage expectancy is derived using equations that provide for the degree of protection built into the installation (termed "hardness" and specified in pounds-per-square-inch [psi] of dynamic overpressure a silo could survive; American ICBM silos were generally given 1,000–1,200 psi ratings, older Soviet silos were estimated in the 500–700 psi range, and the newest Russian ICBMs were believed to be going into "super-hardened" silos built to withstand up to 2,700 psi); the reliability of the delivery missile in each aspect of its performance, the yield of the attacking nuclear warhead, and the accuracy of impact. As a rule of thumb, missile accuracy is roughly four times more important in this calculation than is nuclear yield. Soviet missile warheads had relatively high yields but poor accuracy. The Team B critique led U.S. intelligence analysts to double their accuracy estimates. Under this set of equations, warheads with that level of accuracy had a probability of destroying an ICBM silo of more than 90 percent, increased to a virtual certainty in the case of a two-on-one attack in which two warheads were targeted on each ICBM silo (at a 95 percent confidence level). Post–Cold War research indicates that Soviet ICBM accuracy corresponded closely to original CIA estimates, and Soviet missile reliability was significantly less than postulated. In the reverse case, moreover, the recent data puts maximum Soviet silo hardness at about 1,500 psi, in which circumstance a one-on attack by a U.S. warhead in itself produces virtual certainty of destruction. Many Soviet ICBMs had silos of only 450–900 psi, and 40

percent (the older-generation ICBMs) occupied silos hardened to only 150 psi. See Pavel Podvig, "The Window of Vulnerability That Wasn't: Soviet Military Buildup in the 1970s—A Research Note," *International Security* 33, no. 1 (Summer 2008): 118–38. Podvig calculates that by 1981 the Soviet nuclear force could have eliminated less than 600 of the 1,000 U.S. ICBMs and that this level of effectiveness remained constant through 1987, though improving somewhat thereafter (to roughly 700 by 1990). In the 1990 (worst) case, U.S. ICBMs would have had the capacity to retaliate with between 900 and 1,250 warheads, depending upon the proportion of Minuteman III and Peacekeeper ICBMs among the survivors.

12. In its classic formulation, the window-of-vulnerability argument considered the Minuteman force disarmed if a strike against it could reasonably result in over 90 percent silo destruction. From 1978 on, the NIEs showed levels of destruction (for a 1981 scenario) of about 80 percent, still suggesting significant survival of U.S. ICBMs, but this did not seem to matter to proponents of the threat. In addition, here we have not touched on the vagaries of simulations used to war-game these results or on scientific factors that significantly affected the analysis. In particular, until the early 1980s, planners did not take into account micro-changes in the earth's magnetic field, which could have a marked effect on ballistic trajectories and therefore on navigation along a flight path, hence warhead accuracy. The United States not only possessed a far more articulated network of scientific satellites, which enabled targeteers to map magnetic effects and insert corrections into guidance systems, but it had far more sophisticated (and plentiful) computers to make the complex calculations necessary to derive these navigational instructions. The United States also fielded warheads capable of taking a midcourse picture of the stellar field along their trajectory, making course corrections based on determining the difference between that fix and stored data in the inertial guidance system. This technology was deployed on the Minuteman III, Peacekeeper, and Trident D-5. It was so effective it virtually eliminated traditional accuracy differences between land-based and submarine missiles. (ICBMs, because the precise location of their silos could be calculated for purposes of inertial guidance, had always been more accurate than submarine-launched missiles.) In addition, the United States began development of a *maneuverable* reentry vehicle that could make further corrections based on GPS satellite data even while entering the atmosphere. The GPS satellite network in fact originated

as a military program designed to support this and other precision navigation applications. The Soviet Union had no GPS network, no maneuverable
reentry vehicles, and no stellar-inertial navigation system. All of this worked in
favor of U.S. missile accuracy and against the Soviets. (I will spare the reader
citation of all the technical sources behind this thumbnail sketch. Suffice it
to say that I trained in strategic analysis at Columbia University's Institute of
War and Peace Studies and worked with, and among, the defense intellectual
community at the forefront of all these issues. The leading U.S. institution on
guidance and navigation matters was the Charles Stark Draper Laboratory in
Cambridge. For a history of Draper and a primer on these issues see Donald
MacKenzie, *Inventing Accuracy: An Historical Sociology of Nuclear Missile Guidance*
[Cambridge, MA: MIT Press, 1990].)

13. Adm. Stansfield Turner, comments at the conference "Estimating Soviet Mili-
tary Power, 1950 to 1984" (CIA Center for the Study of Intelligence and the
Charles Warren Center for Studies in American History, Harvard University,
December 2–3, 1994, in author's notes). Also see Christopher B. Daly, "Ex-
Director Faults CIA of Carter Era," *Washington Post*, December 3, 1994.

14. Douglas MacEachin, interview with the author, Princeton, NJ, March 10,
2001.

15. CIA, Directorate of Intelligence, "Intelligence Forecasts of Soviet Intercontinental Attack Forces: An Evaluation of the Record," Research Paper, SOV
89-10031, April 1989 (declassified October 1993). Copy courtesy of Douglas
MacEachin.

16. Using standard calculations and assuming the U.S. ICBM silo hardness above
(note 7), the SS-19 as projected in the 1985 NIE would have had to expend
seven warheads per silo to achieve kill probabilities at confidence levels equal
to those of the original "window" scenario (Prados, *Soviet Estimate*, 343n. 6). In
its most capable configuration, the SS-19 carried six warheads. This hypothetical does not even begin to take into account the technical issues involved in
"laying down" seven separate nuclear charges on a target within a short space
of time, nor does it consider the questions associated with performance of
the warheads themselves, given the physical and electromagnetic effects of the
first and succeeding nuclear detonations. At the time, the U.S. technical community, to say nothing of the Russian one, had barely begun to grapple with
the latter issues. As this, and the brief discussions in earlier footnotes indicate,
nuclear war planning was nothing if not a highly complex exercise.

17. John Prados, "National Intelligence Estimates, 1976–1988: Successes and Failures," in *From Détente to the Soviet Collapse*, 84–86.

18. Robert Bowie served as deputy director for intelligence under Stansfield Turner. In 1993 he recounted his concerns: "I was very troubled by the use of a dollar figure for defense spending and I raised the question not only with our people but with the committee [of outside experts] which we had. They explained the methodology: 'You're *starting* with a totally fictitious figure, you have to adjust that, and then you have to convert that into American dollars.' That was done by very crude techniques because there was really no other way. And I strongly objected to the use of these figures and I was told not merely by our people but by the outside consultants that Congress absolutely insisted that there be dollar figures. [The analysts] have always tried to make clear to the Congress the limitations even on the ruble figures, but especially on the dollar ones, but then what happened was that people on the [congressional] committee and others simply dropped all the qualifications." Robert Bowie, comments at the panel discussion "Before the Fall: CIA Estimates and the Soviet Economy, 1970–1990" (Cold War International History Project, Woodrow Wilson International Center for Scholars, Washington, DC, November 16, 1993).

19. CIA, "Can the Soviets 'Stand Down' Militarily?" Intelligence Assessment, SOV 82-10101, June 1982 (declassified 1999), v, 13, 12.

20. Gates, *From the Shadows*, 172–74, 184–85. Though Gates presents this favorable picture of accurate reporting, a number of the agency's line analysts would disagree, not because they were unaware of Soviet problems but, given conservative attacks on the agency, because judgments of that type often ended up on the cutting room floor. One stream of the reporting to which Gates refers, the CIA's annual presentations to the Joint Economic Committee of the U.S. Congress—which were indeed among the most useful and accurate materials on Soviet (and Chinese) economic developments—was remarkable in part because specialists' testimony on Soviet problems seemed to be so poorly reflected in the finished intelligence.

21. After the Cold War, the House Permanent Select Committee on Intelligence commissioned an expert review of the CIA's estimates on the Soviet economy (HPSCI Review Committee, "Survey Article: An Evaluation of the CIA's Analysis of Soviet Economic Performance, 1970–1990," *Comparative Economic Studies* 35, no. 2 [Summer 1993]: 33–57). The review group recommended that

the CIA terminate its use of this economic model, called "SOVSIM" (p. 38–39), noting that it could not understand the CIA's methodology.

22. Quoted in James Noren, "CIA's Analysis of the Soviet Economy," in *Watching the Bear: Essays on CIA's Analysis of the Soviet Union*, ed. Gerald K. Haines and Robert E. Leggett (Langley, VA: CIA, Center for the Study of Intelligence, 2003), 32.

23. Schweizer, *Victory*, 5, 7–8, 20–21, 165–66, 245. Schweizer points to a bad Soviet economy, manufacturing shortages, and the fall of Moscow's hard currency earnings as specific elements of this CIA data. At the time, the agency did know of manufacturing problems and inadequate investment in energy production, which it had been pointing to since the late 1970s, but it believed in a steady rate of Soviet GNP growth, while hard currency earnings from oil exports were near peak. *Victory* identifies Herbert Meyer as a CIA economics expert; in fact, Meyer was an individual Casey brought in from the outside, not an economist at all but an ideologue with a background in business publishing (as editor of *Forbes* magazine). At a point in early 1983, Schweizer recounts, Meyer produced intelligence given to the White House that said the Soviet economy could potentially implode (p. 165)—data contrary to anything else the CIA was reporting, says the author, *because* Meyer had overwritten a typical CIA economic analysis piece with what came to be termed "opportunity intelligence" (excerpts of Meyer's exegesis are printed in the documentary appendix). Here Schweizer's account obscures the fact that other elements of the agency *were not being permitted to report intelligence of that nature.* He also appears to invent dialogue—for example, a key meeting of the National Security Planning Group on January 30, 1981 (p. 7; Ronald Reagan's diary does not note this meeting at all and, in fact, says this was a short day, after which he left for Camp David), and a conversation between Director Casey and his Saudi Arabian counterpart in March 1981 (p. 29), during which the CIA chief allegedly made a secret deal for the Saudis to lower oil prices in order to rob the Soviets of hard currency earnings (that Saudi official had no authority to make such a deal and the generally accepted explanation for why Saudi Arabia would eventually lower its oil price was to compete with British North Sea oil after London dropped its own prices). It bears noting that Casey died in 1987, long before he could have recounted these and other alleged conversations to Peter Schweizer, who was writing in the 1990s. Robert Gates notes an interagency

meeting on Poland on January 30, 1981, but *not* one of the National Security Planning Group (*From the Shadows*, p. 227–28).

24. Gates, *From the Shadows*, 199.

25. Goodman, *Failure of Intelligence*, 113.

26. CIA/DIA, "Beyond *Perestroika:* The Soviet Economy in Crisis," Intelligence Study, DDB-1900-164-91, June 1991, table, 26, CIA Electronic Reading Room, http://www.foia.cia.gov/browse_docs_full.asp (accessed August 5, 2008).

27. In general see John Prados, *Safe for Democracy: The Secret Wars of the CIA* (Chicago: Ivan R. Dee, 2006), 467–585.

28. Gates, *From the Shadows*, 238.

29. Quoted in Schweizer, *Victory*, 69. There are no published cost estimates for the Poland operation save those given by Schweizer himself from his inside sources, peaking at $1–2 billion a year. The following account of the Polish operation depends entirely on Schweizer's material (pp. 67–72, 83–92, 120–23, 144–47, 159–61, 222–25, 244, 257–58, 266).

30. Given what happened in the Iran-contra affair a few years later, had the Poland operation been an unauthorized activity, it is very probable that the fact would have emerged then, which casts doubt on the Pipes statement just quoted.

31. CIA, "Military Reliability of the Soviet Union's Warsaw Pact Allies," NIE 12/11-83, June 28, 1983 (declassified 1999), 3, 5, CIA Electronic Reading Room, http://www.foia.cia.gov/browse_docs_full.asp (accessed August 5, 2008).

32. Thomas C. Reed, *At the Abyss: An Insider's History of the Cold War* (New York: Ballantine Books, 2004), 267–69; and Schweizer, *Victory*, 185–87, 249.

33. Gates, *From the Shadows*, 341–45, 358. The interpretation here is mine.

34. Alfred Reisch, who participated in the overt program until 1974, is at work on a detailed account of this facet of the Cold War. The data here emerged during Reisch's presentation, "The West's Secret Plan for the Mind: Book Distribution to East Europe during the Cold War" (Cold War International History Project, Woodrow Wilson International Center for Scholars, Washington, DC, February 6, 2008).

35. Westad, *Global Cold War*, 2007.

36. Prados, *Safe for Democracy*, 490.

37. A proponent of this view is Anthony Arnold in his *The Fateful Pebble: Afghanistan's Role in the Fall of the Soviet Empire* (Novato, CA: Presidio, 1993). The casualty and cost figures are from Arnold, pp. 185–93. The State Department

estimated the cost at $3 billion a year in the early 1980s, but a Soviet economist told a Western reporter in 1989 that the war had cost about $8.2 billion annually (Arnold, p. 185). The following account relies primarily on Prados, *Safe for Democracy*, 467–92.

38. The idea that Moscow was after Indian Ocean ports was a long-standing distortion of history. In the Soviet-German negotiations of 1939, the ones referenced in chapter 4 that led to the Molotov-Ribbentrop Pact, the *Germans*, seeking a free hand in Europe, suggested to the Russians that their ambitions should be aimed toward the Indian Ocean. During the early years of the Cold War, this notion was resurrected, morphed into a Soviet imperial ambition. By the 1970s this had hardened into a fixed idea for many Western cold warriors, to the degree that when the Soviets did intervene in Afghanistan the move was interpreted in many places as the first step in this expected Soviet move to reach the Indian Ocean.

39. Andrew and Mitrokhin, *Sword and the Shield*, 534. Mitrokhin was a KGB officer reassigned from operations to the central records section of the agency's First Chief Directorate—KGB foreign intelligence—in the late 1950s. For almost three decades, he laboriously accumulated notes on KGB operational files, which he took with him when he defected to Britain through the Baltics in 1992. The Mitrokhin Archive was vetted by British intelligence and used extensively by the CIA, and it represents the most authoritative source on KGB operations anywhere. In addition to the volume cited above, the Mitrokhin Archive included a second narrative volume, also coauthored by Christopher Andrew, *The World Was Going Our Way: The KGB and the Battle for the Third World* (New York: Basic Books, 2005); a special monograph by Mitrokhin alone, *The KGB in Afghanistan* (Cold War International History Project, Working Paper no. 40 [Washington, DC: Woodrow Wilson International Center for Scholars, February 2002]); and a selection of notes and KGB original documents maintained by the Cold War International History Project. This section depends primarily on the Mitrokhin material.

40. Andrew and Mitrokhin, *Sword and the Shield*, 522. For material on the network see pp. 508–16.

41. Vasili Mitrokhin, *The KGB in Afghanistan*, passim.

42. John Barron, *KGB Today: The Hidden Hand* (New York: Reader's Digest Press, 1983), 262–93.

43. Chapman Pincher, *The Secret Offensive* (New York: St. Martin's Press, 1985), 235, 226.

44. Alexander R. Alexiev, *The Soviet Campaign Against INF: Strategy, Tactics, Means,* Report N-2280-AF (Santa Monica, CA: Rand Corporation, February 1985).

45. CIA, "Soviet Strategy to Derail US INF Deployment," Intelligence Assessment, SOVA 83-10025X, February 1983 (declassified 1999).

46. Andrew and Mitrokhin, *Sword and the Shield*, passim.

47. Anthony Glees, *The Stasi Files: East Germany's Secret Operations Against Britain* (London: Free Press, 2003).

48. Ronald Kessler, *Moscow Station: How the KGB Penetrated the American Embassy* (New York: Pocket Books, 1990).

49. Thierry Wolton, *Le KGB en France* (Paris: B. Grasset, 1986), 242–43.

50. Sergei Kostine, *Bonjour, Farewell: La vèritè sur la taupe française du KGB* (Paris: R. Laffont, 1997). Kostine's is the only full-length treatment of the affair. In English see Jeffrey T. Richelson, *A Century of Spies: Intelligence in the Twentieth Century* (New York: Oxford University Press, 1995), 376–78.

51. Department of Defense, *Soviet Acquisition of Militarily Significant Western Technology: An Update* (Washington, DC: September 1985).

52. General Electric (#1), Westinghouse (#6), and Allied/Bendix (#9). The others, in order (excluding those mentioned), were Boeing, Lockheed, Rockwell International, McDonnell-Douglas, Martin-Marietta, and General Dynamics. This was in spite of the fact that electronics accounted for by far the largest number of Soviet technology intelligence requirements (over 40 percent), with the next highest category for armor and electro-optical systems (about 13 percent). Aviation, missiles, and space together accounted for roughly 14–16 percent of Moscow's wish list. In other words, there was a mismatch between Soviet collection activity and intelligence requirements.

53. Michael E. Marotta, "Soviet Computer Technology: A Summary," *Loompanics Catalog* 88, http://www.trust-us.ch/habi2/054_soviet_computer_technology.html (accessed October 30, 2008).

54. Shultz, *Turmoil and Triumph*, 864–68.

55. Gates, *From the Shadows*, 377.

56. Shultz, *Turmoil and Triumph*, 867.

57. Goodman, *Failure of Intelligence*, 151.

58. CIA, "Gorbachev's Approach to Societal Malaise: A Managed Revitalization," Intelligence Assessment, SOV 85-10141, August 1985, excerpted in Douglas

J. MacEachin, *CIA Assessments of the Soviet Union: The Record Versus the Charges: An Intelligence Monograph*, CSI 96-001 (Langley, VA: CIA, Center for the Study of Intelligence, May 1996), 19. All the following reports are quoted from this source. Almost all of the full-length papers were released by the CIA at a conference at Princeton University in the spring of 2001 and may also be read in the CD-ROM set (Princeton Papers) made available at that time.

59. CIA, "Domestic Stress in the Soviet Union," NIE 11-18-85, November 1985, in ibid., 21.

60. CIA, "The 27th CPSU Congress: Gorbachev's Unfinished Business," Intelligence Assessment, SOV 86-10023, April 1986, in ibid., 23.

61. CIA, "Gorbachev's Domestic Challenge: The Looming Problems," Intelligence Assessment, SOV 87-10009, February 1987, in ibid., 25.

62. Douglas MacEachin, excerpted testimony to the Joint Economic Committee, April 1988, in ibid., 27.

63. CIA, "Soviet National Security Policy: Responses to the Changing Military and Economic Environment," Research Paper, SOV 88-10040CX, June 1988, in ibid., 29.

64. Douglas MacEachin to Richard Kerr (Deputy Director for Intelligence), memorandum, September 27, 1988, with attached research paper by Kay Oliver, "Prospects for a Leadership Crisis," in ibid., 30–31.

65. Senate Select Committee on Intelligence, Soviet Task Force, transcript of CIA Briefing on the Soviet Union, December 7, 1988, in U.S. Senate, Select Committee on Intelligence, *Hearing on Nomination of Robert M. Gates to Be Director of Central Intelligence*, 102 Cong., 1st sess. (Washington: Government Printing Office, 1992), 2: 483–564.

66. Quoted in ibid., 544–45.

67. Quoted in R. Jeffrey Smith, "CIA Assesses Effect of Gorbachev Cuts," *Washington Post*, December 13, 1988.

68. Quoted in Kirsten Lundberg, *The CIA and the Fall of the Soviet Union: The Politics of "Getting It Right,"* Case Study C16-94-1251.0, Intelligence and Policy Project, John F. Kennedy School of Government (Cambridge, MA: Harvard University, 1994), 32. This is one of a series of case studies the CIA commissioned from the Kennedy School on a variety of intelligence subjects. Copy courtesy of the Kennedy School of Government. For another view see Bruce D. Berkowitz and Jeffrey T. Richelson, "The CIA Vindicated: The Soviet Collapse *Was* Predicted," *National Interest*, no. 41 (Fall 1995): 36–47.

69. CIA, "Gorbachev's Domestic Gambles and Instability in the USSR," Intelligence Assessment, SOV 89-10077X, September 1989, reprinted in Benjamin B. Fischer, ed., *At Cold War's End: U.S. Intelligence on the Soviet Union and Eastern Europe, 1989–1991* (Reston, VA: CIA, 1999), v, 27–48.

70. George H. W. Bush and Brent Scowcroft, *A World Transformed* (New York: Knopf, 1998),154.

71. CIA, "The Soviet System in Crisis: Prospects for the Next Two Years," NIE 11-18-89, November 1989 (declassified 1999), in *At Cold War's End*, 49–81.

72. Patrick E. Tyler, "Webster Sees No Revival of Soviet Threat," *Washington Post*, March 2, 1990; CIA, "Rising Political Instability Under Gorbachev: Understanding the Problems and Prospects for Resolution," Intelligence Memorandum, SOV M89-10040X, April 1989, in MacEachin, *CIA Assessments of the Soviet Union*, 33–34.

73. CIA, "The Deepening Crisis in the USSR: Prospects for the Next Year," NIE 11-18-90, November 1990 (declassified 1999), in *At Cold War's End*, 83–109.

74. CIA, "The Soviet Cauldron," Intelligence Memorandum, SOV M 91-20177, April 25, 1991 (declassified 1999), in ibid., 111–19.

Chapter 7: How the Cold War Ended

1. Roger R. Trask and Alfred Goldberg, *The Department of Defense, 1947–1997: Organization and Leaders* (Washington, DC: Historical Office, Office of the Secretary of Defense, 1997), tables, 166–72.

BIBLIOGRAPHY

Government Publications

Congressional Research Service. *Soviet Diplomacy and Negotiating Behavior, 1979–1988: New Tests for U.S. Diplomacy.* Washington, DC: Government Printing Office, 1988.

Fischer, Benjamin B., ed. *At Cold War's End: U.S. Intelligence on the Soviet Union and Eastern Europe, 1989–1991.* Reston, VA: CIA, 1999.

Haines, Gerald K., and Robert E. Leggett. *Watching the Bear: Essays on CIA's Analysis of the Soviet Union.* Langley, VA: CIA, Center for the Study of Intelligence, 2003.

MacEachin, Douglas J. *CIA Assessments of the Soviet Union: The Record Versus the Charges: An Intelligence Monograph.* CSI 96-001. Langley, VA: CIA, Center for the Study of Intelligence, May 1996.

———. *US Intelligence and the Polish Crisis, 1980–1981.* Washington, DC: Center for the Study of Intelligence, 2000.

Trask, Roger R., and Alfred Goldberg. *The Department of Defense, 1947–1997: Organization and Leaders.* Washington, DC: Historical Office, Office of the Secretary of Defense, 1997.

U.S. Congress. House. Committee on Foreign Affairs. *Soviet Negotiating Behavior.* 3 vols. Special Studies Series. Washington, DC: Government Printing Office, 1979, August 1988, April 1991.

U.S. Congress. House. Permanent Select Committee on Intelligence Review Committee. "Survey Article: An Evaluation of the CIA's Analysis of Soviet Economic Performance, 1970–1990." *Comparative Economic Studies* 35, no. 2 (Summer 1993): 33–57.

U.S. Congress. Joint Economic Committee. *Hearings: Allocation of Resources in the Soviet Union and China.* Washington, DC: Government Printing Office, annual series.

———. *Joint Hearings: Political Economy of the Soviet Union.* 98th Cong., 1st sess. Washington, DC: Government Printing Office, 1983.

U.S. Congress. Senate. Armed Services Committee. *Hearings: Current Developments in the Former Soviet Union.* 103rd Cong., 1st sess. Washington, DC: Government Printing Office, 1993.

U.S. Congress. Senate. Select Committee on Intelligence. *Hearing on Nomination of Robert M. Gates to Be Director of Central Intelligence.* 102 Cong., 1st sess. Washington: Government Printing Office, 1992.

U.S. Department of State. *Soviet-American Relations: The Détente Years, 1969–1972.* Washington, DC: Government Printing Office, 2007.

Other Sources

Alexiev, Alexander R. *The Soviet Campaign Against INF: Strategy, Tactics, Means.* Report N-2280-AF. Santa Monica, CA: Rand Corporation, February 1985.

Andrew, Christopher M., and Oleg Gordievsky, eds. *Instructions from the Centre: Top Secret Files on KGB Foreign Operations, 1975–1985.* London: Hodder & Stoughton, 1991.

———. *KGB: The Inside Story of Its Foreign Operations from Lenin to Gorbachev.* New York: HarperCollins, 1990.

Andrew, Christopher M., and Vasili Mitrokhin. *The Sword and the Shield: The Mitrokhin Archive and the Secret History of the KGB.* New York: Basic Books, 1999.

———. *The World Was Going Our Way: The KGB and the Battle for the Third World.* New York: Basic Books, 2005.

Arbatov, Georgi. *The System: An Insider's Life in Soviet Politics.* New York: Times Books, 1992.

Arnold, Anthony. *The Fateful Pebble: Afghanistan's Role in the Fall of the Soviet Empire.* Novato, CA: Presidio, 1993.

Baker, James A., III. *The Politics of Diplomacy: Revolution, War, and Peace, 1989–1992.* With Thomas M. DeFrank. New York: Putnam, 1995.

Barron, John. *KGB Today: The Hidden Hand.* New York: Reader's Digest Press, 1983.

Berkowitz, Bruce D., and Jeffrey T. Richelson. "The CIA Vindicated: The Soviet Collapse *Was* Predicted." *National Interest*, no. 41 (Fall 1995): 36–47.

Beschloss, Michael R., and Strobe Talbott. *At the Highest Levels: The Inside Story of the End of the Cold War.* Boston: Little, Brown, 1993.

Bialer, Seweryn. *Stalin's Successors: Leadership, Stability, and Change in the Soviet Union.* Cambridge: Cambridge University Press, 1980.

Bush, George H. W., and Brent Scowcroft. *A World Transformed.* New York: Knopf, 1998.

Cahn, Anne Hessing. *Killing Détente: The Right Attacks the CIA.* University Park: Pennsylvania State University Press, 1998.

Cannon, Lou. *President Reagan: The Role of a Lifetime.* New York: Public Affairs Press, 2000.

———. *Reagan.* New York: Putnam, 1982.

Chernyaev, Anatoly S. *The Diary of Anatoly S. Chernyaev, 1985–1989* (National Security Archive Electronic Briefing Books nos. 192, 220, 250, and 275). Translated by Anna Melyakova and edited by Svetlana Savranskaya. Washington, DC: National Security Archive, 2006–2009. http://www.gwu.edu/~nsarchiv/NSAEBB/NSAEBB275/index.htm.

———. *My Six Years with Gorbachev.* Translated and edited by Robert D. English and Elizabeth Tucker. University Park: Pennsylvania State University Press, 2000.

Cold War International History Project Bulletin, nos. 1–16 (1992–2008).

Cold War International History Project Virtual Archive, www.CWIHP.org.

Combs, Dick. *Inside the Soviet Alternate Universe: The Cold War's End and the Soviet Union's Fall Reappraised.* University Park: Pennsylvania State University Press, 2008.

Cortright, David. *Peace Works: The Citizen's Role in Ending the Cold War.* Boulder, CO: Westview Press, 1993.

Cowley, Robert, ed. *The Cold War: A Military History.* New York: Random House, 2005.

Dobbs, Michael. *Down with Big Brother: The Fall of the Soviet Empire.* New York: Alfred A. Knopf, 1997.

Dobrynin, Anatoly. *In Confidence: Moscow's Ambassador to America's Six Cold War Presidents (1962–1986).* New York: Times Books, 1995.

Duffy, Michael, and Dan Goodgame. *Marching in Place: The Status Quo Presidency of George Bush.* New York: Simon & Schuster, 1992.

Ekedahl, Carolyn M., and Melvin A. Goodman. *The Wars of Eduard Shevardnadze.* University Park: Pennsylvania State University Press, 1997.

Firth, Noel E., and James H. Noren. *Soviet Defense Spending: A History of CIA Estimates, 1950–1990.* College Station: Texas A & M University Press, 1998.

Fischer, Beth A. *The Reagan Reversal: Foreign Policy and the End of the Cold War.* Columbia: University of Missouri Press, 1997.

FitzGerald, Frances. *Way Out There in the Blue: Reagan, Star Wars, and the End of the Cold War.* New York: Simon & Schuster, 2000.

Gaddis, John Lewis. *The Cold War: A New History.* New York: Penguin Press, 2005.

———. *The United States and the End of the Cold War: Implications, Reconsiderations, Provocations.* New York: Oxford University Press, 1992.

Gaidar, Yegor. *Collapse of an Empire: Lessons for Modern Russia.* Translated by Antonina W. Bouis. Washington, DC: Brookings Institution Press, 2007.

Garthoff, Raymond L. *Détente and Confrontation: American-Soviet Relations from Nixon to Reagan.* Rev. ed. Washington, DC: Brookings Institution, 1994.

———. *The Great Transition: American-Soviet Relations and the End of the Cold War.* Washington, DC: Brookings Institution, 1994.

———. *A Journey Through the Cold War: A Memoir of Containment and Coexistence.* Washington, DC: Brookings Institution Press, 2001.

———. *Policy versus the Law: The Reinterpretation of the ABM Treaty.* Washington, DC: Brookings Institution, 1987.

Gates, Robert M. *From the Shadows: The Ultimate Insider's Story of Five Presidents and How They Won the Cold War.* New York: Simon & Schuster, 1996.

Glees, Anthony. *The Stasi Files: East Germany's Secret Operations Against Britain.* London: Free Press, 2003.

Goodman, Melvin A. *Failure of Intelligence: The Decline and Fall of the CIA.* Lanham, MD: Rowman & Littlefield, 2008.

Gorbachev, Mikhail S. *At the Summit: Speeches and Interviews, February 1987–July 1988.* New York: Richardson, Steirman & Black, 1988.

———. *Memoirs.* Translated by Wolf J. Seidler. New York: Doubleday, 1996.

Grachev, Andrei. *Gorbachev's Gamble: Soviet Foreign Policy and the End of the Cold War.* Cambridge, UK: Polity, 2008.

Graham, Thomas, Jr. *Disarmament Sketches: Three Decades of Arms Control and International Law.* Seattle: University of Washington Press, 2002.

Gromyko, Andrei. *Memoirs.* Translated by Harold Shukman. New York: Doubleday, 1989.

Herf, Jeffrey. *War by Other Means: Soviet Power, West German Resistance, and the Battle of the Euromisiles.* New York: Free Press, 1991.

Herspring, Dale R. *The Soviet High Command, 1967–1989: Personalities and Politics.* Princeton, NJ: Princeton University Press, 1990.

Hutchings, Robert L. *American Diplomacy and the End of the Cold War: An Insider's Account of U.S. Policy in Europe, 1989–1992.* Baltimore: Johns Hopkins University Press, 1997.

Huygen, Maarten. "Dateline Holland: NATO's Pyrrhic Victory." *Foreign Policy*, no. 62 (Spring 1986).

International Institute for Strategic Studies. *Strategic Surveys, 1986–1987, 1987–1988*, and *1988–1989*. London: IISS, 1987–1989.

Israelyan, Victor. *On the Battlefields of the Cold War: A Soviet Ambassador's Confession.* Translated and edited by Stephen Pearl. University Park: Pennsylvania State University Press, 2003.

Kaiser, Robert G. *Why Gorbachev Happened: His Triumphs and His Failure.* New York: Simon & Schuster, 1991.

Kengor, Paul. *The Crusader: Ronald Reagan and the Fall of Communism.* New York: Regan Books, 2006.

Kessler, Ronald. *Moscow Station: How the KGB Penetrated the American Embassy.* New York: Pocket Books, 1990.

Kostine, Sergei. *Bonjour, Farewell: La vèritè sur la taupe française du KGB.* Paris: R. Laffont, 1997.

Kotkin, Stephen. *Armageddon Averted: The Soviet Collapse, 1970–2000.* Oxford: Oxford University Press, 2001.

Krishtoff, Lena, and Eva Skelley, eds. *Perestroika: The Crunch Is Now: A Collection of Press Articles and Interviews.* Moscow: Progress Publishers, 1990.

Leffler, Melvyn P. *For the Soul of Mankind: The United States, the Soviet Union, and the Cold War.* New York: Hill & Wang, 2007.

Lettow, Paul. *Ronald Reagan and His Quest to Abolish Nuclear Weapons.* New York: Random House, 2005.

Lévesque, Jacques. *The Enigma of 1989: The USSR and the Liberation of Eastern Europe.* Berkeley: University of California Press, 1997.

Ligachev, Yegor. *Inside Gorbachev's Kremlin: The Memoirs of Yegor Ligachev.* Translated by Catherine A. Fitzpatrick, Michele A. Berdy, Dobrochna Dyrcz-Freeman, and Marian Schwartz. Boulder, CO: Westview Press, 1996.

Mann, James. *The Rebellion of Ronald Reagan: A History of the End of the Cold War.* New York: Viking, 2009.

Matlock, Jack F., Jr. *Autopsy on an Empire: The American Ambassador's Account of the Collapse of the Soviet Union.* New York: Random House, 1995.

Maynard, Christopher. *Out of the Shadow: George H. W. Bush and the End of the Cold War.* College Station: Texas A & M University Press, 2008.

Medvedev, Grigori. *The Truth About Chernobyl.* Translated by Evelyn Rossiter. New York: Basic Books, 1991.

Merkl, Peter H. *German Unification in the European Context*. University Park: Pennsylvania State University Press, 1993.

Mitrokhin, Vasili. *The KGB in Afghanistan*. Cold War International History Project, Working Paper no. 40. Washington, DC: Woodrow Wilson International Center for Scholars, February 2002.

Morris, Edmund. *Dutch: A Memoir of Ronald Reagan*. New York: Random House, 1999.

Muir, Malcolm, Jr., ed. *From Détente to the Soviet Collapse: The Cold War from 1975 to 1991* Lexington: Virginia Military Institute, 2006.

Nahaylo, Bohdan, and Victor Swoboda. *Soviet Disunion: A History of the Nationalities Problem in the USSR*. New York: Free Press, 1990.

Nuti, Leopoldo, ed. *The Crisis of Détente in Europe: From Helsinki to Gorbachev, 1975–1985*. London: Routledge, 2009.

Oberdorfer, Don. *From the Cold War to a New Era: The United States and the Soviet Union, 1983–1991*. Updated edition. Baltimore: Johns Hopkins University Press, 1998.

———. *The Turn: From the Cold War to a New Era: The United States and the Soviet Union, 1983–1991*. New York: Poseidon Press, 1991.

O'Sullivan, John. *The President, the Pope, and the Prime Minister: Three Who Changed the World*. Washington, DC: Regnery Publishing, 2006.

Palazchenko, Pavel. *My Years with Gorbachev and Shevardnadze: The Memoir of a Soviet Interpreter*. University Park: Pennsylvania State University Press, 1997.

Parrish, Thomas. *The Cold War Encyclopedia*. New York: H. Holt, 1996.

Pincher, Chapman. *The Secret Offensive*. New York: St. Martin's Press, 1985.

Podvig, Pavel. "The Window of Vulnerability That Wasn't': Soviet Military Buildup in the 1970s—A Research Note." *International Security* 33, no. 1 (Summer 2008): 118–38.

Pond, Elizabeth. *Beyond the Wall: Germany's Road to Unification*. Washington, DC: Brookings Institution, 1993.

Prados, John. *Safe for Democracy: The Secret Wars of the CIA*. Chicago: Ivan R. Dee, 2006.

———. *The Soviet Estimate: U.S. Intelligence Analysis and Soviet Strategic Forces*. Rev. ed. Princeton, NJ: Princeton University Press, 1986.

Pry, Peter V. *War Scare: Russia and America on the Nuclear Brink*. Westport, CT: Praeger, 1999.

Reagan, Ronald. *An American Life*. New York: Simon & Schuster, 1990.

———. *The Reagan Diaries*. Edited by Douglas Brinkley. New York: Harper Collins, 2007.

Reed, Thomas C. *At the Abyss: An Insider's History of the Cold War.* New York: Ballantine Books, 2004.

Reeves, Richard. *President Reagan: The Triumph of Imagination.* New York: Simon & Schuster, 2005.

Richelson, Jeffrey T. *A Century of Spies: Intelligence in the Twentieth Century.* New York: Oxford University Press, 1995.

Rodman, Peter W. *More Precious Than Peace: The Cold War and the Struggle for the Third World.* New York: C. Scribner's Sons, 1994.

Savranskaya, Svetlana, and Thomas Blanton, eds. *The Reykjavik File: Previously Secret U.S. and Soviet Documents on the 1986 Reagan-Gorbachev Summit* (National Security Archive Electronic Briefing Book no. 203). Washington, DC: National Security Archive, October 13, 2006. http://www.gwu.edu/~nsarchiv/NSAEBB/NSAEBB203.

Schweizer, Peter. *Reagan's War: The Epic Story of His Forty-Year Struggle and Final Triumph over Comunism.* New York: Doubleday, 2002.

———. *Victory: The Reagan Administration's Secret Strategy That Hastened the Collapse of the Soviet Union.* New York: Atlantic Monthly Press, 1994.

Shattan, Joseph. *Architects of Victory: Six Heroes of the Cold War.* Washington, DC: Heritage Foundation, 1999.

Shevardnadze, Eduard. *The Future Belongs to Freedom.* Translated by Catherine A. Fitzpatrick. New York: Free Press, 1991.

Shultz, George P. *Turmoil and Triumph: My Years as Secretary of State.* New York: Scribner's, 1993.

Smyser, W. R. *From Yalta to Berlin: The Cold War Struggle over Germany.* New York: St. Martin's Press, 1999.

Sullivan, David S. *Soviet SALT Deception.* Boston, VA: Coalition for Peace Through Strength, 1979.

Talbott, Strobe. *Deadly Gambits: The Reagan Administration and the Stalemate in Nuclear Arms Control.* New York: Knopf, 1984.

Thatcher, Margaret. *The Downing Street Years.* New York: HarperCollins, 1993.

Thomas, Daniel C. *The Helsinki Effect: International Norms, Human Rights, and the Demise of Communism.* Princeton, NJ: Princeton University Press, 2001.

USSR Ministry of Defense. *Whence the Threat to Peace?* Moscow: Military Publishing House, 1982.

Volkogonov, Dmitri. *Autopsy for an Empire: The Seven Leaders Who Built the Soviet Regime.* Edited and translated by Harold Shukman. New York: Free Press, 1998.

Wagnleitner, Reinhold. *Coca-Colonization and the Cold War: The Cultural Mission of the United States in Austria after the Second World War.* Translated by Diana M. Wolf. Chapel Hill: University of North Carolina Press, 1994.

Walker, Martin. *The Cold War: A History.* New York: H. Holt, 1994.

Weiser, Benjamin. *A Secret Life: The Polish Colonel, His Covert Mission, and the Price He Paid to Save His Country.* New York: Public Affairs, 2004.

Westad, Odd Arne. *The Global Cold War: Third World Interventions and the Making of Our Times.* New York: Cambridge University Press, 2007.

Westwick, Peter J. "'Space-Strike Weapons' and the Soviet Response to SDI." *Diplomatic History* 32, no. 5 (November 2008): 955–79.

Whitfield, Stephen J. *The Culture of the Cold War.* 2nd ed. Baltimore: Johns Hopkins University Press, 1996.

Winik, Jay. *On the Brink: The Dramatic, Behind-the-Scenes Saga of the Reagan Era and the Men and Women Who Won the Cold War.* New York: Simon & Schuster, 1996.

Wittner, Lawrence S. *The Struggle Against the Bomb.* Vol. 3: *Toward Nuclear Abolition: A History of the World Nuclear Disarmament Movement, 1971 to the Present.* Stanford: Stanford University Press, 2003.

Wohlforth, William C., ed. *Witnesses to the End of the Cold War.* Baltimore: Johns Hopkins University Press, 1996.

Wolton, Thierry. *Le KGB en France.* Paris: B. Grasset, 1986.

Zelikow, Philip, and Condoleezza Rice. *Germany Unified and Europe Transformed: A Study in Statecraft.* Cambridge: Harvard University Press, 1997.

Zubok, Vladislav M. *A Failed Empire: The Soviet Union in the Cold War from Stalin to Gorbachev.* Chapel Hill: University of North Carolina Press, 2007.

ACKNOWLEDGMENTS

I WISH TO THANK DON JACOBS, THEN OF POTOMAC BOOKS, and Robert McMahon of Ohio State University for convincing me to take on this project. McMahon, series editor for these texts, earns a huge dollop of additional thanks for his deft editing of the manuscript. My colleagues at the National Security Archive, Thomas Blanton, Svetlana Savranskaya, and William Burr, working in this substantive area, traded ideas and helped me refine my thinking on certain points, and for that they deserve thanks. Leopoldo Nuti of the University of Rome (III) helped in this regard as well, in particular with respect to European issues, and the conference he helped organize through the Machiavelli Center for Cold War Studies brought back for me much of the substantive terrain over which I once roamed. I also wish to further acknowledge Dr. Savranskaya for her efforts at teasing out archival resources from the former Soviet Union and for her translations of key texts, particularly from the diaries and notes of Soviet official Anatoly Chernyaev, which must henceforth be a prime source for anyone working on the Gorbachev era. Ellen Pinzur deserves special thanks for reading and commenting on this entire manuscript. These and other participants and commentators are responsible for much that is good in this study. I am solely responsible for its errors.

INDEX

ABOUT THE AUTHOR

JOHN PRADOS is a senior fellow at the National Security Archive in Washington, D.C., and holds a PhD in political science (international relations) from Columbia University. He is the author of numerous books, including *William Colby and the CIA: The Secret Wars of a Controversial Spymaster*, *Vietnam: The History of an Unwinnable War, 1945–1975*, and *Safe for Democracy: The Secret Wars of the CIA*. His work has focused on national security, presidential decision making, intelligence and military history, and Southeast Asia. He lives in Silver Spring, Maryland.

Also by John Prados

William Colby and the CIA: The Secret Wars of a Controversial Spymaster

Vietnam: The History of an Unwinnable War, 1945–1975

Safe for Democracy: The Secret Wars of the CIA

Hoodwinked: The Documents That Reveal How Bush Sold Us a War

Inside the Pentagon Papers (written and edited with Margaret Pratt Porter)

The White House Tapes: Eavesdropping on the President (written and edited)

Lost Crusader: The Secret Wars of CIA Director William Colby

America Confronts Terrorism: Understanding the Danger and How to Think About It (edited with an introduction by)

The Blood Road: The Ho Chi Minh Trail and the Vietnam War

Presidents' Secret Wars: CIA and Pentagon Covert Operations from World War II Through the Persian Gulf

Combined Fleet Decoded: The Secret History of U.S. Intelligence and the Japanese Navy in World War II

The Hidden History of the Vietnam War

Valley of Decision: The Siege of Khe Sanh (with Ray W. Stubbe)

Keepers of the Keys: A History of the National Security Council from Truman to Bush

Pentagon Games: Wargames and the American Military

The Soviet Estimate: U.S. Intelligence Analysis and Soviet Strategic Forces

The Sky Would Fall: Operation Vulture: The Secret U.S. Bombing Mission to Vietnam, 1954